PRAISE FOR
A Heartbreaking Work of Staggering Genius

"What is really shocking and exciting is the book's sheer rage.
AHWOSG is truly ferocious, like any work of genius. Eggers—
self-reliant, transcendent, expansive—is Emerson's ideal Young
American. [The book] does itself justice: it is a settling of accounts.
And it is almost too good to be believed."
—*London Review of Books*

"There's a restless energy all over this book … [It's] a keen mixture
of self-consciousness and hope, of horror and hysteria and
freshness and wisdom."
—*The Village Voice*

"[*AHWOSG*] never comes on as oppressive or self-pitying. Eggers
has instead pitched his tone at an uncommon sort of irony, using it
not as a device to keep us at arm's length but to involve us—to
make the story of his life tellable, and thus, somehow, survivable.
Heartbreaking? Certainly. Staggering? Yes … And if genius is cap-
turing the universal in a fresh and memorable way, call it that too."
—*The Times* (London)

"Scathingly perceptive and hysterically funny … Eggers reveals a
true, and truly broken, heart."
—*People*

"For 40 years readers have been waiting around on J. D. Salinger
to send down a new manuscript from high atop his reclusive
Vermont mountain. Well, the vigil is over and we can forget
about hearing from Salinger. He's been replaced by a stunning
new writer. His name is Dave Eggers."
—*Tampa Tribune*

"This thing took off for me in the basement and didn't stop.
It's a merciless book."
—David Foster Wallace

DAVE EGGERS

A HEARTBREAKING WORK
OF STAGGERING GENIUS

Dave Eggers is the founder of *McSweeney's,* a quarterly journal and website (www.mcsweeneys.net). His work has appeared in *The New Yorker* and *Ocean Navigator.* He is the recipient of the Addison Metcalf Award from the American Academy of Arts and Letters, and was a 2001 finalist for the Pulitzer Prize. He lives in Northern California.

THIS WAS
UNCALLED FOR.

A
HEARTBREAKING WORK
OF STAGGERING GENIUS.

BY DAVE EGGERS

VINTAGE BOOKS
A Division of Random House, Inc.
New York

FIRST VINTAGE BOOKS EDITION: February 2001

All rights reserved under International and Pan-American Copyright Conventions.
Published in the United States by Vintage Books, a division of Random House, Inc.,
New York. Random House is owned *in toto* by an absolutely huge German company
called Bertelsmann A.G. which owns too many things to count or track. That said,
no matter how big such companies are, and how many things they own, or how
much money they have or make or control, their influence over the daily lives and
hearts of individuals, and thus, like 99 percent of what is done by official people
in cities like Washington, or Moscow, or São Paulo or Auckland, their effect on
the short, fraught lives of human beings who limp around and sleep and dream
of flying through bloodstreams, who love the smell of rubber cement and think
of space travel while having intercourse, is very very small, and so hardly
worth worrying about.

A portion of this book appeared in *The New Yorker* in a somewhat different form.

Originally published in hardcover in slightly different form in the United States by
Simon & Schuster, New York, 2000.
Vintage Books and colophon are registered trademarks of Random House, Inc.

Library of Congress Catalog Card Number:
00-043832
ISBN 0-375-72578-4
Manufactured in the United States of America
28 30 29 27

Height: 5'11"; Weight: 175; Eyes: blue; Hair: brown; Hands: chubbier than one
would expect; Allergies: only to dander; Place on the sexual-orientation scale,
with 1 being perfectly straight, and 10 being perfectly gay:

NOTE: This is a work of fiction, only in that in many cases, the author could not
remember the exact words said by certain people, and exact descriptions of certain
things, so had to fill in gaps as best he could. Otherwise, all characters and incidents
and dialogue are real, are not products of the author's imagination, because at the
time of this writing, the author had no imagination whatsoever for those sorts of
things, and could not conceive of *making up* a story or characters—it felt like driving
a car in a clown suit—especially when there was so much to say about his own, true,
sorry and inspirational story, the actual people that he has known, and of course the
many twists and turns of his own thrilling and complex mind. Any resemblance to
persons living or dead should be plainly apparent to them and those who know them,
especially if the author has been kind enough to have provided their real names and,
in some cases, their phone numbers. All events described herein actually happened,
though on occasion the author has taken certain, very small, liberties with
chronology, because that is his right as an American.

First of all:

I am tired.
I am true of heart!

And also:

You are tired.
You are true of heart!

RULES AND SUGGESTIONS
FOR ENJOYMENT OF THIS BOOK:

1. There is no overwhelming need to read the preface. Really. It exists mostly for the author, and those who, after finishing the rest of the book, have for some reason found themselves stuck with nothing else to read. If you have already read the preface, and wish you had not, we apologize. We should have told you sooner.

2. There is also no overarching need to read the acknowledgments section. Many early readers of this book (see p. xlv) suggested its curtailment or removal, but they were defied. Still, it is not necessary to the plot in any major way, so, as with the preface, if you have already read the acknowledgments section, and wish you had not, again, we apologize. We should have said something.

3. You can also skip the table of contents, if you're short of time.

4. Actually, many of you might want to skip much of the middle, namely pages 239–351, which concern the lives of people in their early twenties, and those lives are very difficult to make interesting, even when they seemed interesting to those living them at the time.

5. Matter of fact, the first three or four chapters are all some of you might want to bother with. That gets you to page 123 or so, which is a nice length, a nice novella sort of length. Those first four chapters stick to one general subject, something manageable, which is more than what can be said for the book thereafter.

6. The book thereafter is kind of uneven.

PREFACE TO THIS EDITION

For all the author's bluster elsewhere, this is not, actually, a work of pure nonfiction. Many parts have been fictionalized in varying degrees, for various purposes.

DIALOGUE: This has of course been almost entirely reconstructed. The dialogue, though all essentially true—except that which is obviously not true, as when people break out of their narrative time-space continuum to cloyingly talk about the book itself—has been written from memory, and reflects both the author's memory's limitations and his imagination's nudgings. All the individual words and sentences have been run through a conveyor, manufactured like so: 1) they are remembered; 2) they are written; 3) they are rewritten, to sound more accurate; 4) they are edited to fit within the narrative (though keeping with their essential truth); 5) they are rewritten again, to spare the author and the other characters the shame of sounding as inarticulate as they invariably do, or would, if their sentences, almost invariably begun with the word "Dude"—as in, for example, "Dude, she died"— were merely transcribed. It should be noted, however, that what's remarkable is that the book's most surreal dialogue, like that with the Latino teenagers and that with the beleaguered Jenna, is that which is most true to life.

CHARACTERS, AND THEIR CHARACTERISTICS: The author, though he was loath to do it, had to change a few names, and further disguise these name-changed characters. The primary example is the character named John, whose real-life name is not actually John, because John's real-life counterpart justifiably did not want some of the dark portions of his life chronicled—though after reading the manuscript, he did not object to his deeds and words being spoken by another. Especially if the character were less a direct facsimile, and more of an amalgam. Which he is, in fact. Now, to make John work, and create a manageable narrative, his alteration had a sort of domino effect, making necessary a few other fictions. Among them: In real life, Meredith Weiss, who is real, does not know John all that well. The person who in real life acted as intermediary was not Meredith, but another person, whose presence would give away the connection, indeed, would give away poor John, and we could not have that. Thus, the author called Meredith:

"Hey."

"Hey."

"So, do you mind doing [such and such] and saying [such and such], which in real life you did not actually do and say?"

"No, not at all."

So that was that. It should be noted, though, that Meredith's main scene, in Chapter V, contains no fabrications. You can ask her. She lives in Southern California.

Otherwise, name changes are addressed in the body of the text. Moving on:

LOCATIONS AND TIME: First, there have been a few instances of location-switching. In Chapter V, there were two in particular. The conversation with Jenna, wherein the narrator tells her that Toph has fired a gun at his school and then disappeared, did not happen that night in that location, but instead happened in the backseat of a car, traveling from one party to the next, on New Year's Eve, 1996. Later in the same chapter, the narrator, with the same Meredith mentioned above, encounters some youths on a San Francisco beach. This episode, though otherwise entirely factual, actually occurred in Los Angeles. Also, in this chapter, as in a few other chapters, there has been compression of time. It is, for the most part, referenced in the text, but we will reiterate here that in the latter third of the book, much happens in what seems to be a short period of time. Though most of the events rendered did in fact happen within a very close span of time, a few did not. It should be noted, however, that the following chapters feature no time-compression: I, II, IV, VII.

A NOTE ABOUT COLUMBINE: This book was written, and the dialogue it recounts was spoken, many years before the horrific events at that school and elsewhere. No levity is being attached to such things, intentionally or not.

OMISSIONS: Some really great sex scenes were omitted, at the request of those who are now married or involved. Also removed was a fantastic scene—100 percent true—featuring most of the book's primary characters, and a whale. Further, this edition reflects the omission of a number of sentences, paragraphs, and passages.

Among them:

p. 38: As we lie on the bed, there are only a few long hours when Beth is asleep and Toph is asleep and my mother is asleep. I am awake for much of that time. I like the dark part of the night, after midnight and before four-thirty, when it's hollow, when ceilings are harder and farther away. Then I can breathe, and can think while others are sleeping, in a way can stop time, can have it so—this has always been my dream—so that while everyone else is frozen, I can work busily about them, doing whatever it is that needs to be done, like the elves who make the shoes while the children sleep.

As I lie, drenched in the amber room, I wonder if I will nap in the morning. I think I can, believe I can sleep from maybe five until ten, before the nurses start coming in, adjusting and wiping, and so am content to stay up.

But this hideabed is killing me, the flimsiness of the mattress, the way that bar is digging into my back, bisecting my spine, grinding into it. Toph turning, kicking. And on the other side of the room, her uneven breathing.

p. 126: How do you handle this? Bill is up visiting, and he and Toph and I are driving over the Bay Bridge, and we are talking about stockbrokering. We are talking about how, after Toph spent a weekend in Manhattan Beach with Bill and Bill's two stockbroker roommates, Toph now wants to be a stockbroker, too. Bill is so excited about it all he can hardly stand it, wants to buy him a pair of suspenders, a starter-sized ticker...

"We were thinking that, with Toph so good with numbers and all, that something like that would be a perfect career—"

I almost drive the car off the bridge.

p. 197: *Why the scaffolding?*

See, I like the scaffolding. I like the scaffolding as much as I like the building. Especially if that scaffolding is beautiful, in its way.

p. 207: Alcoholism and death make you omnivorous, both reckless & afraid, amoral, desperate.

Do you really believe that?

Sometimes. Sure. No. Yes.

p. 217: ... But see, in high school, I did a series of paintings of members of my family. The first was of Toph, from a photograph I had taken. Because for the assignment we were required to grid the picture out for accuracy, the painting, in tempera, was dead-on; it looked just like him. Not so with the rest of them, without aid of a picture under a grid. I did one of Bill, but his face came out too rigid, his eyes too dark, and his hair looked matted, Caesar-like, which was not at all the case in real life. The painting of Beth, from a photograph of her dressed for the prom, was off, too, all bloodred flesh under pink taffeta—I abandoned it right away. The one of my mom and dad, from an old slide, showed them on a boat together on a gray day. My mother takes up most of the frame, facing the camera, while my dad is over her shoulder, at the front of the boat, looking off to the side, unaware a picture is being taken, or feigning same. I screwed that one up, too—couldn't get the likenesses. Any time one of them would see one of the paintings, they hated them. Bill was incensed when the one of him was shown at the public library. "Is that legal?" he demanded of my father, the lawyer. "Can he even do that? I look like a monster!" And he was right. He did. So during my junior year, when Ricky Storr asked me to do a portrait of his father, I hesitated, because I had been so repeatedly frustrated by my limits, by my inability to render someone without distorting them, clumsily, horribly. But to Ricky I said yes, out of respect, thrilled in a way that he had bestowed the honor on me with the painting of a memorial for his father. So Ricky provided a formal black-and-white photograph, and I worked at it for weeks, with tiny brushes. When I was done, the likeness, to me, was unassailable. I told Ricky to come to the school's art room, that it was ready. He finished his lunch early one day and came down. I turned it around, with a flourish, with great pride, ready for us both to glow in its presence.

There was quiet. Then he said:

"Oh. Oh. That's not what I expected. That's not ... what I expected."

Then he left the room, and the painting with me.

p. 217: When we would drive past a cemetery we would click our tongues and marvel, unbelieving. Especially the big ones, the crowded one, obscene places, so few trees, all that gray, like some sort of monstrous ashtray. When we went by Toph could not look, and I looked only to know, to reconfirm my own promise, that I would never be in such a place, would never bury anyone in such a place—who were these graves for? Who did they comfort?— would never allow myself to be buried in such a place, that I would either disappear completely—

I have visions of my demise: When I know I have only so much more time left—for example if I do in fact have AIDS as I believe I probably do, if anyone does, it's me, why not—when the time comes, I will just leave, say goodbye and leave, and then throw myself into a volcano.

Not that there seems to be any appropriate place to bury someone, but these municipal cemeteries, or any cemetery at all for that matter, like the ones by the highway, or the ones in the middle of town, with all these bodies with their corresponding rocks—oh it's just too primitive and vulgar, isn't it? The hole, and the box, and the rock on the grass? And we glamorize this process, feel it fitting and dramatic, austerely beautiful, standing there by the hole as we lower the box. It's incredible. Barbaric and base.

Though I should say I once saw a place that seemed fitting. I was walking—I would say "hiking," if we were doing anything but walking, but since we were just walking, I will not use the word "hiking," which everyone feels compelled to use anytime they're outside and there's a slight incline—in a forest above the Carapa, a tributary of the Amazon. I was on a junket, with a few other journalists—two from *Reptile* magazine—and a group of herpetologists, a bunch of chubby American snake experts with cameras, and we had been brought through this forest, on an upward-meandering path, looking for boa constrictors and lizards. After maybe forty-five minutes under this dappled dark forest, suddenly the trees broke, and we were at the top of the trail, in a clearing, over the river, and at that point you could see for honestly a hundred miles. The sun was setting, and in that huge Amazonian sky there were washes of blue and orange, thick swashes of each, mixed loosely, like paint pushed with fingers. The river was moving slowly below, the color of caramel, and beyond it was the forest, the jungle, green broccoli chaos as far as you could see. And immediately before us there were about twenty simple white crosses, without anything in the way of markings. A burial ground for local villagers.

And it occurred to me that I could stay there, that if I had to be buried, my rotting corpse heaped on with dirt, I could stand to have it done there. With the view and all.

It was odd timing, too, because earlier that day, I was almost sure I was leaving this world, via piranha.

We had anchored our boat, a three-story riverboat, in a small river cul-de-sac, and the guides had begun fishing for piranha, using only sticks and string, chicken as bait.

The piranhas took to it immediately. It was a cinch—they were jumping onto the boat, flopping around with their furious little faces.

And then, on the other side of the boat, our American guide, a bearded Bill, was swimming. The water, like tea, made his underwater limbs appear red, making all the more disconcerting the fact that he was swimming amid a school of piranhas.

"Come in!" he said.

Oh God no way.

Then everyone else was in, the chubby herpetologists were in, all their limbs in the bloodred tea. I had been told that piranha attacks were extremely rare (though not unheard of), that there was nothing to fear, and so soon enough I jumped from the boat and was swimming, too, relatively content that, even if there was some feeding frenzy, at least my odds were better than if I were in the water alone—while the fish were gorging on someone else, I'd have time to swim to safety. I actually did the math, the math of how long it would take the fish to eat the other four people vis-à-vis how long I'd have to get to the riverbank. After about three or four minutes, each one panic-stricken, trying not to touch my feet to the muddy ground, keeping my movements minimal so as not to attract attention, I got out.

Later, I tried out one of the guides' dugout canoes. After a few of the herpetologists had failed to stay afloat in it, I was convinced that I, being so very agile, could paddle and keep it afloat. I got in the tiny canoe, steadied myself, and paddled away. And for a while I did it. I set off from the main boat, downriver, alternating sides with the small paddle, the very picture of skill and grace.

But about two hundred yards down the river, the canoe began to sink. I was too heavy. It was taking in water.

I looked back to the boat. The Peruvian guides were all watching, were hysterical. I was sinking into the brown water, the current taking me farther downstream, and they were laughing, doubled over. They were loving it.

The canoe tipped, and I fell in, at this point in the middle of the river, where it was much deeper, a darker shade of brown. I could not see my limbs. I climbed onto the capsized canoe, desperate.

I was sure I was gone. Yes, the piranhas over there by the main boat had not touched us, but how could you be sure that out here, that they wouldn't take a nip from a finger? They often nipped fingers and toes, and that would draw blood and from there...

Oh God Toph.

I was there, and the canoe was sinking again, capsized but sinking under my weight, and soon I would be wholly in this river again, the river infested with piranhas, and my thrashing would draw them to me—I was trying, trying to keep it to a minimum, just kicking my legs, staying afloat—and then I would be picked at slowly, chunks from my calves and stomach, then, once the flesh was torn, and blood ribboning out, there would be the flurry, a hundred at once, I would look down and see my extremities overcome by a terrible blur of teeth and blood, and I would be picked clean, to the bone, and why? Because I had to show the entourage that I could do whatever any Peruvian river guide could do—

And I thought of poor Toph, this poor boy, three thousand miles away, staying with my sister—

How could I leave him?

p. 218: [M]y mother read a horror novel every night. She had read every one in the library. When birthdays and Christmas would come, I would consider buying her a new one, the latest Dean R. Koontz or Stephen King or whatever, but I couldn't. I didn't want to encourage her. I couldn't touch my father's cigarettes, couldn't look at the Pall Mall cartons in the pantry. I was the sort of child who couldn't even watch *commercials* for horror movies—the ad for *Magic*, the movie where the marionette kills people, sent me into a six-month nightmare frenzy. So I couldn't look at her books, would turn them over so their covers wouldn't show, the raised lettering and splotches of blood—especially the V. C. Andrews oeuvre, those turgid pictures of those terrible kids, standing so still, all lit in blue.

p. 414: Bill and Beth and Toph and I are watching the news. There is a small item about George Bush's grandmother. It is apparently her birthday.

We debate about how old the grandmother of a man in his late sixties must be. It seems impossible that she's still breathing.

Beth changes the channel.

"That's disgusting," she says.

p. 427: [S]he was living in a sort of perpetual present. Always she had to be told of her context, what brought her here, the origins and parameters of her current situation. Dozens of times each day she had to be told everything again—What made me? Whose fault am I? How did I get here? Who are these people?—the accident recounted, sketched in broad strokes, her continuously reminded but always forgetting—

Not forgetting. Having, actually, no capacity to grip the information—

But who does? Fuck it, she was alive and she knew it. Her voice sang the same way it always did, her eyes bulged with amazement over the smallest things, anything, my haircut. Yes, she still knew and had access to those things that had been with her for years—that part of her memory was there, intact—and while I wanted to punish those responsible, would relish it and presumed that I would never tire of it, being with her, so close to her skin and the blood rushing beneath it, drains me of hatred.

The music from the pool changed.

"Ooh, I like this song," she said, doing a zig-zag with her neck.

Finally, this edition reflects the author's request that all previous epigraphs—including "The heart's immortal thirst to be completely known and all forgiven." *(H. Van Dyke)*; "[My poems] may hurt the dead, but the dead belong to me." *(A. Sexton)*; "Not every boy thrown to the wolves becomes a hero." *(J. Barth)*; "Everything will be forgotten and nothing will be redressed." *(M. Kundera)*; "Why not just write what happened?" *(R. Lowell)*; "Ooh, look at me, I'm Dave, I'm writing a book! With all my thoughts in it! La la la!" *(Christopher Eggers)*—be removed, as he never really saw himself as the type of person who would use epigraphs.

—AUGUST 1999

CONTENTS

PART I.

THROUGH THE SMALL TALL BATHROOM WINDOW, ETC.

Scatology—video games—blood—"blind leaders of the blind"
[Bible]—some violence—embarrassment, naked men—mapping

PART II.

PLEASE LOOK. CAN YOU SEE US, ETC.

California—ocean plunging, frothing—Little League, black mothers—
rotation and substitution—hills, views, roofs, toothpicks—numbing
and sensation—Johnny Bench—motion

PART III.

THE ENEMIES LIST, ETC.

Demotion—teachers driven before us—menu—plane crash—light—
knife—State of the Family Room Address—half-cantaloupes—so like a
fragile girl—old model, new model—Bob Fosse Presents

PART IV.

OH I COULD BE GOING OUT, SURE

But no. No no!—the weight—seven years one's senior, how fitting—
John Doe—decay v. preservation—burgundy, bolts

PART V.

OUTSIDE IT'S BLUE-BLACK AND GETTING DARKER, ETC.

Stephen, murderer, surely—The Bridge—Jon and Pontius Pilate—
John, Moodie, et al.—lies—a stolen wallet—the 99th percentile—
Mexican kids—lineups, lights—a trail of blood, and then silence

PART VI.

WHEN WE HEAR THE NEWS AT FIRST

[Some mild nudity]—all the hope of history to date—an interview—
death and suicide—mistakes—keg beer—Mr. T—Steve the Black
Guy—a death faked, perhaps (the gray car)—a possible escape, via rope,
of sheets—a broken door—betrayal justified

PART VII.

Some bitterness, some calculation—Or anything that looks un-us—more nudity, still mild—of color, who is of color?—Chakka the Pakuni— hairy all the crotches are, bursting from panties and briefs—The Marina—The flying-object maneuver—drama or blood or his mouth foaming or—a hundred cymbals—would you serve them grapes? Would that be wrong?—"So I'm not allowed"—Details of all this will be good

PART VIII.

The Future—"Slacker? Not me," laughs Hillman—Meath: Oh yeah, we love that multicultural stuff—Fill out forms—"a nightmare WASP utopia"—a sexual sort of lushness—There has been Spin the Bottle— "I don't know"—"Thank you, Jesus"—"I'm dying, Shal"

PART IX.

Laura Branigan, Lori Singer, Ed Begley, Jr.—to be thought of as smart, legitimate, permanent. So you do your little thing—a bitchy little thing about her—a fall—the halls, shabbily shiny, are filled with people in small clumps—that Polly Klaas guy giving me the finger at the trial— Adam, by association, unimpressive

PART X.

The cold when walking off the plane—plans for a kind of personal archaeological orgy or something, from funeral homes to John Hussa, whose mom heated milk once, after Grizzly—weddings—a lesbian agnostic named Minister Lovejoy—Chad and the copies—leaf pile— another threat—of course she knows—wouldn't everyone be able to tell?—the water rising, as if under it already

PART XI.

No hands—down the hill, the walk—not NAMBLA—birthday, parquet—Skye—hot, poisoned blood—jail, bail, the oracle—more maneuvers—a fight—finally, finally.

ACKNOWLEDGMENTS

The author wishes first and foremost to acknowledge his friends at NASA and the United States Marine Corps, for their great support and unquantifiable help with the technical aspects of this story. *¡Les saludo, muchachos!* He wishes also to acknowledge the many people who have stretched the meaning of generosity by allowing their real names and actions to appear in this book. This goes doubly for the author's siblings, especially his sister Beth, whose memories were in most places more vivid, and triply for Toph (pronounced "Tofe"—long *o*), for obvious reasons. His older brother Bill is not being singled out because he is a Republican. The author would like to acknowledge that he does not look good in red. Or pink, or orange, or even yellow—he is not a spring. And until last year he thought Evelyn Waugh was a woman, and that George Eliot was a man. Further, the author, and those behind the making of this book, wish to acknowledge that yes, there are perhaps too many memoir-sorts of books being written at this juncture, and that such books, about real things and real people, as opposed to kind-of made up things and people, are inherently vile and corrupt and wrong and evil and bad, but would like to remind everyone that we could all do worse, as readers and as writers. ANECDOTE: midway through the writing of this…this…*memoir*, an acquaintance of the author's accosted him at a Western-themed restaurant/bar, while the author was eating a hearty plate of ribs and potatoes served fried in the French style. The accoster sat down opposite, asking what was new, what was *up*, what was he working on, etc. The author said Oh, well, that he was kind of working on a book, kind of mumble mumble. Oh great, said the acquaintance, who was wearing a sport coat made from what seemed to be (but it might have been the light) purple velour. What kind of book? asked the acquaintance. (Let's call him, oh, "Oswald.") What's it about? asked Oswald. Well, uh, said the author, again with the silver tongue, it's kind of hard to explain, I guess it's kind of a memoir-y kind of thing— *Oh no!* said Oswald, interrupting him, loudly. (Oswald's hair, you might want to know, was feathered.) *Don't tell me you've fallen into that trap!* (It tumbled down his shoulders, Dungeons & Dragons–style.) *Memoir! C'mon, don't pull that old trick, man!* He went on like this for a while, using the colloquial language of the day, until, well, the author felt sort of bad. After all, maybe Oswald, with the purple velour and the brown corduroys, was right—maybe memoirs were *Bad*. Maybe writing about actual events, in the first person, if not from Ireland and before you turned seventy, was *Bad*. He had a point! Hoping to change the subject, the author asked Oswald, who shares a surname with the man who killed a president, what it was that *he* was working on. (Oswald was some sort of professional writer.) The author, of course, was both expecting and dreading that Oswald's project would be of grave importance and grand scope—a renunciation of Keynesian economics, a reworking of *Grendel* (this time from the point of view of nearby conifers), whatever. But do you know what he said, he of the feathered hair and purple velour? What he said was: a screenplay. He didn't italicize it then but we will here: *a screenplay.* What sort of screenplay? the author asked, having no overarching problem with screen-plays, liking movies enormously and all, how they held a mirror to our violent society and all, but suddenly feeling slightly better all the same. The answer: A screenplay "about William S. Burroughs, and the drug culture." Well, suddenly the clouds broke, the sun shone, and once again, the author knew this: that even if the idea of relating a true story is a bad idea, and even if the idea of writing about deaths in the family and delusions as a result is unappealing to everyone but the author's high school classmates and a few creative writ-ing students in New Mexico, there are still ideas that are *much, much worse.* Besides, if you are bothered by the idea of this being real, you are invited to do what the author should have done, and what authors and readers have been doing since the beginning of time:

PRETEND IT'S FICTION.

As a matter of fact, the author would like to make an offer. For those of you on the side of Oswald, he will do this: if you send in your copy of this book, in hardcover or paperback, he will send you, for a fee of $10.00 (make check out to D. Eggers), a 3.5" floppy disk, on which will be a complete digital manuscript of this work, albeit with all names and locations changed, in such a way that the only people who will know who is who are those whose lives have been included, though thinly disguised. *Voila!* Fiction! Further, the digital version will be interactive, as we expect our digital things to be (hey, have you heard of these new mole-cule-sized microchips? The ones that can do, like all the functions ever performed by all computers since the beginning of time, in one second, in a grain of salt? Can you believe that? Well, it's as true now as ever: technology is changing the way we live). About the digital version, for starters, you'll have the option of choosing the protagonist's name. We'll provide dozens of suggestions, including "the Writer," "the Author," "the journalist," and "Paul Theroux"—or you can go it alone and make up your own! Matter of fact, using the search-and-replace function your computer surely fea-tures, readers should be able to change all the names within, from the main characters down to the smallest cameos. (This can be about *you*! You and *your* pals!) Those interested in this fictional version of this book should send their books to A.H.W.O.S.G. Special Offer for Fiction-Preferrers, c/o Vintage Books, 299 Park Avenue, New York, NY 10171. NOTE: This offer is real. ALTHOUGH: Books sent in, unfortunately, cannot be returned. INSTEAD: They will be remaindered with the rest. Moving on: The author wishes to acknowledge the existence of a planet just beyond Pluto, and further, wishes, on the basis of his own casual research and faith, to reassert Pluto's planethood. *Why did we do that to Pluto?* We had it good with Pluto. The author wishes to acknowledge that because this book is occasionally haha, you are permitted to dismiss it. The author wishes to acknowledge your problems with the title. He too has reservations. The title you see on the cover was the winner of a round-robin sort of title tourney, held outside Phoenix, Arizona, over a long weekend in December 1998. The other contenders, with reasons for failure: *A Heartbreaking Work of Death and Embarrassment* (true but unappealing); *An Astounding Work of Courage and Strength* (Stephen Ambrose would have cause for action); *Memories of a Catholic Boyhood* (also taken, more or less); and *Old and Black in America* (risque, some say). We preferred the last one, alluding as it does to both aging and an American sort of *otherness*, but it was dismissed out of hand by the publisher, leaving us with *A Heartbreaking Work of Staggering Genius*. Yes, it caught your eye. First you took it at face value, and picked it up immediately. "This is just the sort of book for which I have been looking!" Many of you, particularly those among you who seek out the maudlin and melodramatic, were struck by the "Heartbreaking" part. Others thought the "Staggering Genius" element seemed like a pretty good recommendation. But then you thought, Hey, can these two elements work together? Or might they be like peanut butter and chocolate, plaid and paisley—never to peacefully coexist? Like, if this book is, indeed, heartbreaking, then why spoil the mood with the puffery? Or, if the title is some elaborate joke, then why make an attempt at sentiment? Which is to say nothing of the faux (real? No, you beg, please no) boastfulness of the whole title put together. In the end, one's only logical interpretation of the title's intent is as a) a cheap kind of joke b) buttressed by an interest in lamely executed titular innovation (employed, one suspects, only to shock) which is c) undermined of course by the cheap joke aspect, and d) confused by the creeping feeling one gets that the author is dead serious in his feeling that the title is an accurate description of the content, intent, and quality of the book. Oh, pshaw—does it even matter now? Hells no. You're here, you're in, we're havin' a party!

The author would like to acknowledge that he did, indeed, vote for Ross Perot in 1996, and is not the least ashamed about it, because he is an ardent fan of the rich and insane, particularly when their hearts bleed, which Mr. Perot's does, it really does. On a different note, the author feels obligated to acknowledge that yes, the success of a memoir—of any book, really—has a lot to do with how appealing its narrator is. To address this, the author offers the following:

a) That he is like you.

b) That, like you, he falls asleep shortly after he becomes drunk.

c) That he sometimes has sex without condoms.

d) That he sometimes falls asleep when he is drunk having sex without condoms.

e) That he never gave his parents a proper burial.

f) That he never finished college.

g) That he expects to die young.

h) That, because his father smoked and drank and died as a result, he is afraid of food.

i) That he smiles when he sees young black men holding babies.

One word: appealing.

And that's just the beginning!

Now, the author also wishes to acknowledge the major themes of this book.

They are:

It is every child's and teen's dream. Sometimes it is
born of bitterness. Sometimes it is born of self-pity.
Sometimes one wants attention. Usually all three factors play a part. The point is that everyone at one point
or another daydreams about their parents dying, and
about what it would be like to be an orphan, like
Annie or Pippi Longstocking or, more recently, the
beautiful, tragic naifs of *Party of Five*. One pictures, in
place of the love perhaps unpredictably given and more
often withheld by one's parents, that, in their absence,
that love and attention would be lavished upon them,
that the townspeople, one's relatives, one's friends and
teachers, the world around, would suddenly be swept
up in sympathy and fascination for the orphaned child,
that his or her life would be one of celebrity mixed
with pathos, fame sprung from tragedy—the best
kind, by far. Most daydream it, some live it, and this
aspect of the book will intimate that just as it was in
Pippi, it is in real life. Thus, an incomparable loss
begets both constant struggle and heart-hardening,
but also some unimpeachable rewards, starting with
absolute freedom, interpretable and of use in a number
of ways. And though it seems inconceivable to lose
both parents in the space of 32 days—there was that
line from *The Imp. of Being Earnest*: "To have lost one

parent, Mr. Worthing, might be considered a misfortune. To have lost both smacks of carelessness"—and to lose them to completely different diseases (cancer, sure, but different enough, in terms of location, duration, and provenance), that loss is accompanied by an undeniable but then of course guilt-inducing sense of mobility, of infinite possibility, having suddenly found oneself in a world with neither floor nor ceiling.

B) THE BROTHERLY LOVE / WEIRD SYMBIOSIS FACTOR
This thread will be going throughout, and was as a matter of fact supposed to be the surprise conclusion reached at the end of the book, the big pay-off, as it were, that, while the author searches for love—there will be some episodes involving that—and his brother searches for, you know, whatever little kids search for (gum and pennies?) and together they try to be normal and happy, they actually will probably always be unsuccessful in any and every extracurricular relationship, given that the only people who they truly admire and love and find perfect are each other.

C) THE PAINFULLY, ENDLESSLY
SELF-CONSCIOUS BOOK ASPECT
This is probably obvious enough already. The point is, the author doesn't have the energy or, more important, skill, to fib about this being anything other than him

telling you about things, and is not a good enough liar to do it in any competently sublimated narrative way. At the same time, he will be clear and up-front about this being a self-conscious memoir, which you may come to appreciate, and which is the next theme:

C.2) The Knowingness About the Book's Self-consciousness Aspect

While the author is self-conscious about being self-referential, he is also knowing about that self-conscious self-referentiality. Further, and if you're one of those people who can tell what's going to happen before it actually happens, you've predicted the next element here: he also plans to be clearly, obviously aware of his knowingness about his self-consciousness of self-referentiality. Further, he is fully cognizant, way ahead of you, in terms of knowing about and fully admitting the gimmickry inherent in all this, and will preempt your claim of the book's irrelevance due to said gimmickry by saying that the gimmickry is simply a device, a defense, to obscure the black, blinding, murderous rage and sorrow at the core of this whole story, which is both too black and blinding to look at— *avert...your...eyes!*—but nevertheless useful, at least to the author, even in caricatured or condensed form, because telling as many people as possible about it helps, he thinks, to dilute the pain and bitterness and thus facilitate its flushing from his soul, the pursuit of which is the basis of the next cluster of themes:

D) THE TELLING THE WORLD OF SUFFERING AS MEANS OF FLUSHING OR AT LEAST DILUTING OF PAIN ASPECT

For example, the author spends some time later relating his unsuccessful, though just barely unsuccessful, attempt to become a cast member of *The Real World* in 1994, when the show's third season was being filmed in San Francisco. At that point, the author sought to do two related things: 1) to purge himself of his past by trumpeting his recent life's events to the world, and thus, by spreading his pain, his heartbreaking story, to the show's thousands or millions of watchers, he would receive in return a thousand tidal waves of sympathy and support, and never be lonely again; and 2) To become well known for his sorrows, or at least to let his suffering facilitate his becoming well known, while at the same time not shrinking from the admission of such manipulations of his pain for profit, because the admission of such motivations, at least in his opinion, immediately absolves him of responsibility for such manipulations' implications or consequences, because being aware of and open about one's motives at least means one is not lying, and no one, except an electorate, likes a liar. We all like full disclosure, particularly if it includes the admission of one's 1) mortality and 2) propensity to fail. (Related, but not the same.)

E) THE PUTTING THIS ALL DOWN AS TOOL
FOR STOPPING TIME GIVEN THE OVERLAP
WITH FEAR OF DEATH ASPECT

and E)'s self-explanatory corollary,

E.2) IN ADDITION TO PUTTING THIS DOWN AS TOOL
FOR STOPPING TIME, THE SEXUAL RENDEZVOUS
WITH OLD FRIENDS OR GRADE SCHOOL CRUSHES
AS TOOL FOR COLLAPSING OF TIME
AND VINDICATION OF SELF-WORTH

F) THE PART WHERE THE AUTHOR EITHER EXPLOITS
OR EXALTS HIS PARENTS, DEPENDING ON YOUR
POINT OF VIEW

G) THE UNMISTAKABLE FEELING ONE GETS, AFTER
SOMETHING TRULY WEIRD OR EXTRAORDINARY, OR
EXTRAORDINARILY WEIRD, OR WEIRDLY TERRIBLE,
HAPPENS TO THEM, THAT IN A WAY THEY HAVE
BEEN *CHOSEN* ASPECT

This of course happened to the author. After the double deaths, and his guardianship, he felt suddenly
watched—he could not help but think, in much the
same way someone who had been struck by lightning

might, that he had somehow been singled out, and that his life was thereafter charged with purpose, with the gravest importance, that he could not be wasting time, that he must act in accordance with his destiny, that it was so plainly obvious that...that...*he had been chosen...to lead!*

H) THE ASPECT HAVING TO DO WITH
(PERHAPS) INHERITED FATALISM

This part concerns the unshakable feeling one gets, one thinks, after the unthinkable and unexplainable happens—the feeling that, if this person can die, and that person can die, and this can happen and that can happen...well, then, what exactly is preventing everything from happening to this person, he around whom everything else happened? If people are dying, why won't he? If people are shooting people from cars, if people are tossing rocks down from overpasses, surely he will be the next victim. If people are contracting AIDS, odds are he will, too. Same with fires in homes, car accidents, plane crashes, random knifings, stray gunfire, aneurysms, spider bites, snipers, piranhas, zoo animals. It's the confluence of the self-centeredness discussed in G), and a black sort of outlook one is handed when all rules of impossibility and propriety are thrown out. Thus, one starts to feeling that death is literally around each and every corner—and more specifically, in every elevator; even more literally, that, each and every time an elevator door opens, there will be standing, in a trenchcoat, a man, with a gun, who will fire one bullet, straight into him, killing him instantly, and deservedly, both in keeping with his role as the object of so much wrath in general, and for his innumerable sins, both Catholic and karmic. Just as some police—particularly those they dramatize on television—might be familiar with death, and might expect it at any instant—not necessarily their own, but death generally—so does the author, possessing a naturally paranoid disposition, compounded by environmental factors that make it seem not only possible but *probable* that whatever there might be out there that snuffs out life is probably sniffing around for him, that his number is perennially, eternally, up, that his draft number is low, that his bingo card is hot, that he has a bull's-eye on his chest and target on his back. It's fun. You'll see.

And finally:

1) THE MEMOIR AS ACT OF SELF-DESTRUCTION ASPECT
It can and should be the shedding of a skin, which is something one should do, as necessary and invigorating as the occasional facial, or colonic. Revelation is everything, not for its own sake, because most self-

revelation is just garbage—*oop!*—yes, but we have to purge the garbage, toss it out, throw it into a bunker and burn it, because it is fuel. It's fossil fuel. And what do we do with fossil fuel? Why, we dump it into a bunker and burn it, of course. No, we don't do that. But you get my meaning. It's endlessly renewable, usable without diminishing one's capacity to create more. The author falls asleep shortly after he becomes drunk. The author has sex without condoms. The author falls asleep when he's drunk having sex without condoms. There. That's something. You have something. But what do you *have*?

1.2) The Easy and Unconvincing Nihilistic Poseurism Re: Full Disclosure of One's Secrets and Pain, Passing It Off Under a Semi-high-minded Guise When in Fact the Author Is Himself Very Private About Many or Most Matters, Though He Sees the Use in Making Certain Facts and Happenings Public

1.3) The Fact That, Below, or Maybe Next to, the Self-righteousness, and the Self-hatred, Is a Certain Hope, Instilled Far Before Any of This Happened.

There will also be these threads, which are all more or less self-explanatory:

j) THE FLOUTING OF SUBLIMATION AS EVIDENCE OF ENFORCED SOLIPSISM ASPECT

k) THE SOLIPSISM AS LIKELY RESULT OF ECONOMIC, HISTORICAL AND GEOPOLITICAL PRIVILEGE ASPECT

l) THE TOPH DIALECTIC: HE SERVING AS BOTH INSPIRATION FOR AND IMPEDIMENT TO WRITING OF MEMOIR

m) THE TOPH DIALECTIC II: HE SERVING AS BOTH MAGNET AND, WHEN THE NEED ARISES, WEDGE VIS-À-VIS RELATIONS WITH WOMEN

Similarly:

n) THE PARENTAL LOSS DIALECTIC: IN TERMS OF THAT FACTOR LENDING ITSELF WELL TO SITUATIONS NECESSITATING THE GARNERING OF SYMPATHY AND ALSO TO THOSE REQUIRING A QUICK EXIT

Not to mention:

o) THE ASPECT CONCERNING THE UNAVOIDABILITY, GIVEN THE SITUATION WITH BROTHER, OF NEAR-CONSTANT POIGNANCE

P) THE SELF-AGGRANDIZEMENT AS ART FORM ASPECT

Q) THE SELF-FLAGELLATION AS ART FORM ASPECT

R) THE SELF-AGGRANDIZEMENT DISGUISED AS SELF-FLAGELLATION AS EVEN HIGHER ART FORM ASPECT

S) THE SELF-CANONIZATION DISGUISED AS SELF-DESTRUCTION MASQUERADING AS SELF-AGGRANDIZEMENT DISGUISED AS SELF-FLAGELLATION AS HIGHEST ART FORM OF ALL ASPECT

T) THE SEARCH FOR SUPPORT, A SENSE OF COMMUNITY, IF YOU WILL, IN ONE'S PEERS, IN THOSE ONE'S AGE, AFTER ONE LOOKS AROUND AND REALIZES THAT ALL OTHERS, ALL THOSE OLDER, ARE EITHER DEAD OR PERHAPS SHOULD BE ASPECT

U) THE FACT THAT T) DOVETAILS QUITE NICELY WITH G) ASPECT

Or, in graph form (next page):

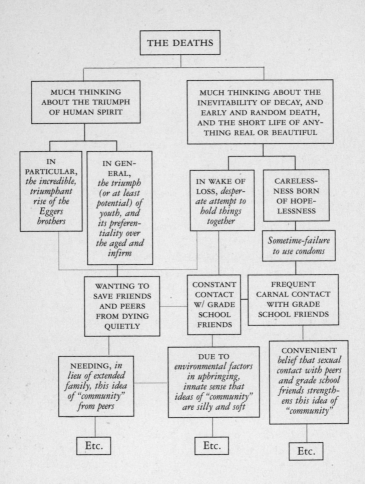

The author would also like to acknowledge what he was paid to write this book:

TOTAL (GROSS) $100,000.⁰⁰

DEDUCTIONS

Agent's fee (15%) $15,000.⁰⁰

Taxes (after agent's fee) $23,800.⁰⁰

EXPENSES RELATED TO PRODUCTION OF BOOK

Portion of rent, two years (btw $600 & $1,500/mo) . . . *approx:* $12,000.⁰⁰

Trip to Chicago (research) $850.⁰⁰

Trip to San Francisco (research) $620.⁰⁰

Food (consumed while ostensibly writing) $5,800.⁰⁰

Sundries $1,200.⁰⁰

Laser printer $600.⁰⁰

Paper $242.⁰⁰

Postage (to send manuscript, for approval, to siblings Beth (somewhere in No. California), and Bill (an advisor to the Comptroller of Texas, in Austin), Kirsten (San Francisco, married), Shalini (living at home in L.A., doing well), Meredith Weiss (freelance wardrobe stylist, San Diego), Jamie Carrick (in L.A., part of management team for Hanson, a popular music outfit), "Ricky" (San Francisco, investment banker—high-tech IPOs), etc. etc.) $231.⁰⁰

Copy of *Xanadu* Original Movie Soundtrack $14.³²

Information retrieval service (unsuccessful attempt to retrieve two years' worth of journal entries from external hard drive, expired) $75.⁰⁰

NET TOTAL $39,567.⁶⁸

Which still isn't so bad, come to think of it—more than the author, who is not a pet owner, can spend. Therefore, he pledges some of it to you, or at least some of you. The first 200 readers of this book who write with proof that they have read and absorbed the many lessons herein will each receive a check, from the author, for $5, drawn from a U.S. bank, probably Chase Manhattan, which is not a good bank—do not open an account there. Now: how to prove that you have bought and read the book? Let's say we do this: Take the book, which you are required to have purchased*—enclose your receipt, or a copy of the receipt—and have someone take a picture of you reading the book, or maybe putting it to better use. Special consideration for a) the inclusion in the picture of a baby (or babies), as everyone knows that babies are nice; b) the inclusion in the picture of a baby with an exceptionally large tongue; c) pictures taken in exotic locales (with the book, remember); d) pictures of the book being rubbed against by a red panda, a small bear + raccoon-looking mammal, also known as the "lesser panda," native of central China and frequent-rubber-against of things for marking

---

* It should go without saying that if you've checked this book out from the library, or are reading it in paperback, you are much, much too late. Come to think of it, you may be reading this far, far in the future—it's probably being taught in all the schools! Do tell: What's it like in the future? Is everyone wearing robes? Are the cars rounder, or less round? Is there a women's soccer league yet?

of territory. DO NOT FORGET TO: center yourself, or whatever your subject, in the picture. If you're using an auto-focus camera with a 35mm lens, get closer than you feel you should; the lens, because it's convex, has the effect of backing you up 5–8 feet. ALSO: Keep your clothes on, please. Those readers who are savvy enough to have picked up a copy of one quarterly publication in particular will already know the most expeditious address to receive this free-ish money (though that address is only good until maybe August 2000), and will therefore be at an advantage, timewise. Otherwise, send your tasteful photographs to:

A.H.W.O.S.G. Offer

Vintage Books

299 Park Avenue

New York, NY 10171

If, by the time the author receives your letter, he has already distributed the 200 checks, good fortune may yet strike. If your picture is amusing or your name or hometown unfortunate-sounding, and you include a self-addressed stamped envelope, he will put something (not money) inside the envelope and will send it back, because he does not have cable, and needs diversion. Now.* The author would like to acknowledge your desire to get started with the plot, the body of the book, the *story*.

*Interesting story: My father once related how he and his friend Les had come up with a way, when stalling for time in a meeting or deposition (he and Les were lawyers [Les, alive and well, still is a lawyer]), instead of saying "Um...," or "Uh...," one could say "Now...," a word which accomplishes two things: it serves the same stalling purpose as "Um...," or "Uh...," but instead of being dumb-sounding offputting, it creates suspense for what is coming next, whatever that might be, that which the speaker doesn't yet know.

He will do that, and, contrary to what was said in D),
he will be giving you, for a good 100 pages or so, unin-
terrupted, unself-conscious prose, which will entertain
and make sad and, here and there, hearten. He will get
on with that story any moment now, because he recognizes when the time has come, when the time is right,
when the getting's good. He acknowledges the needs
and feelings of a reader, the fact that a reader only has
so much time, so much patience—that seemingly endless screwing about, interminable clearing of one's
throat, can very easily look like, or even *become*, a sort
of contemptuous stalling, a putting-off of one's readers, and no one wants that. (Or do they?) So we will
move on, because the author, like you, wants to move
on, into the meat of it, dive right in and revisit this
stuff, because it's a story that ought to be told, involving,
as it does, death and redemption, bile, and betrayal. So
dive in we will, after a few more acknowledgments.
The author would like to acknowledge the brave men
and women serving in the United States Armed Forces.
He wishes them well, and hopes they come home soon.
That is, if they want to. If they like it where they are,
he hopes they stay there. At least until such time as
they want to come home. Then they should come
straight home, on the very next plane. The author
would also like to acknowledge the makers of comic
book villains and superheroes, those who invented, or

at least popularized, the notion of the normal, mild-mannered person transformed into mutant by freak accident, with the mutant thereafter driven by a strange hybrid of the most rancid bitterness and the most outrageous hope to do very, very odd and silly things, many times in the name of Good. The makers of comic books seemed to be onto something there. Now, in a spirit of interpretive *glasnost*, the author would like to save you some trouble by laying out a rough guide to a little over half of the metaphors in the book. (Next page.) The author would also like to acknowledge his propensity to exaggerate. And his propensity to fib in order to make himself look better, or worse, whichever serves his purposes at the time. He would also like to acknowledge that no, he is not the only person to ever lose his parents, and that he is also not the only person ever to lose his parents and inherit a youngster. But he would like to point out that he is currently the only such person with a book contract. He would like to acknowledge the distinguished senator from Massachusetts. And Palestinian statehood. And the implicit logic of the instant replay rule. And that he too is well aware of all of the book's flaws and shortcomings, whatever you consider them to be, and that he tips his hat to you for noticing them. And come to think of it, he would actually like to acknowledge his brother Bill after all; his brother Bill is such a good

INCOMPLETE GUIDE
TO SYMBOLS AND METAPHORS

Sun	=	Mother
Moon	=	Father
Family room	=	Past
Nosebleed	=	Decay
Tumor	=	Portent
Sky	=	Emancipation
Ocean	=	Mortality
Bridge	=	Bridge
Wallet	=	⎡ Security
		Father
		Past
		⎣ Class

Lattice	=	Transcendental-equivalent
White bed	=	Womb
Furniture, rugs, etc.	=	Past
Tiny stuffed bear	=	Mother
Toph	=	Mother
Dolls	=	Mother
Lake Michigan	=	⎡ Mother
		Past
		Peace
		Chaos
		⎣ Unknown

Mother	=	Mortality
Mother	=	Love
Mother	=	Rage
Mother	=	Cancer
Betsy	=	Past
John	=	Father
Shalini	=	Promise
Skye	=	Promise
Me	=	Mother

Note: No symbolism is meant by the use of Journey's "Any Way You Want It."

man. And this book's gracious and trusting editor, Geoff Kloske, and Mr. Kloske's assistant, Nicole Graev, who has her vowels transposed but is otherwise very nice. Also C. Leyshon, A. Quinn, J. Lethem, and V. Vida, for the assuaging of fears, not to mention Adrienne Miller, John Warner, Marny Requa and Sarah Vowell, whose readings of this book before it was readable were much appreciated (even though, come to think of it, the author did toss Warner $100, which makes his acknowledgment kind of unnecessary). And once again, all the people who star in this story, especially Mr. C.M.E., who knows who he is. Finally, the author would also like to acknowledge the men and women of the United States Postal Service, for performing a sometimes thankless task with great aplomb and, given the scale and scope of the endeavor, with stunning efficiency.

Here is a drawing of a stapler:

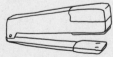

I.

Through the small tall bathroom window the December yard is gray and scratchy, the trees calligraphic. Exhaust from the dryer billows out of the house and up, breaking apart while tumbling into the white sky.

The house is a factory.

I put my pants back on and go back to my mother. I walk down the hall, past the laundry room, and into the family room. I close the door behind me, muffling the rumbling of the small shoes in the dryer.

"Where were you?" my mother says.

"In the bathroom," I say.

"Hmph," she says.

"What?"

"For fifteen minutes?"

"It wasn't that long."

"It was longer. Was something broken?"

"No."

"Did you fall in?"

"No."

"Were you playing with yourself?"

"I was cutting my hair."

"You were contemplating your navel."

"Right. Whatever."

"Did you clean up?"

"Yeah."

I had not cleaned up, had actually left hair everywhere, twisted brown doodles drawn in the sink, but knew that my mother would not find out. She could not get up to check.

My mother is on the couch. At this point, she does not move from the couch. There was a time, until a few months ago, when she was still up and about, walking and driving, running errands. After that there was a period when she spent most of her time in her chair, the one next to the couch, occasionally doing things, going out, whatnot. Finally she moved to the couch, but even then, for a while at least, while spending most of her time on the couch, every night at 11 p.m. or so, she had made a point of making her way up the stairs, in her bare feet, still tanned brown in November, slow and careful on the green carpet, to my sister's old bedroom. She had been sleeping there for years—the room was pink, and clean, and the bed had a canopy, and long ago she resolved that she could no longer sleep with my father's coughing.

But the last time she went upstairs was weeks ago. Now she is on the couch, not moving from the couch, reclining on the couch during the day and sleeping there at night, in her nightgown, with the TV on until dawn, a comforter over her, toe to neck. People know.

While reclining on the couch most of the day and night, on her back, my mom turns her head to watch television and turns it back to spit up green fluid into a plastic receptacle. The plastic receptacle is new. For many weeks she had been spitting the green fluid into a towel, not the same towel, but a rotation of towels, one of which she would keep on her chest. But the towel on her chest, my sister Beth and I found after a short while, was not such a good place to spit the green fluid, because, as it turned out, the green fluid smelled awful, much more pungent an aroma than one might expect. (One expects some sort of odor, sure, but *this*.) And so the green fluid could not be left there, festering and then petrifying on the terry-cloth towels. (Because the green fluid hardened to a crust on the terry-cloth towels, they were almost impossible to clean. So the green-fluid towels were one-use only, and even if you used every corner of the towels, folding and turning, turning and folding, they would only last a few days each, and the supply was running short, even after we plundered the bathrooms, closets, the garage.) So finally Beth procured, and our mother began to spit the green fluid into, a small plastic container which looked makeshift, like a piece of an air-conditioning unit, but had been provided by the hospital and was as far as we knew designed for people who do a lot of spitting up of green fluid. It's a molded plastic receptacle, cream-colored, in the shape of a half-moon, which can be kept handy and spit into. It can be cupped around the mouth of a reclining person, just under the chin, in a way that allows the depositor of green bodily fluids to either raise one's head to spit directly into it, or to simply let the fluid dribble down, over his or her chin, and then into the receptacle waiting below. It was a great find, the half-moon plastic receptacle.

"That thing is handy, huh?" I ask my mother, walking past her, toward the kitchen.

"Yeah, it's the cat's meow," she says.

I get a popsicle from the refrigerator and come back to the family room.

They took my mother's stomach out about six months ago. At that point, there wasn't a lot left to remove—they had already taken out [I would use the medical terms here if I knew them] the rest of it about a year before. Then they tied the [something] to the [something], hoped that they had removed the offending portion, and set her on a schedule of chemotherapy. But of course they didn't get it all. They had left some of it and it had grown, it had come back, it had laid eggs, was stowed away, was stuck to the side of the spaceship. She had seemed good for a while, had done the chemo, had gotten the wigs, and then her hair had grown back— darker, more brittle. But six months later she began to have pain again— *Was it indigestion?* It could just be indigestion, of course, the burping and the pain, the leaning over the kitchen table at dinner; people have indigestion; people take Tums; *Hey Mom, should I get some Tums?*—but when she went in again, and they had "opened her up"—a phrase they used—and had looked inside, it was staring out at them, at the doctors, like a thousand writhing worms under a rock, swarming, shimmering, wet and oily—*Good God!*— or maybe not like worms but like a million little podules, each a tiny city of cancer, each with an unruly, sprawling, environmentally careless citizenry with no zoning laws whatsoever. When the doctor opened her up, and there was suddenly light thrown upon the world of cancer-podules, they were annoyed by the disturbance, and defiant. *Turn off. The fucking. Light.* They glared at the doctor, each podule, though a city unto itself, having one single eye, one blind evil eye in the middle, which stared imperiously, as only a blind eye can do, out at the doctor. *Go. The. Fuck. Away.* The doctors did what they could, took the whole stomach out, connected what was left, this part to that, and sewed her back up, leaving the city as is, the colonists to their manifest destiny, their fossil fuels, their strip malls and suburban sprawl, and replaced the stomach with a tube and a portable external IV bag. It's kind of cute, the IV bag. She used to carry it with her, in a gray backpack—it's futuristic-looking, like a synthetic ice pack crossed with those liquid food pouches engineered for space travel. We have a name for it. We call it "the bag."

My mother and I are watching TV. It's the show where young amateur athletes with day jobs in marketing and engineering compete in sports of strength and agility against male and female bodybuilders. The bodybuilders are mostly blond and are impeccably tanned. They look great. They have names that sound fast and indomitable, names like American cars and electronics, like Firestar and Mercury and Zenith. It is a great show.

"What is this?" she asks, leaning toward the TV. Her eyes, once small, sharp, intimidating, are now dull, yellow, droopy, strained—the spitting gives them a look of constant exasperation.

"The fighting show thing," I say.

"Hmm," she says, then turns, lifts her head to spit.

"Is it still bleeding?" I ask, sucking on my popsicle.

"Yeah."

We are having a nosebleed. While I was in the bathroom, she was holding the nose, but she can't hold it tight enough, so now I relieve her, pinching her nostrils with my free hand. Her skin is oily, smooth.

"Hold it tighter," she says.

"Okay," I say, and hold it tighter. Her skin is hot.

Toph's shoes continue to rumble.

A month ago Beth was awake early; she cannot remember why. She walked down the stairs, shushing the green carpet, down to the foyer's black slate floor. The front door was open, with only the screen door closed. It was fall, and cold, and so with two hands she closed the large wooden door, click, and turned toward the kitchen. She walked down the hall and into the kitchen, frost spiderwebbed on the corners of its sliding glass door, frost on the bare trees in the backyard. She opened the refrigerator and looked inside. Milk, fruit, IV bags dated for proper use. She closed the refrigerator. She walked from the kitchen into the family room, where the curtains surrounding the large front window were open, and the light outside was white. The window was a bright silver screen, lit from behind. She squinted until her eyes adjusted. As her eyes focused, in the middle of the screen, at the end of the driveway, was my father, kneeling.

It's not that our family has no taste, it's just that our family's taste is inconsistent. The wallpaper in the downstairs bathroom, though it came with the house, is the house's most telling decorative statement, featuring a pattern of fifteen or so slogans and expressions popular at the time of its installation. *Right On*, *Neat-O*, *Outta Sight!*—arranged so they unite and abut in intriguing combinations. *That-A-Way* meets *Way Out* so that the A in *That-A-Way* creates *A Way Out*. The words are hand-rendered in stylized block letters, red and black against white. It could not be uglier, and yet the wallpaper is a novelty that visitors appreciate, evidence of a family with no pressing interest in addressing obvious problems of decor, and also proof of a happy time, an exuberant, fanciful time in American history that spawned exuberant and fanciful wallpaper.

The living room is kind of classy, actually—clean, neat, full of heirlooms and antiques, an oriental rug covering the center of the hardwood floor. But the family room, the only room where any of us has ever spent any time, has always been, for better or for worse, the ultimate reflection of our true inclinations. It's always been jumbled, the furniture competing, with clenched teeth and sharp elbows, for the honor of the Most Wrong-looking Object. For twelve years, the dominant chairs were blood orange. The couch of our youth, that which interacted with the orange chairs and white shag carpet, was plaid—green, brown and white. The family room has always had the look of a ship's cabin, wood paneled, with six heavy wooden beams holding, or pretending to hold, the ceiling above. The family room is dark and, save for a general sort of decaying of its furniture and walls, has not changed much in the twenty years we've lived here. The furniture is overwhelmingly brown and squat, like the furniture of a family of bears. There is our latest couch, my father's, long and covered with something like tan-colored velour, and there is the chair next to the couch, which five years ago replaced the bloodoranges, a sofa-chair of brownish plaid, my mother's. In front of the couch is a coffee table made from a cross section of a tree, cut in such a way that the bark is still there, albeit heavily lacquered. We brought it back, many years ago, from California and it, like most of the house's furniture, is evidence of an empathetic sort of decorating philosophy—for aesthetically disenfranchised furnishings we are like the families that adopt troubled children and refugees from around the world—we see beauty within and cannot say no.

One wall of the family room was and is dominated by a brick fireplace. The fireplace has a small recessed area that was built to facilitate indoor barbecuing, though we never put it to use, chiefly because when we moved in, we were told that raccoons lived somewhere high in the chimney. So for many years the recessed area sat dormant, until the day, about four years ago, that our father, possessed by the same odd sort of inspiration that had led him for many years to decorate the lamp next to the couch with rubber spiders and snakes, put a fish tank inside. The fish tank, its size chosen by a wild guess, ended up fitting perfectly.

"Hey *hey!*" he had said when he installed it, sliding it right in, with no more than a centimeter of give on either side. "Hey *hey!*" was something he said, and to our ears it sounded a little too Fonzie, coming as it did from a gray-haired lawyer wearing madras pants. "Hey hey!" he would say after such miracles, which were dizzying in their quantity and wonderment—in addition to the Miracle of the New Fish-tank Fitting, there was, for example, the Miracle of Getting the TV Wired Through the Cool New Stereo for True Stereo Sound, not to mention the Miracle of Running the Nintendo Wires *Under* the Wall-to-Wall Carpet So as Not to Have the Baby Tripping Over Them All the Time Goddammit. (He was devoted to Nintendo.) To bring attention to each marvel, he would stand before whoever happened to be in the room and, while grinning wildly, grip his hands together in triumph, over one shoulder and then the other, like the Cub Scout who won the Pinewood Derby. Sometimes, for modesty's sake, he would do it with his eyes closed and his head tilted. Did *I* do *that*?

"Loser," we would say.

"Aw, screw you," he would say, and go make himself a nice tall Bloody Mary.

The ceiling in one corner of the living room is stained in concentric circles of yellow and brown, a souvenir from heavy rains the spring before. The door to the foyer hangs by one of its three hinges. The carpet, off-white wall-to-wall, is worn to its core and has not been vacuumed in months. The screen windows are still up—my father tried to take them down but could not this year. The family room's front window faces east, and because the house sits beneath a number of large elms, it receives little light. The light in the family room is not significantly different in the day and the night. The family room is usually dark.

I am home from college for Christmas break. Our older brother, Bill, just went back to D.C., where he works for the Heritage Foundation—something to do with eastern European economics, privatization, conversion. My sister is home because she has been home all year—she deferred law school to be here for the fun. When I come home, Beth goes out.

"Where are you going?" I usually say.

"Out," she usually says.

I am holding the nose. As the nose bleeds and we try to stop it, we watch TV. On the TV an accountant from Denver is trying to climb up a wall before a bodybuilder named Striker catches him and pulls him off the wall. The other segments of the show can be tense—there is an obstacle course segment, where the contestants are racing against each other and also the clock, and another segment where they hit each other with sponge-ended paddles, both of which can be extremely exciting, especially if the contest is a close one, evenly matched and with much at stake—but this part, with the wall climbing, is too disturbing. The idea of the accountant being chased while climbing a wall... no one wants to be chased while climbing a wall, chased by anything, by people, hands grabbing at their ankles as they reach for the bell at the top. Striker wants to grab and pull the accountant down—he lunges every so often at the accountant's legs—all he needs is a good grip, a lunge and a grip and a good yank—and if Striker and his hands do that before the accountant gets to ring the bell... it's a horrible part of the show. The accountant climbs quickly, feverishly, nailing foothold after foothold, and for a second it looks like he'll make it, because Striker is so far below, two people-lengths easily, but then the accountant pauses. He cannot see his next move. The next grip is too far to reach from where he is. So then he actually *backs up*, goes down a notch to set out on a different path and when he steps down it is unbearable, the suspense. The accountant steps down and then starts up the left side of the wall, but suddenly Striker is there, out of nowhere—*he wasn't even in the screen!*—and he has the accountant's leg, at the calf, and he yanks and it's over. The accountant flies from the wall (attached by rope of course) and descends slowly to the floor. It's terrible. I won't watch this show again.

Mom prefers the show where three young women sit on a pastel-colored couch and recount blind dates that they have all enjoyed or suffered through with the same man. For months, Beth and Mom have watched the show, every night. Sometimes the show's participants have had sex with one another, but use funny words to describe it. And there is the funny host with the big nose and the black curly hair. He is a funny man, and has fun with the show, keeps everything buoyant. At the end the show, the bachelor picks one of the three with whom he wants to go on another date. The host then does something pretty incredible: even though he's already paid for the three dates previously described, and even though he has nothing to gain from doing anything more, *he still gives the bachelor and bachelorette money for their next date.*

Mom watches it every night; it's the only thing she can watch without falling asleep, which she does a lot, dozing on and off during the day. But she does not sleep at night.

"Of course you sleep at night," I say.

"I don't," she says.

"Everyone sleeps at night," I say—this is an issue with me—"even if it doesn't feel like it. The night is way, way too long to stay awake the whole way through. I mean, there have been times when I was pretty sure I had stayed up all night, like when I was sure the vampires from *Salem's Lot*—do you remember that one, with David Soul and everything? With the people impaled on the antlers? I was afraid to sleep, so I would stay up all night, watching that little portable TV on my stomach, the whole night, afraid to drift off, because I was sure they'd be waiting for just that moment, just when I fell asleep, to come and float up to my window, or down the hall, and bite me, all slow-like…"

She spits into her half-moon and looks at me.

"What the hell are you talking about?"

In the fireplace, the fish tank is still there, but the fish, four or five of those bug-eyed goldfish with elephantiasis, died weeks ago. The water, still lit from above by the purplish aquarium light, is gray with mold and fish feces, hazy like a shaken snow globe. I am wondering about something. I am wondering what the water would taste like. Like a nutritional shake? Like sewage? I think of asking my mother: *What do you think that would taste like?* But she will not find the question amusing. She will not answer.

"Would you check it?" she says, referring to her nose.

I let go of her nostrils. Nothing.

I watch the nose. She is still tan from the summer. Her skin is smooth, brown.

Then it comes, the blood, first in a tiny rivulet, followed by a thick eel, venturing out, slowly. I get a towel and dab it away.

"It's still coming," I say.

Her white blood cell count has been low. Her blood cannot clot properly, the doctor had said the last time this had happened, so, he said, we can have no bleeding. Any bleeding could be the end, he said. Yes, we said. We were not worried. There seemed to be precious few opportunities to draw blood, with her living, as she did, on the couch. *I'll keep sharp objects out of proximity*, I had joked to the doctor. The doctor did not chuckle. I wondered if he had heard me. I considered repeating it, but then figured that he had probably heard me but had not found it funny. But maybe he didn't hear me. I thought briefly, then, about supplementing the joke somehow, pushing it over the top, so to speak, with the second joke bringing the first one up and creating a sort of one-two punch. *No more knife fights*, I might say. *No more knife throwing*, I might offer, heh heh. But this doctor does not joke much. Some of the nurses do. It is our job to joke with the doctors and nurses. It is our job to listen to the doctors, and after listening to the doctors, Beth usually asks the doctors specific questions—*How often will she have to take that? Can't we just add that to the mix in the IV?*—and sometimes I ask a question, and then we might add some levity with a witty aside. I know that I should joke in the face of adversity; there is always humor, we are told. But in the last few weeks, we haven't found much. We have been looking for funny things, but have found very little.

"I can't get the game to work," says Toph, who has appeared
from the basement. Christmas was a week ago.

"What?"

"I can't get the Sega to work."

"Is it turned on?"

"Yes."

"Is the cartridge plugged all the way in?"

"Yes."

"Turn it off and on again."

"Okay," he says, and goes back downstairs.

Through the family room window, in the middle of the white-
silver screen, my father was in his suit, a gray suit, dressed for
work. Beth paused in the entrance between the kitchen and the
family room and watched. The trees in the yard across the street
were huge, gray-trunked, high-limbed, the short grass on the lawn
yellowed, spotted with fall leaves. He did not move. His suit, even
with him kneeling, leaning forward, was loose on his shoulders and
back. He had lost so much weight. A car went by, a gray blur. She
waited for him to get up.

You should see the area where her stomach was. It's grown like a
pumpkin. Round, bloated. It's odd—they removed the stomach,
and some of the surrounding area if I remember correctly, but even
with the removal of so much thereabouts, she looks pregnant. You
can see it, the bulge, even under the blanket. I'm assuming it's the
cancer, but I haven't asked my mother, or Beth. Was it the bloat-
ing of the starving child? I don't know. I don't ask questions.
Before, when I said that I asked questions, I lied.

The nose has at this point been bleeding for about ten minutes.
She had had one nosebleed before, two weeks ago maybe, and Beth

could not make it stop, so she and Beth had gone to the emergency room. The hospital people had kept her for two days. Her oncologist, who sometimes we liked and sometimes we did not, came and visited and glanced at stainless steel charts and chatted on the side of the bed—he has been her oncologist for many years. They gave her new blood and had monitored her white blood cell count. They had wanted to keep her longer, but she had insisted on going home; she was terrified of being in there, was finished with hospitals, did not want—

She had come out feeling defeated, stripped, and now, safely at home, she did not want to go back. She had made me and Beth promise that she would never have to go back. We had promised.

"*Okay*," we said.

"I'm serious," she said.

"Okay," we said.

I push her forehead as far back as possible. The arm of the couch is soft and pliable.

She spits. She is used to the spitting, but still makes strained, soft vomiting noises.

"Does it hurt?" I ask.

"Does what hurt?"

"The spitting."

"No, it feels good, stupid."

"Sorry."

A family walks by outside, two parents, a small child in snowpants and a parka, a stroller. They do not look through our window. It is hard to tell if they know. They might know but are being polite. People know.

My mother likes to have the curtains open so she can see the yard and the street. During the day it is often very bright outside, and though the brightness is visible from inside the family room, somehow the light does not travel effectively into the family room, in terms of bringing to the family room any noticeable illumination. I am not a proponent of the curtains being open.

Some people know. Of course they know.

People know.

Everyone knows. Everyone is talking. Waiting.

I have plans for them, the nosy, the inquisitive, the pitying, have developed elaborate fantasies for those who would see us as grotesque, pathetic, our situation gossip fodder. I picture strangulations—*Tsk tsk, I hear she's*-gurgle!—neck-breakings—*what will happen to that poor little bo*-crack!—I picture kicking bodies as they lie curled on the ground, spitting blood as they—*Jesus Christ, Jesus fucking Christ, I'm sorry, I'm sorry!*—beg for mercy. I lift them over my head and then bring them down, break them over my knee, their spines like dowels of balsa. Can't you see it? I push offenders into giant vats of acid and watch them struggle, scream as the acid burns, breaks them apart. My hands fly into them, breaking their skin—I pull out hearts and intestines and toss them aside. I do head-crushings, beheadings, some work with baseball bats—the variety and degree of punishment depending on the offender and the offense. Those whom I don't like or my mother doesn't like in the first place get the worst—usually long, drawn-out strangulations, faces of red then purple then mauve. Those I barely know, like the family that just walked by, are spared the worst—nothing personal. I'll run them over with my car.

We are both distantly worried about the bleeding nose, my mother and I, but are for the time being working under the assumption that the nose will stop bleeding. While I hold her nose she holds the half-moon receptacle as it rests on the upper portion of her chest, under her chin.

Just then I have a great idea. I try to get her to talk funny, the way people talk when their nose is being held.

"Please?" I say.

"No," she says.

"C'mon."

"Cut it out."

"*What?*"

My mother's hands are veiny and strong. Her neck has veins. Her back has freckles. She used to do a trick where it looked like she would be pulling off her thumb, when in fact she was not. Do you know this trick? Part of one's right thumb is made to look like part of one's left hand, and then is slid up and down the index finger of the left finger—attached, then detached. It's an unsettling trick, and more so when my mother used to do it, because she did it in a way where her hands sort of shook, vibrated, her neck's veins protruding and taut, her face gripped with the strain plausibly attendant to pulling off one's finger. As children, we watched with both glee and terror. We knew it was not real, we had seen it dozens of times, but its power was never diminished, because my mother's was a uniquely physical presence—she was all skin and muscles. We would make her do the trick for our friends, who were also horrified and enthralled. But kids loved her. Everyone knew her from school—she directed the plays in grade school, would take in kids who were going through divorces, knew and loved and was not shy about hugging any of them, especially the shy ones—there was an effortless kind of understanding, an utter lack of doubt about what she was doing that put people at ease, so unlike some of the mothers, so brittle and unsure. Of course, if she didn't like someone, that kid knew it. Like Toby Willard, the beefy, dirty-blond boy up the block, who would stand in the street and, unprovoked, give her the finger as she drove by. "Bad kid," she would say, and she meant it— she had an inner hardness that under no circumstances did you want to trifle with—and would have him struck from her list until the second he might say sorry (Toby unfortunately did not), at which time he would have gotten a hug like anyone else. As strong as she was physically, most of the power was in her eyes, small and blue, and when she squinted, she would squint with a murderous intensity that meant, unmistakably, that, if pushed, she would deliver on her stare's implied threat, that to protect what she cared about, she would not stop, that she would run right over you. But she wore her strength casually, had a trusting carelessness with her flesh and muscles. She would cut herself while slicing vegetables, cut the living shit out of her finger, usually her thumb, and it would bleed everywhere, on the tomatoes, the cutting board, in the sink, while we watched at her waist, awed, scared she would die. But she would just grimace, wash the thumb clean under the tap, wrap the thumb in a paper towel and keep cutting, while the blood slowly soaked through the paper towel, crawling, as blood crawls, outward from the wound's wet center.

Beside the TV there are various pictures of us children, including one featuring me, Bill, and Beth, all under seven, in an orange dinghy, all expressions panicked. In the picture, we seem surrounded by water, for all anyone knows, miles from shore—our expressions certainly indicate that. But of course we couldn't have been more than ten feet out, our mother standing over us, ankle-deep, in her brown one-piece with the white fringe, taking the picture. It is the picture we know best, the one we have seen every day, and its colors—the blue of Lake Michigan, the orange of the dinghy, our tan skin and blond hair—are the colors we associate with our childhoods. In the picture we are all holding the side of the little boat, wanting out, wanting our mother to lift us out, before the thing would sink or drift away.

"How's school?" she asks.

"Fine."

I don't tell her I've been dropping classes.

"How's Kirsten?"

"She's good."

"I always liked her. Nice girl. Spunky."

When I rest my head on the couch I know that it's coming, coming like something in the mail, something sent away for. We know it is coming, but are not sure when—weeks? months? She is fifty-one. I am twenty-one. My sister is twenty-three. My brothers are twenty-four and seven.

We are ready. We are not ready. People know.

Our house sits on a sinkhole. Our house is the one being swept up in the tornado, the little train-set model house floating helplessly, pathetically around in the howling black funnel. We're weak and tiny. We're Grenada. There are men parachuting from the sky.

We are waiting for everything to finally stop working—the organs and systems, one by one, throwing up their hands—*The jig is up*, says the endocrine; *I did what I could*, says the stomach, or what's left of it; *We'll get em next time*, adds the heart, with a friendly punch to the shoulder.

After half an hour I remove the towel, and for a moment the blood does not come.

"I think we got it," I say.

"Really?" she says, looking up at me.

"Nothing's coming," I say.

I notice the size of her pores, large, especially those on her nose. Her skin has been leathery for years, tanned to permanence, not in an unflattering way, but in a way interesting considering her Irish background, the fact that she must have grown up so fair—

It begins to come again, the blood thick and slow at first, dotted with the black remnants of scabs, then thinner, a lighter red. I squeeze again.

"Too hard," she says. "That hurts."

"Sorry," I say.

"I'm hungry," says a voice. Toph. He is standing behind me, next to the couch.

"What?" I say.

"I'm hungry."

"I can't feed you now. Have something from the fridge."

"Like what?"

"I don't care, anything."

"Like what?"

"I don't know."

"What do we have?"

"Why don't you look? You're seven, you're perfectly capable of looking."

"We don't have anything good."

"Then don't eat."

"But I'm hungry."

"Then eat something."

"But what?"

"Jesus, Toph, just have an apple."

"I don't want an apple."

"C'mere, sweetie," says Mom.

"We'll get some food later," I say.

"Come to Mommy."

"What kind of food?"

"Go downstairs, Topher."

Toph goes back downstairs.

"He's scared of me," she says.

"He's not scared of you."

In a few minutes, I lift the towel to see the nose. The nose is turning purple. The blood is not thickening. The blood is still thin and red.

"It's not clotting," I say.

"I know."

"What do you want to do?"

"Nothing."

"What do you mean, nothing?"

"It'll stop."

"It's not stopping."

"Wait awhile."

"We've been waiting awhile."

"Wait more."

"I think we should do something."

"Wait."

"When's Beth coming back?"

"I don't know."

"We should do something."

"Fine. Call the nurse."

I call the nurse we call when we have questions. We call her when the IV isn't dripping properly, or when there's a bubble in the tube, or when bruises the size of dinner plates appear on our mother's back. For the nose the nurse suggests pressure, and keeping her head back. I tell her that I have been doing just that, and that it has not yet worked. She suggests ice. I say thank you and hang up and go to the kitchen and wrap three cubes of ice in a paper towel. I bring them back and apply them to the bridge of her nose.

"Ah!" she says.

"Sorry," I say.

"It's *cold*."

"It's *ice*."

"I know it's ice."

"Well, *ice* is *cold*."

I still have to apply pressure to the nose, so with my left hand I apply pressure, and with my right I hold the ice to the bridge of her nose. It's awkward, and I can't do both things while sitting on the arm of the couch and still be in a position to see the television.

I try kneeling on the floor next to the couch. I reach over the arm of the couch to apply the ice with one hand, and pressure with the other. This works fine, but after a short while my neck gets sore, having to turn ninety degrees to see the screen. It's all wrong.

I have an inspiration. I climb onto the top of the couch, above the cushions, on top of the back of the couch. I stretch out on the top, the cushions shhhing as I settle my weight upon them. I reach down so my head and arms are both aiming in the same direction, with my arms just reaching her nose and my head resting comfortably on the top of the couch, with a nice view of the set. Perfect. She looks up at me and rolls her eyes. I give her a thumbs up. Then she spits green fluid into the half-moon receptacle.

My father had not moved. Beth stood in the entranceway to the family room and waited. He was about ten feet from the street. He was kneeling, but with his hands on the ground, fingers extended down, like roots from a riverbed tree. He was not praying. His head tilted back for a moment as he looked up, not to the sky, but to the trees in the neighbor's backyard. He was still on his knees. He had gone to get the newspaper.

The half-moon container is full. There are now three colors in the half-moon container—green, red, and black. The blood, which is coming through her nose, is also coming through her mouth. I study the container, noting the way the three fluids do not mix, the green fluid being more viscous, the blood, this blood so thin, just swishing around on top. There is some black liquid in the corner. Maybe that is bile.

"What's the black stuff?" I ask, pointing to it from my perch above her.

"That's probably bile," she says.

A car pulls into the driveway and into the garage. The door connecting the garage to the laundry room opens and closes and then the door to the bathroom opens and closes. Beth is home.

Beth has been working out. Beth likes it when I am home from college for the weekends because then she can work out. She needs her workouts, she says. Toph's shoes continue to rumble. Beth comes into the room. She is wearing a sweatshirt and spandex leggings. Her hair is up though it's usually down.

"Hi," I say.

"Hi," Beth says.

"Hi," Mom says.

"What are you doing on top of the couch?" Beth asks.

"It's easier this way."

"What is?"

"Nosebleed," I say.

"Shit. How long?"

"Forty minutes maybe."

"Did you call the nurse?"

"Yeah, she said to put ice on."

"That didn't work last time."

"You tried ice before?"

"Of course."

"You didn't tell me that, Mom."

"Mom?"

"I'm not going back in."

My father, a man of minor miracles, had done something pretty incredible. This is what he did: six months or so ago, he had sat us down, Beth and I—not Bill, Bill was in D.C., and not Toph, who for reasons that are obvious enough was not invited—in the family room. Our mother was not there for some reason, I can't remember exactly where she was—but so we were there, sitting as far

away as possible from the customary cloud of smoke around him
and his cigarette. The conversation, if it had followed the standard
procedure for such things, would have included warm-up talk,
some talk of things generally, and how what he was about to say
was very difficult, etcetera, but we were just settling in, kind of
well obviously not expecting—

"Your mother's going to die."

I have Beth take my place, holding the ice and squeezing the nose.
Eschewing my innovation, she sits on the arm of the couch instead
of on the top of the couch. The towel is soaked. The blood is warm
and wet against my palm. I go to the laundry room and toss the
towel into the washbasin, where it lands with a slap. I shake the
cramps out of my hands and get another towel, and Toph's shoes,
out of the dryer. I give the towel to Beth.

I go downstairs to check on Toph. I sit on the stairs, which
afford a view of the basement, a rec room converted into a bedroom
and then converted again into a rec room.

"Hi," I say.

"Hi," Toph says.

"How's it going?"

"Fine."

"Are you still hungry?"

"What?"

"Are you still hungry?"

"What?"

"Pause the stupid game."

"Okay."

"Can you hear me?"

"Yes."

"Are you listening?"

"Yes."

"Do you still want food?"

"Yeah."

"We'll get some pizza in a while."

"Okay."

"Here's your shoes."

"Are they dry?"

"Yeah."

I go back upstairs.

"We need to empty this," Beth says, indicating the half-moon receptacle.

"Why me?"

"Why not you?"

I slowly lift the half-moon receptacle over Mom's head and walk it to the kitchen. It is full to the brim. It is swishing forward and back. Halfway into the kitchen I spill most of it down my leg, immediately wondering how acidic the contents of the half-moon receptacle are, with the bile and all. *Will the fluid burn through my pants?* I stand still and watch to see if it burns through, like acid, expecting to see smoke, a gradually growing hole—as happens when one spills alien blood.

But it does not burn. I decide to change my pants anyway.

Beth holds the nose for a while. She sits on the arm of the couch, next to Mom's head. From the kitchen, I turn up the volume on the TV. It's been an hour.

With the nose still bleeding, Beth meets me in the kitchen.

"What are we going to do?" she whispers.

"We have to go in, right?"

"We can't."

"Why?"

"We promised."

"Oh c'mon."

"What?"

"This can't be it."

"It could be it."

"I know it could be it, but it shouldn't be it."

"She wants it to be it."

"No, she doesn't."

"I think she does."

"No she doesn't."

"She said so."

"She didn't mean it."

"I think she might."

"No way. That's ridiculous."

"Did you hear her?"

"No, but even so."

"What do you think?"

"I think she's scared."

"Yeah."

"And I think she's not ready. I mean, are you ready?"

"No, of course not. You?"

"No. No, no."

Beth goes back to the family room. I wash out the half-moon receptacle, my head struggling with the logistics. So. Okay. At this rate, with the blood coming out slowly but continuously, how long would it actually take? A day? No, no, less—it's not *all* the blood, well before all the blood was gone it would be— We wouldn't actually be waiting for *all* the blood to drain; rather, after a while, things would break down, would— *Jesus, how much blood?* A gallon? Less? We could find out. We could call the nurse again. No, no, we can't. If we ask someone they'll make us bring her in. And if they knew we needed to bring her in, and we didn't bring her in, we'd be murderers. We could call the emergency room, ask hypothetically: "Hi, I'm doing a report for school about slow blood leakage and…" Fuck. Would we have enough towels? God no. We could use sheets, we have plenty of sheets— It might be only a few hours. Would that be enough time? What's enough time? We would talk a lot. Yes. We would sum up. Would we be serious, sober, or funny? We would be serious for a few minutes— Okay okay okay okay. Fuck, what if we ran out of things to say and— We've already made the necessary arrangements. Yes, yes, we wouldn't need to talk details. We'd have Toph come up. Would we have Toph come up? Of course, but... oh he shouldn't be there, should he? Who wants to be there at the very end? No one, no one. But for her to be alone...of course she won't be alone, you'll be there, Beth'll be there, dumb-ass. Fuck. We'd have to get Bill on the phone. Who else? Which relatives? No grandparents, her parents long gone, in-laws gone, her sister Ruth gone, her sister Ann not dead but gone, out of touch, hiding, that hippie freak— Fuck. Some of those people hadn't called in years. Friends then. Which? The ones from volleyball, from Montessori— Shit, we'll definitely forget some people... Hell, we'll forget some people, people will understand, they'll have to— Fuck it, we're leaving anyway, we're moving away after all this, fuck it— A conference call? No, no— tacky. Tacky but practical, definitely practical, and it might also be fun, people chatting, lots of voices, we could use noise and distraction, not quiet, not quiet, quiet not good—need noise. We'd have to prime them, warn them, but shit, what to say? "Things are happening quickly"—something like that, vague but clear enough, do it quietly, everything implicit, get on the kitchen extension, out of earshot, say something before Mom gets on the phone— That would do the trick, all the people on the line at once— I'll have to call the phone company, get some kind of hookup— Are we already signed up for that kind of thing? Call-waiting, sure, but conference calling—probably not, definitely not, fuck— We need a speakerphone is what we need. That would do it, a speakerphone— I could go get one, I'd have to go all the way up to Kmart, take Dad's car even, faster than Mom's, much

faster— Is that a stick? No, no, automatic, I can drive it, haven't
driven it before but could drive it, no problem, fast car, open it up
there on the highway— But fuck, it's easily twenty minutes there
and back, plus shopping time and what if they didn't have— I
could call first, of course I'd call, dumbshit, ask them if they have
the speakerphone... I'd have to know what kind of phone I've got
here, for compatibility, okay, Sony and then— But why the fuck
should I go? Beth's been here all year, had all the extra time, Beth
should go, of course Beth, Beth'll go Beth'll go— But she won't
think the speakerphone is necessary, she'll say forget it— Fuck,
maybe we should just screw it— Screw it. Screw it. Screw it.
Would the speakerphone really make it easier? Of course not, we'd
still need the conference-call hookup deal— We'll call Bill and
Aunt Jane and the cousins, Susie and Janie, Ruth's daughters,
maybe cousin Mark, too. That's it. So the phone call would be
twenty minutes maybe, then we'd bring Toph upstairs for a while,
a little visit, again, casual, light, fun, loose, loose, fun, light— So
twenty minutes or so of Toph upstairs, then— All right, all right,
wait: how much time total are we talking? How long for the nose?
Two hours maybe, easily more, for sure, could be a day—Jesus,
does anyone know this?—the conservative estimate would be two
hours— Wait. I can stop the nosebleed. I will stop the nosebleed.
Yes. I will find a way. More ice. Rearrange her—a reverse incline;
gravity, yes. I will hold the nose tighter, tighter this time; I probably wasn't holding tight enough before— Fuck. What if it doesn't
work? It won't work. We shouldn't spend the last hours fighting
it; no, we will know and let it go—turn the TV off right away, of
course— But would that be too dramatic? Fuck, we can be dramatic here, we can— Well, we'd ask her, of course, dumbshit, it'd
be up to Mom of course, the TV, whether it was on or off—it's her
show of course—that's a dumb way of putting it, "her show," so
crass, such disrespect, you fucking dumbshit. Fuck. Okay, so we'd
have some time, we could sit there, hang out, just sit there, it'd be

nice— Jesus, it's not going to be *nice*, not with the blood everywhere— The blood is going to make it unbearable— But maybe
not, it's so slow, the blood— Oh, it'll be days, days before it
drains, enough drains, but maybe that'll be good, natural, a slow
draining, like a leeching—not like a leeching, asshole you *sick
fucking asshole*—not a *goddamn motherfucking leeching*— Would we
tell people how it happened? No, no. This would be a "died at
home" thing, nice phrase, the phrase they used, come to think of
it, for that one guy from high school who shot himself after grad-
uating, the guy from art class with those Marty Feldman eyes. Also
when that one woman, the one with bone cancer, locked herself in
the house and burned it down. That was incredible. Was it brave,
or unhinged? Would that have made it easier, the burning of
everything? Yes. No. "Died at home." That's how we'll do it, say
nothing else. People will know anyway. No one'll say a thing. Fine.
Fine. Fine. Fine.

I pour the contents of the container over the food collected
inside the disposal. I turn on the water, then the disposal, and it
grinds everything up. I can hear Beth in the family room.

"Mom, we should go in."

"No."

"Seriously."

"No."

"We have to."

"We do not."

"What do you want to do?"

"Stay here."

"We can't. You're bleeding."

"You said we would stay here."

"But, Mom. C'mon."

"You promised."

"This is crazy."

"You promised."

"You can't just keep bleeding."

"Call the nurse again."

"We already called the nurse again. The nurse said we had to go in. They're waiting for us."

"Call another nurse."

"Mom, please."

"This is stupid."

"Don't call me stupid."

"I didn't call you stupid."

"Who were you calling stupid?"

"No one. I said it was stupid."

"What's stupid?"

"Dying of a bloody nose."

"I'm not going to die of a bloody nose."

"The nurse said you could."

"The doctor said you could."

"If we go in, I'll never leave."

"Yes you will."

"I won't."

"Oh Jesus."

"I don't want to go back in there."

"Don't cry, Mom, Jesus."

"Don't say that."

"Sorry."

"We'll get you out."

"Mom?"

"What!"

"You'll get out."

"You want me in there."

"Oh, God."

"Look at you two, Tweedledum and Tweedledee."

"Huh?"

"You want to go out tonight, that's what it is."

"Jesus."

"It's New Year's Eve. You two have plans!"

"Fine, bleed. Sit there and bleed to death."

"Mom, please?"

"Just bleed. But we don't have enough towels for all the blood. I'll have to get more towels."

"Mom?"

"And you'll ruin the couch."

"Where's Toph?" she asks.

"Downstairs."

"What's he doing?"

"Playing his game."

"What will he do?"

"He'll have to come with."

At the end of the driveway my father knelt. Beth watched and it was kind of pretty for a second, him just kneeling there in the gray winter window. Then she knew. He had been falling. In the kitchen, the shower. She ran and flung open the door, threw the screen wide and ran to him.

I clear out the backseat of the station wagon and put a blanket down, then put a pillow against the side door and lock it. I come back into the living room.

"How am I going to get in the car?" she says.

"I'm gonna carry you," I say.

"You?"

"Yeah."

"Ha!"

We get her jacket. We get another blanket. We get the half-moon receptacle. We get the IV bag. Another nightgown. Slippers. Some snacks for Toph. Beth puts everything in the car.

I open the basement door.

"Toph, let's go."

"Where?"

"To the hospital."

"Why?"

"For a checkup."

"Now?"

"Yes."

"Do I have to go?"

"Yes."

"Why? I can stay with Beth."

"Beth's coming with."

"I can stay alone."

"No, you can't."

"Why?"

"Because you can't."

"But why?"

"Jesus, Toph, get up here!"

"Okay."

I am not sure I can lift her. I don't know how heavy she'll be. She could be a hundred pounds, she could be a hundred and fifty pounds. I open the door to the garage and come back. I move the table away from the couch. I kneel in front of her. I put one arm under her legs, and the other behind her back. She has tried to sit up.

"You'll never get up if you're kneeling."

"Okay."

I get off my knees and crouch.

"Put your arm around my neck," I say.

"Be careful," she says.

She puts her arm around my neck. Her hand is hot.

I remember to use my legs. I keep her nightgown between my hand and the back of her knees. I do not know what her skin there will feel like. I am afraid of what is under her nightgown—bruises, spots, holes. There are bruises, soft spots...where things have rotted through? As I stand up, she reaches her other arm around to meet the one around my neck, and grabs one hand with the other. She is not as heavy as I thought she would be. She is not as bony as I feared she would be. I step around the chair next to the couch. I had once seen them both, my mother and father, on the couch, both sitting there. I head toward the hallway to the garage. The whites of her eyes are yellow.

"Don't let my head hit."

"I won't."

"Don't."

"I won't."

We pass the first doorway. The wood molding cracks.

"Ow!"

"Sorry."

"Owwwwwwooooooh."

"Sorry, sorry, sorry. You okay?"

"Mmmmm."

"Sorry."

The door to the garage is open. The air in the garage is frozen. She pulls her head in and I clear the doorway. I think of honeymoons, the threshold. She is pregnant. She is a knocked-up bride. The tumor is a balloon. The tumor is a fruit, an empty gourd. She is lighter than I thought she would be. I had expected the tumor to create more weight. The tumor is large and round. She wears her pants over it, wore her pants over it, the ones with the elastic waistband, the last time she wore pants, before the nightgowns. But she is light. The tumor is a light tumor, empty, a balloon. The tumor is rotten fruit, graying at the edges. Or an insects' hive, something festering and black and alive, fuzzy on its sides. Something with eyes. A spider. A tarantula, the legs fanning out, metastasizing. A balloon covered in dirt. The color is the color of dirt. Or blacker, shinier. Caviar. Like caviar in color and also in the shape and size of its components. She had had Toph late. She was forty-two then. She had prayed in church every day while pregnant. When she was ready, they cut her stomach open to get him but he was fine, perfect.

I step down into the garage and she spits. It is audible, the gurgling sound. She does not have the towel or the half-moon receptacle. The green fluid comes over her chin and lands on her nightgown. A second wave comes but she holds her mouth closed, her cheeks puffed out. There is green fluid on her face.

The car door is open and I aim her head in first. She shrugs her shoulders, tries to make herself smaller for an easier fit. I shuffle my feet, adjust my grip. I move in slow motion. I am barely moving. She is a vase, a doll. A giant vase. A giant fruit. A prize-winning vegetable. I pass her through the door. I lean down and place her on the seat. She is suddenly girlish in the nightgown, self-consciously pushing it down to cover her legs. She adjusts the pillow against the door, behind her, and slides back into it.

When she is settled she reaches for a towel on the floor of the car and brings it to her mouth and spits into it and wipes off her chin.

"Thank you," she says.

I close the door and wait in the passenger seat. Beth comes out with Toph, who is in his winter coat and is wearing mittens. Beth opens the station wagon's hatchback and Toph climbs in.

"Hi, sweetie," Mom says, craning her head back, looking up at him.

"Hi," says Toph.

Beth gets in the driver's seat, turns around and claps her hands together.

"Road trip!"

• • •

You should have seen my father's service. People came, third-grade teachers, friends of my mother, a few people from my father's office, no one knew them, parents of our friends, everyone bundled up, huffing inside, glassy-eyed from the cold, kicking their snowy feet on the mats. It was the third week in November, and prematurely freezing, the roads covered with ice, the worst in years.

All the guests looked stricken. Everyone knew my mother was sick, were expecting this sort of thing from *her*, but this, this from him was a surprise. No one knew what do to, what to say. Not that many people knew him—he didn't socialize much, at least not in town, had maintained only a handful of friends—but they knew my mother, and they must have felt like they were at the funeral for the husband of a ghost.

We were embarrassed. It was all so gaudy, so gruesome—here we were, inviting everyone to come and watch us in the middle of our disintegration. We smiled and shook hands with everyone as they walked in. *Oh hi!* I said to Mrs. Glacking, my fourth-grade teacher, whom I hadn't seen in easily ten years. She looked good, looked the same. Huddled together in the lobby, we were sheepish and apologetic, trying to keep things breezy. My mom, wearing a flower-print dress (it was the best thing she had in which she could conceal her intravenous apparatus), tried to stand and receive the comers, but she soon had to sit, grinning up at everyone, hello hello, thank you thank you, how are you? I thought about sending Toph to another room, half for his own benefit and half so the guests didn't have to see the whole horrific tableau, but then he went off with a friend anyway.

The minister, a corpulent stranger in black and white and that churchy neon green they wear, was at a loss. My father was an atheist, and thus this minister, who knew my father only through what he had been told an hour before, talked about how much my father enjoyed his work (*Did* he? we wondered, having no idea one way or the other), and how much he enjoyed golf (he did, we knew that much). Then Bill got up. He was dressed well; he knew how to wear suits. He made some jokes, bantered brightly, a little too brightly, perhaps, a little too a-few-jokes-to-warm-up-the-crowd (he was at the time doing a lot of public speaking). Beth and I nudged my mother a few times in solidarity, embarrassed further, always looking for fun at his expense, mocking the leavened earnestness. And then we filed out, everyone watching our mother and her slow careful steps, she smiling to all, happy to see every-one, all these people she hadn't seen in so long. We milled a little in the foyer, and then told everyone that we'd be having a little party at home, we had so much food people had brought by, thanks by the way, if anyone wanted to come by.

Many came, my mother's friends, brother's, sister's, my friends from high school and college, home for Thanksgiving, and with everyone there and it dark out and winter, I spent much of the time trying to convert what was a sort of dour affair into something fun. I hinted that someone should get some beer—*Someone should get a case, man*, I whispered to Steve, a college friend—but no one did. I thought we should be getting drunk, not out of misery or whatev-er, but just—it was a party, right?

Bill was out from D.C. with the girlfriend we didn't like. Kirsten got jealous because Marny, an old girlfriend of mine, was there. Sitting in the family room, we tried to play Trivial Pursuit, still dressed in jackets and ties, but it wasn't much fun, especially without the beer. Toph played Sega in the basement with a friend. My mother sat in the kitchen while her old volleyball friends stood around her, drinking wine, laughing loudly.

Les came by. He was the only friend of our father's who we actually knew, who we had ever really heard anything about. Years ago, they had been at the same downtown law firm, and even after they each left and went elsewhere they still commuted into

Chicago together occasionally. As Les and his wife were gathering their coats and scarves to leave, Beth and I met him at the door, thanked him. Les, a kind and funny man, meandered into talking about my father's driving.

"He was the best driver I've ever seen," said Les, marveling. "So smooth, so in control. He was incredible. He would see three, four moves ahead, would drive with a only few fingers on the wheel."

Beth and I were eating it up. We had never heard anything about our father, knew nothing about him outside of what we'd seen ourselves. We asked Les for more, anything. He told us how our father used to call Toph the caboose.

"Yeah, I didn't even know his name for a long time," Les said, shaking his shoulders into his coat. "Always 'the caboose.'"

Les was great, so great. We had never heard this term. It was not used in the house, not once. I pictured my father saying it, pictured him and Les at a restaurant off Wacker, him telling Les jokes about Stosh and Jon, the two Polish fishermen. We wanted Les to stay. I wanted Les to tell me what my father thought about me, about us, the rest of us, if he knew he was in trouble, if he had given up (why had he given up?). And Les, why was he still going to work, a few days before he expired? Did you know that, Les? That he was at work four days before? When did you last talk to him, Les? Did he know? What did he know? Did he tell you? What did he say about all this?

We ask Les if he'll come for dinner sometime. He says yes, of course. Just call, whenever.

I did not know that the last time I saw my father would be the last time I would see my father. He was in intensive care. I had come up from college to visit, but because it had been so soon after his diagnosis, I didn't make much of it. He was expected to undergo some tests and treatment, get his strength back, and return home in a few days. I had come to the hospital with my mother, Beth, and Toph. The door to my father's room was closed. We

pushed it open, heavy, and inside he was smoking. In intensive
care. The windows were closed and the haze was thick, the stench
unbelievable, and in the midst of it all was my father, looking
happy to see us.

No one talked much. We stayed for maybe ten minutes, huddled on the far side of the room, attempting as best we could to
stay away from the smoke. Toph was hiding behind me. Two green
lights on the machine next to my father blinked, alternately, on,
off, on, off. A red light stayed steady, red.

My father was reclining on the bed, propped against two pillows. His legs were crossed casually, and he had his hands clasped
behind his head. He was grinning like he had won the biggest
award there ever was.

After a night in the emergency room and after a day in intensive
care, she is in a good room, a huge room with huge windows.

"This is the death room," Beth says. "Look, they give you all
this space, room for relatives, room to sleep…"

There is another bed in the room, a big couch that folds out,
and we are all in the bed, fully dressed. I forgot to change my pants
before we left the house, and the stain from the spill is brown, with
black edges. It is late. Mom is asleep. Toph is asleep. The foldout
bed is not comfortable. The metal bars under the mattress dig.

A light above her bed is kept on, creating a much-too-dramatic
amber halo around her head. A machine behind her bed looks
like an accordion, but is light blue. It is vertical and stretches and
compresses, making a sucking sound. There is that sound, and the
sound of her breathing, and the humming from other machines,
and the humming from the heater, and Toph's breathing, close and
constant. Mom's breaths are desperate, irregular.

"Toph snores," Beth says.

"I know," I say.

"Are kids supposed to snore?"

"I don't know."

"Listen to her breathing. It's so uneven. It takes so long for every breath."

"It's terrifying."

"Yeah. It's like twenty seconds sometimes."

"It's fucking nuts."

"Toph kicks in his sleep."

"I know."

"Look at him. Out cold."

"I know."

"He needs a haircut."

"Yeah."

"Nice room."

"Yeah."

"No TV, though."

"Yeah, that's weird."

After most of the guests left, Kirsten and I had gone into my parents' bathroom. The bed would squeak, and we didn't really want to sleep there anyway, the way it smelled, like my father, the pillows and walls soaked in it, the gray smell of smoke. The only reason any of us ever went in there was either to steal change from his dresser or to go through their window to get onto the roof—you had to go through their window to get to the roof. Everyone in the house was asleep, downstairs and in the various bedrooms, and we were in my parents' walk-in closet. We brought blankets and a pillow into the carpeted area between the wardrobe and the shower, and spread the blanket on the ground, in front of the mirrored sliding closet doors.

"This is weird," Kirsten said. Kirsten and I met in college, had dated for many months, and for a long time we were tentative—

we liked each other a great deal but I expected someone so normal and sweet-looking to find me out soon enough—until one weekend she came home with me, and we went to the lake, and I told her my mother was sick, had been given time parameters, and she told me that that was weird, because her mother had a brain tumor. I had known that her father had disappeared when she was young, that she had been working, year-round, since she was fourteen, I knew she was strong but then there were these new words coming from her face, these small shadowy words. From then on we were more serious.

"Too weird," she said.

"No, this is good," I said, undressing her.

Everywhere people were sleeping—my mother in Beth's room, my friend Kim on the living room couch, my friend Brooke on the family room couch, Beth in my old room, Bill in the basement, Toph in his room.

We were quiet. There was nothing left of anything.

Beth remembers first, with a gasp, in the middle of the night. We had been vaguely conscious of it, in recent days, but then we had forgotten, until just now, at 3:21 a.m., that tomorrow—today—is her birthday.

"Shit."

"Shh."

"He can't hear. He's asleep."

"What should we do?"

"There's a gift shop."

She will not know that we had almost forgotten.

"Yeah. Balloons."

"Flowers."

"Sign Bill's name."

"Yeah."

"Maybe a stuffed animal."

"God, it's all so gift-shoppy."

"What else can we do?"

"Ow!"

"What?"

"Toph just kicked me."

"He turns in his sleep. A hundred eighty degrees."

"Hear that?"

"What?"

"Listen!"

"What?"

"Shhh! She hasn't breathed."

"How long?"

"Seems like forever."

"Fuck."

"Wait. There she goes."

"God that's weird."

"It's terrible."

"Maybe we should wait until we get home before the birthday thing."

"No, we have to do something."

"I hate that this room is on the first floor."

"Yeah, but it's a nice room."

"I don't like the headlights."

"Yeah."

"Should we close the curtains?"

"No."

"What about in the morning?"

"No, why?"

At 4:20 Beth is asleep. I sit up and look at Mom. She has hair again. For so long she did not have hair. She'd had five wigs, at least, over a number of years, all of them sad in the way wigs are sad. One was too big. One was too dark. One was too curly. One was frosted. Still, most of them had looked more or less real. The odd thing was that her current hair was real, but had grown back much curlier than her original hair, and curlier even than her curliest wig. And darker. Her hair now looked more like a wig than any of the wigs.

"Funny how your hair grew back in," I had said.

"What's funny about it?"

"Well, how it's darker than before."

"It is not."

"Of course it is. Your hair was gray almost."

"No it wasn't. I had it frosted."

"That was ten years ago."

"It was never gray."

"Fine."

I lie back down. Beth's breathing is heavy, quiet. The ceiling looks like milk. The ceiling is moving slowly. The corners of the ceiling are darker. The ceiling looks like cream. The metal bar that bisects and supports the bed's mattress digs into our backs. The ceiling is fluid.

When my father was in intensive care, about a day and a half from throwing in the towel, a priest was sent, presumably to administer last rites. After meeting him and ascertaining the purpose of the visit, my father quickly dismissed him, sent him out. When the doctor related this story later—it had become something of a legend on the floor—he made reference to the axiom that denies the existence of atheists in the proverbial trenches: "They say there are no atheists in the trenches," the doctor said, looking at the floor, "but...*whew!*" He wouldn't even let the man do some sort of cursory prayer, Hail Mary, anything. The priest had come in likely knowing that my father was not a churchgoer, not affiliated with any church at all. But thinking that he was doing my dad a favor, he offered some sort of chance at repentance, a one-in-a-thousand raffle ticket for redemption. But see, my father had as much patience for religion as he did for solicitors ringing the bell. To them, he would open the door, grin his dopey grin, say no thanks quickly and brightly, then close the door firmly. Which is what he did with this poor, well-meaning priest: He grinned his big grin, and, being unable to get up and show the poor man the business side of the door himself, just said, "No thanks."

"But, Mr. Eggers—"

"No thanks, goodbye."

We'll get her out in a few days. Beth and I have vowed to get her out, have planned to break her out, even if the doctors say no; we will hide her under a gurney, will pose as doctors, will wear sunglasses and go quickly and will take her to the car, and I will lift her and Toph will provide some distraction if necessary, something, a little dance or something; and then we'll jump in the car and be gone, will bring her home, triumphant—we did it! we did it!—and we'll get a hospital bed and put it in the living room, where the couch was. We'll arrange for a nurse, twenty-four hours a day—actually, the bed and the nurse will be arranged by a woman, Mrs. Rentschler, who used to live across the street, in the house whose yard my father was looking at, on his knees, a woman who had moved away long ago, but only to another part of town, and then suddenly she is again there, she is part of the hospital's hospice program, and she will make the arrangements and she will hug us and we will like her though we never knew her before. One of the nurses will be a large, middle-aged black woman from North Chicago who will speak with a southern accent and will bring her own Bible, and will cry sometimes, her shoulders shaking. There will be a sullen younger woman from Russia who will show up angry and will perform her duties in a clipped, rushed manner and will nap when we aren't watching. There will be a nurse who comes one day and will not return the next. There will be women, our mother's friends, who will come and visit, in make-up and fur coats. There will be Mrs. Dineen, an old family friend, who will come out from Massachusetts for a week, because she wants to be here, to see Mom again, and will sleep in the basement and will talk about spirituality. It will snow prodigiously. The nurses will clean my mother when we are not in the room or awake. There will be vigils. We will enter the room at any hour of the day or night and, if our mother is not awake, we will freeze, then get ready, then walk over and put our hands over her mouth to see if she's breathing. One day she will let us summon her sister Jane, and we will pay to fly her out, just in time. When Aunt Jane arrives at the bedside, after we have picked her up at the airport, our mother, who at this point will not have sat up in days, will shoot up like a child from a nightmare, and will hold her sister who will smile wide and close her eyes. There will be an endless stream of visitors, who will sit casually at our mother's side and chat about recent happenings, because, because a dying person doesn't want to talk about dying, would rather hear about who's getting divorced, whose kids are in rehab or will be soon. There will be baked goods. There will be Father Mike, a young red-haired priest who will make it clear that he's not going to try to convert anybody, and will do Mass while she stays in bed, will skip the wafer part for her lack of stomach, and Mrs. Dineen will take communion too; I'll watch some of it as I'm cooking a frozen pizza in the kitchen. There will be the rosary fetched from the cabinet upstairs. We will light candles to stave off the smell that emanates from her pores after her liver stops working. We will sit next to the bed and hold her hands, which are hot. She will sit up suddenly in the middle of the night, talking loudly, incomprehensibly. All words will be considered her last, until they are followed by others. When Kirsten walks into the room one day she will rise suddenly and insist that Kirsten see the naked man in the fish tank. We will suppress laughs—she will have been insisting on the naked man for days—and Kirsten, with a certain degree of seriousness, will actually go over to the fish tank to look, a gesture Mom will take, with first a roll of the eyes and then a deeply satisfied smile, as vindication. Then she will lie back down, and in a few days her mouth will dry up, and her lips will chap and scab, and the nurse will moisten them every twenty minutes with a Q-tip. There will be morphine. Between her hair, which for some reason will continue to look oddly pert, fluffy, and her skin, shiny, tan-and-jaundiced, and her glossy lips, she will look great. She will be wearing the satin pajamas Bill bought for her. We will play music. Beth will play Pachelbel and, when that seems a bit much, we will put on sweeping New Age music produced by my father's sister, Aunt Connie, who lives in Marin County with a talking cockatoo. The morphine drip will not be enough. We will call again and again for more. Finally we will have enough, and will be allowed to choose the dosage ourselves, and soon will administer it every time she moans, by allowing it to flow through the clear tube and into her, and when we do the moaning stops.

We will leave while they take her away and when we come back the bed will be gone, too. We will move the couch back, against the wall, where it was before the bed came. A few weeks later a friend will arrange for Toph to meet the Chicago Bulls, after they practice at that gym in Deerfield, and Toph will bring his basketball cards, one or two of each of them, rookie cards mostly, those being worth more, so the players can sign them and make them more valuable. We will watch them scrimmage through the window, then, after practice, there they are, in their sweat suits—they come out specially, had been asked to—and Scottie Pippen

and Bill Cartwright will ask Toph, as they're signing his cards
with the permanent marker that he's brought, why he isn't in
school, it being a Wednesday or Monday or whatever day it will
be, and he will just shrug— Beth and I will pull him from school
from time to time that spring, when something comes up or just
whenever, because while we want to keep alive an air of normalcy,
half the time we just say fuck it, and he's so happy, glowing to have
met the Bulls, now has all these ludicrously valuable cards, and on
the way home we will discuss getting them notarized to make sure
people know that he was there. Bill will change jobs to be closer,
will move from D.C. to L.A., just after the riots, and will do his
think-tanking there. He'll handle all the money, from insurance
and the house—there was nothing saved, nothing really at all—
and Beth will handle the bills and forms and other paperwork and,
because we're the closest in age and it was never really up for
debate, Toph will be with me. But first he'll finish third grade, and
I'll drop some classes and, though whatever number of credits
short, will go through the graduation ceremony, with Beth and
Toph and Kirsten there, dinner afterward but low-key, let's keep it
low-key, no big thing. And afterward, a week at most, while people, old people, are frowning and clicking their tongues and shaking their heads, we will sell that house, will sell most of its contents, would have burned the fucker down had we been able, and
we will move to Berkeley, where Beth will start law school and
we'll all set up somewhere, a nice big house in Berkeley with all of
us, with a view of the Bay, close to a park with a basketball court
and enough room to run—

She stirs and her eyes open slightly.

I get out of the bed and it squeaks. The floor is cold. It is 4:40
a.m. Toph rolls into the spot on the bed I have been occupying. I
step over to my mother. She is looking at me. I lean over her bed
and touch her arm. Her arm is hot.

"Happy birthday," I whisper.

She is not looking at me. Her eyes are not open. They were open a slit, but are not now open. I am not sure if they were seeing me. I walk to the window and close the curtains. Outside, the trees are bare and black, quickly sketched. I sit in the taut pleather chair in the corner and watch her and the light-blue suction machine. The light-blue suction machine, working rhythmically, seems fake, a stage prop. I sink into the chair and lean back. The ceiling is swimming. It is milky, stuccoed in sweeping half-circles, and the half-circles are moving, turning slowly, the ceiling shifting like water. The ceiling has depth or—the ceiling is moving forward and back. Or the walls are not solid. The room is maybe not real. I am on a set. There are not enough flowers in the room. The room should be full of flowers. Where are the flowers? When does the gift shop open? Six? Eight? I bet myself. I bet it is six. All right, it's a bet. I consider how many flowers I can buy. I do not know what they cost; I have never bought flowers. I will see what they cost and then buy all the flowers that they have that I can afford, move them from the gift shop to this room. Fireworks.

She will wake up and see them.

"What a waste," she will say.

She stirs and opens her eyes. She looks at me. I get up off the chair and stand by the bed. I touch her arm. It is hot.

"Happy birthday," I whisper, smiling, looking down into her. She does not answer. She is not looking at me. She is not awake. I sit down again.

Toph is on his back, his arms splayed. He sweats when he sleeps, regardless of the room's temperature. When he sleeps, he moves and turns around and around, like the hand of a clock. His breathing is audible. His eyelashes are long. His hand hangs over the foldout bed. As I am looking at him, he wakes up. He gets up and comes to me as I am sitting in the chair and I take his hand and we go through the window and fly up and over the quickly sketched trees and then to California.

II.

Please look. Can you see us? Can you see us, in our little red car?
Picture us from above, as if you were flying above us, in, say, a helicopter, or on the back of a bird, as our car hurtles, low to the
ground, straining on the slow upward trajectory but still at sixty,
sixty-five, around the relentless, sometimes ridiculous bends of
Highway 1. Look at us, goddammit, the two of us slingshotted
from the back side of the moon, greedily cartwheeling toward
everything we are owed. Every day we are collecting on what's
coming to us, each day we're being paid back for what is owed,
what we deserve, with interest, with some extra motherfucking
consideration—we are *owed*, goddammit—and so we are expecting
everything, everything. We get to take what we want, one of each,
anything in the store, a three-hour shopping spree, the color of our
choice, any make, any color, as much as we want, when we want,
whatever we want. Today we have nowhere to be so we're on our
way to Montara, a beach about thirty-five minutes south of San
Francisco, and right now we are singing:
She was alone!
She never knew!

{Something something something!}
When we touched!
When we {rhymes with "same"}!
All {something something}!
All night!
All night!
Alll every night!
So hold tight!
Hoo-ld tight
Baby hold tight!
Any way you want it!
That's the way you need it!
Any way you want it!

Toph does not know the words, and I know few of the words, but you cannot fucking stop us from singing. I'm trying to get him to do the second All night part, with me doing the first part, like:

ME: *All night!* (higher)

HIM: *All-ll night!* (slightly lower)

I point to him when his part comes but he just looks at me blankly. I point to the radio, then to him, then to his mouth, but he's still confused, and it's hard doing any of this while trying not to career off the road and into the Pacific and I guess in a way the gestures look like I want him to eat the radio. But Jesus, he should be able to figure this out. He isn't cooperating. Or he could be dumb. Is he dumb?

Fuck it—I go solo. I hit the Steve Perry notes, I do the Steve Perry vibrato. I can do these things because I am an extraordinary singer.

"Can I sing or what?" I yell.

"What?" he yells.

The windows are open, too.

"I said, 'Can I sing or what?'"

He shakes his head.

"What do you mean?" I yell. "I can sing, *god*dammit."

He rolls up his window.

"What did you say? I didn't hear you," he says.

"I said, can I sing or what?"

"No." He smiles hugely. "You can't sing at all."

I worry about exposing him to bands like Journey, the appreciation of which will surely bring him nothing but the opprobrium of his peers. Though he has often been resistant—children so seldom know what is good for them—I have taught him to appreciate all the groundbreaking musicmakers of our time—Big Country, Haircut 100, Loverboy—and he is lucky for it. His brain is my laboratory, my depository. Into it I can stuff the books I choose, the television shows, the movies, my opinion about elected officials, historical events, neighbors, passersby. He is my twenty-four-hour classroom, my captive audience, forced to ingest everything I deem worthwhile. He is a lucky, lucky boy! And no one can stop me. He is mine, and you cannot stop me, cannot stop us. Try to stop us, you pussy! You can't stop us from singing, and you can't stop us from making fart sounds, from putting our hands out the window to test the aerodynamics of different hand formations, from wiping the contents of our noses under the front of our seats. You cannot stop me from having Toph, who is eight, steer, on a straightaway, while I take off my sweatshirt because suddenly it's gotten really fucking hot. You cannot stop us from throwing our beef jerky wrappers on the floor, or leaving our unfolded laundry in the trunk for, fuck, eight days now, because we have been busy. You cannot stop Toph from leaving a half-full cardboard orange juice container under the seat, where it will rot and ferment and make the smell in the car intolerable, with that smell's provenance remaining elusive for weeks, during which the windows must be kept open at all times, until finally it is found and Toph is buried to his neck in the backyard and covered in honey—or should have been—for his role in the debacle. We cannot be stopped from looking with pity upon all the world's sorry inhabitants, they unblessed by our charms, unchallenged by our trials, unscarred and thus weak, gelatinous. You cannot stop me from telling Toph to make comments about and faces at the people in the next lane.

ME: Look at this loser.

HE: What a *spaz*!

ME: Look at this one.

HE: Oh my *God*.

ME: A dollar to wave at this guy.

HE: How much?

ME: A buck.

HE: That's not enough.

ME: Okay, five bucks to give this guy a thumbs up.

HE: Why a thumbs up?

ME: Cause he's got it goin' on!

HE: Okay. Okay.

ME: Why didn't you do it?

HE: I just couldn't.

It's unfair. The matchups, Us v. Them (or you) are unfair. We are dangerous. We are daring and immortal. Fog whips up from under the cliffs and billows over the highway. Blue breaks from beyond the fog and sun suddenly screams from the blue.

To our right is the Pacific, and because we are hundreds of feet above the ocean, often with nothing in the way of a guardrail between us and it, there is sky not only above us but below us, too. Toph does not like the cliff, is not looking down, but we are driving in the sky, with clouds whipping over the road, the sun flickering through, the sky and ocean below. Only up here does the earth look round, only up here does the horizon dip at its ends, only up here can you see the bend of the planet at the edges of your peripheries. Only here are you almost sure that you are careening on top of a big shiny globe, blurrily spinning—you are never aware of these things in Chicago, it being so flat, so straight—and and and we have been *chosen*, you see, chosen, and have been given this, it being owed to us, earned by us, all of this—the sky is blue for us, the sun makes passing cars twinkle like toys for us, the ocean undulates and churns for us, murmurs and coos to us. We are owed, see, this is ours, see. We are in California, living in Berkeley, and the sky out here is bigger than anything we've ever seen—it goes on forever, is visible from every other hilltop—hilltops!— every turn on the roads of Berkeley, of San Francisco— We have a house, a sublet for the summer, that overlooks the world, up in the Berkeley hills; it's owned by people, Scandinavians, Beth says, who must have some money, because it's all the way up there, and it's all windows and light and decks, and up there we see everything, Oakland to the left, El Cerrito and Richmond to the right, Marin forward, over the Bay, Berkeley below, all red rooftops and trees of cauliflower and columbine, shaped like rockets and explosions, all those people below us, with humbler views; we see the Bay Bridge, clunkety, the Richmond Bridge, straight, low, the Golden Gate, red toothpicks and string, the blue between, the blue above, the gleaming white Land of the Lost/Superman's North Pole Getaway magic crystals that are San Francisco... and at night the whole fucking area is a thousand airstrips, Alcatraz blinking, the flood of halogen down the Bay Bridge, oozing to and fro, a string of Christmas lights being pulled slowly, steadily, and of course the blimps—so many blimps this summer—and stars, not too many visible, with the cities and all, but still some, a hundred maybe, enough, how many do you need, after all? From our windows, from our deck it's a lobotomizing view, which negates the need for movement or thought—it is all there, it can all be kept track of without a turn of the head. The mornings are filmstrip white and we eat breakfast on the deck, and later we eat lunch there, we eat dinner there, we read there, play cards, always with the whole thing, the postcard tableau, just there, all those little people, too much view to seem real, but then again, then again, nothing really is all that real anymore, we must remember, of course, of course. (Or is it just the opposite? Is everything *more* real? Aha.) Behind our house, not too far, is Tilden Park, an endless expanse of lakes and trees and hills, mohair hills touched by patches of shrubs—as in, mohair hill, mohair hill, mohair hill, then an armpit of dark green, then the mohair hills that go on and on, like sleeping lions, as far as— Especially when you're on your bike, starting from Inspiration Point, pedaling into the wind on your way in and with the wind on the way back, the hills going on until Richmond, miles away, where the factories and power plants and big tanks full of deadly or life-giving things are, and the bike path goes the whole way there, all the while with the Bay visible in the distance to the left, the hills on and on to the right, until Mount Diablo, the biggest of all of them, king of the mohair hills, twenty miles east, northeast, whatever. The paths are paralleled with and perpendiculared by wood and wire fences that hold cows, and sometimes sheep, and all this is minutes away, all there, from our house, our house behind which there's even a hiking trail that reaches, just about reaches, the huge rock, Grotto Rock, that juts out twenty feet beyond our back deck, and on some days, when Toph and I are eating our breakfast out on the porch, with the sun crazy and happy for us, smiling and teary-eyed with pride, there will suddenly appear hikers, male and female, always coupled, in their khaki shorts and brown shoes and hats on backward, who will step up from below the rock, and then be atop it, and then be there, holding their backpack straps with their thumbs, at eye level with us, as we eat our breakfast on our redwood deck, twenty feet away.

"Hello!" we say, Toph and I, with compact waves.

"Hello," they say, surprised to see us there, eating our breakfast, at eye level.

It is nice, this moment. Then it's awkward, because they are at the top, the end, of their hike, and want only to sit down for a while and admire the view, but can't help be conscious of these two people, impossibly handsome people, Toph and I, who are sitting not twenty feet behind them, eating Apple Jacks from the box.

We drive past Half Moon Bay and Pacifica and Seaside, the condos on the left and the surfers on the right, the ocean exploding pink. We pass through cheering eucalyptus and waving pines, cars reflect wildly as they come at us, they seem to come right for us, and I look through their windshields for the faces of those coming at us, for a sign, for their understanding, for their trust, and I find their trust and they go by. Our car thrums loudly and I turn up the radio because I can. I drum the steering wheel with open palms, then fists, because I can. Toph looks at me. I nod gravely. In this world, in our new world, there will be rocking. We will pay tribute to musicmakers like Journey, particularly if this is Two-for-Tuesday, which means inevitably that one of the songs will be:

Just a small-town girl...

There are times when I am concerned about Toph's expression when I'm really singing, with vibrato and all, singing the guitar parts—his expression one that to the untrained eye might look like abject terror, or revulsion—but I know well enough that it is awe. I understand his awe. I deserve his awe. I am an extraordinary singer.

We have found a school for Toph, a peculiar little private school called Black Pine Circle, which has given him what amounts to a full scholarship, even though we could pretty comfortably pay for the tuition. We have some money, from the house, from the insurance policy our father took out shortly before his death. Things have been taken care of. But because we are owed, we take the free ride. It's largely Beth's doing, Beth being as much or more owed than Toph and I, and she being gloriously adept at

wringing money from our situation. It worked for her law school
tuition, which, considering her (stated) status as a single parent,
was waived. Even if it wasn't free, Beth would still be, as she is,
half delirious with joy about getting back onto campus in the fall,
a few months hence, slipping back into that world and letting it
overtake her, flushing out the everything about last year. She is
giddy, hyper, and we are both blowing the summer, because we are
owed. I am doing nothing much. Toph and I are playing frisbee,
are going to the beach. I am taking a class in furniture-painting,
and I am taking the class very seriously. I am spending a good deal
of time painting furniture in the backyard, and while I am applying my twelve years of art education to the painting of furniture, I
am wondering what I will do, in a more general, futuristic sense,
what exactly I will do. My furniture is good, I think—I am taking
thrift-store furniture, end tables mostly, sanding them down, and
then painting on them pictures of fat men's faces, blue goats, and
lost socks. I have it in my head that I will sell these tables, will find
a boutique somewhere in town and will sell them for, say, $1,000
per, and when I am hard at work on one of my tables, deep "inside"
one, you might say, solving the unique problems of a new piece—
is this rendering of a severed foot too facile, too commercial?—it seems
that what I am doing is noble, meaningful, and will all too likely
make me celebrated and wealthy. I come inside in the afternoon,
remove my thick rubber gloves, and on the deck, as the sun sets I
permit my own bright glow to subside for the evening. Maybe I
will have to get a job at some point, but for the time being, for the
summer at least, I am allowing us time to enjoy this, this lack of
anything, this lack of humidity, this time to look around. Toph is
going to summer camp on the Berkeley campus, run by the university's athletes, and his skills at everything from lacrosse to football to baseball and frisbee make it obvious that soon enough he
will be a three-sport (at least) professional athlete and will marry
an actress. We assume more scholarships, more gifts spread before

us by the embarrassed and sorry world. Beth and I take turns driving him to and fro, down the hill and up again and otherwise we lose weeks like buttons, like pencils.

The cars flash around the turns of Highway 1, jump out from cliffs, all glass and light. Each one could kill us. All could kill us. The possibilities leap into my head—we could be driven off the cliff and down and into the ocean. But fuck, we'd make it, Toph and I, given our cunning, our agility, our presence of mind. Yes, yes. If we collided with a car at sixty miles per hour on Highway 1, we could jump out in time. Yes, Toph and I could do that. We're quick-thinking, this is known, yes, yes. See, after the collision, as our red Civic arced through the sky, we would quickly plan out— no, no, we would instantly *know the plan*—what to do, the plan of course being obvious, so obvious: as the car arced downward, we would each, simultaneously, open our doors, car still descending, then each make our way to the outside of the car, car still descending, each on one side of the car, and then we would we would we would *stand on the car's frame* for a second, car still descending, each holding on to the open car door or the car roof, and then, ever so briefly, as the car was now only thirty feet or so above the water, seconds until impact, we would look at each other knowingly—"*You know what to do*"; "*Roger that*" (we wouldn't actually say these words, wouldn't need to)—and then we'd both, again simultaneously of course, push off the car, so as to allow the appropriate amount of space between our impact and the car's once we all landed, and then, as the Civic crashed into the ocean's mulchy glass, we would, too, though in impeccable divers' form, having changed our trajectory mid-flight, positioning our hands first, forward and cupped properly, our bodies perpendicular to the water, our toes pointed—*perfect!* We'd plunge under, half-circle back to the surface and then break through, into the sun, whip our heads

to shake the water from our hair and then swim to each other, as
the car with bubbles quickly drowned.

ME: Whew! That was close!

HE: I'll say!

ME: You hungry?

HE: Hey, you read my mind.

Toph is in Little League too, on a team coached by two black men,
these two black men being Nos. One and Two among the black
men that Toph has ever known. His team (and the coaches, too, as
a matter of fact) wear red uniforms and practice on a field in a pine-
surrounded park two blocks up the hill from our sublet, where the
view is even more startling. I bring a book to the practices, guessing that watching eight-to-ten-year-olds run drills will be boring,
but it is anything but. It's enthralling. I watch every movement,
watch them gather around the coach for instructions, watch them
shag balls, watch them go to the drinking fountain. No, I don't
watch all of them, of course not, I watch Toph, follow his new,
oversized red felt hat moving through the drills, watch him waiting his turn, watch him field a ground ball, turn and throw it to
the coach at second, watch only him, even as he's waiting in line,
to see if he's talking with the other kids, if he's getting along,
strain to see if he's being accepted, if—though I occasionally catch
one of the black kids doing something extraordinary—there are
two stars, a boy and girl, both tall and fast and preternaturally gift-
ed, miles ahead of all the rest, loose and lazy with their talent.
During the drills, I wait for Toph's turn, and when it comes time
for him to field a grounder or cover second for a 4-3-2, I almost die
from the pressure.

Should have had that one.

Good, good, good.

Oh, God, c'mon!

I say nothing, but it's all I can do to avoid making noises. He catches well, can catch anything really—we've been working on that since he was four—but the hitting... why can't the kid hit? *A lighter bat?* Choke up! *Quick bat!* Quick bat! Jesus Christ, that was served up like a fat fucking steak. Hit the ball. *Hit that coconut, boy!*

I was never much of a baseball player, but did pretend to know enough to land a job as a T-ball coach and sports camp director during half of my high school and college summers. When Toph was old enough, he attended, came in with me every day, gloating shyly in the celebrity born of being the brother of the camp director, as dashing as he was.

I watch, and the mothers watch. I do not know how to interact with the mothers. *Am I them?* They occasionally try to include me in a conversation, but it's clear they don't know what to make of me. I look over and smile when one of them makes a joke that is laughed at by all. They laugh, I chuckle—not too much, I don't want to seem overeager, but enough to say "I hear you. I laugh with you. I share in the moment." But when the chuckling is over I am still apart, something else, and no one is sure what I am. They don't want to invest their time in the brother sent to pick up Toph while his mother cooks dinner or is stuck at work or in traffic. To them I'm a temp. A cousin maybe. The young boyfriend of a divorcee? They don't care.

Fuck it. I don't want to be friends with these women, anyway. Why would I care? I am not them. They are the old model and we are the new.

I watch Toph interact with the other kids, scanning, guessing, suspecting.

Why are those kids laughing?

What are they laughing at? Is it Toph's hat? It's too big, right?

Who are those little pricks? I'll break those little fuckers.

Oh.

Oh, it was that. Just that. Heh heh. Heh.

After practice, we walk home, down the road, Marin Road, a pure forty-five-degree monster. It's almost impossible to walk it without looking ridiculous, but Toph has invented a walk that surmounts the problem—it's a kind of groovy walk, with his legs bent extravagantly, his arms sort of swimming in front of him, a grabbing of air and sending it behind him in a way that makes him look, in the end, much more normal than the arm-flailing, sole-slapping awkwardness the road normally necessitates. It's an extremely happening walk.

As we hit our street, Spruce, and the ground flattens out, I inquire, as gently as I possibly can, about his hitting, or lack thereof.

"So why do you suck so much at hitting?"

"I don't know."

"Maybe you need a lighter bat."

"You think?"

"Yeah, maybe we'll get a new bat."

"Can we?"

"Yeah, we'll look for a new bat or something."

Then I push him into a bush.

We are still driving. We are going to the beach. While we drive, when there is not watershed rock and roll on the radio, watershed rock and roll conceived and executed by masters of modern music-making, we play word games. There must be noise, there must be music and games. No silence. We are playing the game where you have to come up with the names of baseball players, using the first letter of the last name to start the next first name.

"Jackie Robinson," I say.

"Randy Johnson," he says.

"Johnny Bench," I say.

"Who?"

"Johnny Bench. Reds catcher."

"Are you sure?"

"What do you mean?"

"I've never heard of him."

"Johnny Bench?"

"Yeah."

"So?"

"So maybe you're making him up."

Toph collects baseball cards. He can name the going price for every card he owns—thousands, if you count the collection he inherited from Bill. Still, though, he doesn't know anything about anything. I stay cool, though he deserves to have his head knocked against the window. You should hear the sound that makes. It's amazing, even he says so.

Johnny *Bench?* Johnny fucking *Bench?*

"Trust me," I say. "Johnny Bench."

We stop at a beach on the way. I stop at this beach because I have heard about the existence of beaches like these, and then, on the fat side of a wide bend, a few miles from Montara, there is this certain beach, this beach with a sign that says "Nude Beach." I am suddenly reeling with curiosity. I pull over, jump out of the car—

"Is this it?" he asks.

"Maybe," I say, lost, dizzy—

and almost run across the highway, to the entrance before pausing for Toph, and my thoughts, to catch up. *Is this okay?* I think this is okay. *This is not okay.* I know what to do, I know what is right. Is this right? This is fine. *This is fine.* Nude beach? Fine. *Nude beach. Nude beach.* We walk to the entrance. A bearded man, sitting on a stool with a gray metal box on his lap, wants ten dollars, each, to enter.

"Is he ten dollars, too?" I ask, indicating the eight-year-old boy next to me, wearing a Cal sweatshirt and a Cal baseball hat, worn backward.

"Yes," the bearded man says.

I glance beyond the bearded man, down the cliff, trying to catch a glimpse of the beach below, trying to see if it's worth it. *Twenty dollars!* For ten dollars there had better be some very impressive nude women down there—and not just life-drawing-class nude women. This is okay. This is educational. It's natural. *We're in California! All is new! No rules! The future!*

I'm almost convinced. I step over to the bearded man, out of Toph's earshot, and try to get the lowdown.

"So like, are kids allowed down there?"

"Of course."

"But, is it like... *weird*?"

"*Weird?* What about it would be weird?"

"You know, for a little kid? Is it too much?"

"Too much of what? Of the *human body?*" He says it in a way that's meant to make *me* seem like the freak, he Mr. Natural and me some kind of clothes fascist.

"Never mind," I say. Stupid beach—probably just a bunch of naked guys with beards, bony and pale.

We run back across the highway, back into the red Civic and keep driving. Past the surfers, through the eucalyptus forest before Half Moon Bay, birds swooping up and over then back, circling around us—they too, for us!—then the cliffs before Seaside—then flat for a little while, then a few more bends and can you see this motherfucking sky? I mean, have you fucking *been* to California?

We left Chicago in a blur. We sold most of the stuff in the house, the stuff we didn't want to move with, had this busy little woman come in and price everything, to tell the appropriate people about it—she apparently has a mailing list of devout shoppers, enthusi-
~ts of possessions of the recently dead—about the estate sale for
    Waveland, and then we got out of the way. When they were
        ~t about everything was gone, and we picked through the

remains—some of Toph's old He-Man dolls, some coffee mugs, random pieces of silverware. We packed up the things we had saved—quite a lot, actually, sixty boxes maybe—and the things that hadn't sold, put them all on a truck and now all of it sits in our Spruce Street sublet's low-slung garage. Bill kept Mom's car, sold it, Beth sold Dad's car and bought a Jeep, and I made the rest of the payments on the Civic that Dad and I had bought together, just before, so I could get home on the weekends.

In Berkeley we're living with Beth, and her best friend Katie—also an orphan, both gone by the time she was twelve—and my girlfriend Kirsten, who always wanted to live in California and so came out, too. Between the five of us there was only one parent still living—Kirsten's mother—and so at first we were smug about our independence; we orphans would surely re-create domestic life, from scratch, without precedent. It seemed like a great idea, all of us in the house together—just like college! like a commune! sharing the babysitting, the cleaning, the cooking! Big meals together, parties, joy!—for at least three or four days, after which it became obvious, for all the obvious reasons, that it was not at all a good idea. We are all vibrating with the stress of the sundry adjustments, new schools and jobs, and we all quickly begin to snip and snap and complain about whose newspapers are whose, who should know not to buy granular dishwasher detergent, doesn't everyone know such things my God. Kirsten, with student loans to pay and little savings, is trying frantically to get a job, but has no car. And she won't let me pay her portion of the rent—

"I can pay it, don't worry about it."

"I'm not letting you pay it."

"The martyr rides again!"

—even though I can pay it, she won't allow things to be easy, even for the summer. So I drive her to the BART in the morning, on the way to taking Toph to camp, and together Kirsten and I twitch and jiggle with tension, looking for reasons to attack, explode, let it go, not knowing if we'll be living together in the fall, if we'll have jobs by the fall, if we'll even still be in love in the fall. The house amplifies our problems, its alliances—Toph and I, Katie and Beth, Beth and Kirsten and Katie—and resulting skirmishes making the place claustrophic, even with the view, and generally putting a damper on the fun Toph and I are trying desperately to create.

For example, we soon discover that, because the floors of the house are wood, and the house sparsely furnished, there are at least two ideal runways for sock sliding. The best is the back-deck-to-stairway run (fig. 1), which allows, with only a modest running start, one to glide easily thirty feet, all the way to the stairs leading to the lower floor, the first half of which can be jumped, provided one is prepared to drop and shoulder-roll upon hit-

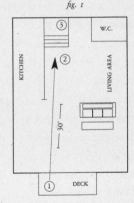

fig. 1

ting the landing, which, if "stuck," should be punctuated with a Mary Lou Retton arm-raise and back-arch. Yes! America!

Our best trick, though, is to pretend, for the benefit of the neighbors and who-ever's around, that I'm beating Toph with a belt. This is how: with the back deck door open, we stand in the living room and then, with the belt buckled into a circle, I yank it quickly on either end, snapping it taut and making a sound not unlike that produced if I were striking Toph's bare legs at full force. When it cracks, Toph squeals like a pig.

BELT: Whack!

TOPH: (Squeal!)

ME: How does that feel, kid?

TOPH: I'm sorry, I'm sorry! I'll never do it again!

ME: Yeah? You'll never walk again!

BELT: Whack!

(Squeal), etc.

It's great fun. We are attacking California, Toph and I, devour-

ing what we can before the fall comes and hems us in, and so while
Beth and Katie do whatever they do, and Kirsten does job interviews, Toph and I drive down to Telegraph and look at the
weirdos. We walk around the campus searching for the Naked
Guy, or tie-dye people, or Hare Krishnas, Jews for Jesus, for the
topless women who walk around, daring people to complain, who
troll for TV cameras and cops issuing unfair citations. We see no
breasts, and never find the Naked Guy, but one day we do see the
Naked Older Man, gray-bearded, chatting casually on a pay phone,
naked but for flip-flops. We eat at Fat Slice, maybe drive down to
the Berkeley Marina, and, at the park at the end of the jetty, green
and hilly and right there in the middle of the Bay practically, we
take out the bats and mitts, a football and a frisbee, always in the
car, all of it, and we throw things and roll around. There are
errands, groceries and bad haircuts to get, and then the slow, quiet
nights, no TV in the house, and then bed, where we read, talk on
his little bed—"It's weird, already I can hardly remember them,"
he says one night, the words burning and unstoppable, and then
has to sit through an hour of pictures and Remember? Remember?
See, you remember, of course you do—and then Kirsten and I sleep
in a room overlooking everything, the same view as the living
room and porch above, with Beth next door and Toph sleeping—
he sleeps like a dream; two, three minutes and he's out—in a
makeshift home for him we've made, with a curtain and a futon,
out of the area between our bedrooms.

We get to Montara, the beach, and park above it, next to a van,
behind which a blond man is taking off a rubber suit. We get our
stuff and walk down, from above the cliff to below, on a set of
rickety steps, the Pacific cheering heartily for us.

Look at us, lying parallel, he with his shirt on, embarrassed to
take it off. This is us talking:

"Are you bored?"

"Yeah," he says.

"Why?"

"Because you're just lying there."

"Well, I'm tired."

"Well, I'm bored."

"Why don't you go down and build a sand castle?"

"Where?"

"Down there, by the water."

"Why?"

"Because it's fun."

"How much do I get?"

"What do you mean, how much do you get?"

"Mom used to pay me."

"To build a sand castle?"

"Yeah."

I pause to think. I am slow.

"Why?"

"Because."

"Because why?"

"I don't know."

"How much did she give you?"

"A dollar."

"That's crazy."

"Why?"

"Pay you to play in the sand? Forget it. You won't play in the sand unless I pay you?"

"I don't know. I might."

The ocean is too cold, and the drop-off too steep, and the under-tow too strong to allow for swimming. We are sitting, watching the water and foam run madly through our moats and tunnels. He is not the best swimmer, and the waves hit the shore hard, and I get a flash— I'm watching another Toph drowning, twenty feet out. He got pulled out, into the maw, the wave came in and scooped him and—that fucking undertow. I run and jump and swim like a miracle to get him—I was on a swim team! I can swim and dive, fast and strong!—but am too late—I go under again and again but it's all gray, the sand churning, swirling, the water hazy, and then it's too late—he's been pulled hundreds of feet out by now... when I come up for air I can see his little arm, tan and thin, one last wave and... Gone! We should not swim here, ever—

"Hey."

We can swim in pools—

"Hey."

"What, what?"

"What's the deal with your nipples?" he asks.

"What do you mean?"

"Well, they sort of stick out."

I look him in the eye.

"Toph, I want to tell you something. I want to tell you about my nipples. I want to tell you about my nipples, and generally about the nipples of the men in our family. Because someday, son [I do this thing, and he does this thing, where I call him son and he calls me dad, when we are having funny father-son-type chats, mocking them in a way while also being secretly, deeply queasy about using these terms], someday my nipples will be your nipples. Someday you too will have nipples that protrude unnaturally far from your chest, and which will harden at the slightest provocation, preventing you from wearing anything but the heaviest cotton T-shirts."

"No way."

"Yes, Toph," I say, looking out to the ocean thoughtfully, seeing the future. "You will inherit these nipples, and you will inherit a scrawny, rib-showing frame that will not at all fill out until your early twenties, and puberty will hit you impossibly late, and soon the beautiful blond straight hair that you like so much, that you wear long and which helps you look like the young River Phoenix, this hair will thicken, harden, darken, and curl so tightly and wildly that when you wake up you will appear to have permed your hair three times and then ridden for six hours in a convertible. You will slowly grow ugly, with skin riddled with acne so persistent that on top of the general zittiness that will roughen your cheeks and chin, you will get red skin-globules— your dermatologist will call them 'cysts'—that will every other week set up shop in the crevice above your nostril, and will be so large and so red that strangers at twenty yards will gasp, small children will point and cry—"

"No."

"Yes."

"No way. I'll be different I bet."

"Pray for it."

It's windy but when you are lying down, listening to the sand, it's warm, warm, warm. Toph is sitting up, burying my feet.

There is so much to do. I try not to think yet about everything coming soon, all the things we need to do when school starts and all this becomes real, but one thing—that Toph must see a doctor, must get a physical—breaks through and now my head floods, fuck— I have to get a résumé together, and we have to find a new place to live when the sublet ends, and how will Toph get to school if I get an early job? Will Beth pull her weight, will she be too busy, will we kill each other? How often will Bill come up from L.A.? How much should I/can I/will I burden Kirsten? Will she even be around? Will she mellow when she finds a job and a car? Should I lighten my hair? Does that whitening toothpaste really work? Toph needs health insurance. I need health insurance.

Maybe I'm already sick. It's already growing inside me. Something, anything. A tapeworm. AIDS. I have to get started, have to get started soon because I will die before thirty. It will be random, my death, even more random than theirs. I will fall somehow, will fall like she fell, when I found her. I was six and it was midnight, and I found her when she fell down the stairs and opened up her head on the black-slate floor. I had heard her moaning and I walked down the hallway, the green-carpet floor, and at the top of the stairs I saw a figure, in a nightgown, crumpled at the bottom. I walked slowly down the stairs, in my pajamas, with feet, my hand on the railing, having no idea who this was, almost knowing but not knowing at all, and when I was near enough I heard her, the voice hers: "I wanted to see the flower." "I wanted to see the flower," she was saying, three or four times, "I wanted to see the flower." Then there was the blood, black, on the black slate floor, her hair matted with blood, now red, brown, glistening. I woke my father up and then there was the ambulance. She came home wearing a bandage around her head, and for weeks I was not sure she was her. I wanted it to be her, believe it was her, but there was the possibility that she had died and this now was someone else. I would have believed anything.

It's too cold to lie bare-chested. I get up and Toph gets up and he runs and I throw the frisbee ahead of him, leading him by a good twenty yards but the frisbee, because I have thrown it perfectly, floats up, floats slowly, and he reaches it with time to spare, overtakes it, stops, turns, and catches it between his legs.

Oh, we are good. He's only eight but together we are spectacular. We play by the shore, and we run barefoot, padding and scratching into the cold wet sand. We take four steps for each throw, and when we throw the world stops and gasps. We throw so far, and with such accuracy, and with such ridiculous beauty. We are perfection, harmony, young and lithe, fast like Indians. When I run I can feel the contracting of my muscles, the strain of my

cartilage, the rise and fall of pectorals, the coursing of blood, everything working, everything functioning perfectly, a body in its peak
form, albeit on the thin side, just a bit shy of normal weight, with
a few ribs visible, which, come to think of it, might look weird to
Toph, might look kind of anemic, might frighten him, might
remind him of our father's weight loss, of the way his legs, as he
sat at breakfast in his suit, that fall, after he had given up on
chemotherapy but was still going to work, his legs were like
dowels under his flannel pants, thin dowels under those gray flannel pants, now so baggy. I should work out. I could join a gym. I
could get a weight bench. At least get some free weights, a few
dumbbells. I should. I have to. I have to present to Toph a body
exploding with virility, flawless. I need to be the acme of health
and strength, instilling confidence, dashing doubt. I need to be
indomitable, a machine, a perfect fucking machine. I'll join a gym.
I'll start jogging.

We throw the frisbee farther than anyone has ever seen a frisbee go. First it goes higher than anyone has thrown before, so that
in the middle of the pale blue there is only the sun's glazed head-
light and the tiny white disc, and then it goes farther than anyone
has known a frisbee to go, with us having to use miles of beach,
from one cliff to the other, thousands of people in between, to
catch it. It's the trajectory that's important, we know that, that the
distance relies on both velocity and angle of flight, that you have
to throw the living shit out of the thing, and also put it on the
correct trajectory, an upward trajectory both straight and steady,
not too high, not too low, because if it's sent on the right upward
path, its momentum will carry it almost twice the distance, the
second half on its way down, the second half a gimme, meaning
that you need to only provide for half of its distance yourself, its
momentum providing for the second half, when finally its forward
progress slows and slows and stops and it falls, as if parachuting,
and then we move and run under it, our quick steps scratching into

the wet sand and when it falls, it falls into our hands, because we are there.

We look like professionals, like we've been playing together for years. Busty women stop and stare. Senior citizens sit and shake their heads, gasping. Religious people fall to their knees. No one has ever seen anything quite like it.

III.

The enemies list is growing quickly, unabated. All these people
impeding us, trifling with us, not knowing or caring who we are,
what has happened. The squirrelly guy who sold Toph that cheap
lock for his bike—his new bike, the one we bought last year, for
his birthday, just before we left Chicago—I wanted to punish that
man—he said it was the best lock they had, "invincible, no sweat"
he said—and the bike was stolen within the week. And that idiot
in the van, who backed over our little Civic, with both of us in it,
at a stoplight, in the middle of Berkeley, me forced to picture it
happening that second, the van continuing, monster-truck-style,
over the hood, onto us, Toph crushed, slowly, me watching,
helpess— And something should be done about (or to) that gaunt
and severe woman on the BART, the one with the hair pulled back
so tight she looked half-onion, who sat across from us, kept looking over her book, at us, disapproving, as I rested my feet on Toph's
lap, like I was a molester— And the secretary at school, with her
blaming look at me when he's late for school— And that other
woman, the across-the-street neighbor, a haggy creature with the
chubby son, who stops her gardening and stares every time we

leave the house. And the owners of the Berkeley hills sublet, who kept our deposit, citing (or claiming) damage to just about everything in the house. And most of all, those real estate people. Cruel, vicious, subhuman. Those fuckers were unbelievable.

"Where do you work?"

"I don't have a job yet."

"Are you in school?"

"No."

"And this is your...son?"

"Brother."

"Oh. Well. We'll let you know."

We had no idea where to look. Toph's new school has no bus service, so from the start I knew I'd be driving him to and fro regardless of where we lived. Thus, in late July, when we started looking for a place for the fall, we cast our net wide, considered, at least initially, almost every neighborhood in Berkeley, Albany, and southern Oakland. After discerning that between my income— assuming at some point that notion would become reality—and Toph's Social Security money—he's entitled to a monthly stipend, equivalent to what would have been paid our parents, we presume—we could pay about $1,000 a month, we set out.

And were soon struck with the relatively dingy reality of our new lives. There would no longer be hills, or views—that sublet was a freak occurrence. We would have no garage, no washer and dryer, no dishwasher, no disposal, no closets, no bathtub. Some of the places we saw didn't even have doors on the bedrooms. I felt terrible, felt personally responsible; I began to look without Toph, to spare him the gore. We were in decline. In Chicago we had a house, an ample kind of house, four bedrooms, a yard, a creek running behind, huge, hundred-year-old trees, a little hill, some woods. Then there was the sublet, the golden house in the hills, its glass and light, overlooking everything, mountains, oceans, all of those bridges. And now, in part due to the inevitable implosion of our household—Katie doesn't want to live with all of us, Kirsten and I need some time apart, and Beth and I, like any grown siblings with any kind of history behind them, knew one of us would be found bloody and dismembered if we continued to occupy the same four walls—we had all accepted smaller, humbler situations. Beth would live alone, Kirsten with a roommate found in the classifieds, and Toph and I would find a two-bedroom, would try to live close, but not too close, to one or both of them.

I had wanted a loft. For years I had pictured my first postcollegiate rental as a huge raw space, all high ceilings and chipped paint, exposed brick, water pipes and heating ducts, a massive open area where I could paint, could build and house enormous canvases, throw stuff around, maybe set up a basketball hoop, a smallish hockey rink. It would be close to the Bay, and a park, and the BART, grocery stores, everything. I called a few places listed in Oakland.

"What's the neighborhood like?" I asked.

"Well, it's kinda funky. But our lot has a gate."

"A gate? What about a park?"

"A park?"

"Yeah, I have an eight-year-old. Is there a park nearby?"

"Oh please. Get serious."

Even when we accepted the prospect of a one-story two-bedroom in the flatlands, people were unkind, ungiving. I had expected open arms from all, everyone grateful that we, as God's tragic envoys, had stepped down from the clouds to consider dwelling in their silly little buildings. What we were getting was something eerily close to indifference.

Early on, we had seen a listing—two bedrooms, yard, North Berkeley—and had made the call; the man sounded enthused, definitely not evil. But then, on a warm and blue day, we drove to his house. As we got out of our little red car and walked toward him, he was standing out on the porch, he looked stricken.

"This is your brother?"

"Yeah."

"Ooh," he said, with difficulty, as if the O were an egg he was forcing through his mouth. "Jeez, I expected you two to be older. How old are you guys?"

"I'm twenty-two. He's nine."

"But on the application you said he had an income. I don't see how that's possible."

I explained Social Security to him. I explained to him the inheritance of money. I was cheerful about it, emphasizing that we were well aware that it was a little unusual, but anyway, now that that's out of the way—

He tilted his head, his arms folded. We were still on the driveway. We were not being invited into the house.

"Listen guys, I don't want to waste your time. I'm really looking for a couple, an older couple preferably."

The wind sent to us the smell of those white flowers that are everywhere, the ones on the bushes. Rhododendrons?

"Can you see where I'm coming from?" he asked.

On the BART, on the way to an A's game, we sat, Toph and I, reading side by side, and across from us was a young woman, Latina, a little older than me, with her daughter, a bit younger than Toph. The woman, small and in a white shirt, was playing with the hair of the girl, who was sucking on a drinkbox. They could be sisters, with a wider age-gap than Toph and me—or could she be her mother? If she's 25 and the girl 7... it could be. They seemed nice. The woman was not wearing any rings. I wondered if we could all move in together. She would understand. She would already know how it is. We could combine our households. It would be so good, we could share all the responsibilities, babysitting no problem. Toph and this girl would be friends and maybe

would end up getting married— And maybe the woman and I
should be together, too. But she looked like she had a boyfriend.
Did she? That secure look. So at ease. Not just a boyfriend, but a
good man, too. A large man maybe. A boyfriend who lifts heavy
things for a living. Or could, if he wanted to. She was now turning the girl's hair around her fingers, around and around, the black
threads tighter and— But we wouldn't have to be romantic. We
could just have a happy household. The boyfriend, whose name
could be Phil, would be a okay with it, part of the mix. But he
wouldn't be living with us. That would be too much. No sleep-
overs, either. No underwear or bathrooms or showers. But maybe
she's not with anyone. Phil went away. Phil was drafted. He was a
Peruvian citizen and was drafted, and we were sad for him, but
that's how it goes, sorry Phil. So. How would we decorate? That
would be a problem. But I would defer. Yes, defer. To have a happy
easy house with help from this woman and to have her and Toph
content in their room with their stomachs on the carpet and sharing some book I would defer.

In mid-August, by now desperate, I walked into a small adobe
house a few blocks from Beth's new apartment. The owner was a
large, middle-aged black woman, looking not unlike the Bible-
reading woman who had been with my mother at the end. The
house was perfect. Or rather, it was not at all perfect, but was far
less imperfect than anything else we'd seen. The woman's son had
just gone to college—she was also a single mother—and she was
picking up and moving to New Mexico. The house was about the
right size for us, snug on a street dappled through a canopy of
interlocking greenery. There was a backyard, a porch, a shed, a sun-
room even, no dishwasher or laundry but it hardly mattered, with
us a few weeks from school starting—when she asked about financial matters, I threw down my ace.

"I'm worried about your lack of a job," she said.

"Listen," I blurted. "We can pay. We have money. We could pay the year's rent all at once, if you want."

Her eyes widened.

So we wrote the check. At this point, all sense of thrift has fallen away. We grew up in a tightfisted house, where there was no allowance, where asking for $5 from our father elicited the heaviest of sighs, required detailed plans for repayment. Our mother was far worse—would not even shop in Lake Forest, where everything was overpriced, would instead drive ten, twenty, thirty miles to Marshall's, to T.J. Maxx, for bargains, for bulk. Once a year we'd all pile into the Pinto and would drive to a place on the west side of Chicago, Sinofsky's, where for $4, $5 each we'd buy dozens of slightly flawed rugby shirts, holes here and there, extra buttons, collars ruined by bleach, pink bleeding into white. We grew up with a weird kind of cognitive dissonance; we knew we lived in a nice town—our cousins out East often made that point to us—but then, if this was true, why was our mother always fretting aloud about not having the money to buy staples? "How will I even buy milk tomorrow?" she would yell at him from the kitchen. Our father, who was out of work a year here, a year there, never seemed impressed with her worry; he seemed to have it all worked out. Still, we were ready for and expected sudden indigence, to be forced out of the house in the middle of the night and into one of the apartments on the highway, at the edge of town. To become one of *those kids*.

It never happened, of course, and now, though we are not rich, and there is very little money actually coming in, Beth and I have tossed away the guilt associated with spending it. When it's a matter of expense versus convenience, the choice is not a choice. While my mother would have driven forty miles for a half-priced tomato, I'll pay $10 for it if it means I don't have to get in the car. It's a matter of exhaustion, mostly. Fatigue loosens my wallet, Beth's even more, loosens the checkbook tied to Toph's account. We are done sacrificing, Beth and I have decided—at least when it's unnecessary, when it involves money, which, for the time being at least, we have. Even the larger expenditures, those that require Bill's approval, are pushed through with little resistance.

We lasted about a month without a washer/dryer. Every weekend, Toph and I would stuff our laundry into four plastic garbage bags, grab two each, his pair smaller, throw them over our shoulders and stagger, peasant-like, to the place around the corner and down the street. Because there is no way to carry two large, over-stuffed garbage bags at once, after half a block Toph would have dropped one of his bags. With its cheap plastic ripped and his shorts and Bulls T-shirts spilling across the sidewalk, he'd run back to the house to get another bag to replace it. Seconds later, he'd return, with his bicycle—

"What are you doing?"

"Wait. Let me try something…"

—thinking he could balance the laundry bags on the seat and the frame, and of course that wouldn't work for shit, so we'd be on the sidewalk, picking it all up, four bags of laundry, the clothes stuck in his bike chain, on the neighbor's lawn, ants making homes inside— twenty minutes later and only fifty feet from our front door. There was exhaustion, there was exasperation, there were thoughts of washing clothes in the sink or shower. The next day we called Bill, hummed loudly through his mild objections, and finally bought ourselves a washer and dryer.

They're used, both found and delivered for $400, and they're loud, and they don't match—one is beige and one is white—but good lord, they're beautiful, beautiful machines.

. . .

The house is about half the size of the last place, but it's full of light, and there is room in this house, there is flow. The floors are wooden floors, and because the first room becomes the kitchen, there is room, if one is so inclined, to run from one end of the house to the other, without hitting a door or a wall. As a matter of fact, if one happens to be wearing socks, one can run, hypothetically, from the back of the house, through the kitchen, and when one gets to the hardwood of the living room, one can jump, slide, and make it all the way to the front door, sometimes still at full speed (fig. 2).

fig. 2

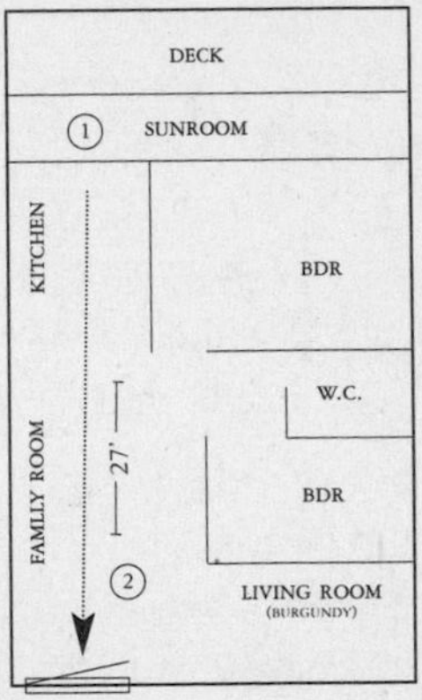

We feel temporary here, like house-sitters, vacationers, and so we do very little in the way of mingling with the community. The immediate neighbor-hood includes an older lesbian couple, an elderly Chinese couple, a black man/white woman pair in their early for-ties, and Daniel and Boona next door, sandaled and beaded, unmarried—and just friends, it seems—both in some kind of social work. Elsewhere on the block are single mothers, divorcees, widows, widowers, single women living with single men, single women living with single women, and, a few blocks away, there is even Barry Gifford. Only here would we blend. Only here, by comparison, would we seem ho-hum.

We repaint the entire house. Toph and I do it all in one week, with rollers, skipping the corners, the molding, leaving the rooms loose, fuzzy, Rothkoesque. We do the family room a sort of light blue, and the living room a deep burgundy. My room is salmon, the kitchen is an off-yellow, and Toph's we leave white—until one

night, the night before his 10th birthday and in the middle of a
spell of nightmares, for decoration and protection I paint two huge
superheroes, Wolverine and Cable, on his walls, one flying down
from above, one standing over his bed. He sleeps through the
entire process, the paint dripping onto his bedspread, his exposed
left leg.

The place is ours now, but it's a mess.

We discuss the problem.

"You suck," I say.

"No, you suck," he says.

"No, you suck."

"Nooooo, you suck."

"Well, you suckity suck suck."

"What?"

"I said, you—"

"That's so stupid."

We are on the couch, surveying. We are arguing over who has
to clean what. More important, we are debating who should have
done the work in the first place, before there was this much work
to do. There was a time, I am reminding Toph, when a condition
of his allowance was the completion of a bare minimum of household chores.

"Allowance?" he says. "You never give me my allowance."

I rethink my strategy.

The coffee table is our home's purgatory, the halfway point for
everything eaten or worn or broken. It is covered with papers and
books, two plastic plates, a half-dozen dirty utensils, an opened
Rice Krispie bar, and a Styrofoam container containing french fries
that last night one of us decided were "too thick and squishy" and
were left uneaten. There is a package of pretzels that has been
opened by the one person in the house who can't open bags properly and so cuts holes in the middle with steak knives. There are at
least four basketballs in the room, eight lacrosse balls, a skate-

board, two backpacks, and a suitcase, still partially packed, which has not moved in four months. Next to the couch, on the floor, are three glasses that once held milk and now hold its hardened remains. The family room and its perpetual state of disrepair is the problem that we are attempting to resolve.

I have just delivered a State of the Family Room Address, sweeping in scope, visionary in strategy, inspirational to one and all, and the issue has now moved to committee. And though the committee has been looking at it from many angles, addressing matters of both the provenance of the various elements of its unkemptness and matters of precisely who would be best suited to carry out the committee's recommendations, we are stalemated, solution-wise.

"But it's mostly your stuff," he says.

He's right.

"Immaterial!" I say.

Early in the negotiations, I, the senior committee member, had proposed a plan whereby the junior committee member, Toph, being young and in need of valuable life lessons and no doubt eager to prove his mettle to his peers, would clean the living room not only this time, but also on a regular basis, perhaps twice a week, in exchange for not only $2 a week in tax-free allowance, but also the guarantee that if all expressed duties are performed satisfactorily and on time, he will not be beaten senseless in his sleep by the senior committee member. The junior committee member, insolent and obviously lacking both good sense and any notion of bipartisanship, does not like this plan. He dismisses it out of hand.

"No way" is what he said.

However, with great charity and in the spirit of compromise, the senior member immediately proposed an altered plan, a generous plan whereby Toph, being so wonderfully youthful and in need of diversion and exercise, would clean the house on a regular basis, now only once a week instead of twice, in exchange for not $2 but now $3 ($3!) a week in tax-free allowance, and along with the guarantee that if all such cleaning duties are performed satisfactorily and on time, the junior committee member will not be buried to his neck in the backyard and left helpless, able only to scream as hungry dogs tear the flesh from his head. Again, showing how bullheaded and shortsighted he can be, Toph passes on the proposal, this time without comment—only a roll of the eyes—and his refusal to consider any reasonable plan at all is what prompts the charged exchange detailed previously and which continues presently:

"You know how much you suck?" I ask Toph.

"No, how much?" he answers, feigning boredom.

"A lot," I say.

"Oh, that much?"

We are at an impasse, two parties with the same goal but, seemingly, no way to reconcile our ideas about getting there.

"You know what we need?" Toph asks.

"What?" I say.

"A robot maid."

None of it is his fault. Though he's relatively neat—brought up in Montessori, all those careful children and their butcher-block cubbyholes—I'm converting him slowly, irrevocably, to my way, the slovenly way, and the results are getting a little gruesome. We have an ant problem. We have an ant problem because we have not yet grasped the difference between paper mess and food mess. We leave food out, we leave food on the plates in the sink, and when I finally turn myself to the task of washing the dishes, I must first wash away all the ants, those tiny black ones, off the plates and silverware and down the drain. Then we spray the ant column, which extends from the sink, across the counter, down the wall and through the floorboards, with Raid, which of course we hide when guests come—oh, this is Berkeley.

Certain things get us motivated. One day, his friend Luke, all

of eleven, walked in and said: "Jesus. How can you live like this?"
And for a week or so afterward we cleaned thoroughly, set schedules of maintenance, bought supplies. But we soon lost our inspiration and settled back in, allowing things to fall and stay fallen.
If we throw and miss the garbage can, the item, usually remnants
of a fruit item, stays where it lands, until a few weeks later when
someone, Beth or Kirsten, making a big show of how appalled they
are, picks it up and throws it out. They worry for us. I worry for
us. I worry that any minute someone—the police, a child welfare
agency, a health inspector, someone—will burst in and arrest me,
or maybe just shove me around, make fun of me, call me bad
names, and then take Toph away, will bring him somewhere where
the house is kept clean, where laundry is done properly and frequently, where the parental figure or figures can cook and do so
regularly, where there is no running around the house poking each
other with sticks from the backyard.

The running around hitting each other with things is pretty
much the only thing we're both interested in, and thus the rest of
our operation suffers. We scrape through every day blindly, always
getting stumped on something we should know—how to plunge
a toilet, how to boil corn, his Social Security number, the date of
our father's birthday—such that every day that he gets to school,
that I get to work and back in time for dinner, each day that we
cook and eat before nine and he goes to bed before eleven and doesn't
have blue malnourished-looking rings around his eyes like he did
for all those months last year—we never figured out why—feels
like we've pulled off some fantastic trick—an escape from a burning station wagon, the hiding of the Statue of Liberty.

By mid-fall, we settle into something like a schedule. In the morning, a little after I go to bed, Toph wakes up at, say, 3 or 4 or 4:30
in the morning, so as to allow ten minutes to shower, ten minutes

to dress, half an hour to make and eat breakfast and finish his homework, and at least three and a half, four hours for cartoons. At 8:45, he wakes me up. At 8:50 he wakes me up again. At 8:55 he wakes me up one more time and, while yelling at him because he's late, I drive him to school. I park our little red car next to the school, on the side I have been told, in four separate flyers and one personal note, is not to be used for the loading or unloading of children. Then I grab a piece of paper from his backpack and compose a note.

> Dear Ms. Richardson,
>   I am sorry Chris is late this morning. I could make something up about an appointment or a sickness, but the fact is that we woke up late. Go figure.
>   Best,
>   Brother of Chris

We are always late, always half-done. All school forms need to be sent to me twice, and I have to hand them in late. Bills are paid in ninety days minimum. Toph is always squeezed onto sports teams late, and exceptions must be made—I am never sure whether our incompetence derives from our situation, or just my lack of organization—though of course I publicly blame the former. Our relationship, at least in terms of its terms and its rules, is wonderfully flexible. He has to do certain things for me because I am his parent, and I have to do certain things for him. Of course, when I am called upon to do something I don't want to do, I do not have to do it, because I am not, actually, his parent. When something doesn't get done, we both shrug, because technically, neither of us is responsible, being just these two guys, brothers maybe, but we hardly even look alike, making duty even more questionable. But when someone has to be blamed, he allows me to finger him, and when he resists, I only need to look at him that certain way, that way that says "We are partners, here, little jerk, and yesterday, when I was exhausted, and sick with pinkeye, you wanted to get some of those Magic cards, absolutely had to have

them for the next day, because everyone was bringing new cards in
to show during lunch, and because I was afraid that you'd be
unpopular and would be cast out for being a near-orphan and having funny ears and living in a rental and would grow up with an
interest in guns and uniforms, or worse, I'll find you under the covers reading *Chicken Soup for the Prepubescent Soul* and lamenting your
poor lot, I got dressed and went to that comics store that's open 'til
eight, and we got two packs of cards and one of them had a holo-
gram in it, and you were the envy of all, and your life continued
on its recent course of ease, of convenience, of relative stardom, of
charmed bliss"—and he relents.

Parked in front of the school, I try to get him to give me a hug.
I reach my arm around him, pull him near and say what I find
myself saying too often:

"Your hat smells like urine."

"No it doesn't," he says.

It does.

"Smell it."

"I'm not going to smell it."

"You should wash it."

"It doesn't smell."

"It does."

"Why would it smell of urine?"

"Maybe you peed on it."

"Shut up."

"Don't say that. I told you not to say that."

"Sorry."

"Maybe you shouldn't sweat so much."

"Why?"

"It must be your sweat that's making it smell like urine."

"Bye."

"What?"

"Bye. I'm already late."

"Fine. Bye."

He gets out. He has to knock on the school's door to get in, and when the door opens, the secretary tries to give me the customary dirty look but now as always I am not watching, cannot see her, no. Toph disappears inside.

On my way to whatever temping assignment I have that day or week, usually somewhere in the sweltering (Far) East Bay, I muse idly about home schooling. I have been lamenting all the time he is there, at school, being taught God knows what, away from me. I calculate that his teachers see him, on a daily basis, as much as or more than I do, and I am convinced there is something fundamentally wrong with this situation; a jealousy creeps over me, of his school, his teachers, the parents who come in and help...

For weeks I've been working for a geological surveying company, re-creating topographical maps, line by line, with archaic Macintosh drawing programs. It's monotonous, but also soothing and meditative, the utter lack of thinking necessary, no worry possible in the utter safety of life there, in their immaculate Oakland office, with its water coolers and soda machines and soft, quiet carpet. While temping there are breaks, and lunch, and one can bring a Walkman if one so desires, can take a fifteen-minute break, walk around, read— It's bliss. The temp doesn't have to pretend that he cares about their company, and they don't have to pretend that they owe him anything. And finally, just when the job, like almost any job would, becomes too boring to continue, when the temp has learned anything he could have learned, and has milked it for the $18/hr and whatever kitsch value it may have had, when to continue anymore would be a sort of death and would show a terrible lack of respect for his valuable time—usually after three or four days—then, neatly enough, the assignment is over. *Perfect*.

In her sunglasses and new Jeep, Beth picks Toph up from school, and he spends the afternoon at her little place, sharing her futon, the two of them studying side by side, until I get home. At

that point, Beth and I do our best to fight about something vital
and lasting—"You said six o' clock" / "I said six thirty" / "You said
six"/ "Why would I have said six?"—and once we have done so, she
leaves us to our dinner.

Which we wouldn't bother with if we didn't have to. Neither
Toph nor I, though raised by our mother thirteen years apart, ever
developed any interest in food, and much less in cooking—both of
our palates were stunted at five, six years old, at fruit rolls and
plain hamburgers. And though we daydream aloud about the existence of a simple pill, one pill a day, that would solve our daily
dietary requirements, I recognize the importance of cooking regularly, though I have no idea why cooking regularly is important. So
we cook about four times a week, for us a heroic schedule of operation. This is the menu from which we choose, with almost all
dishes modeled closely after those which our mother, while still
cooking more varied and robust meals for our siblings and father,
prepared specially for us, each of us at one time her youngest:

1. THE SAUCY BEEFEATER
(Sirloin strips, sliced and sauteed in Kikkoman-brand soy sauce, cooked until black,
served with tortillas and eaten by hand, the tortilla being torn into small pieces, each
small piece being used to envelope one, two, maybe three but no more than three beef
fragments at a time. Served with potatoes, prepared in the French manner, with oranges
and apples, sliced the only logical way—first in half, width-wise, then lengthwise, ten
slices per—and served in a bowl, on the side.)

2. THE SAUCY CHICKEN
(Sliced chicken breasts, sautéed in Kikkoman soy sauce, cooked until tangy, almost
crispy, and served with tortillas and eaten by hand in the manner described above.
Accompanied with potatoes, served in the French manner—which it should be mentioned are exclusively Ore-Ida brand Crispers! frozen french fries, they being the only
one of their species that actually become crispy during their oven-time. Also with sliced
oranges and apples, served on the side.)

3. THE CRUNCHY CHICKEN
(Courtesy of Church's Fried Chicken, drive-through, at San Pablo and Gilman. White
meat insisted on, along with biscuits, mashed potatoes, and added to, at home, with a
small green salad of iceberg lettuce and one sliced cucumber. No dressing.)

4. The Crumbling Wall

(Hamburger, prepared medium well, with bacon and barbecue sauce. Courtesy of that place on Solano, where, it should be mentioned, they use much too much barbecue sauce, which anyone should know has the almost immediate effect of soaking the bun, the bun becoming like oatmeal, inedible, the burger ruined, all in a matter of minutes— so quick that even when the burger is picked up and patrons attempt to save the bun ("Separate them! Quick! Get the bun away from the sauce! Now scrape! Scrape!"), it's always too late, necessitating the keeping, at home, of a stash of replacement buns, which are then toasted, heavily, to provide maximum resistance to the sauce's degenerative effects. Served with potatoes of the French kind, and fruit, as above.

5. The Mexican-Italian War

(Tacos: Ground beef sauteed in Prego spaghetti sauce (Traditional style), served with tortillas, but without beans, salsa, tomatoes, cheese, guacamole, and whatever that white creamy substance is that is sometimes found on the dish's inferior, less pure incarnations. On the side: Pillsbury brand crescent rolls and iceberg salad. No dressing.)

6. [We didn't actually name any of these meals. Would we seem cooler, or somehow less cool, had we done so? I am thinking less cool.]

(Pizza, served with pepperoni. Tombstone, Fat Slice, Pizza Hut, or Domino's, if the price cannot be resisted. With a ready-made small green salad.)

7. The Old Man and the Sea

(Mrs. Paul's frozen fried clams, one package each ($3.49—not cheap), served with Crispers!, crescent rolls, and sliced oranges and apples. Or sometimes cantaloupe.)

8. Gavin MacLeod and Charo

(For him: Grilled cheese served with one slice of Kraft American cheese set in middle of two pieces of seeded Jewish rye, toasted in pan and cut diagonally. For other him: Quesadillas—one slice of Kraft American cheese, between one tortilla, prepared in skillet. With sliced honeydew.)

(NOTE: no spices are available, except oregano, which is shaken, sparingly, onto two items: a) pepperoni pizza; and b) sliced Jewish rye bread, which is folded around oregano, a la Tufnel. No vegetables are available, except carrots, celery, cucumbers, green beans and iceberg lettuce, which are all served raw and only raw. Unavailable is food that swims in its own excrement. Pasta is not available, especially not that regurgitated mess known as lasagna. Further, all such foods, those containing more than two or three ingredients mixed together indiscriminately, including all sandwiches except salami, are not chewed, but eschewed. All meals are served with a tall glass of 1% milk, with the gallon jug resting on the floor next to the table, for convenient refills. Alternative beverages are not available. Anything not on the menu is not available. Any complaints will be handled quickly, and with severity.)

"Hey, I need your help," I say, when I need his help cooking.

"Okay," he says, and then helps out with the cooking.

Sometimes we sing while we are cooking. We sing regular words, words about pouring the milk or getting the spaghetti sauce, though we sing them in opera-style. We can sing opera-style, too. It is incredible.

Sometimes, while cooking, we have sword fights using wooden spoons or sticks that we bring into the house for such occasions. It is an unsaid mission of mine, the source of which is sometimes clear and sometimes not, to keep things moving, to entertain the boy, to keep him on his toes. For a while we would chase each other around the house, mouths full of water, threatening to spit. Of course, neither of us would have ever thought of actually spitting a mouthful of water at the other inside the house, until one night, when I had him cornered in the kitchen, I just went ahead and did it. Things have been devolving ever since. I have stuck half a cantaloupe into his face. I have rubbed a handful of banana onto his chest, tossed a glassful of apple juice into his face. It's an effort, I'm guessing, to let him know, if it weren't already obvious, that as much as I want to carry on our parents' legacy, he and I will also be doing some *experimenting*. And constantly entertaining, like some amazing, endless telethon. There is a voice inside me, a very excited, chirpy voice, that urges me to keep things merry, madcap even, the mood buoyant. Because Beth is always pulling out old photo albums, crying, asking Toph how he feels, I feel I have to overcompensate by keeping us occupied. I am making our lives a music video, a game show on Nickelodeon—lots of quick cuts, crazy camera angles, fun, fun, *fun*! It's a campaign of distraction and revisionist history—leaflets dropped behind enemy lines, fireworks, funny dances, magic tricks. *Whassat? Lookie there! Where'd it go?*

In the kitchen, when the inspiration calls, I take out the family's seventeen-inch turkey knife, plant my legs in an A, squat a little and hold the knife over my head, samurai-style.

"Hiyyyyy!" I yell.

"Don't," he says, backing away.

"Hiyyyyy!" I yell, stepping toward him, because threatening children with seventeen-inch knives is funny. Always the best games have involved some kind of threatened injury, or near-accident, as when he was a toddler and I would run around with him on my shoulders, pretending to be dizzy, spinning, stumbling—

"Not funny," he says, backing into the family room.

I put the knife away; it clinks into the silverware drawer.

"Dad used to do that all the time," I say. "Out of the blue. He'd get this look on his face, this bug-eyed look, and act like he was going to split our heads open with the knife."

"Sounds funny," he says.

"Yeah, it was funny," I say. "It actually was funny."

Sometimes while we cook he tells me about things that happened at school.

"What happened today?" I ask.

"Today Stuart told me that he hopes that you and Beth are in a plane and that the plane crashes and that you both die just like Mom and Dad."

"They didn't die in a plane crash."

"That's what I said."

Sometimes I call the parents of Toph's classmates.

"Yeah, that's what he said," I say.

"It's hard enough, you know," I say.

"No, he's okay," I continue, pouring it on this incompetent moron who has raised a twisted boy. "I just don't know why Stuart would say that. I mean, why do suppose your son wants Beth and me to die in a plane crash?

"No, Toph's fine. Don't worry about us. We're fine. I'm worried about you— I mean, you should worry about young Stuart there," I say.

Oh, these poor people. What is to be done?

. . .

During dinner, during the basketball season, we watch the Bulls on cable. Otherwise, needing to keep constantly occupied, we play one of an endlessly rotating series of games—gin, backgammon, Trivial Pursuit, chess—with our plates next to the board. We have been trying to eat in the kitchen, but since we got the Ping-Pong net, it's been more difficult.

"Unhook the net," I say.

"Why?" he asks.

"For dinner," I say.

"No, you unhook it," he says.

So usually we eat on the coffee table. If the coffee table is beyond clearing, we eat on the family room floor. If the family room floor is covered with plates from the night before, we eat on my bed.

After dinner, we play games for our own amusement and the edification of the neighbors. In addition to the belt-cracking game mentioned earlier, there is the game that involves Toph pretending that he's a kid, while I pretend I'm a parent.

"Dad, can I drive the car?" he asks as I sit, reading the paper.

"No, son, you can't," I say, still reading the paper.

"But why?"

"Because I said so."

"But Daaaad!"

"I said no!"

"I hate you! I hate you I hate you I hate you I hate you!"

Then he runs to his room and slams the door.

A few seconds later he opens the door.

"Was that good?" he asks.

"Yeah, yeah," I say. "That was pretty good."

. . .

Today is Friday, and on Friday he gets out of school at noon, so I usually come home early, too, if I can. We are in his room.

"Where are they?"

"They're in there."

"Where?"

"Hiding."

"Where?"

"In that mountain thing we made."

"Inside the papier-maché?"

"Yeah."

"When was the last time you saw them?"

"I don't know. A while. A week maybe."

"You sure they're still in there?"

"Yeah. Almost positive."

"How?"

"They still eat their food."

"But you never see them?"

"No, not really."

"What crappy pets."

"Yeah, I know."

"Should we return them?"

"Can we?"

"I think so."

"Stupid iguanas."

We walk the two blocks, through the backyard of that one mossy gnome house, to the park with the small half court.

"Now, why do you go all the way over there when you do it?"

"All the way over where?"

"You had an open-court layup, but you went all the way over there to do it. Watch. I'll be you............ See?"

"See what?"

"I went all the way over—like eight feet over there."

"So?"

"That's what you were doing!"

"I was not."

"You were too."

"I was not."

"You were!"

"Let's just play."

"You gotta learn this—"

"Fine, I learned it."

"Jerk."

"Pussy."

The game invariably ends with this:

"What's the big deal?"

"—"

"You get so emotional when we play."

"—"

"C'mon. Talk. Say something."

"—"

"I have a right to tell you how to do stuff."

"—"

"Don't be such a sullen little dork."

"—"

"What's your problem? You have to walk ten feet behind me? You look like an idiot."

"—"

"Here, you carry this. I'm going to the store."

"—"

"—"

"Is the door open? I don't have a key."

"Here."

5:30 p.m.

"I'm taking a nap."

"So?"

"I need you to wake me up in an hour."

"What time?"

"Six-twenty."

"Fine."

"Really. You have to wake me up."

"Fine."

"I'll be incredibly upset if I don't get up."

"Fine."

7:40 p.m.

"Jesus!"

"What?"

"Why didn't you wake me up?"

"What time is it?"

"Seven-forty!"

"Oh!" he says, actually putting his hand over his mouth.

"We're late!"

"For what?"

"Goddamn it! For your open house, idiot!"

"Oh!" he says, again actually putting his hand over his mouth.

We have twenty minutes to make it. We are firemen and there is a fire. I run this way, he the other. Toph goes up to his room to change. In a few minutes I knock on his door.

"Don't come in!"

"We have to go."

"Hold on."

I wait by the door and the door opens. He is dressed.

"What is that? You can't wear that."

"What?"

"No way."

"What?"

"Don't mess with me. Just change, retard."

The door closes. Drawers are opened and there is stomping.

The door reopens.

"Are you kidding?"

"What?"

"That's worse than the last thing you had on."

"What's wrong with it?"

"Look at it. There're permanent grease stains all over it. And it's too big. And it's a sweatshirt. You can't wear a sweatshirt. And don't you have any other shoes?"

"No. Someone didn't get me any."

"I didn't what?"

"Nothing."

"No, tell me—what didn't I do for you?"

"Nothing."

"Screw you."

"No, screw you."

"Change!"

The door closes. A minute, then the door opens.

"That's bet— What the— Can't you tuck in the shirt? I mean, didn't anyone ever teach you how to tuck in your shirt? You look like a moron."

"Why?"

"You're nine years old and I'm going to have to come over there and help you tuck in your shirt."

"I can do it."

"I'm doing it. We've got five minutes left to get there. Jesus, we're always late. I'm always waiting for you. Don't move. And where's your belt? God, you're a mess."

7:40–7:50 p.m.

"Goddamn it. We're always late. Why the hell can't you get dressed yourself? Roll down your window. It's too hot in here. How come you refuse to open your window when it's boiling in here? And your buttons are off. Look at your buttons. Look at your

collar, up around your ear. Oh my God. Now I'll have to dress you
every day. At least help with your buttons. Man are they off. You
missed about ten, retard."

"*Retard.*"

"*Retard.*"

"*Retard.*"

We are flying down San Pablo, in the left lane, then the right
lane, passing Beetles and Volvos, their pleading bumper stickers.

"I was dressed fine."

"Dressed fine? Goddamn it, you were so not dressed fine. Open
the window more. You looked like a retard. A little more. That's
good. You cannot dress like that to an open house. This is what
people wear. This is special occasion rules, my man. This is like,
give me a break, you know? This is obvious stuff. This is just
common sense. I mean, give me a goddamn break, okay? You have
got to help me out every once in a while, little man. I'm exhausted, overworked, dead half the time, and I just can't be dressing
someone who's nine years old and should be perfectly capable of
dressing himself. I mean, Jesus Christ, Toph, give me a goddamn
break every once in a while, please? Can I have a break every once
in a while? A little break? A little cooperation? Jesus Christ—"

"You just passed the school."

7:52 p.m.

The open house is still full—it goes until nine, not eight, as I
had thought—and we are both overdressed. We walk in. Toph
immediately untucks his shirt.

The walls are covered with corrected papers about slavery, and
the first-graders' unsettling self-portraits.

Heads turn. This is our first open house, and people are not
sure what to make of us. I am surprised, having expected that
everyone would have been briefed about our arrival. Kids look at
Toph and say hi.

"Hi, Chris."

And then they look at me and squint.

They are scared. They are jealous.

We are pathetic. We are stars.

We are either sad and sickly or we are glamorous and new. We walk in and the choices race through my head. Sad and sickly? Or glamorous and new? Sad/sickly or glamorous/new? Sad/sickly? Glamorous/new?

We are unusual and tragic and alive.

We walk into the throng of parents and children.

We are disadvantaged but young and virile. We walk the halls and the playground, and we are taller, we radiate. We are orphans. As orphans, we are celebrities. We are foreign exchange people, from a place where there are still orphans. Russia? Romania? Somewhere raw and exotic. We are the bright new stars born of a screaming black hole, the nascent suns burst from the darkness, from the grasping void of space that folds and swallows—a darkness that would devour anyone not as strong as we. We are oddities, sideshows, talk show subjects. We capture everyone's imagination. That's why Matthew wants Beth and me dead in a plane crash. His parents are old, bald, square, wear glasses, are wooden and gray, are cardboard boxes, folded, closeted, dead to the world— We ate at their house actually, not long ago, accepting a neighborly invitation sometime before Matthew's plane crash comment. And we were bored to tears in their stillborn house, its wooden floors and bare walls—the daughter even played the piano for us, the father so haughtily proud of her, the poor bald guy. They owned no TV, there were no toys anywhere, the place was airless, a coffin—

But we!—we are great-looking! We have a style, which is messy, rakish, yet intriguingly so, singular. We are new and everyone else is old. We are the chosen ones, obviously, the queens to their drones—the rest of those gathered at this open house are aging, past their prime, sad, hopeless. They are crinkly and no longer have random sex, as only I among them am still capable of. They are done with such things; even thinking about them having sex is unappealing. They cannot run without looking silly. They cannot coach the soccer team without making a mockery of themselves and the sport. Oh, they are over. They are walking corpses, especially that imbecile smoking out in the courtyard. Toph and I are the future, a terrifyingly bright future, a future that has come from Chicago, two terrible boys from far away, cast away and left for dead, shipwrecked, forgotten, but yet, but yet, here, resurfaced, bolder and more fearless, bruised and unshaven, sure, their pant legs frayed, their stomachs full of salt water, but now unstoppable, insurmountable, ready to kick the saggy asses of the gray-haired, thickly bespectacled, slump-shouldered of Berkeley's glowering parentiscenti!

Can you see this?

We walk around the classrooms. In his homeroom, on the walls, there are papers about Africa. His paper is not on the wall.

"Where's your paper?"

"I don't know. Ms. Richardson didn't like it, I guess."

"Hmmph."

Who is this Ms. Richardson? I need an explanation. Answers.

The school is full of nice children but eccentric children, delicate and oddly shaped. They are what my friends and I, growing up in public schools, always envisioned private school kids were like— a little too precious, their innate peculiarities amplified, not muted, for better and worse. Kids who think that they are pirates, and are encouraged to dress the part, in school. Kids who program computers and collect military magazines. Chubby boys with big heads and very long hair. Skinny girls who wear sandals and carry flowers.

After about ten minutes, we're bored. My main reason for coming has gone bust.

I was looking to score.

I expected flirting. I expected attractive single mothers and flirting. My goal, a goal I honestly thought was fairly realistic, was to meet an attractive single mother and have Toph befriend the mother's son so we can arrange playdates, during which the mother and I will go upstairs and screw around while the kids play outside. I expected meaningful glances and carefully worded propositions. I imagine that the world of schools and parents is oozing with intrigue and debauchery, that under its concerned and well-meaning facade, its two-parent families, conferences with teachers and thoughtful questions directed to the history teacher about Harriet Tubman, everyone is swinging.

But by and large they're ugly. I scan the crowd milling in the courtyard. The parents are interesting only in their prototypical Berkeley-ness. They wear baggy tie-dyed, truly tie-dyed, pants, and do not comb their hair. Most are over forty. All of the men have beards, and are short. Many of the women are old enough to have mothered me, and look it. I am disheartened by the lack of possibility. I am closer in age to most of the children. Oh but there is one mother, a small-headed woman with long, long, straight black hair, thick and wild like a horse's tail. She looks exactly like her daughter, same oval face, same sad dark eyes. I've seen her before, when I've driven Toph to school, and have guessed that she's single; the father is never present.

"I'm gonna ask her out," I say.

"Please, don't. Please," Toph says. He really thinks I might.

"Do you like the daughter at all? This could be fun—we could double date!"

"Please, please don't."

Of course I won't. I have no nerve. But he does not know that yet. We walk the halls decorated with construction paper and student work. I meet Ms. Richardson, the homeroom teacher, who is tall and black and severe—with distended, angry eyes. I meet the science teacher who looks precisely like Bill Clinton and stutters. There is a girl in Toph's class who, at nine, is taller than her parents, and heavier than me. I want Toph to be her friend and make her happy.

A woman nearby is looking at us. People look at us. They look and wonder. They wonder if I am a teacher, not knowing how to place me, thinking maybe that because I have scraggly facial hair and am wearing old shoes that I will take and molest their children. I surely look threatening. The woman, this one looking at us, has long gray hair and large glasses. She is wearing a floor-length patterned skirt and sandals. She leans toward us, points her finger to me and to Toph and back, smiles. Then we find our places and read the script:

MOTHER

Hi. This is your... son?

BROTHER

Uh... no.

MOTHER

Brother?

BROTHER

Yeah.

MOTHER
(squinting to make sure)

Oh, you can tell right away.

BROTHER
(though knowing that it is not really true, that
he is old and severe-looking, and his brother glows)

Yeah, people say that.

MOTHER

Having fun?

BROTHER

Sure. Sure.

MOTHER

You go to school at Cal?

BROTHER

No, no, I finished school a few years ago.

MOTHER

And you live around here?

BROTHER

Yeah, we live a few miles north. Close to Albany.

MOTHER

So you live with your folks?

BROTHER

No, just us.

MOTHER

But...where are your parents?

BROTHER
(thinking, thinking: "They're not here." "They couldn't make it." "I have no idea, actually; if only you knew just little idea I have. Oh it's a doozy, that story. Do you know what it's like, to have no idea, no idea at all of their exact whereabouts, I mean, the actual place that they are right now, as we speak? That is a weird feeling, oh man. You want to talk about it? You have a few hours?")

Oh, they died a few years ago.

MOTHER
(grabbing BROTHER's *forearm)*
Oh, I'm *sorry.*

BROTHER

No, no, don't worry.

(wanting to add, as he sometimes does, "It wan't your fault." He loves that line, especially when he tacks on: "Or was it?")

MOTHER

So he lives with you?

BROTHER

Yeah.

MOTHER

Oh, gosh. That's interesting.

BROTHER

(thinking of the state of the house. It is interesting.)

Well, we have fun. What grade is your...

MOTHER

Daughter. Fourth. Amanda. If I may, can I ask how they died?

BROTHER

(again scanning possibilities for the entertainment of him and his brother. Plane crash. Train crash. Terrorists. Wolves. He has made up things before, and he was amused, though younger brother's amusement level was unclear.)

Cancer.

MOTHER

But...at the same time?

BROTHER

About five weeks apart.

MOTHER

Oh my god.

BROTHER
(with inexplicable little chuckle)

Yeah, it was weird.

MOTHER

How long ago was this?

BROTHER

A few winters ago.

(BROTHER *thinks about how much he likes the "a few winters ago" line. It's new. It sounds dramatic, vaguely poetic. For a while it was "last year." Then it was "a year and a half ago." Now, much to* BROTHER's *relief, it's "a few years ago." "A few years ago" has a comfortable distance. The blood is dry, the scabs hardened, peeled. Early on was different. Shortly before leaving Chicago,* BROTHERs *went to the barber to have* TOPH's *hair cut, and* BROTHER *doesn't remember how it came up, and* BROTHER *was really hoping it wouldn't come up, but when it did come up,* BROTHER *answered, "A few weeks ago." At that the hair-cutting woman stopped, went through the antique saloon-style doors to the back room, and stayed there for a while. She came back red-eyed.* BROTHER *felt terrible. He is always feeling terrible, when the innocent, benign questions of unsuspecting strangers yield the bizarre answer he must provide. Like someone asking about the weather and being told of nuclear winter. But it does have its advantages. In this case,* BROTHERs *got a free haircut.)*

MOTHER
(holding BROTHER's *forearm again)*

Well. Good for you! What a good brother you are!

BROTHER
(Smiling. Wonders: What does that mean? *He is often told this. At soccer games, at school fund-raisers, at the beach, at the baseball card shows, at the pet store. Sometimes the person*

telling him this knows their full biography and sometimes she or he does not. BROTHER *doesn't understand the line, both what it means and when it became a standard sort of expression that many different people use.* What a good brother you are! BROTHER *had never heard the saying before, but now it comes out of all kinds of people's mouths, always phrased the same way, the same words, the same inflections— a rising sort of cadence:*

What   a   good bro-ther   you   are!

What *does* that mean? *He smiles, and if Toph is close, he'll punch him in the arm, or try to trip him*—look at us horsing around! Light as air!*—then* BROTHER *will say the same thing he always says after they say their words, the thing that seems to deflate the mounting tension, the uncomfortable drama swelling in the conversation, while also throwing it back at the questioner, because he often wants the questioner to think about what he or she is saying. What he says, with a cute little shrug, or a sigh, is:)*

Well, what are you gonna do?

*(*MOTHER *smiles and squeezes* BROTHER's *forearm one more time, then pats it.* BROTHERs *look to* AUDIENCE, *wink, and then break into a fabulous Fossean dance number, lots of kicks and high-stepping, a few throws and catches, a big sliding-across-the-stage-on-their-knees thing, then some more jumping, some strutting, and finally, a crossing-in-midair front flip via hidden trampoline, with both of them landing perfectly, just before the orchestra, on one knee, hands extended toward audience, grinning while breathing heavily. The crowd stands and thunders. The curtain falls. They thunder still.)*

FIN

As the crowd stomps the floor for a curtain call, we sneak through the back door and make off like superheroes.

IV.

Oh I could be going out, sure. It's Friday night and I should be out, across the Bay, I should be out every night, with the rest of the young people, fixing my hair, spilling beer, trying to get someone to touch my penis, laughing with and at people. Kirsten and I are *taking a break*, which we have done twice already and will do ten or twelve times in the future, meaning that we (ostensibly) date other people. So yes, I could be out, enjoying this freedom specifically and that of youth generally, exulting in the richness of my time and place.

But no.

I will be here, at home. Toph and I will cook, as usual—

"Can you get the milk?"

"It's right there."

"Oh. Thanks."

—and then we will play Ping-Pong, and then we'll probably drive to that place on Solano and rent a movie, and, on the way back, buy a few push-ups at 7-Eleven. Oh I could be out, rollicking in the ripeness of my flesh and others', could be drinking things and eating things and rubbing mine against theirs, speculating about this person or that, waving, indicating hello with a sudden upward jutting of my chin, sitting in the backseat of someone else's car, bumping up and down the San Francisco hills, south of Market, seeing people attack their instruments, afterward stopping at a bodega, parking, carrying the bottles in a paper bag, the glass clinking, all our faces bright, glowing under streetlamps, down the sidewalk to this or that apartment party, hi, hi, putting the bottles in the fridge, removing one for now, hating the apartment, checking the view, sitting on the arm of a couch and being told not to, and then waiting for the bathroom, staring idly at that ubiquitous Ansel Adams print, Yosemite, talking to a short-haired girl while waiting in the hallway, talking about teeth, no reason really, the train of thought unclear, asking to see her fillings, no, really, I'll show you mine first, ha ha, then no, you go ahead, I'll go after you, then, after using the bathroom she is still there, still in the hallway, she was waiting not just for the bathroom but for me, and so eventually we'll go home together, her apartment, where she lives alone, in a wide, immaculate railroad type place, newly painted, decorated with her mother, then sleeping in her oversized, oversoft white bed, eating breakfast in her light-filled nook, then maybe to the beach for a few hours with the Sunday paper, then wandering home whenever, never—

Fuck. We don't even have a baby-sitter.

Beth and I are still thinking it's too early to leave Toph with anyone but family, that to do otherwise would cause him to feel unwanted and alone, leading to the warping of his fragile psyche, then to experimentation with inhalants, to the joining of some *River's Edge* kind of gang, too much flannel and too little remorse, the cutting of his own tats, the drinking of lamb's blood, the inevitable initiation-fulfilling murder of me and Beth in our sleep. So when I go out, once a week, on a day Beth and I have chosen together, Toph gets his things together, stuffs them into his backpack, uses both straps, and walks over to her house and spends the night on half of her futon.

The no-baby-sitter rule is only one of many, so so many, all necessary to keep this thing together, keep it from spinning out of control. For instance, Beth is no longer allowed to have Toph around if any of those feeble and obnoxious friends of hers will be there—Katie, as an orphan herself, knows what is what, but the others do not, at all—drinking or even not drinking, because they insist on talking about inappropriate things, the proclivities of boyfriends, the degree of their last drunkenness, and do so in a stunted, Valley sort of way that spreads stupidity by osmosis. Further, if either Beth or I am dating someone, that someone will not be introduced to Toph immediately, and Toph will not be required to go on junkets—football games, zoos, rodeos—so we can show him off to these new boyfriends. No, there will be a wait-ing period, so that by the time Toph meets this someone, this someone will actually be a someone that Toph may see again, so that he will not be required to meet dozens, fifty, hundreds of people over the years, all introduced as some sort of special person, eventually souping them together, getting himself confused, growing up with no sense of propriety, identity, no discernible and changeless family core, thus weak and flighty, thus susceptible to the dubious allure of ashrams, kibbutzes and Jesus. As for my own dating, if I am going out on something like a date, and we go out early, and the date involves an activity that Toph might enjoy, then of course Toph comes along. If the star of the something-like-a-date expresses any reservations about having Toph along, she is clearly a very bad person. If she thinks that because Toph is brought along to dinner, that it means that I like her less, that he is serving as some kind of buffer, then she is misguided and self-centered and also a bad person. If when she comes over she questions anything about the state of the house—"Oh God, there's food under the couch!" or even "Holy bachelor pad!"—or worse, any parental decisions made in her company or otherwise, she is first glared at in Toph's presence, later lectured out of his earshot, and then becomes fodder for month-long trashings in conversations with Beth about people who know nothing about anything and how dare they say anything, these people, these lotus-eating simpletons who have never known struggle, who would never question other parents, but feel the right to question me, us, simply because we are new at it, are young, are siblings. Then again, of course, if she, the date-person, does not ask about the passed-on parents, she is unthoughtful, rude, weightless, too young, selfish. If she does, but assumes that it was a car crash—

"Who said it was a car crash?"

"I just assumed."

"You just... What?"

—then she is a very bad person. However, asking too many questions is not at all allowed, either, because—

"Don't you want to talk about it?"

"What, now? With you?"

"Yes. Please."

"At a bar?"

"You don't have to carry this around alone."

Oh Jesus.

"Oh Jesus."

—that's not her place, and there's no coming out of that alive. If she wants me to *make more of an effort*, to come up to Stanford to see *her* as opposed to her always having to come down, she is reminded, politely, with all due restraint, of the vast, vast, immeasurable chasm between our respective situations, hers being one of breezy frivolity, of limitless cable TV and "Let's watch a movie," and "Let's go out to dinner," and "Let's go here," and "Let's go there," and cafés and drinking whatever whenever, and Tahoe, and camping, and shopping, and skydiving, and doing anything at any time, while mine, in sharp, razor-sharp contrast—let's not be unclear about this (Terrie, this should be so imminently clear)— being put-upon, purposeful, stressful, spartan, down-time-less, limiting, exhausting, a world of young knees needing stitching and young lunches needing packing and young minds needing help with elaborate projects about east Africa, not to mention grueling parent-teacher conferences and bizarre and threatening notices from Social Security—HAS CHRISTOPHER EGGERS BEEN RECENTLY MARRIED? CHECK YES OR NO AND RETURN THIS FORM IMMEDIATELY. FAILURE TO DO SO WILL RESULT IN CESSATION OF BENEFITS—my existence almost wholly dedicated to being the only thing standing in the way of for-him-otherwise-certain oblivion, given to trying to pull off what might very well be one of the great achievements of recorded history. If she does not understand this she is a bad person. If she says she understands, but wonders why maybe I couldn't *still* try to make an effort, some sort of better effort, it only proves how much she does not understand, will never understand, will not understand until one day, when something unspeakable happens, she should pray something bad does not happen but it probably will, when her own life-fabric is pulled taut, when there is suddenly no margin for error, no room for the loosey-goosey, the lolling and dilly-dallying and time-management decadence—and just how difficult it is to maintain this kind of self-righteous front while knowing full well that such an effort to meet her at Stanford, or even halfway, would of course be made if the relationship seemed worth it and if she hadn't, on the second time out, asked to be spanked. Seeking some kind of understanding, though, I find myself seeking out others mangled by bizarre familial machinery, those whose parents are dead, or dying, at least divorced—hoping that these people will know what I know, and thus will not hassle me about the details, about give and take, about *my contributions*. Toph-wise, if, as we paw each other on the couch in the burgundy living room after Toph has gone to asleep, she wants to stay the night, and does not understand why she cannot, does not understand why Toph must not wake up to see random people sleeping

in his brother's bed, she is too young and unthoughtful and does
not appreciate the importance of creating for Toph as simple a
childhood as possible, and so she is not seen again. If she does not
know how to talk to Toph, if she treats him like a hearing-impaired
dog or worse, like a *child*, she is not seen again and is made fun of
with Beth. If, on the other hand, she treats Toph like an adult, fine,
but in such a way that inappropriate things are said, things unfit
for his young ears, such as "Can you believe what they were charging for condoms at Walgreen's?" then she is unpreferred. In general, if, even with the observance of said rules, Toph does not like her,
for whatever reason—he never says so but it becomes clear (he
retreats to his room when she arrives or he does not show her his
lizards or does not want to go for candy after the movie)—then she
is slowly faded away, unless of course she is extraordinarily good-
looking, in which case it doesn't matter what the little dickhead
says. If she brings Toph something, for instance a pack of new Ping-
Pong balls, the need for which she somehow gleaned, then she is a
good person, not a bad one, and she is loved unconditionally. If she
comes over for dinner and actually eats our version of tacos, without all that ludicrous shit people usually put in them, she is a saint
and is welcome anytime. If she recognizes that the way we cut
oranges—width-wise, not length-wise—is the only logical way, the
only aesthetically pleasing way, and eats the whole slice as opposed
to just sucking the juice and leaving that anemone mess, then she
is perfect and will be talked about glowingly—remember Susan?
We liked Susan—for months to come, even if she is not seen again,
because she is otherwise too skinny and nervous-seeming.

Not that we're demanding. No—we're fun! Easy, laid-back.
Ha ha. Yes. Fun. There is no reason for anyone to be nervous; the
rules are for us only, are never stated, never discussed. We are,
truth be told, exceptionally effort-making, jovial, comfort-giving,
even if we spend most of our time, in her presence, trying not so
much to entertain her, but to entertain each other, often at her

expense. *But in a fun way!* Everything is low-key with us, it should be noted that it's demonstrably low-key, that we're accepting of everyone, and, best of all, Toph takes to just about everyone immediately. Sure, it helps if you're interested in iguanas and can make words while belching, but even without such features, he actually recognizes the difficult spot a given date-person is in, and makes things easy, showing them his Magic cards when they say they'd like to see them, getting them beverages, with ice, sitting next to them, almost on top of them, so happy he is for the new company, someone who might, if he goes and gets it before his bedtime and maybe while his brother is in the bathroom and so can't protest, play Trivial Pursuit, as long as it's the fast way—one pie piece per answer correctly provided.

At the moment I'm seeing a woman who is twenty-nine. The twenty-nine-year-old, an actual woman-woman, is the managing editor at the weekly where I do some design and freelance illustrating. Though it becomes clear early on, after she wears a beret one day, of purple velour, that we're not meant to be, I continue the relationship, gloating about my ability to procure and relate to this woman-woman, seven years older. She is smart, with long blond hair and laugh lines, and is also midwestern, from Minnesota I think, and knows how to order and drink actual drinks. And she's twenty-nine. Was that mentioned, that she's twenty-nine? This I consider fitting, fitting that I, who am bearing the weight of both Toph and the world, I who have been through so much and already feel so old, should be dating a woman seven years my senior. But of course!

Her motivations are unclear, but I have a theory: at twenty-nine, she, like most people at or near thirty, is feeling wretched, old, as if their chance has passed—and the only way to regain even a smidgen of their squandered youth would be to drink in someone like me, bursting with virility—

But whoa I feared seeing her naked body. Before we got to that stage, I wondered, often, if she would be wrinkled, prunelike, sagging. I had never seen the naked flesh of anyone over twenty-three, and, when we went out one night, without Toph, drank some specific vodka drink that I had never heard of, until we held hands at that table in the back while pretending to listen to the ex–lead singer of that certain seminal Los Angeles punk band, this man blurrily singing blah blah far below us, $14 background music, and then went to her apartment, I was ready to be horrified, was debating what I would do if I had to touch her pimpled or varicose flesh, and when we stumbled up and into her place I was happy that it was so dark, even darker in her bedroom— But then she was not grizzled and drooped, her flesh was still firm and full and I was thrilled and relieved, and in the morning, in the white light, she was pale and smooth, her hair blonder and longer than I remembered, streaming all over her white sheets, and for a few minutes it was really nice— But I had to leave. It was the first time I had spent the night elsewhere since we had moved to California, and though Toph was sleeping at Beth's, I wanted to be home in case he came back early—if I was not, he would know I had stayed elsewhere, and would not understand this, and would grow up to sell crack or sing in a harmonizing pop group from Florida. I dressed and left, passed her roommate on the way out and drove back, over the bridge, glorious, the ships plowing to and fro, and made it in time. The house was empty, and I dove into bed, fell back asleep, and when he came home his brother was there, of course had been there the whole time, of course had never left.

But tonight there is no going out. I went out on Wednesday, so now and for the rest of the week am staying in, holding the world together.

"Time for bed."

"What time is it?"

"Time for bed."

"Is it ten?"

"Yes." [Loud exhale.] "It's past ten." [Roll of eyes.] "I'll meet you there in a second."

He gets into bed and under the covers. I sit next to him, my back against the headboard. Bill bought the headboard months ago—every time he's in town we have to go furniture shopping, with him trying to stock the house with antique knockoffs from the warehouse near the highway—but the headboard didn't fit Toph's bedframe, so we've just set the thing, this big piece of wood, between his bed and the wall, for effect, a headboard playing the role of a headboard.

I get our book from the floor. We read every night, sometimes for a while but usually for just fifteen minutes or so, the longest I can do it before falling asleep myself, but long enough to provide Toph with a degree of comfort, stability, of peace and well-being before drifting off to his child's slumberland—

We're reading John Hersey's *Hiroshima*. Oh sure, there's all the horror, the indescribable suffering, the people's skin coming off like cottage cheese, but, see, I have decided that as much as there will be fun and hilarity in this house, I am determined to also fill this place with sober and lasting learning. Sometimes during dinner, I open randomly and read from the encyclopedia, the massive one-volume thing we bought from the skinny kid selling them door to door. Before this was *Maus*. Before that was *Catch-22*, though we didn't finish that—with the obscure (for him) references and all the characters, it was taking us an hour to get through each page. In *Hiroshima*, I skip over really horrific parts, and he listens with the utmost attentiveness because he is perfect—he is just as enthusiastic about our experiment as I am, wants to be the ideal, new-model boy as much as I want to be the ideal, new-model parent. And after I read, carefully explaining the significance of this and that, the historical context (all made up or

approximated), it's always nice just to lie for a minute, on his narrow twin bed, with him under the comforter and me over it, so
nice and warm here—

"Get out."

"Ehmp?"

"Out."

"Noo."

"Wake up."

"No, no, no."

"Go to your own bed."

"Oh please, no. We can both fit."

"Out. Out. Please."

"Fine."

I roll over him, making myself as heavy as possible, then get
up. I go into the bathroom and then return to his room while
brushing my teeth, humming and doing a little softshoe. He gives
me a fake thumbs-up. I go back to the sink and spit, and come
back. I lean against his door.

"So. Big day, huh?" I say.

"Yeah," he says.

"I mean, a lot happened. A full day, this was."

"Yeah. The half day at school, then the basketball, and then
dinner, and the open house, and then ice cream, and a movie— I
mean, it was almost as if it was too much to happen in one day, as
if a number of days had been spliced together to quickly paint a
picture of an entire period of time, to create a whole-seeming idea
of how we are living, without having to stoop (or rise) to actually
pacing the story out."

"What are you getting at?"

"No, I think it's good, it's fine. Not entirely believable, but it
works fine, in general. It's fine."

"Listen, you, we've had plenty of days like this, and many that
were much more complicated. Remember your big camp-out

sleepover birthday party? The Lake Tahoe–with-your-large-headed-friend trip? Really, if anything, this is a much more pedestrian day than most. This is just a caricature, this, the skeleton of experience— I mean, you know this is just one slivery, wafer-thin slice. To adequately relate even five minutes of internal thought-making would take forever— It's maddening, actually, when you sit down, as I will once I put you to bed, to try to render something like this, a time or place, and ending up with only this kind of feebleness— one, two dimensions of twenty."

"So you're reduced to complaining about it. Or worse, doing little tricks, out of frustration."

"Right. Right."

"The gimmicks, bells, whistles. Diagrams. *Here is a picture of a stapler*, all that."

"Right."

"You know, to be honest, though, what I see is less a problem with form, all that garbage, and more a problem of conscience. You're completely paralyzed with guilt about relating all this in the first place, especially the stuff earlier on. You feel somehow obligated to do it, but you also know that Mom and Dad would *hate* it, would crucify you—"

"I know, I know."

"But then again, I should say, and Bill and Beth would say— well, probably not Bill, but definitely Beth—that your guilt, and their disapproval, is a very middlebrow, middle-class, midwestern sort of disapproval. It's superstition as much as anything—like the primitives who fear the camera will take their soul. You struggle with a guilt both Catholic and unique to the home in which you were raised. Everything there was a secret—for instance, your father being in AA was not to be spoken of, ever, while he was in and after he stopped attending. You never told even your closest friends about anything that happened inside that house. And now you alternately rebel against and embrace that kind of suppression."

"How do you mean?"

"Well, you think you're so open about stuff now, you believe that you and me are the New Model, that because of our circumstances, you can toss away all the old rules, can make it up as we go along. But at the same time, so far you've been very priggish and controlling, and for all your bluster you end up maintaining most of their customs, the rules imposed by our parents. Especially the secrecy. For instance, you hardly ever let my friends come over, because you don't want them to see how messy the house is, how we live."

"Well—"

"I know. I understand. You fear the knock on the door from the child welfare agency, whatever. But then again, you're not so afraid, and you know it. You've planned out what you'd say, excuses you'd make, how you'd break me out of a foster home if it came to that, where we'd flee, how we'd live, new identities, plastic surgery. But first of all, if any child welfare person, or any person at all, ever tries to move in on us, on this, what is now your turf, your project, you go absolutely ballistic, you lose your mind."

"I do not."

"Allow me to recount a scene from just last week, between you and one of your best friends:

'So he was at Luke's the whole time, but he hadn't called. For about five hours. I had dinner ready, was waiting around, was going out of my brain. And he had just flaked. Drives me insane. He needs to learn the value of my time, that I cannot wait around all day for his call. I'm going to ground him.'
    'Oh, the poor thing. Don't ground him.'
    'What?'
    'He's sorry, I'm sure—'
    'Are you telling me what to—'
    'No, I just think that...'
    'See, that's just such bullshit, that you think that you have a say in something like that, just because I'm young. I mean, you would never contradict some forty-year-old mother, would you?'

'Well—'

'Well don't. Because I am a forty-year-old mother. As far as you and every-one else is concerned, I am a forty-year-old mother. Don't ever forget that.'

"Poor Marny, one of your oldest friends. She meant nothing by it, just an innocent comment. She's probably the last person in the world who would ever be insensitive, but see, you're always ready to fight. You've got that single-parent rage, that black-single-mother defensiveness, combined with your own naturally ready-be-indignant/aggressive tendencies, inherited from our mom. I mean, tonight, when you finally go to bed, you'll lie there and think of things you'd do to people who would come in here and do me harm. You'll picture all manner of murders in my defense. Your visions will be vivid and horrifically violent, mostly you and a baseball bat, with you taking out on whoever would invade our sanctuary the cumulative frustration you feel from all of this, our present situation, the walls and parameters set up already, the next ten, thirteen years laid out, more or less spoken for, and also the general anger you feel, have felt not just since Mom and Dad died—that would be convenient if it were true—but it began well before that, you know this, the anger coursing through the marrow of kids growing up in loud, semi-violent alcoholic households, where chaos is always... What is it? What's funny?"

"You have toothpaste on your chin."

"Where?"

"Lower."

"Here?"

"Lower."

"Still there?"

"No, you got it."

"The point is, with me—"

"It looked like a bird dropping."

"Fine. Ha ha. Anyway, with me you have this amazing chance to right the wrongs of your own upbringing, you have an opportunity to do everything better—to carry on those traditions that made sense and to jettison those that didn't—which is something every parent has the chance to do, of course, to show up one's own parents, do everything better, to upwardly evolve from them—but in this case, it's even more heightened, means so much more, because you get to do this with me, *their own progeny*. It's like finishing a project that someone else could not, gave up on, gave to you, the only one who could save the day. Do I have it right so far, big man? And best of all, for you at least, you finally have the moral authority you've craved, and have often exercised, ever since you were very young—you used to go around the playground chastising the other kids for swearing. You didn't drink alcohol until you were eighteen, never did drugs, because you had to be more pure, had to have something over the other people. And now your moral authority is doubled, tripled. And you use it any way you need to. That twenty-nine-year-old, for instance, you'll break up with her after a month because she smokes—"

"And the beret. The purple beret."

"That's not the reason you'll give her."

"Fine, but that'll be justified. Please. For obvious reasons. It's incredibly hard, hearing those sounds, smelling the smells, watching the kissing of that paper, the sucking from those tubes—"

"Yes, but it's the way you'll tell her, the way you'll sort of shame her, mentioning that not only did your parents die of cancer, your father of lung cancer, but that you don't want the smoke around your little brother, blah blah, and it's the way you'll say it, you'll want to make this poor woman feel like a leper, particularly because she rolls her own cigarettes, which even I admit is kind of doubly sad, but see, you want her to feel like a pariah, like a lower form of life, because that's what, deep down, you feel she is, what you feel anyone tethered to any addiction is. And now you feel that you have the moral authority to pass judgment on these people, that because of your recent experiences, you can expound on anything, you can play the conquering victim, a role that gives you power drawn from sympathy and disadvantage—you can now play the dual role of product of privilege and disenfranchised Job. Because we get Social Security and live in a messy house with ants and holes in the floorboards you like to think of us as lower class, that now you know the struggles of the poor—how dare you!—but you like that stance, that underdog stance, because it increases your leverage with other people. You can shoot from behind bulletproof glass."

"All this energy from you! Were you drinking soda before bed?"

"And poor Dad. Why not just leave him alone? I mean—"

"God. Please. So I'm not allowed to talk about—"

"I don't know. I guess so. If you feel you have to."

"I do."

"Fine."

"I can't see past it."

"Fine. So you're going to stay up tonight, most of the night, like every night, staring at your screen—remember when you were a senior in college? You were in that creative writing class, and you were writing about these deaths, not two months afterward; you were writing about Mom's last breaths even, one paragraph describing your mother's last breaths, and the whole class kind of not knowing what the hell to do with you, they were like, 'We-hell now...,' didn't know whether to talk about the story, all of them sitting there nervously with their Xerox copies of it, or to send you to counseling. But that did not deter you. You have been determined, then and since, to get this down, to render this time, to take that terrible winter and write with it what you hope will be some heartbreaking thing."

"Listen, I'm tired."

"Now you're tired. You were the one who started talking. I've been ready to sleep for half an hour."

"Fine."

"Fine."

"Night."

I kiss him on his smooth, tanned forehead. The smell of urine. He has a tan line, a U of pale skin where the fastener of his hat, worn backward, covers his forehead.

"Do the thing," he says.

I do the thing where I rub his back quickly, through the comforter, to make the bed warm.

"Thanks."

"Night."

I leave the light on, close his door halfway, and walk out to the family room. I straighten the rug, a frayed oriental we inherited. This rug, so faded and sorry, and the long thin one in the kitchen, are unraveling, thread by thread. Toph and I run on them, and when we do the threads grow, ooze out like tendrils. I don't know what to do to keep them intact. I wonder about protecting them, having them restored, and know that I will not bother. I tuck a wormlike blue thread, seven or eight inches of it, underneath.

I fix the cover on the couch. That couch was perfect and white in our living room in Chicago, but got so filthy so quickly here, streaked with black at the corners where we lean our bikes, the pillows yellowed and stained with grape juice, chocolate. We had rented an upholstery cleaner, but its effect was laughable. The couch will continue its decline, as will all the things we've been given. Maintenance is impossible. There is a pile of shoes near the door that I should straighten. The floor needs to be swept, but I'm discouraged before I begin—the dirt is intrinsic to this house, is in the molding and the grouting, in the nooks and the carpet and the flaws in the structure. There are holes in the floorboards, and the baseboards are crooked. I had tried a vacuum, borrowed one from the neighbors, and it had worked well, but the place was dusty, the floor covered with stuff the next day. Now I only sweep.

I get one of Toph's popsicles out of the freezer. There is noise next door. I step out onto the back porch. Robert and Benna, the neighbors to our left, are having a thing, maybe ten of them out there on the deck.

"Hey there," Robert says. He's always friendly, always cheerful, thoughtful, caring. It's unnerving.

He's a few years older and lives with Benna, who's about thirty and runs a battered-women's shelter. Their friends look like Berkeley grad students.

"Hi," I say.

"Come on over!" he says.

"Yeah, come and have a drink," says Benna.

"No, I can't," I say. It's warm, the moon is out.

I talk about the work I have to do, Toph being in bed, etc. I lie about a phone call I'm waiting for because I don't want to have to come over, meet their friends, explain our story, why we live here, the whole thing.

"C'mon, just a drink," says Robert. He's always asking me to come over. As friendly as he and Benna are, radiating *welcome*, I feel more affinity with the black man/blond woman couple to our right, with their unmoving white curtains, their snugly closed door, the two Dobermans. They rarely talk to anyone, usually stay out of sight—it's so much easier.

I thank Robert and step back inside.

I retreat into the living room, the room I have painted burgundy. The walls are cluttered with ancient pictures of our parents, grandparents, their parents, and their various diplomas, notices, portraits, needlepoints, etchings. I sit on the couch I found in the shed in back, a velvety thing, maroon, its springs broken, wood chipped. Most of the antiques we kept are here—the chairs, the end table, that beautiful cherry desk. It's dark. I need to cut the bushes in front, because they've grown so high that almost no light comes through the front window, even during the day, making it so dim here, always, rubiate, the walls blood red. I haven't found a lamp yet that will fit the room.

So much suffered in the moves, from Chicago to the hills, from the hills down here. Picture frames broken, glass rattling in all the boxes. We've lost things. I'm almost sure there's a rug missing, a whole rug. And so many books, our grandmother's. I had been keeping them in the shed in back, in the boxes we packed them in, until I went in there, after four months or so, and found a leak in the roof; most of them were soaked, mildewed. I try not to think of the antiques—the mahogany bookshelf, scratched, or the circular end table with the nicks in it, the needlepoint-covered chair with the cracked leg. I want to save everything and preserve all this but also want it all gone—can't decide what's more romantic, preservation or decay. Wouldn't it be something just to burn it all? Throw it all in the street? I resent having to be the one—why not Bill? Beth?—who has to lug all this stuff from place to place, all the boxes, the dozens of photo albums, the dishes and linens and furniture, our narrow closets and leaky shed overflowing with it all. I know I offered to keep it, insisted on it, wanted Toph to be able to live among it all, be reminded— Maybe we could store it until we have a real house. Or sell it and start over.

"Hey," he yells from his room.

"What?"

"Did you lock the front door?"

He usually locks the front door.

"I will."

I walk to the front door and turn the bolt.

V. (WHERE IS YOUR BROTHER?)

Outside it's blue-black and getting darker. There is a man walking up the steps. He is unshaven and is wearing sandals and a poncho made from, one can be almost sure, hemp. I do not want to talk to this man. I have talked to the man from the California Public Interest Research Group (CalPIRG). I have donated to the couple from the women's shelter, and to that little boy from the youth group, to the woman from the Green Party, the kids from the Boys Club, the pair of solemn teenagers from SANE/FREEZE. The Berkeley-ness of Berkeley, so charming at first, is getting old.

The bell rings.

"You get it," I say. "I'm not here."

"You're right next to it."

"So?"

"So?"

"*Topher.*"

He gets up, sock-footed. I am given a look.

"Tell them you're home alone," I say. "You're an orphan."

He opens the door and says something to the man and suddenly the man is in our living room. *What did I just say—*

Oh. The baby-sitter. Stephen.

Stephen is a grad student at Berkeley, from England or Scotland. Or Ireland. He is quiet, bores Toph to tears, and rides a bicycle with a huge wicker basket attached to the front. Beth found him at school; he had posted a flyer.

"Hey," I say.

"Hello," he says.

He brings his bicycle into the living room.

I go to my room to change. I come out, tell him that I'll be back by midnight—

"Actually, can you stay until one?"

"I don't see why not."

"Good. Then let's say one."

"Fine."

"But I might be early."

"Okay then."

"Depends on what happens."

—and I tell him that Toph should be in bed by eleven.

This is our third time with Stephen, who is replacing Nicole, who we liked a great deal—Toph liking her almost as much as I was hoping to like her—but who graduated a few months ago and had the temerity to move away. There was also Janie, the Berkeley student who insisted on having Toph come to her Telegraph Avenue apartment, and who was fine until one night, after she and Toph had been playing soccer in her hallway with a balloon—he usually came home drenched with sweat—she had joked, "You know, Toph, you're fun to hang out with. We should go out sometime, get a few beers..."

Thus Stephen.

I kiss Toph on the head, which is covered by a baseball hat, worn backward. The hat smells like urine.

"Your hat smells like urine," I say.

"It does not," Toph says.

It does.

"It does."

"How could it smell like urine?"

"Maybe you peed on it."

He sighs, takes my hands off his shoulders.

"I didn't pee on it."

"Maybe by accident."

"Shut up."

"Don't tell me to shut up. I've told you that."

"Sorry."

"Stephen," I ask, "will you smell this hat and tell me if it smells like urine?"

Stephen does not think the question is a serious one. He smiles nervously, but does not make a move to smell the hat.

"Well then," I say. "We'll see you later. Toph, we'll...well, I guess we'll see you tomorrow."

Then out the door, down the steps and into the car and as I'm backing out of the driveway there is the usual euphoria—

Free!

—which pretty much overtakes me. Often I laugh out loud, giggle, bang the steering wheel a few times, grinning, put the right tape in the stereo—

This time it lasts for ten, twelve seconds.

Then, at the moment that I am turning the corner, I become convinced, in a flash of pure truth-seeing—it happens every time I leave him anywhere—that Toph will be killed. Of course. The baby-sitter was acting peculiar, was too quiet, too unassuming. His eyes had plans. Of course. So obvious from the beginning. I ignored the signals. Toph had told me Stephen was weird, repeatedly had mentioned his scary laugh, the veggie food he brought and cooked, and I just shrugged it all off. If something happens it'll be my fault. He will try bad things on Toph. He will try to molest Toph. While Toph is sleeping he will do something with wax and rope. The possibilities snap through my head like pedophilia flashcards—handcuffs, floorboards, clown suits, leather, videotape, duct tape, knives, bathtubs, refrigerators—

Toph will never wake up.

I should turn around. This is stupid. We don't need this kind of risk. I don't need to do this, don't need to go out. It's silly, juvenile, inconsequential. I need to go back.

But I have to do this. There is no risk.

But there is risk.

But the risk is worth it.

I'm so, so evil.

I open the window, turn up the volume. I pass two cars at once and get on the highway and speed toward the Bay Bridge, doing 70 in the left lane, along the water.

Through the toll, the light, onto the ramp, onto the bridge. Now I can't turn back. The Oakland shipyards to the left, a billboard encouraging the saving of water.

I will come home and the door will be open, wide. The babysitter will be gone and there will be silence. And at once I will know. There will be the smell of everything being perfectly wrong. At the steps up to Toph's room there will be blood. Blood on the walls, handprints soaked in blood. A note to me, from Stephen, taunting; maybe a videotape of everyth— I will be to blame. His little body, bent, blue— The baby-sitter was standing there and he had already known what he would do—as they stood there, I felt something wrong, knew something was off, I knew it was wrong... *and still I left*. What does that say? What kind of monster— Everyone will know. I will know, I will not fight. There will be a hearing, a trial, a show trial—

How did you come to meet this man, this baby-sitter?

We found a posting, on a bulletin board.

And how long did your interview of him take?

Ten, twenty minutes.

And that was enough?

Yes. I guess so.

You didn't really know anything about this man, did you?

I knew he was Scottish. Or English.

Or Irish.

Could have been.

And you left your brother to go where?

Out. To bars.

To bars. And what was at these bars?

Friends, people, beer.

Beer.

There was a special, I think.

A special.

On the beer. Certain kinds.

Oh, you know, I just wanted to be *out*. I didn't care much what we did. You have to understand that at that point I was getting out once a week, tops, maybe once every ten days, and so when I could get a baby-sitter on a night when anything was happening I threw myself at it, would leave early so I could be out for a while, would have the baby-sitter come at six, seven, whatever, and I'd race into the city, to eat there with whoever was eating—maybe they'd just be sitting around, at Moodie's usually, watching cable, getting ready, and I would be there, on the couch, with a beer from the fridge, savoring every minute, not knowing when it would come again, and they would be casual, having no idea what it meant to me, even when I'd be a little manic about it all, a little overeager, laughing too much, drinking too quickly, getting another from the fridge, no problem, okay, hoping for something to happen, hoping we'd go somewhere good, anything to make the night *count*, make it worth it, justify the constant red/black worry, the visions—I felt so detached sometimes, went for weeks at a time without really being around people my age, like living in a country where no one understands your words—

Over the bridge, the crosscutting wind floods in. I turn the volume up. Far to the left, down and half a mile south, tankers float in the black bay, waiting to touch Oakland.

Is it bravery to stay?

Or bravery to go?

A betrayal. There will already be ambulances there. There will be lights. The neighborhood will pop and glow like a carnival— But quiet. Just the lights, the whispering. Everyone asking where I am. *Where are the boy's parents? They what? Well, where is the boy's brother? He what?*

To the right there is Treasure Island, then Alcatraz, then the inlet, the ocean. Through the tunnel we are spaceships, the cars changing lanes, hungry, searching, shooting through the barrel, quick and lateral like water bugs—and after the tunnel there is the city, the thousands of Lite Brite tubes stuck through the night's paper black.

There will be a small casket. I'll be at the service but everyone will know. They'll try me and convict me and I'll be killed in a chair. Or hanged; I'll be hanged because I'll want the pain, slow, the veins burning, bursting—

Oh but that embarrassing erection at the end—

In the brown light of the cavernous bar, Brent is still trying to name his band. At the moment they're called The Gods Hate Kansas, after a '60s science fiction novel, but that name has been held for almost six months, and it's time for moving on. He is straw-polling the alternatives, which he has scribbled on a long, thin piece of paper, like a little scroll:

Scott Beowolf

Van Gogh Dog Go

Jon & Pontius Pilate

Jerry Louis Farrakhan

Pat Buchanitar

Kajagoogubernatorial Process

Spike Lee Major Tom Dick and Harry Connick, Jr. Mints

Most of the names are like this, the melding of two or more cultural elements, ideally one high and one low, the smugly clever, utterly meaningless result. There are other, mostly local, bands that have planted their flag in this territory—JFKFC; Thomas Jefferson Slave Apartments; Prince Charles Nelson Reilly.

Brent and I, and everyone else, are standing on the bar's second level, looking down upon the heads of the hundred or so below us, while drinking beer that has been brewed on the premises. We know that the beer has been brewed on the premises because, right there, behind the bar, are three huge copper vats, with tubes coming out of them. That is how beer is made.

Everyone is here: Brent, Moodie, Jessica, K.C., Pete, Eric, Flagg, John—all these people from high school, from before high school, from grade school, earlier, all from Chicago, all just out of school, all living out here—it's the manifestation of an inexplicable sort of mass migration, about fifteen of us out here, with more of us landing in San Francisco every month, all for different reasons, for no particular reason. Certainly no one has come to take advantage of this job market, which is anything but enticing. For now, we're all scraping by with temping, with anything. Jessica is nannying in Santa Rosa; K.C. teaches sixth grade at a Catholic girls' school; Eric's in grad school at Stanford; and Pete, as part of some dubious Jesuit volunteer corps (cult?), is living with a half-dozen other conscripts in Sacramento, where he works for the Prisoners' Rights Union, editing a popular periodical called *The California Prisoner*.

The presence of all these people is both surreal and immeasurably comforting. They constitute the only ties Toph and I still have to home, because already, less than a year since we left Chicago, we have lost touch with each and every one of our parents' friends, even our mother's friends. Which was odd, Beth and I felt—we expected our progress to be more closely followed, to be checked up on. But it's just as well. Those conversations and epistolary exchanges, when they happened, early on, were always awkward, fraught, their worry for us palpable, poorly hidden, their distrust (we thought) implicit.

These people, though, these friends, they create for us and for Toph a willy-nilly world of faux-cousins, -aunts, -uncles. They eat with us, do the beach with us; the girls, K.C. and Jessica, buy kitchen implements for us, come over to casually straighten up, make beds, clear the dishes from the sink and the bedrooms, are available at any time for questions regarding the boiling of corn, the unthawing of frozen beef. And all have known Toph since he was born, held him when he was bald, and so do not question his presence at movies, barbecues, at any social gathering. And he knows them, too, can discern their voices on the phone, their cars in the driveway, remembers most of the words to our high school talent show act, the one we all rehearsed in the basement for months. At that point Toph was maybe four, five years old, but he was there every time, would beg our mother to stay for every minute, watching us from the stairs, giggling wildly. He knew every word.

And so I try to entice these people out to Berkeley as often as possible, want them around, as much for my own amusement as for continuity, to step in as extended family, to play roles: the aunt who cooks, the aunt who sings, the uncle who can do the trick where he puts the stack of quarters on his bent elbow and catches them in his palm, a snap of the arm. And they do come out, stay out, as much by choice as not. Moodie, for one, is over all the time, lately has been sleeping on the couch at least three nights a week. We have been close since high school, when we shared foot odor powder, compared acne remedies—we were both abused by it— and drank Miller Genuine Draft in his basement– bedroom–supra-pad. Picking up from our highly successful high school fake I.D. business—we were the first in town to utilize the then-new Macintosh technology, obliterating the competition, those still using Polaroids and posterboard—and from my back room we've begun a tiny graphic design operation, complete with laser-printed letterhead and raised-shiny-ink business cards ($39.99 for 500), catering to clients, much like our fake I.D. patrons, who want things done quickly, cheaply, and don't mind so much if they're riddled with errors and—

"Thank you."

John has gotten me a beer.

John is broken and I've known him forever.

He's got a nice tan, as usual. He always liked to be tan.

He grew up in the neighborhood, and our parents were close. I've known him since I knew anyone. There are pictures of us under the kitchen table eating popsicles, of me in their backyard, drinking out of the bird feeder with a straw. Together, at nine, ten years old, we would painstakingly write letters to the makers of Lego, suggesting design improvements and offering ideas for future products. Enfield, Connecticut is where the Lego headquarters sit—I still remember. And I was as much his parents' child as he was ours, and even in junior high and on, when we had less and less to say to each other, we were still inextricably tied, were stuck with each other, our closets full of the other's borrowed clothes.

His parents are gone, too. His mother, tall, blond, loud, had done cancer our second year in high school, a huge mess, bringing him even more snugly into our family. Five years later, after a year at Penn, he transferred to Illinois, to be closer to his father, who was not doing well, had had a stroke, had been treated for depression— And a year later, he went too, an aneurysm, such a fucking mess we were—it was only a few months after my own father, that whole year cloudy for both of us; we didn't even see each other that much—it just made it worse, the sight of each other reminding us

only of what we had in common, and the wondering if we needed
to ask how the other was doing but ending only in mumbling,
hands-over-mouths, nervous sniffing—

After his dad's funeral, John had missed only a few days of
school, was back on Wednesday.

"You're back," I said.

"Yeah," he said.

He had nowhere else to go.

"What's with the knuckles?" They were cut, scabbed.

"Oh I broke a window. You know."

I said I did know. Did I know?

And now he's out here, living in Oakland for now. After grad-
uating he tried Chicago first, but tired of constantly running into
people from Champaign. They were all there, the whole school—
so few make it out of the state. To most, Chicago was Oz, anything
beyond it was China, the moon.

"So. How's Toph?" he says.

"Fine," I say.

Pliers, handcuffs—

"Where is he?" he asks.

Paint thinner, vaseline—

"He's home. Baby-sitter."

Other stuff—*stuff he brought from Scotland!*—

"Oh."

I change the subject.

"How's the job search going?"

"I don't know. Good maybe. I just saw a job counselor."

"A what?"

"A job counselor."

"What does that mean?"

"He's a guy who helps you figure out—"

"Okay, I know, but how does it work, exactly?"

"You talk to him about your interests, he gives you a test—"

"Like, a multiple-choice test?"

"Yeah. It took about three hours."

"He gives you a test to find out what kind of job you want?"

"Right."

"You're kidding."

"Why would I be kidding?"

We watch the crowd below. They are wearing clothes they bought secondhand in the Mission or, for twice the price, in the Haight. They have unbuttoned the first two buttons of their tight synthetic-fibered shirts, worn over T-shirts with logos for non-existent companies. They have shaved heads or carefully messy Westerberg hair. There are young men up from Stanford in light blue oxfords with shortshorn, shiny heads, hard with gel. There are small women in big shoes, with snug, ribbed shirts.

Everyone is talking. People have come with friends and are talking with the friends they've come with. They're out with people from work. They are looking into the faces they see every day and are saying things they've said a hundred times. Like us, they have in their hands beer that has been brewed on the premises.

"Should we order some food?" we/they say.

"I don't know. Should we?" we/they say.

From here, the bar's second floor, their mouths are moving, but their words are only groans, one continuous, monotonal groan, a sort of mooing, punctuated by the occasional squeal—"*Ohmygod!*"

There's too many of them, of us. Too many, too similar. What are they all doing here? All this standing, all this standing, sitting, talking. There isn't even a pool table, darts, anything. Just this loitering, lolling, this drinking of beer in thick glasses—

I've risked everything for this?

Something needs to happen. Something huge. The taking over of something, a building, a city, a country. We should all be armed and taking over small countries. Or rioting. Or no: an orgy. There should be an orgy.

All these people—we should close the doors and dim the lights and be naked together. We could start with all of us, K.C. and Jessica, go from there. That would make it all worthwhile, that would justify everything. We could move the tables, bring in some couches, mattresses, pillows, towels, stuffed animals...

But this—this is obscene. How dare we be standing around, talking about nothing, not running in one huge mass of people, running at something, something huge, knocking it over? Why do we all bother coming out, gathering here in numbers like this, without starting fires, tearing things down? How dare we not lock the doors and replace the white bulbs with red and commence with the massive orgy, the joyous mingling of a thousand arms, legs, breasts?

We are wasting this.

What could we possibly be talking about?

Pete sidles up.

"Hey there," he says, with a trace of the British accent he cultivated in high school.

"Tell me," he asks. "How is young Toph?"

"Fine," I say.

"Where is he, anyway?"

I love Pete, and he means no harm, but why this question? Why this question twice in one night? Much like the "What a good brother!" refrain, "Where is your brother?" has become a sort of required question, but with no internal logic. Why ask me, when I am out trying to drink and incite orgies, where my brother is? What answer could Pete, could John, be expecting? A ridiculous question. *How* would be fine. *How is your brother?* makes sense, and can be answered easily: Toph is fine. But why *Where?*

"At home," I say.

"Oh. With who?"

Razors, chain saws, freezers—

"I have to go."

I plow my way to the bathroom.

These questions. These people should know better. *Are all my friends morons?*

In the bathroom someone is peeing in the sink. As I am noticing that there is someone peeing in the sink, that someone notices me noticing and naturally thinks I was looking at his penis, which I was not, which was sitting there on the sink like a newborn chick, purple and wrinkled, reaching for water.

I want to leave but immediately realize that would make me look even more suspicious, as if I entered the bathroom *specifically* to see the man's penis on top of the porcelain sink, and having done that—*yes, I see*—I was free to leave. I get a stall, close the door behind me. And there, at eye level, is one of our stickers.

SCREW THOSE IDIOTS.

MIGHT MAGAZINE.

Moodie and I designed them a month ago, passed them out to friends with instructions to put them in bathrooms, on walls, lampposts, cars. It was to be the first step of a three-month preliminary marketing campaign, getting everyone's tongues wagging with the word "Might." *What is Might?* They will ask, intrigued. *I do not know, but when it becomes clear what it is that they will be doing, I will be interested in their doings.*

There was not much of a debate involved in deciding what the stickers should say. It was obvious, and as far as we were concerned, it said it all:

SCREW THOSE IDIOTS.

But now, looking at the sticker, crookedly slapped on the cinder-block wall, I realize there's a problem: It's unclear *who* is being screwed. Who are the idiots that should be getting screwed? Oh fuck. Sure, we intended it to be fairly vague, the "idiots" interpretable as anyone—other magazines, employers, parents, hippies, the corner grocer. But now, a terrible question rears its head: Are we implying that the sticker's reader should be screwing *us*?

Oh God, it does, it does. After all, just after it implores the reader to "Screw those idiots," it says "Might Magazine." We're the ones to screw! It offers no choice!

It's a disaster. We've covered the city with stickers telling people to screw us. There are so many ways it could have been better phrased. For instance:

MIGHT MAGAZINE SAYS:
SCREW THOSE IDIOTS.

Or

"SCREW THOSE IDIOTS,"
SAYS MIGHT MAGAZINE.

Or

SCREW THOSE IDIOTS
("THOSE IDIOTS" NOT REFERRING TO THOSE BEHIND
MIGHT MAGAZINE, THE MAKERS OF THIS STICKER,
WHO ARE GOOD PEOPLE AND SHOULD NOT BE SCREWED).

This is terrible, this is Armageddon. We've already printed 500 of these things. I lean over the toilet and try to peel this one off—I'll remove every one, by hand!—but it only shreds, feebly. I pick and pick, with no discernible progress, my fingernails black with gobs of sticker-matter. My shins are wet from toilet-bowl moisture. And I'm still hanging through my zipper.

When I leave the stall, the purple-chick-penis man is gone, and when I get back to our spot by the railing, half of the people are gone; Jenna is standing alone.

We chat idly for a good two or three minutes before:

"So how's your little brother?"

"Fine, thanks."

I am worrying, but there's no way...

"What's his name again?"

"Toph."

...that she would ever...

"Where is he?" she asks.

Jesus. These people. I look down at the crowd, all the dumb people down there.

"Toph? Oh, I haven't seen him in weeks."

"What do you mean?"

"I mean, he's probably somewhere in the Dakotas about now."

"What?"

"Yeah, it's fucked up. He just took off one day. Hitchhiking. Around the country, with some friends."

"You're kidding."

"I wish."

"I'm so sorry."

"Oh don't worry. It's partly my fault, I guess. He was a little pissed at me, I guess. Typical adolescent stuff."

"What do you mean?"

I have been looking down, watching a middle-aged man in a beret and black leather jacket mingle with two college-aged women, the poor man, not knowing that it's all over for him, forever, beret and all. I glance over at Moodie to make sure he isn't hearing us. He'd kill me. He's not paying attention, so I look at Jenna, both for dramatic effect and also to make sure she's still with me.

She is, so I continue. I am not sure why I continue. People ask questions, and before I can formulate a truth-oriented answer, I lie. I lie about how my parents died—"You remember that embassy bombing, the one in Tunisia?"—about how old I am—I always say forty-one—how old Toph is, how tall he is; when they ask about him they get the most elaborate lies—he just lost an arm, he's got the brain of an infant, a halfwit, a badger (I only use that one in his presence); that he's in the merchant marine, he's in jail, in juvie, is back out, selling crack—"Oh, give him some crack and you should see his face light up!"—that he's playing in the CBA.

"Well, he got into some trouble at school," I tell Jenna.

"What kind of trouble?"

"Well, you know how you're not supposed to bring guns to school?"

"Right."

"Well, I had told him not to bring his gun to school. Simple as that. Everyone knows that. You can play with it in the house, in the neighborhood—whatever, I told him, but not at school, because rules are rules, right?"

"Wait. He has a gun?"

"Of course, sure."

"How old is he?"

"Nine. Almost ten."

"Huh. So they caught him with the gun?"

"Oh it was much worse than that. See, Toph has sort of a temper, you know, and so this kid, Jason somebody, had been bugging him, singing some annoying song all day, some song Toph didn't like at all, and finally he just snapped—whack, just like that, he takes the gun from his locker and squeezes one into him."

"Oh my God."

"Yeah, I know."

No, I tell her, little Jason isn't dead, he's fine now, pulled out of his coma a week ago. And that naturally I took away Toph's gun privileges, and of course beat him within an inch of his life, so zealously that something snapped in his leg somewhere, a tendon maybe, and he fell to the floor, squealed like a pig, couldn't get up, had to be taken to the emergency room. That while we were at the hospital some doctor must have snitched or something, because a cop shows up and—

"What did you tell the cop about his leg?" Jenna wants to know.

"Oh, that was easy. I told her he and a friend were whipping each other with wet towels."

"And she believed you?"

"Of course. Of course. You wouldn't believe what people will believe once they know our story. They're ready for anything, basically—will believe anything, because they've been thrown off-balance, are still wondering if any of this is true, our story in general, but aren't sure and are terrified of offending us."

"Yeah," she says, not getting it. I decide to wrap it up.

"Anyway, then he's on crutches for three weeks, really resenting me and everything, really holding a grudge, and then boom, the second he's off the crutches he's gone."

"Hitchhiking."

"Right."

"I'm so sorry. Listen, if there's anything I can do…"

"One thing?"

"What?"

"Don't tell Moodie about this."

"Okay."

"He'll worry."

He's going to kill me. I better leave. She'll tell him, and then he'll kill me. He'll punch me. He'll punch me like he did in high school, after Homecoming, at the lake, when I was drunk and fell on him, from a tree. He'll hit me like he hit me then—one good shot, in the sternum, sending a quick, simple message—You're an asshole—that I felt for months, every time I breathed.

I find my car and drive across town, all the passing headlights glaring, mocking—that was probably bad, what I just did to Jenna; a therapist would say that was bad—up Ninth, across Market, up Franklin and down to Cow Hollow, where Therese lives. Down the hill and over a few blocks and her turreted third-floor apartment comes into view. Therese lives in the top floor of a huge light blue house on Gough, a few blocks up from Union Street, in an apartment she decorated with her mother, complete with pot holders and curtains and about a hundred overstuffed pillows. The plan is for me to end up in her bed. Her bed is huge and has posts.

I pull up across the street, which is set on a forty-five-degree angle, and look up for a light in her window. It's dark. There's that little plastic owl on her fire escape. She is asleep. No, no, a faint light near the kitchen. A TV? She could be up. She could have gone out and come home and could be up. It's only eleven-thirty— *Oh, to be inside!* No, no, no. This is stupid. I drive around the block. I have no excuse to be there.

I turn and go back. I will think of something.

I park in the driveway behind her car and jump up the wooden steps of her porch and ring the bell. I will say I want to sleep there. I will say that I need to sleep there—that I was locked out of my house. This is so embarrassing, I will say, chuckling. Heh heh. One of those weird things, I will say. Was close by, was in the city when I realized. Toph's at Beth's, I'll say. Sorry. *How are you? Were you asleep?*

She'll let me in. We'll go to the beach, like we did that other time, the last time I showed up at midnight, needy. When I asked her to come to the beach she had been in her pajamas but had gotten excited about going, had gotten dressed, and while she got dressed I packed a bag full of bananas, Fig Newtons, and a bottle of wine. She brought blankets and when we got in the car, dark, seats cold, we turned on the heat, squeezed each other's hands, and sped over the Golden Gate and through the Headlands, the black road winding through purple hills, like driving around the contours of huge sleeping bodies. Past the old rickety wooden military buildings, the gun turrets high over the Pacific, and to the beach at Fort Cronkite. We parked by the darkened barracks and got out and took off our shoes and walked over that little pond on the gray wooden bridge—so loud—and the ocean was black, the wind was coming straight off the water. We huddled under the blanket, still barefoot, warming our hands in each other's armpits—

She is not answering her bell.

She will shake her head when she sees me but she will let me in. I push the bell twice more. I turn around and face the street.

A car, black, shiny, comes up the hill and stops at the corner. Inside is a woman, maybe thirty-five, dressed up and driving alone. She sets the brake and fumbles for something in her purse. I am no more than twenty feet away. She will look up my way. She will look up at the porch and see me. She will open the passenger door and tell me to come with her and share her bed. *I was hoping you'd ask*, I will say, kind of suavelike. I will not care what we do, anything would be fine, nothing is okay, too. It does not matter. A bed with room and warmth and her legs entwined with mine underneath. I will comment on how cold her toes are and she will rub them against my legs—

Things like that often happened. To people all over the world.

The woman finds what she wants in her purse, relaxes the brake, drives up the hill and turns. Therese is not home. I leave.

At Union Street the bars have just let out and there are people everywhere. Julie bartends at a bar called the Blue Light, which, besides being imbued with just that, is full of mirrors and people wearing loafers and white pants. Julie I met at Moodie's last party; I will drop in on her. I will pretend I'm looking for someone there, or else I'll be forward and tell her I just came to see her, because suddenly I was thinking of her and wanted to see her. She will like that. She will be surprised and flattered. She might say it: *I am both surprised and flattered!*

I park five blocks down. Union Street is bustling with people in white pants and loafers. People from Marin, New York, Europe. At the door the bouncer will not let me in. I've left my driver's license in the car.

"Need I.D."

"I know, but—"

"Sorry. Go away."

"I just—"

"Turn around. And walk away."

Of course I picture killing him. For some reason with a huge, two-handed sword. Just lopping off his bald melon of a head.

"Listen, just— Is Julie here?"

"No."

"Did she leave?"

"Didn't work tonight."

I walk back toward the car, past a few dozen more people in white pants. A few loners in khakis. Oh if only something would happen. Nothing ever happens. This is all some terrible machine, where only the expected passes through.

I go to the White Hen Pantry to use the pay phone. I'll call Meredith. Meredith will come out.

She answers. I ask her what is up. She says that nothing is up. I ask her what she is doing. She says that she is doing nothing. I ask her if she wants to do something. She says okay.

Meredith and I have never been more than friends, and since college, when she's been in L.A. and I've been here, we talk only on the phone. She's up visiting for a week, is staying just off Haight.

I pick her up. We walk down to Nickie's. It's small, full of bodies, sweltering.

"Should we be dancing?"

"I have to drink more," she says.

—and after drinking at the bar, pounding like in a prom limo, we dance. Clumsily, bumping into other people, sweating profusely, immediately. The crowd is tight on the small floor, and we are forced to dance close. Looking for space, we edge toward one corner, under a speaker. It's deafening, whatever it is (Earth, Wind and Fire?), the bass is massive, invasive; the bass knocks loudly and then just pushes like floodwater into our brains and then is everywhere, forcing out all thinking; it brings ten suitcases and sets up in the master bedroom; it rearranges the furniture; the bass vibrates through our heads, adding a sound track to synapses, to everything stored there, to remembered phone numbers and child-hood memories. We let our bodies get closer and of course the only place to look is down, where Meredith's body is gyrating, her parts becoming bigger, smaller, bigger, smaller—

We leave the bar; we'll go to the ocean.

The drive to the ocean is long.

By now, the baby-sitter's done with whatever he wanted, has left on his basketed bike and is back, at his hideout, telling his friends about it. They are having a good laugh. He is showing them the Polaroids—

No, Toph would find a way. He'd pretend to be asleep or dead, and then, after Stephen fell asleep—after gorging himself on everything in the fridge—he'd come up behind him and bash him with something. His bat. That one we just got, the metal one. He'd bust Stephen's head in with the bat, and when I get home he'll be a hero, tired and bruised, but a hero and happy and he will not blame me for leaving, will understand.

ME: Whew! That was close!

HE: I'll say!

ME: You hungry?

HE: Now you're talking.

Meredith and I park and take off our shoes. The sand is cold. As we walk toward the water, bonfires burn up and down the beach. Close to the waves, glowing from the headlights behind us, we set down a small towel and sit, lean into each other. But some-thing has happened to our momentum; we were about to fall into the guiltless pleasure-taking that we had worked hard for earlier, that seemed inevitable only twenty minutes ago, but now we are here and it suddenly feels forced, silly between us, friends who should know better. And so we talk about our jobs. At the moment, she's working in postproduction for the television reprise of *Flipper*.

"Really?" I say. I did not know this.

"It's better than it sounds," she says.

But she wants to be making movies, wants to have a whole studio, wants to be producing more and better movies, weird stuff, have a kind of collective, something like Warhol's Factory, all these people around—

"But you know," she's saying, "it could take five, ten years to get anything like that together. And it'll cost so much money... I mean, even if I started right now... it's the waiting that's the killer—the waiting to be wherever you plan to be. The groping through the days, the temping or postproduction on *Flipper*—"

"Everything takes forever."

"Right. To know exactly what you want to be doing, to know exactly what you'd make, given the means, given some time, all the projects lined up, the body of work, have it all mapped out— who will be involved, what the office will look like, where the desks will go, couches, hot tub..."

"It should be easier."

"It should be automatic."

"Instantaneous."

"Every day a world-clearing sort of revolution, a bloodless one, one more interested in regeneration than any sort of destruction. Every day we start with a fresh world—or, better yet, each day we start with this world, the one we know, and by nine, ten a.m., we've destroyed it."

"You just—"

"I know. I just contradicted myself. So okay, there would be a certain amount of destruction, but it wouldn't be at anyone's expense, or against anyone's will."

"Right, right, and...?"

"Let's say that every day, every morning, millions of people, on cue, take the whole stupid thing apart, all the cities and towns, with hammers and saws and rocks and bulldozers and tanks—

whatever. Shake the Etch-A-Sketch. We just converge on the buildings like ants, then wire the things and knock them down, knock everything down, every day, so the world, by noon or so, is flat again, wiped clean of buildings and bridges and towers."

"I have dreams like this, where we move things."

"Yeah, yeah. And after the taking apart, when the canvas is blank—"

"Then we start over. But not start over in the Rome-wasn't-built-in-a-day sort of way. Not even in the rebuilding-Germany sort of way. I mean, we wake up, tear the world down to its foundations, or below that even, and then, by three in the afternoon, we've got a new world."

"By three?"

"Yeah, two or three, depending on whether it was winter or summer—we'd have to have enough daylight to enjoy it. I mean, I think we could do something there. Like, imagine, if a hundred million people, or more, way more—I mean, worldwide, there's gotta be two billion people like us, right?"

"Two bil—"

"Yeah, so you take all these people, and you spread the word that from now on, every day we create everything from scratch."

"You mean, like a more just and equal—"

"Yeah, sure, more justice and everything, but as much as that, all the political and economic reasons to do it, I mean, beyond that, really, is the feeling of—I mean, imagine walking among the ruins, you know? Wouldn't that be phenomenal? Not ruins like dead people everywhere or anything; I mean, just ruins, like things disassembled, cleared away, so every day you'd be left with just a bare, pure landscape—you'd have to have lots of trucks and trains to haul it away, up to Canada or something—"

"And every day you'd start from scratch, and everyone'd get together and say, Hey, let's put some buildings there, and, um, over there, let's have a five-hundred-foot stuffed hippo, and there, in front of that mountain, a huge fucking, uh, something else."

"Sure, sure. But you'd have to be able to accelerate everything, have everything be a bit easier than it currently is, in terms of construction and everything; you'd need, like, huge robots or something."

"Sure, robots, of course."

"I'm dead serious about all this."

"I am too. I'm with you."

"We can do this."

"Sure."

"We have to get people interested."

"Everyone we know."

"Even the flakes."

"John."

"Right. Good luck."

"I know. You know what he was talking about tonight?"

"You saw him?"

"Yeah."

"I owe him a call."

"He was talking about how he had just taken some test, an aptitude test, to tell him what kind of job he should have, so he could be told what to do with his life—"

"Jesus."

"It's brutal."

"We need to change him."

"Inspire him."

"Him, everyone."

"Get everyone together."

"All these people."

"No more waiting."

"Means through mass."

"It's criminal to pause."

"To wallow."

"To complain."

"We have to be happy."

"To not be happy would be difficult."

"We would have to try to not be happy."

"We have an obligation."

"We've had advantages."

"We have a platform from which to risk."

"A cushion to fall back on."

"This is abundance."

"A luxury of place and time."

"Something rare and wonderful."

"It's almost historically unprecedented."

"We must do extraordinary things."

"We have to."

"It would be obscene not to."

"We will take what we've been given and unite people."

"And we'll try not to sound so irritating."

"Right. From now on."

I tell her how funny it is we're talking about all this because as it so happens I'm already working to change all this, am currently in the middle of putting together something that will address all these issues, that will inspire millions to greatness, that with some high school friends—Moodie and two others, Flagg and Marny—we're putting something together that will smash all these misconceptions about us, how it'll help us all to throw off the shackles of our supposed obligations, our fruitless career tracks, how we will force, at least urge, millions to live more exceptional lives, to [standing up for effect] do extraordinary things, to travel the world, to help people and start things and end things and build things...

"And how will you do this?" she wants to know. "A political party? A march? A revolution? A coup?"

"A magazine."

"Oh… right."

"Yeah," I say, looking out to the ocean, basking in its applause. "It's going to be huge—we'll have a big house somewhere, or a loft, and there'll be an art gallery, and maybe a dorm—"

"Like the Factory!"

"Yeah, but without the drugs, the cross-dressers."

"Right. A collective."

"A movement."

"An army."

"All-inclusive."

"Raceless."

"Genderless."

"Youth."

"Strength."

"Potential."

"Rebirth."

"Oceans."

"Fire."

"Sex."

Our mouths are all over each other. All the talk of plans and new worlds… We sit upright as we kiss, and at first we kiss like friends, with our eyes open, almost laughing. But as our hands start moving, we begin to believe, and our eyes close, and our heads turn this way and that, we're kissing each other but so much more, kissing like warriors saving the world, at the end of the movie, the last two, the only two who can save everything—and because we are too post-drunk tired to keep our heads upright with our eyes shut, we recline, and soon the towel underneath Meredith is just a crooked snakeskin and we have taken off our pants, the air cool where we are now bare. And sex, inevitable, will make us more powerful. A manifesto consummated under this great sky, the approval of the pounding sea—

There's noise down the shore. I squint and can see a group of people coming our way, loud, emitting bursts of noise, shrieks of laughter. I set myself on my elbow to watch, squinting harder. A group of maybe six, seven, are fully dressed, with dark pants, shoes, hats. We move the towel from under Meredith's head to over our naked lower halves. We will act casual. We fall back into an embrace, so they'll leave us alone, not that they would ever bother us in the first place.

The voices get louder, and closer.

"Just wait until they go by," I whisper into Meredith's lips.

"How far awa—"

"Shhh."

Then louder and the scratching footsteps audible and then, instead of passing by, they are suddenly upon us. Legs everywhere. I look up. One has taken my pants and is rifling through them. He throws them toward the ocean. Because I'm stupid I assume they're from Mexico, Mexican American, teenagers. Four boys and three girls. Five boys, two girls. Men, women. Ages unclear.

"What was you two doing?" a voice asks.

"Naughty naughty!" says another.

"Where's your pants, stud?"

Only female voices so far, strong accents. Naked from the waist down, we can't even move. I hold the towel around both of us, disbelieving— What is this? This is the beginning of something very bad— The end?

I look for my boxer shorts. They're in the pants, by the water. I take the other towel, the one underneath us, pull it out, wrap it around my waist and stand up.

"What the fuck are you d— Fuck!" Someone's thrown sand in my eyes. My eyes are full of sand. I blink wildly, epileptically. I stagger then sit down.

"What the fuck—" The sand is under my eyelids. I can't open them. *I'll be blind.*

The girls are on Meredith.

"Hey honey!"

"Hey baby!"

"Fuck you," says Meredith. She is still sitting down, head in her knees. One of the girls shoves her.

I am blind. I blink frantically, swatting the sand out of my eyes. while wondering if I am blind and if we'll both be dead soon. What a stupid way to go. *Is this how people die? Can we outrun them?* I refuse to have these people kill us. *Do they have weapons?* No weapons yet. Toph, Toph. Blinking, tearing madly, I clear one eye out. I stand up again, get the towel back on, holding it around my waist like I've just gotten out of the shower.

They are all around us, almost perfectly spaced, almost perfectly boy-girl-boy. Strange—

One of the girls has come behind me and is trying to take the towel from my waist. It's unclear what they want. I'm assuming already that the guy who went through my pants took my wallet. Now what?

"Get the fuck away!" I want to swing at the girl. I scan the ground for my boxers. "What the fuck do you want?"

"We don't want nothing," says a male voice.

"Hey, you got any money?" says a girl.

"You're not taking any of our fucking money," I say.

Who are these people? One is smiling at me. A small guy with a fedora. I'm pushed from behind, trip on the towel and fall to the sand. Meredith is holding her knees. They've done something with her pants, too.

They stand above us, grinning. There are laughs. There are six of them. Did one leave? Is Meredith crying? Three guys, three girls. The lights from the headlights behind them give everyone three, four shadows. Where did the other one go? There's the one tall guy, a medium-sized guy, and a small guy, the fedora guy, who looks older. The girls wear skirts and black leather jackets.

"Why don't you just leave us the fuck alone?" says Meredith.

The question loiters for a minute, lamely. Stupid question. This has just begun, surely—

"Okay, let's go," says the short one.

They start to—Jesus—walk away. All we had to do was ask? This is unbelievable.

The short one, the oldest of the group, turns to us.

"Hey listen, man, we was just goofing around. Sorry."

Then he jogs down the shore to catch up with the rest of them. It's over.

They are gone and I am soaring. Those motherfuckers! My head is clear and muscular and filled with blood. Something has happened. We're alive, we've won! Powerful us! They were scared. We scared them off. They feared us. We won. We told them to go away and they did. I am the president. I am the Olympics.

I find my boxers in the sand, cold, put them on. Then my pants. Meredith is putting on hers. I feel my pockets.

"Fuck."

"Your wallet?"

"Yeah."

They're walking back the way they came, a hundred yards away now. I am barefoot and running feels good—my legs feel strong, light. My head is clear and straight. Are they armed? Toph, Toph. Will it get worse now? No, no. I am huge, I am Captain America. Halfway there I start yelling.

"Hey!"

Nothing. They are oblivious, disbelieving even.

"Hey! Wait, goddammit!"

A few stop and turn around.

"Hold on!" I say.

They all stop. They wait, watching me run toward them.

Twenty feet before them, I stop, hands on my waist, breathing hard.

"Okay, who took my wallet?"

A beat. They look at each other.

"No one took your wallet," the fedora one says. He looks about thirty. He turns to his friends. "Did anyone take his wallet?" They shake their heads. These fucking people.

"Listen," I say, "what the fuck did you think you were doing? There's going to be hell to pay if we don't fix this shit up. "

No one says anything. I nod to the short, older one:

"Should I be talking to you about this? Are you the man?"

The words come before I know them. *Are you the man?* I just said that. It sounded so good. That's how people talk. But should I have dropped the Are in the question? *You the man?*—

He nods. He is, apparently, the man.

I motion for us to take a few steps aside, to talk. Come here. He complies. This is what one does. He is shorter close up. I look down to him, his face stiff and tan.

"Listen, man, I don't know why you guys were fucking with us, but now my fucking wallet's gone."

"We didn't take the wallet, amigo," he says.

Did he just say amigo? That's so weird, so 21 Jump Street, *that he'd actually say amigo*—

"Listen," I continue, "I've seen all of you. I can identify you, every single one of you guys, and you'll be in deep fucking shit if you're caught."

He considers this for a second. My eyes burrow. *I* am the man! "So, what do you want?"

"I want you to give me the fucking wallet back is what I want."

"But we don't *have* the wallet."

The tall one hears him. "We didn't take the fucking wallet."

"Well," I say to all of them now, loudly, "before you came and started fucking with us, I had a fucking wallet. Then you come and start fucking with us, and now I don't have a fucking wallet. And that's all the fucking cops need to know."

The cops. *My* cops.

The short one looks at me. "C'mon, we don't have the wallet. I swear. What do you want us to do?"

"I guess you guys are gonna have to come back and help me find the thing, because if you don't, I'm gonna call the cops, and the fucking cops'll pick you all up, and *they'll* figure out where the fucking wallet went."

The small one looks at me from under the brim of his hat and then turns to his friends.

"C'mon," he says.

And then they are following me.

We walk back, me walking to the side to prevent any funny business, ambushes, to the spot where we had been. Meredith is standing, dressed and with a towel in hand. She doesn't know what to make of this. *They're back?*

"All right, you better start looking. I hope you find it..." I pause as one of the girls throws me a disgusted look. "Because otherwise you're fucked."

They spread out and start looking, pushing sand around with their feet. I stand to the side, where I can see all of them at once, my hands on my waist, overseeing. I am the foreman, I am the boss. They lift and shake the towel we were lying on. Each one does it at least twice, the shaking of that towel. They shuffle around, picking up sticks, throwing them toward the water.

"Fuck this!" says one of the girls. "We don't have the fucking thing. We didn't do nothing."

"Fuck you you didn't do anything! That was assault, idiot! I mean, who do you think the cops are gonna believe? Two regular people sitting on the beach, or you people? I mean, sorry, but that's the fucking truth. You guys'll be *fucked*."

I am the cop, a friendly but stern cop. I am helping them. I assume one of them still has the thing, that they're just stalling. I have to figure out a way to scare them, to get the thing back. Then I—*should I?*—*I shouldn't say that*—okay, sure:

"I mean, I don't know what your status is with green cards and everything, but this could get really fucking ugly, you guys."

There is no visible reaction.

They keep searching. Meredith starts looking, too, but I take her arm. "Don't. Let them do it."

One of the girls sits down, sullen.

"I sure hope you guys find the fucking thing," I say, thinking that it's best that I be talking the whole time. I decide to throw out my last ace. "This was my goddamn dad's wallet you stole." I'm not sure how much to tell them but because I want the wallet back at all costs—

"And my dad just died," I say. "It's all I have of his."

And it is. He had so few things, personal things, and we sold the clothes, the suits—the wallet was the one thing I kept, outside of a small box of papers, some business cards, paperweights from his office.

They keep looking. I look at their pants pockets, scanning for bulges. I briefly wonder if they'll let me frisk them.

"Listen man," the short one says. "We didn't fucking take it. What do you want?"

I know the answer: I want the wallet, and then I want them in jail, and I want them miserable. I want them, all seven of them, or five of them, all of them, to be wearing gray uniforms that itch and chafe them as they sleep fitfully, on cots, their stupid heads full of regret, their cheeks wet with their weeping for forgiveness, forgiveness not so much from their simple God or jailer, but from me. They will be so sorry. Their tiny heads will implode with guilt and remorse. My dead father's beautiful, frayed, soft leather wallet—

"It's not here," he says.

"Then you guys better come with me," I say. "We'll have to find a phone. You can tell the cops your side of the story, I'll tell mine, and we'll see what happens. But if you guys take off, you're fucked because then they're going to assume you took it."

We look at each other. He starts walking toward the parking lot, his friends follow.

Meredith grabs the second towel, shakes it out. We walk behind the three of them, to keep track. Three total—I can take two of them. All three even. I am massive! I am America!

No one talks. Our shadows, two each, crisscross and jump over the sand. The scratching of our feet. The lights from the houses above the beach are few. That weird windmill at the end of Golden Gate Park is straight ahead, black.

When we get to the parking lot, what I thought was a phone—a box attached to a lamppost—is not a phone.

We stand for a second under the glare. I look around, up at the houses across the Great Highway, all glass facing the ocean, looking for support, maybe someone on a porch, or a jogger, a biker; there is no one awake.

"Okay, we'll have to walk across," I say. "We'll cross the highway and walk up until we get to a phone."

I'm still in charge. We're a team. I am their leader, their stern but fair warden. They seem to consent.

I walk toward them, expecting them to turn and walk toward the highway. As I come among them, they don't move. I am suddenly between all three of them.

Everything is new.

"Fuck you," says the tall one, swinging at my head. I have no time to move, but he misses. Another swing, from behind. Nothing. Then a leg appears and the foot lands in my crotch. I fall to my knees. I stare at the cement. Gum, oil stains—

They run away, arms and legs, like big spiders, laughing.

How long do you stay on your knees in a situation like this?

"Fuck you!" they say. Creative.

The kick wasn't bad. I still have breath. Then I'm up! I am up and running after them. I'm in the middle of the parking lot road and I see them just off to the right, fifty yards ahead, getting into—there are—what? Fuck! fuck!—two cars, in the middle of the street, ready, revving—

How did they know? How did they know?

As I reach the middle of the street the doors shut; the cars start toward me. The front car is an old convertible, dark green with a black top, huge hood. One of the girls from before is driving. Holy fucking shit. *Like a getaway car!* I stand in the middle of the street as they come toward me. I'm going to get the fucking license plates.

They drive at me, slow at first but then faster. I have them. License plates, suckers! License plates, fuckers! As they come toward me, I yell the numbers of their plates out loud, pointing at them with every digit, exaggerating the pointing to make sure they know what I'm doing, that I've got them—*got them!*

"G!

"F!

"Six!

"Seven!

"Nine!

"O!"

Beautiful! Beautiful, you fuckers! You dumb stupid motherfuckers!

They swerve around me, yelling, laughing, waving their little middle fingers at me.

I am yelling, thrilled, *high*.

"Ha ha you fuckers! I got you! I got you motherfuckers!"

They pass, then turn onto the highway, accelerate, are gone. I got the first car's plate but not the second's. I run back to Meredith. A block away we find a phone.

"Wait, calm down, where are you?" the operator says.

"I don't know. The beach."

"What's wrong?"

"We were attacked, robbed."

"By who?"

"Bunch of Mexican kids."

I tell her what the car looked like. I try to tell her the license plate number, but she says she can't take it, to tell it to the officer when he gets there, she says. I hang up.

G-H...6-0...

Fuck.

G-H-0-0-

Fuck!

We sit down.

I'm not hurt. I think about whether or not I'm hurt. I'm not. We sit on the cement wall of the path and for a moment I fear they'll come back. Maybe there'll be guns, maybe to eliminate the witnesses, a drive-by. No, no. They're gone, they're gone. Won't be back. I jump down from the wall; I can't sit, I'm wired. I pace in front of her. *I got their plates!* Stupid assholes.

The police car pulls up two minutes after. It looks huge. The engine roars. It's immaculate, shiny like an enormous toy. The officer steps out and he is burly and mustached and—is he? It's after 2 a.m.—he is wearing sunglasses. He introduces himself and asks us to get in the back of the car and we do. It is a beautiful car, clean, the black vinyl bright, perfect. I answer:

"Yeah, we were just hanging out on the beach."

"Seven of them."

"Mexican."

"I'm sure of it. Their accents, their looks. Completely. They spoke English, but with a Mexican accent." I try to think of what they looked like, who the older one looked like. *Baretta.* He looked like Robert Blake.

"They took my wallet."

"I don't know how much. Maybe twenty dollars."

"We were calling the police to straighten it out."

"Yeah, they came with me."

"I don't know why. Because they said they didn't take it."

"But then they kicked me in the groin [groin being the more

police-report-appropriate word for *crotch*} and then they got in two
cars and took off."

"A big dark green convertible with a black top."

"Yeah, yeah, I had it down before. Fuck. It start with G-H, and
there's a six in it, and a zero. I think it ended with zero. Is that
enough? Can you go on that?"

The car is so clean. I love the car. A shotgun hangs at eye level
in front of us. The computer next to the steering wheel glows blue,
beautiful thing. The radio fitzes and beeps. The officer listens and
answers questions on the CB. He turns around.

"Okay, it looks like we have some suspects. We've stopped a
car just off the highway. We're going to have to go there so you can
make a positive I.D."

I look at Meredith. We have been in the car maybe three or
four minutes. Is that possible?

"You already found the car? Is it the dark green convertible?"
I ask him, leaning into the front seat.

"I'm not sure. But we better go." We go.

Meredith and I look out the window bright-eyed and atten-
tive, like tourists passing through a city on a Saturday night. We
turn onto another highway and suddenly there are lights everywhere. It looks like an accident. At least four police cars. Five. All
parked, lights spinning, popping. There are cops on the street,
walking back and forth, standing outside their cars, talking into
CB's pulled through their windows. It's an event.

Our car stops before an overpass. There is an old convertible
parked about twenty yards ahead, light blue with a black top.

"That's not it," I say. The officer turns around.

"Excuse me?"

"That's definitely not the car," I say. "Theirs is green. Dark
green. With a black top. I'm positive."

He looks at me and turns back around and talks into his CB.
After a minute, he turns back to us.

"Okay, we're going to ask you to take a look at the people in the car, just to make sure," he says.

"That's definitely not the car," I say.

"We have to do this," he says.

There are four cops standing by the blue convertible. One of them opens the front door and reaches in, helping out a handcuffed man. The man shimmies out of the car and stands up. He turns toward us, squints. He has long blond hair, a goatee, is wearing a flannel shirt, army shorts, black boots. The spinning lights make him blue and then red and then flesh-colored again, then blue and then red again. He looks through our windshield and into our car.

"Do you recognize him?"

"No. That's definitely not him. I'm positive they were Mexican. This's definitely not the right car."

"Well, hold on there. We're going to have to look at all of the passengers."

Why?

The cop makes a signal with his hand to one of the officers outside. They bring out a young woman with dyed red hair, a miniskirt and go-go boots. She stands next to the first man.

"My god, those poor people," Meredith whispers.

"No, no," I say to the cop. "You've got to understand, these people were Mexican. You know, shorter, dark-haired. These people are white."

They bring out three more, two more men and one other woman, until they are all standing there, shoulder to shoulder, lit up, tinted red and blue, squinting into our headlights. Maybe they're people we know. Meredith grabs my arm, sliding down in her seat. "God I hope they can't see us."

I lean forward and tell the cop again:

"That's not them."

He talks to his CB for a while and writes something on a clipboard. As he makes a U-turn to drive us back, the kids standing by the road are just getting their handcuffs taken off. The other cops are getting back into their cars. We duck.

We drive back to the beach parking lot. Once there, the cop turns around and gives us his card. Cops have cards.

We get out. I ask him about the likelihood of them finding the Mexican kids, or the wallet.

"It's pretty small odds," he says. "It's a wallet, you know? It's a little thing. Here's an incident report card. That's your incident report number, in case you have anything to report. Or if we need to call you, you'll need that as a reference."

Then he's gone.

Meredith wants to go home and sleep. Half of me wants to get back to my car and cruise for the green convertible, hunt them down, get some kind of weapon first and then drive, hunt, do bad things, to each and every one.

But I need to go home to see what's happened to Toph, whether the baby-sitter's done what I fear he's done.

We don't talk much on the drive back to the Haight, down the wide, barren avenues of the Richmond. At her friend's place she gets out; we agree to see each other again before she goes back to L.A. Then I'm going home, past all the dumb kids at Haight and Masonic, sitting against the wall, smoking in their rasta hats, playing with those sticks, flipping the stupid fucking stick around with the other two sticks, as if that could possibly be diverting for more than twenty or thirty seconds, just the stick up and down, back and forth, my God—and down Fell, onto 80 and toward the Bay Bridge.

Motherfuckers. Stupid motherfuckers steal my dad's fucking wallet, the only fucking thing I have of his, that and some stationery, the paperweights, the business cards, a high school yearbook, some papers about him being in the army—

Those fucking kids. Those fuckers— I'll stake out the beach tomorrow. I will not forget.

The clouds above are fat, moving slowly over the gray bridge like manatee ghosts.

On the bridge I begin to feel the leaden, downward pull of the alcohol in my system. I nod off and on. I slap myself, for the sound and the shock—*awake!* Turn up the radio. On the bridge, the lower tier, it's straight ahead and action-packed. It's a *Battlestar Galactica* runway. It's the circuitry inside a computer, an old rickety computer, a 2XL—

I nod again. *Awake!*

The bridge is a tunnel. On bridges I think of the accident, the one I heard related a hundred times: my mom driving her tiny powder blue Beetle, somewhere in Massachusetts, Bill and Beth toddlers, over a two-lane bridge—a tire blows, she skids, swerves, across traffic and breaks halfway through the opposite guardrail, the car's front hanging over the edge, her seeing it all ending, Bill and Beth screaming, me in her womb—

There are a few other cars. There is a carful of men in a shiny black BMW. The lights of the bridge make the cars shinier, sleeker, faster-seeming. We are all returning home, to our adobe homes, our wooden homes. There is a family in a small blue—good god, put that kid in a seatbelt!

Stupid fuckers take that fucking wallet.

I'm alone and will never go out again. When will I get out again? It will be weeks from now. It will be never. I am lost. I am in the bridge's dark corridor, the lower tier, riding under cars going the other way, to San Francisco. I am heading back to Berkeley, to the flatlands, to our house, where there is no one, where it is just my bed, quiet. And Toph. Blood on the porch. The baby-sitter has taken him away. Or the baby-sitter has left him bleeding, as a warning. Markings on his face, numbers, astrological shit, on his chest, clues to the culprit. All my fault. I will run away. They will be looking somewhere tropical but will not guess that I went to Russia. I will go to Russia and will wander around Russia until I die. How could I have left? My parents never left us as children. They didn't go out. They stayed home, were ensconced, at home, in the family room, reliable, he on the couch, she on her chair—

After the bridge accident she was a mess when driving over water, near cliffs, on two-lane highways. On our one trip to California, all of us under ten, we went to see the Sequoias, all the way up that mountain, and she made it up, around and around, two lanes all the way, but could not make it down, on the outside lane, there was no barrier, just the sheer drop, and Bill tried to calm her—

"Mom, just—"

"I can't! I can't!"

—and so she parked, waited until a trooper could come and drive the car down for us, she in the passenger seat, turning around to smile at us, embarrassed—

I make it off the bridge, down the hill, toward the highway's split, Oakland or Berkeley. I nod awake again, this time after veering toward the median divider. I slap myself again, and again and again. I open the window. The Ashby exit. Good, good. Close, close. University. I am home free. Stephen did something. Maybe I should leave now, go to the airport, assume the worst. I will turn around if I see the flashing lights. I will come from Solano Avenue, down the hill, so I can see if there are ambulances and if so I can turn around and go to the airport before they see me—

The wallet is gone. My father has slipped further down the well. The wallet was the constant reminder; every time I used it, it was always there, in my pocket! Taken by stupid Mexican spiders, the fuckers. The only thing I had of his. The rugs are unraveling, the furniture splitting. I cannot be trusted with anything, everything precarious, lost, broken, soaked—

This is not the way things should be, Toph and I in our dingy little house, holes in the floor, everything decomposing, me losing things, letting a bunch of kids take our father's wallet. And Toph with the baby-sitter, this evil man—

It'll be cold in Russia but maybe not now. I can get a jacket at the airport.

The Gilman exit! I will not crash. I will move in with friends. I will get over it. I will either move to Russia or I will get over it. I turn onto our street, Peralta, and there are no lights, no cops, no amusement park lights of ambulances and cops and fire engines—

The door is closed. There is no blood on the steps. I walk up to the porch and through the window I can see the baby-sitter's bike still parked against the fireplace and then, as I approach the door, I can see Toph sprawled on the couch. Good, good. At least he's here.

Though he might be dead. He could still be dead. The door is not locked—maybe *someone else* has killed Toph *and* the baby-sitter! I hadn't thought of that but of course! A burglar has come in, has taken what he pleased, and then...poisoned both of them! Or else he was Stephen's accomplice. It was all a setup—

I step inside, careful, fists clenched. I step toward Toph. I look for blood—none. Poisoned maybe. Or beaten—internal bleeding. I bring my face close to his. His breath is hot on my cheek.

Alive! Alive!

He could be dying, though, like the boy in that movie, Bruce Davison and Andie MacDowell's son. How will I know? I will trust. Go to the hospital? No. No. He is good. He is fine. There is drool on the arm of the couch.

Where's Stephen? That's it. Stephen is gone because he poisoned Toph. Toph is dying. Toph has an hour to live. There will be no point to taking him to the hospital. The woman's voice from the poison hot line will crack—"There's nothing...nothing you can do—" and, broken, hysterical, I will gather my faculties so I can wake him, so we can talk for our last hour together. Should I tell him? No, no. We will have fun. I will pull it off.

Hey, little man.

What time is it?

One.

He is not dead. He will live. Everything is normal. Normal, normal, normal. Good. Good. Normal. Normal. Fine.

I walk into the kitchen, drop my keys, tick, in the bowl with the change. I peek into the bedroom. No Stephen. To the back bedroom, open the door. There. Stephen is asleep on the bed, school papers spread out everywhere.

I wake him up. He gathers his stuff.

"He was talking in his sleep," he says.

"Huh. What did he say?"

"Nothing, really. Just mumbling."

I write him a check. I open the front door for him. He gets on his bicycle and, still half-asleep, rides away, awkward and jumpy like a butterfly. I lock the door after him.

I go back to the living room, where Toph is splayed, as if boneless, on the couch. He has brought a comforter from his room, which is now on the floor. His mouth is open and there is a dark round pond of drool on his gray T-shirt.

"Hey."

"Mmph."

"Hey. Help me out here."

"Mmph."

"I'm gonna put you in bed. Put your arm around."

He puts one arm around my neck and grabs it with the other, pulls his head toward me so I don't hit it on the door frame.

"Don't hit my head."

"I won't."

The molding cracks.

"Owww."

"Sorry."

"Idiot."

I lay him on the bed, in his jeans and sweatshirt, and put his blanket over him. In the kitchen, I check the answering machine. I look in the fridge. I wonder briefly about people I could call. Who would be awake? Someone will want to come over. Who would be willing?

I walk back to my bedroom, drop my change on the dresser.

The wallet. On the dresser.

It was here.

VI.

When we hear the news at first it means almost nothing. It has just been announced that *The Real World*, MTV's seminal program involving the housing of seven young people in one house and the televising of their lives, will film its next season in San Francisco. MTV is seeking applicants. They are looking for a new cast.

At the office we have a few hearty laughs about it.

"Has anyone seen the show?"

"No."

"No."

"Some of it."

We're all lying. Everyone's seen the show. We all despise it, are enthralled by it, morbidly curious. Is it interesting because it's so bad, because the stars of it are so profoundly uninteresting? Or is it because in it we recognize so much that is maddeningly familiar? Maybe this is indeed us. Watching the show is like listening to one's voice on tape: it's real of course, but however mellifluous and articulate you hear your own words, once they're sent through this machine and are given back to you, they're high-pitched, nasal, horrifying. Are our lives that? *Do we talk like that, look like that?* Yes. *It could not be.* It is. *No.* The banality of our upper-middle-class lives, so gaudily stuck between the mindless drunk-driving of high school—that was meant as a metaphor only—and the death that is homeowning and family-having, especially when packaged within a comfort zone of colorful couches and lava lamps and pool tables—wouldn't this make interesting television only for those whose lives are even more boring than those of *The Real World*'s cast?

But it's impossible to ignore.

As half of the people we know, in secret or unabashedly, are scrambling to get their applications in, we wonder what sort of fun we can make, put our much-needed spin on it all.

One of our contributors, David Milton, writes a letter to them, which we have ready for the first issue. The letter reads:

Dear Producers,
Something is radiating deep within me and it must be transmitted or I will implode and the world will suffer a great loss, unawares. Epic are the proportions of my soul, yet without a scope who cares am I? This is why I must but must be one of the inhabitants of MTV's "Real World." Only there, burning brightly into a million dazzled eyes, will my as yet uncontoured self assume the beauteous forms that are not just its own, but an entire market niche's, due.

I am a Kirk Cameron–Kurt Cobain figure, roguishly quirky, dandified but down to earth, kooky but comprehensible; denizen of the growing penumbra between alternative and mainstream culture; angsty prophet of the already bygone apocalypse, yet upbeat, stylish and sexy!

Oscar Wilde wrote, "Good artists exist in what they make, and consequently are perfectly uninteresting in what they are. A great poet, a really great poet, is the most unpoetical of all creatures. But inferior poets are absolutely fascinating...[they] live the poetry [they] cannot write." As with Dorian Gray, life is my art! Oh MTV, take me, make me, wake me from my formless slumbers and place me in the dreamy Real World of target marketing.
Sincerely,
David Milton

And after the chuckles, and after I get over my fleeting paranoia that Milton's making fun of me in particular, we get serious for a second. We are trying to get advertising, distribution, all that flotsam lined up for our first issue, and right now we are nowhere, because we have nothing and are no one.

We have, though, assembled a crack team. There is Moodie, of course, and now there is Marny, who has moved out, a few months out of college. Yes, in high school we had dated. Yes, she had been a cheerleader, though an improbable one, a serious one, the one who never smiled. And now she is the one among us who reads *Ms.,* who reads *The Nation,* who knows what or who Che Guevara was. And there is Paul, who has just joined up, having grown up twenty miles south of us, along Lake Michigan, on the cold, cruel streets of Chicago's Gold Coast. We had started with one more, my grade school best friend Flagg, whom I had coerced into leaving his girlfriend and job in Washington to move to Berkeley to be a part of the start-up. He had made the trip, set up with us, at a desk by the window, had spent his days doing our "market research"— it was just for show, soft, unprovable statistics to parade in front of advertisers—but he soon learned what the rest of us pretty much knew going in: that there would be no money in this, not for a long time at least, if ever, and the hours were going to be ludicrous, spent in a filthy corner of a shaky warehouse, where dust falls from the rafters when the tenants walk above, where the locks are decorative only, where the rent sets us back $250 a month.

But it's not like anyone here, in San Francisco, in this building, is going to tell you you're wasting your time.

The rest of the floor consists, with occasional musical chairings, of a desk for our landlord, Randy Stickrod (real name), who is a magazine consultant, having recently aided in the launch of *Wired,* the founders of which only recently vacated the precise area we are currently inhabiting, and moved two floors up. Across from us is the desk, desk-organizer, and tiny computer of Shalini

Malhotra, who helps with *just Go!*, a tiny ecotravel magazine, and who is working on her own zine, provisionally titled *Hum*—the Indian word for "Us"—which will be dedicated to uniting and speaking for/to/from twentysomethings of the South Asian American persuasion. There is also *bOING bOING,* a "neurozine" published by Carla Sinclair and Mark Fraunfelder, a plastic/gel/leather-new-wave-circa-1984-looking husband-and-wife team just up from L.A. In the back there is a guy putting out a magazine called *Star Wars Generation*—no explanation necessary. All together, our floor, our building, it has something, is bursting, is not just a place where people are working but a place where people are creating and working to change the *very way we live.*

The warehouse, as luck would have it, is in San Francisco's South Park neighborhood, an area of maybe six blocks which, if the newspapers are right, is itself about to explode, because this is where *Wired* makes its home, as do a handful of other magazines, mostly computer rags but also *SF Weekly, The Nose* (humor) and *FutureSex* ("cybererotica" (naked people wearing virtual reality gear))—not to mention countless start-up software companies, Web developers, Internet providers—and this is 1993, when this stuff is new—graphic designers, architects, all surrounding or very close to a small oval of green called South Park (no relation)— bordered by small Victorians and bisected by an active playground—within which sits, on its perfect lush green grass, an incredibly dense concentration of sophisticated and gorgeous youth—a green oval teeming with the vernal and progressive and new and beautiful. They have tattoos before everyone has tattoos. They ride motorcycles, and their leather is amazing. They practice (or claim to practice) Wicca. They are the luminous young daughter of Charles Bronson, who interns at *Wired,* where the ratio of attractive young women to interns and assistants is 1:1, they being one and the same. There are bike messengers who also write social-ist tracts, and bike messengers who are 200 lb transvestites, and writers who prefer to surf, and raves are still attracting crowds, and the young creative elite of San Francisco are here and only here, do not want to be elsewhere, because technology-wise, New York is ten or twelve years behind—you can't even e-mail anyone there yet—and style-wise L.A. is so '80s, because here, in stark contrast, there is no money, no one is allowed to make money, or spend money, or look like you've spent money, money is suspect, the making of money and caring about money—at least insofar as having more than, say, $17,000 a year—is archaic, is high school, is completely beside the point. Here there are no clothes that are not preworn—when a shirt is not a used shirt, when a shirt has cost more than $8, we say:

"Hey, nice *shirt*."

"Yeah, nice...you know, *shirt*."

And there are no cars that are not old cars, or preferably very old cars, silly cars, cheap cars, the coveted parking spaces around South Park filled with automotive mutants, anomalies. And in San Francisco, for better or worse, there are no ideas dumb enough to be squashed, or people aren't honest enough to tell people the truth about their dumb ideas, and so half of us are doing dumb, doomed things— And there is no prestige like the prestige in working for *Wired*, wearing one of those new black shoulder bags they just had made, or having been at the party thrown by the people from Survival Research Laboratories, who make giant robots and have them fight each other—and though the material rewards are a joke, and the apartment rents are already starting to get silly, we say nothing and complain little because when the cherubic bald anchorman on the news says that this is the "best place on Earth" we cringe but then kind of even believe it, in a way, believe that we have to work eighteen hours a day, whether for ourselves or one of these tech start-ups or whatever, because we're in a certain place, are lucky, feel lucky even though it's been only a few years since the hills burned, since the highways collapsed— But so we are gathered here, each and every perfect warm-but-not-too-warm day, each day lathered in sun and possibility, *prob*ability, and while everyone drinks their lattes and eats their burritos, pretending not to be checking each other out— there is a feeling that we are, at least at this point in time, with our friends, on this lush grass, at the very red molten-hot core of everything, that something is happening here, that, switching metaphors, that we are riding a wave, a big wave—of course, not one that's too big, not like one of those huge Hawaii kinds that kill people on the coral—

Of course, we, and our magazine, can't let on that we're part of this scene, or any scene. We begin to perfect a balance between being close to where things are happening, knowing the people involved and their patterns, while keeping our distance, an outsider's mentality, even among other outsiders. Ridiculing other magazines, especially *Wired* upstairs, we do a What's Hot/What's Not list:

WHAT'S HOT	WHAT'S NOT
the sun	snow
flambé	vichyssoise
branding irons	a cold beverage
lava (molten)	lava (hardened)

We place an ad with the local media organizations, saying that we are not this and we are not that, that this will be, unless something bizarre and terrible happens, the very first meaningful magazine in the history of civilization, that it will be created *by and for us twentysomethings* (we try alternatives, to no avail: people in their twenties? people of twenty?), that we are looking for writers, photographers, illustrators, cartoonists, interns— Anyone who wants to help will be put to work—we need hundreds, can use thousands. We send in the listing-manifesto, and in days (hours?), a cascade of résumés. Most just out of college, some with pictures drawn above their names, designs in the margins, transcripts from their years at Bates, Reed, Wittenberg attached. We call everyone, can't call them quick enough, we want to marry every one of them, are thrilled to have found them, to have *made this connection*. We offer work to everyone.

"What kind of help do you need?" they ask.

"What do you want to do?" we say.

"What kind of hours will it require?"

"What kind of time do you have?"

We'll take anything, anyone we can get, no matter what kind of loser they are, we don't care, even if they went to Stanford, Yale. For us it's all about numbers, amassing sheer numbers of people— Most who come have other jobs, and many, thank God, have no jobs at all, and have been given by their parents a year or so to get on their feet. Every time someone walks through the door and steps over our garbage and around our boxes looking to offer themselves we have met a brother, a sister, already believing so fervently in the utter urgency of what we're doing—

"I saw your notice and I just fucking had to come down. It's about fucking time someone did this."

"Great. Thanks."

"Now, I've got some poetry…"

—and though we can't accommodate everyone's talents, proclivities, and agendas—about five different people want to write about the many, many uses of hemp—we know that we have something, have touched a nerve. We want everyone to follow their dreams, their hearts (aren't they bursting, like ours?); we want them doing things that we will find interesting. Hey Sally, why work at that silly claims adjusting job—didn't you used to sing? Sing, Sally, *sing*! We feel sure that we speak for others, that we speak for millions. If only we can get the word out, spread the word, with this, this magazine… We will make the magazine a platform from which to spring, a springboard from which to speak—

We write the premiere issue's opening essay:

> Could there really be more to a generation than illiterate, uninspired, flannel-wearing "slackers"? Could a bunch of people under twenty-five put out a national magazine with no corporate backing and no clue about marketing? With actual views about actual issues? With a sense of purpose and a sense of humor? With guts and goals and hope? Who would read a magazine like that? You might.

That's where the pun comes in. That last part.

To fund a second phone line, for the fax machine, we hold bake sales in the park. All the contributors bring goods, and we raise about $100. We beg everyone we know to switch to Working Assets for their long distance—

"But you *have* to. They donate money to good causes, and they say if we get a hundred people to change over, they might advertise and—"

We seek out alliances with others, like us, who are taking a formless and mute mass of human potential and are attempting to make it speak, sing, scream, to mold it into a political force. Or at least use it to get themselves in *Time* and *Newsweek*.

There is Lead or Leave, a Washington, D.C., political group which already, in 1993, claims some 500,000 members. There is Third Millennium, a similarly minded advocacy group, one born of a weekend brainstorming session held at the family getaway of one of the young Kennedys. Both organizations want to amass their own thousands, register voters and become the youth version of the AARP, then, once the numbers are marshaled and the weapons distributed, they'll fight the war that we all must fight, the war that will become our Great War, or at least our Vietnam: Social Security.

It appears, from the calculations of many economists, that, when we are all sixty-five or seventy or whatever, when we retire, there will not be enough money left in the pot for us…that Social Security will be bankrupt. Lead or Leave and Third Millennium make news everywhere by registering voters and holding press conferences to call attention to this looming Armageddon, and we make contact with these organizations, pledge solidarity, though to be honest we have absolutely no idea what they're talking about. Though we share with them the desire to motivate and bring to action (some kind of action, though what exactly we are not sure) our 47 million souls, what we are most interested in is their mailing list.

It's not like we don't support them—because we do, conceptually if not materially, or ideologically—it's just that, given little to no contact with economic insecurity of any kind, we have a hard time finding the fire in the belly for such things. We want to join them in complaining about the burdens of student loans, but then remember that of all of us, only Moodie had to take one on. We want to complain about jobs, but we don't really want jobs ourselves—not the kind you'd complain about—so quickly fall mute. And Social Security? Well, personally at least, I cannot in my wildest fantasies see myself making it past fifty or fifty-five, so find the issue moot. All *we* really want is for no one to have a boring life, to be impressive, so we can be impressed.

We try to convince people that we're a lifestyle magazine.

"See, we're talking here about a *style* of *life*."

"Huh."

"Get it? Not lifestyle like *lifestyle*. Life. Style. A *style* of *life*."

"Right."

"A style. Of *life*."

We find strength in people doing things we find worthwhile, heroic, and who are getting great press for doing such things. We lionize Fidel Vargas, the youngest mayor in the country, whose politics we know nothing about but whose age (twenty-three) we do. We glorify Wendy Kopp, at twenty-five the founder of Teach

for America, which places recent college graduates in understaffed
or -financed schools, mostly urban. We love people like this, those
who are starting massive organizations, trying new approaches to
age-old problems, and getting the word out about it, with great
PR, terrific publicity photos, available in black and white or color
transparency.

We are willing and ready. Whomever we need to ally ourselves
with, whatever we need to do, we will be there—if we have to
organize events and sponsor speakers, if we have to go to large, loud
rock concerts and sit at tables and hand out literature and look
down the loose-necked tanktops of late-teenage girls... even if we
have to appear on television and in magazines and be quoted
extensively and live like rock stars and wield power like messiahs—
whatever it takes, we are ready. Just tell us where to be, who we're
talking to, the circulation of your newspaper or approximate view-
ership, and a vague idea of what you want us to say.

It's like the '60s! Look! Look, we say to one another, at the
imbalances, the glaring flaws of the world, aghast, amazed. Look
how things are! Look at how, for instance, there are all these homeless people! Look at how they have to defecate all over the streets,
where we have to walk! Look at how high rents are! Look at how
the banks charge these hidden fees when you use their ATMs! And
Ticketmaster! Have you heard about these service charges? How if
you charge your tickets over the phone, they charge you, like, $2
for every goddamn ticket? Have you heard about this? It's *completely
fucking ridiculous.*

But soon it will be okay. When we begin publishing, and put
in the six months or so until world domination, these things will
be addressed, redressed. We look at portfolios. As I sit down with
a comely photographer named Debra, I see not only a possible dating possibility, but also an image that immediately screams the
theme song of our message. In her book is a picture of a stark
naked man streaking across a beach, blurry with speed.

"This is the cover!" I say.

"Okay!" she says, and I wonder if this will help my chances with her.

The streaker on the cover spawns another idea: We, too, will be naked! Yes, on the cover will be Debra's streaking boyfriend (a live-in, alas) and on the inside will be hundreds of streaking young people! We will imitate the light and look of the first one, but aha! it'll be hundreds of us, all running together on the beach, a herd of bare and hopeful flesh, sprinting from left to right, of course symbolizing all the things that that would obviously symbolize. We call Debra and set it up and then start calling about for naked models—we call friends, everyone we know.

The idea gets scaled back. We don't need hundreds. (How could we have fit hundreds in the frame, anyhow?) We only need a few people, ten maybe, eight, five. Of course we'll be there, for starters. So Moodie, Marny, and me. Now to diversify. We are obsessed with seeming diverse. Not in terms of actually having an incredibly diverse staff or anything—but in terms of appearing diverse, thus when photo opportunities arise, we panic. We *must* look like the perfect cross section of young America! For the cameras we need three men and three women; three whites, one black, one Latino, one Asian— But instead we have just us, three/four white people (*and not even a Jew!*). For the naked shoot we need an African-American, a Latino. A Latina. Whatever. We need somebody Asian. Lily says no. Ed, a circulation expert guy we know at *Wired*, who is black, says no. Desperate, we wonder: would Shalini, being Indian, pass for a more well-known minority? Would she show up in a blurry picture as clearly *of color*?

"Will you—"

"No," she answers.

We call June.

June Lomena is our black friend. She works occasionally in the building, for one of the other magazines, had stopped by to say hi one day, and had subsequently written something oblique about male-female relationships for the first issue. And did we mention she's black? (She also might be Latina, we think, because of the name and all, but then we do not ask.) She is by training (at Brown) an actress and so when we ask her to run around naked, she readily says yes. So there are four of us. Everyone else we know refuses. We finally find one more guy, through a friend, who we figure will be good because his head is shaved.

"We can't pay you," we say.

"That's okay," he says.

We do not know why he wants to do this, to get in a car with four strangers and run naked on a beach and be photographed doing it, and come to think of it, we do not want to know.

So then we are on the beach, Black Sands Beach in the Marin Headlands, on an unseasonably cold October morning. We have just become naked, and have noticed that, right where the fifth guy's regular penis is supposed to be, there is a penis with a gold thing through it. Like a needle, or a nail or something—it's hard to tell without staring. When I glance at it I feel woozy. As a reverent and terrified Catholic I hadn't seen my penis until my teens, hadn't touched it until college, so to see this, which I didn't even know was being done— I turn my attention to Marny's breasts, which look different unclothed than clothed, and, come to think of it, are kind of uneven. June looks normal, lithe and strong, certainly the only one among us with everything perfectly in place. Then I try to discern if Moodie's penis is noticeably bigger than mine, and decide that at least flaccid, it's a draw. Just about. Good. Good.

We are young and naked and on the beach!

Debra gets set up, sitting on a log, facing the water. We get a twenty-yard head start and then we run past her, along the shore, at full sprint. We try to space ourselves out so when we pass her we will be spread out, everyone visible, all colors and sizes. It will be beautiful and poetic and it hurts like a motherfucker. Our penises flop up and down, and then as we pick up speed, slap left to right, back and forth—who would have thought left to right? The pain! People should not do this. Penises were not built for running. I think of a distended muffler scraping the pavement; I think of a bird shaking the life out of a worm— The agony is ridiculous. We run past her, she gets maybe two frames off, and then we do it again. A dozen times at least. I begin to hold my penis for the majority of the run, letting go only when passing directly in front of her. I can't imagine what it's like for the pierced-penis guy. It's definitely not helping to keep it in place. If he had some kind of hookup, like to his navel—

We do one where we run away from Debra and straight into the water, which is frigid, as always. Then we get dressed and go home. When we get the pictures back we are all hopelessly blurry, and the pertinent demographic efforts we have made—two women, one black—are barely visible. All the running past her pictures are unusable, meaning that all the penis abuse was for naught. We are left with the last picture, that which shows all of our bare asses, running into the Pacific. We use that one.

It is the last picture of the first issue's opening six-page spread, a visual montage that precedes the manifesto reprinted earlier. Each page has a grid of sorts, with photographs abutting each other. And over each picture is typeset a word. To wit:

Over a picture of a spoiled-looking young woman: Nope.[1]

Over a display of guns for sale: Nope.[2]

Over two Kewpie dolls in marriage gear: Nope.[3]

Over a televangelist extolling his flock: Nope.[4]

Over a detail of the *Rape of the Sabine Women*: Nope.[5]

Over a close-up of a young man sneering: Nope.[6]

Over a bunch of women's high-heeled business shoes: Nope.[7]

Over a close-up of a collar and tie: Nope.[8]

Over Adam and Eve being expelled from the Garden: Nope.[9]

We are fairly convinced that what we have here is a work of such powerful genius and prophecy that it may very well start riots. Should the meaning prove elusive, a key:

¹ We are *not* spoiled and lazy!

² We do *not* think guns should be sold at counters

³ We are *not* for marriage.

⁴ Or religion.

⁵ And we're *definitely* against rape.

⁶ And sneering.

⁷ *And* heels.

⁸ Same with ties.

⁹ And also being expelled by God from gardens. Or being ashamed of being naked. Or eating apples. [This last one was unclear.]

Then, in the spread, after all this negativity, all the things that we reject out of hand, is the kicker, the finale: a full-page photo of five people running, naked, their backs to the camera, into the ocean. Over that picture, emblazoned in black against the sky (this is in black and white), is one word: Might.

Boom!

In general, we are sure that we are on to something epochal, and our work hours reflect this. They are tests of will and examples of the deleterious effects of peer-pressure and guilt, because as non-traditional as we clearly are, we begin to keep standard daylight hours, nine to five, and add to them two or three bonus rounds, depending on what needs, for the sake of ourselves and mankind, to get done by the next day.

It must be done! Waiting is obscene!

During the day Moodie and I do our graphic design work, primarily for the *San Francisco Chronicle*'s internal promotions department. Moodie is still doing other marketing work, and I am still temping, usually at the Pac Bell headquarters in San Ramon, where I spend eight-hour days designing certificates commemorat-

ing exemplary achievement (fig. 3). Marny is waitressing four
nights a week, but increasingly, our bills are being paid by the
Chronicle, the heads of which
took pity on me early on—
the eyes of Dianne Levy, a
single mother of a teenaged
daughter, welled up when I
told her that I, too, had a
youngster at home—and
now they count on us to do
ads, posters, and campaigns
that promote the paper's

fig. 3

various sections and columnists. We do the work with the radiant
acuity for which we are known.

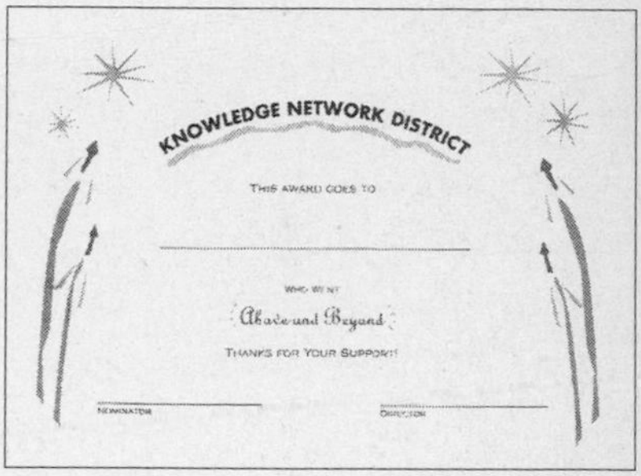

"We need an ad for the business section," they say.

Sure, we say. The result:

THE CHRONICLE. MAKE IT YOUR BUSINESS.

"Now one for the sports section."

CHRONICLE SPORTS. WE KNOW THE SCORE.

We are tired of such misuse of our creative powers, and have
decided that we will not wait to raise money this way to fund
Might. While we tell anyone who asks that *Might* was started on
overworked credit cards, on the runoff from our graphic design
business, the terrible, unspeakable truth is that I simply wrote a
check. It was about ten thousand dollars for the first print bill,
constituting a hulking portion of the insurance and house money
that came my way after the estate was settled. I thought, at first,
that we should tell everyone the truth. What better metaphor for
our endeavor? Rising from the ashes—literally—of our parents,
this smallish amount of money enabling us to do it the way we
want, to save us from having to sell the idea to others, to raise
money, or to abandon it altogether when it would become
obvious—as it surely would—that no one would put such funds

behind such a ridiculous enterprise. But this way there is no waiting for approval. This way there are no strings. Moodie and Marny
know that this is how the magazine has been funded, but no one
else is told, ever. Maybe they wouldn't understand; maybe they
would understand all too well. After that first investment, though,
future contributions will be minimal, as the operation begins
almost immediately to pay for itself, though hopes for it paying *us*
are very dim and far away. Then again, things could change quickly.
Things could turn around if, say, we weren't just a bunch of anony-
mous half-wits putting out an underfunded zine...but, rather, the
same half-wits, admittedly, but one of whom was the star of a
widely watched and wildly influential MTV real-life-revealing
television phenomenon?

We get applications.

Marny and I decide we'll both apply. We fill out the short
questionnaires. As required, we both make videotapes of ourselves
talking and doing something that we hope they will find diverting. Some people skateboard. Some tap-dance, introduce their
families, play with their dogs. For mine, I sit at my desk in the
warehouse, and Moodie videotapes me as I talk about nothing and
then, kind of suddenly, I start drumming, epileptically. I do a
routine where I'm the drummer for Loverboy, who for some reason
couldn't drum without blinking and twitching like he was sitting
on loose wiring. The videotape is kind of funny, we think. It's
likely more scary than funny, but Moodie laughs. We send it in.

Two days later a woman, Laura, calls. She is one of the show's
producers or casting agents or whatever, and she has obviously rec-
ognized me as the sort of person who belongs on TV, inspiring a
nation of disaffected youth. I am to go into the new *Real World*
headquarters for an interview, half an hour or so, which will also be
videotaped.

· · ·

The interview is on a Sunday. As Toph is still sleeping, I drive in from Berkeley, over the bridge, miles above the water, to the makeshift MTV offices in North Beach, next to the Embarcadero and, appropriately enough, lodged among a good portion of the city's ad agencies. I am filled with pride and terror. Of course I wanted to be asked to audition, wanted them to see all there is to see in me, but I had no real intention of following through with it all. And now that I'm actually going through with it, I'm petrified someone—Beth, Toph, David Milton—will find out. I convince myself that this is just for sociological or journalistic reasons. What a funny story this will make! But really: Am I just curious? Or do I want this? And if I did want this, what sort of person am I?

When I arrive, the neighborhood is deserted and I am twenty minutes early. Because people who appear on MTV are not early, are not anxious and responsible enough to be early, I walk around until it's time. When I'm two minutes late, I walk in. The office, only a few weeks old, already has, over the receptionist's desk, a huge, perfect MTV logo fashioned from corrugated steel. As I wait, the young assistants chat with me, attempting to make me feel comfortable. While waiting and chatting, I realize that, duh, I'm already auditioning. I begin to think harder about my words, making them more memorable, wanting to be at once fun, cutting edge, soulful and midwestern. I notice my legs; they're crossed. But how to cross my legs? The guy-guy way or the women's–older man's way? If I do the latter, will they think I'm gay? Will that help?

Then a woman walks in—*glides* in. She looks down at me. She is my mother, my girlfriend, my wife. It is Laura, the producer/casting person who called. She has an Ali MacGraw look about her—her skin lightly tanned, her eyes dark, with straight, milk-chocolate hair, soft on her shoulders, a velvet curtain touching a velvet stage.

She invites me into another room, where she will conduct the interview. I follow. I am ready to give myself to her. She will listen and when she listens, she will know. But my hair is probably all wrong. I meant to check it in the bathroom beforehand but didn't get a chance. Ridiculous. On what could be the most important day ever, for me, for my hair, I leave it to chance—and if I asked to check it now, she'd think I was vain, self-conscious—and we can't let her get the wrong idea. Of course, maybe she wants someone vain. I could be the Vain Person. There's always someone vain. Of course, they're usually models. I could never qualify, never— Unless I was one of those Benetton models, strange and homely. I could do that. Odd-looking, but defiantly so—like the heroin people, or the ones with freckles and huge hair. That could be me—

Oh look at her. More than I want to be on Laura's show I want to settle down with her, to raise a family with her, on ten or so acres on the North Carolina coast. We'll have a dog named Skipper. We'll cook together, for her parents, for the neighbors. Have a crowd of kids that look not like me but like her, with strong, delicate features, that wonderful nose—

"Okay," she says, sitting down behind the video camera.

The tape starts, the red light, everything.

"Where did you grow up?" she asks.

"Oh. I know this. A little suburb of Chicago, Lake Forest. It's about thirty miles north—"

"I know Lake Forest."

"Really?" I say, feeling a format change coming, one where quotation marks fall away and a simple interview turns into something else, something *entirely so much more.* "It's just a little suburb, about seventeen thousand people. I'm surprised that—"

Please. Lake Forest is one of these towns, like Greenwich or Scarsdale—I mean, isn't this one of the wealthiest towns in America?

Is it? I guess it is. I guess. I don't know. But I didn't know any rich people. We weren't rich. My friends' parents were teachers, sold medical supplies, ran frame shops... My parents drove used cars, my mother bought all of our clothes at Marshall's. That kind of thing. We were on what I guess would have been the town's lower socioeconomic half.

What did your parents do?
My mother didn't work until I was about twelve. Then she was a teacher. Montessori. My father was a lawyer, a commodities-oriented lawyer in Chicago. Futures trading.

And your siblings?
My sister's in law school at Cal. My brother Bill works at a think tank in L.A.

What does that mean?
Well, he started out at the Heritage Foundation, traveling eastern Europe, advising the former Soviet republics, whatever they're called, on conversion to free-market economies, et cetera et cetera. Then he wrote a book about downsizing government here, at the local level. It's called *Revolution at the Roots: Making Government Smaller, Better, and Closer to Home.* You should see it. It's even got a quote from Newt Gingrich right there on the cover; something to the effect that all Americans, if they're good Americans, should read this book.

I take it you two don't talk politics much.
No, not too much.

And did you have money growing up?
I don't know. Sometimes. Sometimes not. We were never really lacking for anything, but my mom had a way of making us feel like we were just scraping by. "You're driving us to the poorhouse!" she would yell, usually to our dad but also to anyone, to no one in particular. We never really knew what was going on, but it would be

ridiculous to complain. We lived in a house in this nice town, had
our own bedrooms, clothes, food, toys, went on vacation in
Florida—though we always drove, mind you. We all worked from
the time we were thirteen or so, all summer, Bill and I cut lawns,
Beth was up at the Baskin-Robbins in brown cords, of course had
to buy our own sad, short-lived used cars, Rabbits and rusty
Camaros, all went to public schools, state schools for college. So no,
I wouldn't think of us as having much money—there was certainly
never anything saved, we found that out when they died...

Hmm.
So am I on?

What do you mean?
Did I make the show? Am I on?

Wait a second. We just started.
Oh.

So did you feel different—were there social divisions based on wealth?
Hardly. But if there were, it was an inverse relationship. The kids
who acted and dressed like they had money were outcasts, were
pitied, weren't really allowed to be popular. It's just like anywhere—children in public schools are trained, have it pounded
into them by their peers, that to stand out is to attract possibly
unfavorable attention. So being obviously wealthy was the same as
being too tall, too fat, having a boil on your neck. We all gravitated
toward the middle. This was the case all through school—the
richest kids were usually seen as the wannabes, were the most
desperate, were constantly throwing parties to get the attention of
kids whom everyone really envied, like the guy on the football
team who lived in the old wooden house behind the high school.
The popular kids drove trucks, bought the shittiest cars, had

parents who were divorced or drunk or both, who lived far from the areas considered desirable. The rich kids, like the ones whose shirts were always tucked in, whose hair was always just so, or those who went to the private schools in town, were considered hopeless, troubled, eccentric. I mean, can you imagine being in a town like Lake Forest, with these excellent public schools—and still blowing ten grand a year to send your kid to a school called Country Day? These were the freaks. You know what we called that school?

No.
It was pretty funny.

What did you call it?
Country Gay.

{—}
Country *Gay*. Get it? Country *Gay*?

This was a fairly intolerant town.
Homogeneous, yes; intolerant, no. It was overwhelmingly white, of course, but racism of any kind—at least outwardly expressed—is kind of gauche, so we basically grew up without any sense of prejudice, firsthand or even in the abstract. With the kind of wealth and isolation we had from societal sorts of issues—crime, outside of the vandalism perpetrated by me and my friends, was unheard of—the town was free to see those kinds of things as a kind of entertainment—wrestling matches being contested by other people, in other places. The only instance I ever knew of any truly bigoted stuff was when I was in grade school and this one thin, geek-looking kid with glasses moved in down the street and on the corner, and in his room he hung one of those flags, the southern flag...

The Confederate flag.
Right. So this kid, who was my brother's age, three years older, moved in when I was about nine, and almost immediately turned everything upside down. First, on the bus, my brother Bill saw him draw a swastika on the back of a seat. None of us had ever seen, firsthand, something like that, and thus it became the big story for a while. *An actual racist!* Then, the kid started an informal kind of club, converting—sorry, bad word—a little group of other kids from the neighborhood, and then they all started drawing swastikas on their notebooks, and using the word that people use for these purposes.

What word?
I might get it wrong. The word is kike, right?

Yes.
Is that k-y or k-i?

I think k-i.
Huh. I would have thought k-y. But so, suddenly, that was a word kids were using. We were this enclave of civilization, suddenly corrupted by—it was backward, in a way, with the arrival of this sort of missionary of bigotry... Anyway, one of the neighborhood kids, this guy Todd Golub, was up until this time friends with the rest of the neighborhood kids, but then suddenly he was *Jewish*! And immediately he was off-limits. Of course, I didn't ever hear much of it myself. These guys were older, my brother Bill's age, so I'd hear small bits from Bill, and even then the information was discouraged, my parents not wanting us really to know anything about it at all. "Bad kids," my mom said, and that was that. We knew absolutely nothing. I didn't know any profanity, knew nothing about sex, anything. I was twelve when I realized "balls" referred to testicles, and not the two cheeks of your butt. Don't

laugh. I was terrorized for that kind of thing. At that point, I had the Catholic knowledge of my own anatomy, meaning none at all—

I digress. So Bill tried to hold on to these kids as friends in some way, hoping this swastika stuff was just some temporary viral thing. But just from what I knew, I started having these elaborate fantasies about what went on in the kid's house. Whenever we'd drive by, I'd crane my neck back, looking for that big Confederate flag. You could actually see it pretty easily, it covered the entire window of the kid's room, draped so it sagged in the middle. I had no idea what to think, how deep it ran in that house, so when we drove by, I half expected to see him and his dad out in front, burning crosses, hooded men tossing nooses over tree branches. I really did. We had no frame of reference. This kid was exotic in the same way that the kids who lived in apartments were. I just had no way to process the information. Our town was rigid in many ways, in terms of the uniformity of things, the colors of skin, the makes of cars, the lushness of the lawns, but on top of that it was sort of a blank canvas so—and again, I guess this is true of any child—I was ready to quickly accept the sudden and total substitutions of all I knew to be true.

What about black kids?
We had a few. Maybe four, five at a time. Growing up, in grade school, there was Jonathan Hutchinson. He lived on Old Elm Road, an east-west thoroughfare that acted as the border between Lake Forest and Highland Park, not far from our house; he was okay. A sort of awkward kid, but nice enough. Then he moved away and for a while there weren't any black kids. Then Mr. T moved in.

Mr. T?
Yeah, this was, God, I think we were in junior high, or just in high school, and it was after *The A-Team* had been off the air for a year

or two when we heard about it—Jesus, then it was all anyone could talk about. The town was still reeling from *Ordinary People* being filmed there and all—there were all these pictures of Robert Redford at the McDonald's—but we never had anyone on the level of a Mr. T. I mean, at the time he was still this massive star; I forget what he was doing right then, maybe between series or something, you know how hard that can be, but still this huge star. He moved into this enormous place on Green Bay Road, easily ten acres or so, with a gate, and a big brick wall facing the street. The place was right near town, a few doors down from our church, St. Mary's.

And how was his arrival met?
We lost our brains. Our world exploded. We fucking loved it. The kids, that is. I mean, *The A-Team* had been by far our favorite show—we threw *A-Team* parties, used to run around the seventh grade cafeteria singing the theme song—*Duh duh duh DUH! Duh duh duh...dududududuh!*—while spraying the girls' table with imaginary fire. But our parents, I think now, in retrospect, were a bit more cautiously enthusiastic. First of all, those with money don't want to seem impressed by fame, especially ill-gotten fame, which is what I assume was the thinking in T's case. You don't mind if I just call him T?

Not at all.
After all, this guy was a bouncer when he was discovered. And of course he didn't help matters when he started cutting down all the trees.

I think I remember this.
It made news all over. It was a scandal. Here you had this supposedly uptight white town, and then this large black man with the gold chains and the mohawk comes in and takes this chain saw, and

cuts down, literally, all but about two trees on his property—about two hundred of them, probably, all in plain daylight, by himself, with the chain saw. It was incredible. The nerve! He said he was allergic. But that didn't really fly. See, this was a town that really took pride in its trees. And for good reason; we had some nice god-damn trees. We had the signs all over: "Tree City, U.S.A." We loved those signs. So then he cuts down all these trees and everything, and no one really knows what to say, because they want to condemn him—and some did—but the vast majority of people were kind of afraid of looking racist, or like poor sports or something—this was a place where the black janitor got a *standing ovation* when he sang "Deep River" in the talent show—so everyone eventually just sat back and watched. My dad thought the whole thing was hilarious, loved reading about the debate, giggled wildly about it. "Oh fantastic," he'd say, whenever the town was being embarrassed by the Chicago newspapers. He never identified with Lake Forest, had no friends in town, didn't drive the right kind of car—

So we actually saw him once, Mr. T, when we were on our way to church, saw him right there, in front of his gate, with the chain saw. Amazing. He was doing the shrubs.

How was it that we started talking about all this?
Black kids. Well, he had two daughters, and they went to the high school. So when they showed up, they immediately doubled the black student population, brought it up to four students. I think it was four.

How many kids were in your high school?
About thirteen hundred.

And this is only twenty-odd miles from Chicago.
Right, and there was actually a town to the north, maybe five miles away, called North Chicago, which was mostly black. I think.

How do you mean, you think?
Well, I've never been there or anything. I have been to Highland
Park, that's the Jewish town, and used to buy beer in Highwood,
which was where all the Italian restaurants were, and where all the
Mexican men who cut lawns lived. And there was a mall in
Waukegan, I think—always full of sailors—and Libertyville was
where the kids with the hockey haircuts lived.

So how were Mr. T's girls treated?
Everyone seemed to like them, as far as I could tell. They were supposedly very nice, and kind of funny, but I didn't know them at all,
didn't (and don't) even know their names, actually—they were a
year younger. They were always driving around in that white
Mercedes of theirs—all customized, with those plates: Mr. T 3.
But everyone liked them okay. They were Mr. T's kids, after all,
and as such were a source of great pride for the school, at least as
far as us kids went. It was the first thing we told anyone, really.
That and about *Ordinary People.*

They were the only black kids?
The only other black kid I remember was a guy in my sister's class,
this guy Steve, whose last name I don't know, never did. Not that
I would really know much about anyone in my sister's class, but
the thing with Steve was that, because he was the only black guy
in their class, he was known simply as Steve the Black Guy.

Pardon?
Yeah, to hear my sister tell it, that was basically his name in all
contexts. His *handle*, if you will. He was just this average guy, not
incredibly popular, but nice enough. And so people liked him, and
people I guess thought it was this odd novelty that he was different, odd in the same way that it was odd how that one kid had a
crewcut, or how that one girl, I forget her name, she hung out with

the basketball players—what *was* her name? She was a dwarf. But so he was Steve the Black Guy.

So this was oppressive.
How do you mean? No.

Did you like it?
Yes. I did. Many did not. Many complain about it. Many are ashamed to say that's where they grew up—people in Chicago, in Champaign, can be rough when you tell them; they'll bow, kiss your hand—but I won't apologize for having been brought up in what was, at least in my part of town, a pretty simple suburb— trees and a creek, nice parks. It's not like we had a choice, that at eight or nine, whenever, we could have left home, moved some- where less horribly fraught with this hideous prosperity. I should say, though, that like any seemingly stable and contented context, one with a certain stability and attention to detail and respect for family—comfortable but deeply midwestern, this was—at the same time, it was very quiet sometimes, oddly quiet, and under- neath the quiet there was the tiniest, faintest sound, like air being let out of a narrow hole, a sound like someone screaming from worlds away, and people were dying in dark and bewildering ways.

How do you mean?
Oh, suicides, weird accidents. One kid I knew growing up was apparently in the basement poking around and a stack of wood fell on him. He suffocated. That was our first death. He was ten maybe. Then, like two years later, Ricky's dad.

Ricky's dad?
Ricky was one of my best friends, lived just across the creek—it ran just behind both of our houses—and he and Jeff Farlander and I used to do stuff together, were on the same swim team, every-

thing. It was strange across the creek. Most of the things we did together involved some sort of vandalism, come to think of it, throwing stuff at cars—ice, rocks, crabapples, acorns, snowballs—

In retrospect I have no idea why. Did we resent the passing of these cars? We were bored, and loved the thump of a projectile hitting a passing car, truck, whatever. It kept escalating. First just the throwing of things, then, one winter, we built, using seven or eight full-size snow boulders we rolled from fresh snow, a complete snow wall in the road. We lined them up, packed them together, and watched from the bushes, giddy, giggling. It was a three-foot tall, three-foot deep wall, right on Valley Road, created, because we were very bright and the police knew our handiwork, right in front of Jeff's house. It worked as designed, though, with drivers either stopping and turning around, or stupidly plowing through it, underestimating the wall's depth and craftsmanship.

"There goes the transmission," Jeff would say.

"Yep," I would say, having no idea what he was talking about. I knew nothing about cars.

One summer, we went further. We had always done stuff with lighters and gasoline, lighting this or that. The usual object was to soak a tennis ball in gasoline, light it, and kick it around the street.

"Fireball!" we would yell. "Fireball!" "Fireball!" "Fireball!"

Guess what we called that game?

I give up.
We called that game Fireball.

I see.
But one night a fourth kid, Timmy Rogers, a rangy, stringy-haired kid a year older than us, had the idea that what we'd do, see, would be to take the gasoline and… pour it across the *street*, and then— But we didn't have any matches. Someone would have to go home and quietly get some, not arousing suspicion. But as we were fig-

uring out who would go, and who might have those long-stemmed barbecue matches, Timmy Rogers just took out his lighter, a tiny Bic lighter, leaned down to the gas-soaked pavement — by this point I was literally jumping out of range — and lit the thing, the whole street going up at once. Incredible, flames five feet high, the streets of Lake Forest burning! It didn't last long, not at all, but long enough to attract the police, who came and poked around as we chuckled in the bushes. *We lit the street on fire!* Then we went back to Jeff's and watched *Used Cars* for the sixth time.

What does this have to do with Ricky's dad?
Oh. It was a clear day, in the early summer. I was at home, building a Martian city out of Legos, matching it to the intricate architectural plans I had drawn out in my sketchbook, next to my drawings of flying dinosaurs and friendly aliens with big feet. I had all the foundations laid out, on the gray cratered baseplates I had gotten for my birthday. Then Jeff called and said we had better go over to Ricky's because something terrible had happened.

"What happened?"

"Ricky's dad doused himself with gasoline and lit a match and then ran around the yard on fire, and then stopped running and then had died right there, in front of the house."

I told my mom, then walked down the street to the dead end part, jumped across the creek where it was shallow, went over to Jeff's, and then we walked to Ricky's. He was in the family room, watching TV. His family room was like ours, wood paneled and dark. He said hi. We said hi. There was one of the early music video shows on—this was before MTV—and they were showing a video for a Bob Dylan song called "Jokerman." We liked the video. There were things hurtling toward the screen, like in 3-D. I had just started reading *Rolling Stone*, and had heard of this Bob Dylan, and knew if I was to know anything I had to know and like Bob Dylan, and so I really wanted to like the song, but then Ricky beat me to it.

"I like this song," Ricky said.

I was kind of pissed. I decided to let it go.

Ricky's two little sisters, much younger, floated in and out of the room from time to time. We watched more TV, sitting close to it.

"What did it look like?" Jeff asked. I couldn't believe he asked.

"You know what it looked like?" Ricky said. "It was like at the end of *Raiders of the Lost Ark*."

We knew just the part, the very end, where the Nazis open the Ark of the Covenant and the spirits come out, the spirits that are at first pleasant and beautiful but then turn angry, and flames come from the Ark and kill all the Nazis, impaling them with stiff ropes of fire where they stand, and then the head Nazis, one by one, melt like wax dummies, the skin then cartilage then blood running off their skulls, in order, like differently colored waters. It both terrified and fascinated us.

Wow, we thought. *Raiders of the Lost Ark.*

We sat with Ricky, sat there for a while watching TV, and then got bored and went out into the front yard to see if there were any marks anywhere on the grass, or blood or anything. But there was nothing. The lawn looked perfect, lush and green.

And why are you telling me this?
I don't know. These are the stories I tell. Isn't that what you're looking for? These terrible deaths tearing through this pristine community, all the more strange and tragic given the context, the incongruity—

So tell me something: This isn't really a transcript of the interview, is it?
No.

It's not much like the actual interview at all, is it?
Not that much, no.

This is a device, this interview style. Manufactured and fake.
It is.

It's a good device, though. Kind of a catchall for a bunch of anecdotes that would be too awkward to force together otherwise.
Yes.

And the point of the anecdotes again?
Well, the point of the stuff about Lake Forest should be fairly obvious. It grounds us in a certain world, in a world that will be familiar to many people, especially those who've had the privilege of seeing *Ordinary People*, with Timothy Hutton in a breakthrough role. Best Picture, 1980. The passages describing suicides are formative experiences, of course, which foreshadow both my assumption that I and those I know can be reasonably expected to die in absurd and dramatic ways, and also foreshadows things that happen in the second half of the book. The stuff about race and ethnicity is supposed to make clear the kind of context we grew up in, where there was an incredible sort of homogeneity, where we were deeply embedded into that, in contrast to Toph and me in Berkeley, where there's this outrageous kind of diversity, though within which, ironically enough, we still feel very strange, outside the mainstream—so that's about inclusion and exclusion. The anecdote about Sarah—

Sarah? Who's Sarah?
Oh. I meant to get that in earlier. Let me do that quickly:

We found out about my mom's situation, in between my junior and senior years in college, having been gathered by Dad in the family room. That summer was just a mess. I did some weird things, that summer and that fall. Lots of just simple drinking-based things, and some breaking of things, the clawing at the walls while dreaming, and I started going home from parties in strange cars, drinking with not-good friends. One humid summer night I went to this one party, at this guy Andrew Wagner's place. He lived in an old wooden house, across the highway, kind of remote, and he used to have these massive parties, the outdoor sort that were hard to have in Lake Forest, with so many alert and vigilant police officers at work. And I went there with Marny and a bunch of her friends—they figure in a little later, when I go back home to look for my parents—and drank a lot, keg beer in shiny red cups, the thick kind with the white inside. Soon—it seemed soon, but probably wasn't—the people I came with were leaving. Marny asked me if I wanted a ride, but I said no, that I was talking to Jeff Farlander, that I'd stay. I was talking to Farlander for the first time in years. We had grown up together; I had stayed at his house for days at a time. His house was the first place we went when things were bad at home, his mother was the closest thing to an aunt—

You know what I mean. Jeff and I had drifted in high school, but at this party, Andrew Wagner's party, under the withering porch lights and both of us full of keg-pulled Schaefer, we caught up, punched each other in the arm, everything. When the party was moving from Wagner's to this bar called McCormick's, Jeff and I decided that I'd be going with him.

"You'll come with me," he said.

"Yeah, yeah," I said. I wanted to be eleven again, with him, throwing eggs at cars. But then, as we were walking to his car, I ruined it and said, "Jeff, my mom's dying." Just threw it out before I knew what I was doing—

No, that's not right, I knew what I was thinking, had thought of it, had been thinking of telling him all night, as we talked under the porch light, because he knew her, was there from the beginning—but I kind of sprung it when we were walking to the car, and he slowed down, and in his scratchy voice, scratchy even when we were very young, said, "I know."

And so on the way to the car we were both crying, but just for a second, and then we got in his car and drove on the highway through town, past Lake Forest and Lake Bluff, and to McCormick's, a roadhouse sort of bar on the way to Libertyville and Waukegan. The lot was full. Everyone, from football players to their hangers-on and anyone, really, had been coming here for years. I had never been.

Inside it was full, and I was struck by the fear that if Jeff knew, everyone there would know. There would be silence, gasping. Snickering. But no one said anything. We walked in and there was that one stout, apple-cheeked guy bartending, Jimmy Walker. There was that Hartenstine guy, huge, older, who once played for the Bears.

And there was Sarah Mulhern. Oh, oh.

We had almost grown up together, Sarah and I, had been on the same swim team when I was nine and she was eleven, were on that swim team for some years after. But we had never once spoken. She was older and a better swimmer. And a much better diver. I was a liability to that swim team, to the diving team. I was a slow swimmer and a hapless diver, wouldn't do an inward, couldn't even pull off a one-and-a-half. She could do it all—inwards, one-and-a-halfs, doubles, back one-and-a-halfs, whatever—always with her legs together and toes pointed and the little splash at the end. She was on the medley relay, always won her heats, was the name everyone knew, the name that was broadcast over the loudspeakers. But I never talked to her. Not in junior high or high school, the two years that separated us were too many, and her hair was too straight and blonde, and I had not yet developed the tools to mentally or physically handle the sort of curves she was working with.

But then there she was, Sarah Mulhern, at the bar, and I have no idea how I began talking to her, or much of what we said, but then Jeff was gone and I was getting into the backseat of a car with Sarah, driven by Sarah's friend. The car smelled of smoke and old vinyl. Sarah smoked.

Then we were in her bed, in her parents' big house, and there was some of this and that but I passed out before—

I woke up in a canopy bed, and she was already awake, watching me. The furniture and walls were drenched in yellow-white, as if not only the walls but the air itself had been painted. We sat on her floor and talked about grade school, about the retarded kids who we were told to treat kindly, who would die young. We played records, talked about the fall—she was trying to be a teacher, had gotten her certificate and was doing some tutoring.

Then we snuck out through the garage—her parents were home—and she drove me home. As we sat in my driveway, I wanted to say so many things—that I was actually dating someone else, Kirsten, and that what I had done was a mistake, a terrible crime, that I had slipped because I was confused—

But then I saw a figure through the window, someone sitting up in the family room looking at us, and didn't want to explain about my mother to Sarah and didn't want to explain Sarah to my mother so—

We kissed quickly and I jumped out.

That's Sarah.
Yes. You know, the great thing is that this format makes sense, in a way, because an interview where I opened all this up to a stranger with a video camera actually did take place—MTV could conceivably still have the tape (the application had said: "We will not be able to return the tape to you and a portion of it could end up being aired in conjunction with the series. Your signature on the application gives us the right to do this")—and besides, squeezing all these things into the Q&A makes complete the transition from the book's first half, which is slightly less self-conscious, to the second half, which is increasingly self-devouring. Because, see, I think what my town, and your show, reflect so wonderfully is that the main by-product of the comfort and prosperity that I'm describing

is a sort of pure, insinuating solipsism, that in the absence of struggle against anything in the way of a common enemy—whether that's poverty, Communists, whatever—all we can do, or rather, all those of us with a bit of self-obsession can do—

Wait a second, how many of you do you think are so self-obsessed?
All the good ones. Or rather, there's actually two ways the self-obsession manifests itself: those that turn it inward, and those that turn it outward. For instance, I have this friend John who just channels it all inward—he talks about his problems, his girlfriend, his poor prospects, how his parents died, on and on, to the point of paralysis—he literally isn't interested in anything else. It's his whole world, the endless exploration of his dark mind, this haunted house of a brain.

And the other kind?
The people who think their personality is so strong, their story so interesting, that others must know it and learn from it.

Let me guess here, you—.
Well, I pretend that I'm the latter, but I'm really the former, and desperately so. But still, my feeling is that if you're not self-obsessed you're probably boring. Not that you can always tell the self-obsessed. The best sort of self-obsessed person isn't outwardly so. But they're doing something more public than not, making sure people know that they're doing it, or will know about it sooner or later. I guarantee that the applicants for *The Real World*—I guarantee that if you put all these tapes in a time capsule and opened it in twenty years, you'd find that these are the people who are, in one way or another, running the world—at the very least, they'll be the most visible segment of the demographic. Because we've grown up thinking of ourselves in relation to the political-media-entertainment ephemera, in our safe and comfort-

able homes, given the time to think about how we would fit into this or that band or TV show or movie, and how we would look doing it. These are people for whom the idea of anonymity is existentially irrational, indefensible. And thus, there is a lot of talking about it all—surely the cultural output of this time will reflect that—there'll be a lot of talking, whole movies full of talking, talking about talking, ruminating about talking about wondering, about our place, our wants and obligations—the blathering of the belle epoque, you know. Environmentally reinforced solipsism.

Solipsism.
Of course. It's inevitable, it's ubiquitous. You see it, right? I mean, am I the only one seeing the solipsism?

That was a joke.
Yes, yes. So.

So. What do you think you can offer the show?
Well see, I've thought a lot about this, and I'm figuring I've got it happening two ways: first, I can be the Tragic Guy. Second, we've got this magazine.

Right. Now what's it called again?
Might.

M-i-t-e?
No, M-i-g-h-t. Everyone spells it M-i-t-e. It's ridiculous. Why would it be named after a bug? Mite is such an obscure word, compared to Might, right?

Well, what is *it named after?*
Well, it's a double entendre, see—you'll love this, this is great, it

can mean two things at once, can sit right on the fence between two meanings—with, in this case, "Might" meaning both *power* and *possibility*.

Oooh.
Yeah. I know. It's good.

And what's it about?
Well, see, that's what's great—it'll be this perfect match. It's geared to the same demographic that you're reaching. We're trying to make clear that we aren't just a bunch of people sitting around farting and watching MTV. I mean, not that there's anything wrong with MTV, really, but—you know what I mean. So yeah, I get on the show, the show films us putting this magazine together, reaching millions, defining the zeitgeist, inspiring the world's youth to greatness.

Do you work a lot?
Yes.

How much?
I don't know, maybe seventy hours a week. A hundred maybe. I don't know. We all do. We punish ourselves for our comfortable childhoods. Marny probably more than all of us—she waitresses at a restaurant in Oakland, one in San Francisco, but still keeps up with the rest of us... But that's good, right? Young people, working hard to, you know, achieve their dreams, striving for greatness. That's good TV, yes?

Well...
Or not. We're flexible. I mean, I could work less. I could work part-time. I could let the other people do most of the work. Whatever. You tell me.

Well, that would be something we'd have to talk about.
Right. Does that mean I've got the part? I've got it, right? Don't
I shine through the fog of the rest of these loser applicants? All
these boring people? I mean, isn't it all perfectly clear now? Don't
you want the Tragic Person?

The Tragic Person.
Right. There's seven cast members, right?

Yes.
So, let's work this out. First, you'll get a black person, maybe two—
they'll be hip-hop singers or rappers or whatever—and then you'll
get a couple of really great-looking people, who will be nice to look
at but completely ignorant and prone to terrible faux pas of taste
and ignorance, their presence serving two purposes: they a) look
wonderful on screen, and b) also serve as foils to the black person or
people, who will be much sharper and savvier, but also easily
offended, and will delight in raking the dumb people over the coals
week after week. So that's three or four people. You'll probably throw
in a gay guy or a lesbian, to see how often *they* can get offended, and
maybe an Asian or Latino, or both. Or wait. A Native American.
You should get a Native American! That would be so great. No one
knows any Indians. I mean, I've never met an Indian. Actually,
there was that one guy in college, Cletus, who said he was one-
sixteenth— But so you need to get one who's easily offended, not
a passive sort. You need someone who'll actually care about and
debate the "tomahawk chop," the Redskins and everything. That'd
be great. So. Let's see, that's five or six people so far. Then you'll
need a really straight professional type, a doctor or something, a
lawyer maybe, someone in grad school. And then me.

The Tragic Person.
Right. I realize I seem much too average, at first. I'm white, not

even Jewish, my hair is horrible and I'm poorly dressed and everything—I know how blah that seems, suburban, upper-middle-class, two parents (why do we seem so boring, all of us? Are we as utterly boring as we seem?)—it certainly didn't help with my college admissions experiences, let me tell you. But you need someone like me. I represent tens of millions, I represent everyone who grew up suburban and white, but then I've got all these other things going for me. I'm Irish Catholic, and can definitely play that up if you want. And then the Midwest thing, which I don't need to tell you is pretty valuable. And if you want to go hard-core rural, play that angle, I went to school in the middle of a cornfield, have seen cows, smelled their waste every day there was a south wind. Oh and: it was a state school. So, I can be the average white suburban person, midwestern, knowing of worlds both wealthy and central Illinoisian, whose looks are not intimidating, who's self-effacing but principled, and—and this is the big part—one whose tragic recent past touches everyone's heart, whose struggles become universal and inspiring.

It must be hard.
What?

Raising your brother.
How do you know about him?

It was on your application.
Oh. Right. Well, no, it actually isn't hard at all. It's like...do you have a roommate?

No.
Have you ever?

Yes.

It's like that. We're roommates. It's easy, it's actually often easier
than it would be with a regular roommate, because you can't tell a
regular roommate to sweep the hall, or go get some margarine. So
it's the best of both worlds. We entertain each other. So no, it's
not— Oh, but if it needs to be, it can be. It can be hard. Actually
yes, it is hard. Very hard.

Well, how do you plan to manage being on the show?
How do you mean?

With your brother and all.
Oh, right, right. Well, I've talked it over with my sister, and she'd
be willing to pick up the slack for the duration of the show. She
lives only like a block away— Wait. How long does the filming
go on for?

About four months.
And I'd have to live in the *Real World* house?

Yeah, that's the idea.
Yeah, I mean, I could do that. We talked about it. We made a deal,
Beth and Toph and me, from the beginning. The deal was, that
we'd do everything we could to keep everything normal, to maintain, actually, more normalcy than we grew up with, but at the
same time we wouldn't feel obligated to make the all-encompass-
ing sacrifices that our mom had made, that had for all intents and
purposes killed her, we felt.

On your application you said it was cancer.
Well, sure, technically. But it was stomach cancer, which is
extremely rare, its provenance unknown, and Beth and I—we're
the ones who ruminate on such things, while Bill has moved on, is
mentally much healthier, by all appearances completely normal—

Beth and I got to thinking that its contraction, the development of this cancer, was due to her internalization of all her stress, her many burdens, all the combat within our family over twenty-odd years, it coming down to her to—it was like, in a way, it was like a soldier jumping on a mine to save his... maybe that's a poor analogy. I mean, she swallowed the chaos, sequestered it there, and there it festered and grew and darkened and then was cancer.

Do you really believe that?
Sure. Kind of.

You were saying, about the deal?
The deal was that while Beth and I were holding together and starting over, and creating a world of relative order, and giving Toph as normal a life as possible, under the circumstances, if opportunities arose, that we would do everything we could to— The point is that we would not use each other, to use obligation as an excuse to say no to things. At least not if we could still manage. I mean, you have no idea how thoroughly we shelter him from absolutely everything—honestly, like, he's never even heard more than a few swear words in his life—but we've agreed that we'll do whatever we can to facilitate the things we want to do, will not hold back and become bitter and years later blame him or each other, right? Oh wait, that's a funny story. There was a word my mom used to call us sometimes, that I only figured out in high school. I'll try it out on you. Okay, the word was "mahdda."

What's a mahdda?
Oh ha ha. You're good. You're good. I should have seen that coming. But seriously, that's what I always wondered. When we were sulking about something, or if we had a cold and complained about going to school—we were forbidden from staying home, by the way, never missed a day until late in high school—my mom

would say, Oh don't be such a *mahdda*! We always assumed it had
something to do with being sullen about something we hadn't
gotten. Then in high school I figured it out. The word was
mangled by her Boston accent.

Martyr.
Right, the word was martyr. Of course, my mom was one of the
great martyrs of all time.

About the show...
Right, in terms of *The Real World,* I figured that I'd still see Toph
all the time, but he'd live primarily with Beth for that period.
She'd probably move into our place, and sleep there and everything, with me being there as often as I could—probably not that
much less than now, really. I mean, I have it all pictured, the
traveling back and forth, between the show and my world in
Berkeley, the camera crew maybe with me in the car, following me
driving home each night, or whenever, the music going in the
background, me making the trip home to be with him, like the
divorced dad—you see the potential, no? It would be sort of touching. And then he'd occasionally come into the *Real World* house
with me. It'd be great. He'd be good on TV.

How would he feel about it?
I'm sure he'd love it.

Is he comfortable in front of a camera?
Not really. He's kind of shy, actually.

Hmm.
My heart is pure.
I know what you're thinking.
I know what I mean.

Excuse me?
Nothing.

Why do you want to be on The Real World?
Because I want everyone to witness my youth.

Why?
Isn't it gorgeous?

Who's gorgeous?
Not like that. No, I just mean, that it's in bloom. That's what
you're all about, right? The showing of raw fruit, correct? Whether
that's in videos or on spring break, whatever, the amplifying of
youth, the editing and volume magnifying what it means to be
right there, at the point when all is allowed and your body wants
everything for it, is hungry and taut, churning, an energy vortex,
sucking all toward it. I mean, we're in the same business, really,
though we take vastly different approaches, of course, your *Real
World* being kind of brutally obvious, no offense, whereas the
videos at least don't purport to be anything but what they are—
but you guys, your show claims to do more but then has a strange
ability to flatten all the depth and nuance from these people.

So why are you here?
I want you to share my suffering.

You don't seem to be suffering.
I don't?

You seem happy.
Well, sure. But not always. Sometimes it's hard. Yeah. Sometimes
it's so hard. I mean, you can't always suffer. It's hard to suffer all
the time. But I suffer enough. I suffer sometimes.

Why do you want to share your suffering?
By sharing it I will dilute it.

But it seems like it might be just the opposite—by sharing it you might be amplifying it.
How do you mean?

Well, by telling everyone about it, you purge yourself, but then, because everyone knows this thing about you, everyone knows your story, won't you be constantly reminded of it, unable to escape it?
Maybe. But look at it this way: stomach cancer is genetic, passed more down the female side of our family than otherwise, but because according to Beth and me my mother was done in by dyspepsia, the dyspepsia caused by swallowing too much of our tumult and cruelty, we are determined not to swallow anything, to not keep anything putrefying down there, soaking in its juices, bile eating bile... we are purgers, Beth and I. I don't hold on to anything anymore. Pain comes at me and I take it, chew it for a few minutes, and spit it back out. It's just not my thing anymore.

But if the information is in the eyes of everyone you meet...
Then there's that much more sympathy coming back at us.

But it'll get old.
Then I'll move to Namibia.

Hmm.
I am an orphan of America.

What?
Nothing. Someone else said that, years ago.

So about the dilution...

This is where the lattice comes in.

The lattice.
The lattice that we are either a part of or apart from. The lattice is the connective tissue. The lattice is everyone else, the lattice is my people, collective youth, people like me, hearts ripe, brains aglow. The lattice is everyone I have ever known, mostly those my age or thereabouts—I know little else, know only six or seven people over forty, know nothing to say to them—but my people, we are still there, still able, if we start right now—   I see us as one, as a vast matrix, an army, a whole, each one of us responsible to one another, because no one else is. I mean, every person that walks through the door to help with *Might* becomes part of our lattice: Matt Ness, Nancy Miller, Larry Smith, Shelley Smith (no relation), Jason Adams, Trevor Macarewich, John Nunes, on and on, all these people, the people who come to us or we come to, the subscribers, our friends, their friends, their friends, who knows who knows who, people who have everything in common no matter where they're from, all these people know all the same things and truly hope for the same things, it's undeniable that they do, and if we can bring everyone to grab a part of the other, like an arm at the socket, everyone holding another's arm at the socket, and if we can get everyone to, instead of ripping this arm from the socket, instead hold to it, tight, and thus strengthening—   Then, um—   Like a human ocean moving as one, the undulating, the wave-making—

Ahem.
Or like a snowshoe.

A snowshoe.
You wear snowshoes when the snow is deep and porous. The latticework within the snowshoe's oval distributes the wearer's weight over a wider area, in order to keep him or her from falling

through the snow. So people, the connections between people, the
people you know, become a sort of lattice, and the more people,
good people, they must be good people, who know that they are
here to help, the more of these people you know, and that know
you, and know your situation and your story and your troubles
or whatnot, the wider and stronger the lattice, and the less likely
you are to—

Fall through the snow.
Right.

That is a mediocre metaphor.
Yes. I'm working on it.

You have no problem being inside a fishbowl.
I feel like I'm already inside a fishbowl.

Why?
I feel like I'm being watched at all times.

By whom?
I have no idea. I've always felt like people were watching me, and
knew about what I'd been doing. I imagine it started with my
mom, and the way she had of…she had amazing eyes, these small
sharp eyes, always narrowing to a squint and tearing into you; she
never missed anything, whether she was there seeing it or halfway
around the world. She missed nothing. That's why, for instance,
I like bathrooms. I like bathrooms because usually while inside, I
can be almost sure, at least more sure, that no one is watching me.
I take great comfort in places where people cannot watch me—
windowless rooms, basements, small rooms. I have a pretty good
hunch that people are always watching me, or thinking of watching me. Not all the time, probably very rarely are they actually

watching me, but the point is, the important thing, is that it could be anytime. That's the crucial part, that at any time, someone could be watching me. I know this.

How do you know this?
Because I'm always watching people. When I watch people I too look through them. I learned that from my mother. To glance is not enough; eyes and brains together, acting like a flock of ravenous birds, flapping, tearing, poking...I know everything about people when I look at them for only a moment. I can tell from their clothes, their walks, their hair and hands, I know all the bad things that they've done. I know how they've failed and how they will fail and how miserable they are.

And people are doing the same to you?
Maybe.

So what do you do?
Stay inside. Bedrooms are safe sometimes, if the door is closed and the blinds are down, but if the watchers are in trees, they can see certain things. Windows are fine to look out but harrowing to stand in front of. Even if you check and find that there are no people watching, the people watching can be somewhere not immediately visible. They can be beyond the reach of the naked eye. People use telescopes, binoculars. I have used telescopes, binoculars. People can be in closets. Closets should be checked. Large cabinets should be checked—it only takes a second. And large trunks. Open doors are to be avoided. Bathrooms are good. The only problem with bathrooms is the possibility of one-way mirrors. Years ago I checked all the mirrors in our house, to make sure that there were no windows behind them, with people watching. There were none.

You're exaggerating.

Okay, you want to hear a sad story? Last night I was home, listening to an album. A favorite song came on, and I was singing aloud, loud enough for it to matter but not loud enough to wake up Toph, sleeping in his bedroom adjacent, and as I was singing, I was moving my hands through my hair in a weird obsessive sort of way, like a slow-motion shampooing maneuver—it's something I do with my hair when I am alone and enjoying music—and as I was singing and doing the slo-mo hands-in-hair maneuver, I messed up the words to the song I was singing, and though it was two fifty-one in the morning, I became quickly, deeply embarrassed about my singing gaffe, convinced that there was a very good chance that someone could see me—through the window, across the dark, across the street. I was sure, saw vividly that someone— or more likely a someone and his friends—over there was having a hearty laugh at my expense.

That must drive you insa—

Oh please. What would a brain do if not these sorts of exercises? I have no idea how people function without near-constant internal chaos. I'd lose my mind.

Heh. Heh. Heh. Are you sure you want to be telling me all this?

All what?

About your parents, the paranoia . . .

What am I giving you? I am giving you nothing. I am giving you things that God knows, everyone knows. They are famous in their deaths. This will be my memorial to them. I give you all these things, I tell you about his legs and her wigs—I do so later in this section—and relate my wondering if I should be having sex with my girlfriend in front of their closet the night of my father's service, but after all that, what, in the end, have I given you? It seems like you know something, but you still know nothing. I tell you and it evaporates. I don't care—how could I care? I tell you how many people I have slept with (thirty-two), or how my parents left this world, and what have I really given you? Nothing. I can tell you the names of my friends, their phone numbers, but what do you have? You have nothing. They all granted permission. Why is that? Because you have nothing, you have some phone numbers. It seems precious for one, two seconds. You have what I can afford to give. You are a panhandler, begging for anything, and I am the man walking briskly by, tossing a quarter or so into your paper cup. I can afford to give you this. This does not break me. I give you virtually everything I have. I give you all of the best things I have, and while these things are things that I like, memories that I treasure, good or bad, like the pictures of my family on my walls I can show them to you without diminishing them. I can afford to give you everything. We gasp at the wretches on afternoon shows who reveal their hideous secrets in front of millions of similarly wretched viewers, and yet...what have we taken from them, what have they given us? Nothing. We know that Janine had sex with her daughter's boyfriend, but...then what? We will die and we will have protected...what? Protected from all the world that, what, we do this or that, that our arms have made these movements and our mouths these sounds? Please. We feel that to reveal embarrassing or private things, like, say, masturbatory habits (for me, about once a day, usually in the shower), we have given someone something, that, like a primitive person fearing that a photographer will steal his soul, we identify our secrets, our pasts and their blotches, with our identity, that revealing our habits or losses or deeds somehow makes one less of oneself. But it's just the opposite, more is more is more—more bleeding, more giving. These things, details, stories, whatever, are like the skin shed by snakes, who leave theirs for anyone to see. What does he care where it is, who sees it, this snake, and his skin? He leaves it where he molts. Hours,

days or months later, we come across a snake's long-shed skin
and we know something of the snake, we know that it's of this
approximate girth and that approximate length, but we know very
little else. Do we know where the snake is now? What the snake is
thinking now? No. By now the snake could be wearing fur; the
snake could be selling pencils in Hanoi. The skin is no longer his,
he wore it because it grew from him, but then it dried and slipped
off and he and everyone could look at it.

And you're the snake?
Sure. I'm the snake. So, should the snake bring it with him, this
skin, should he tuck it under his arm? Should he?

No?
No, of course not! He's got no fucking arms! How the fuck would
a snake carry a skin? Please. But like the snake, I have no arms—
metaphorically speaking—to carry these things with. Besides,
these things aren't even mine. None of this is mine. My father is
not mine—not in that way. His death and what he's done are not
mine. Nor are my upbringing nor my town nor its tragedies. How
can these things be mine? Holding me responsible for keeping
hidden this information is ridiculous. I was born into a town and
a family and the town and my family happened to me. I own none
of it. It is everyone's. It is shareware. I like it, I like having been a
part of it, I would kill or die to protect those who are part of it, but
I do not claim exclusivity. Have it. Take it from me. Do with it
what you will. Make it useful. This is like making electricity
from dirt; it is almost too good to be believed, that we can make
beauty from this stuff.

But what about privacy?
Cheap, overabundant, easily gotten, lost, regained, bought, sold.

But what about exploitation? Exhibitionism?
Are you Catholic?

No.
Then why are you talking about exhibitionism? It's a ridiculous term. Someone wants to celebrate their existence and you call it exhibitionism. It's niggardly. If you don't want anyone to know about your existence, you might as well kill yourself. You're taking up space, air.

What about dignity?
You will die, and when you die, you will know a profound lack of it. It's never dignified, always brutal. What's dignified about dying? It's never dignified. And in obscurity? Offensive. Dignity is an affectation, cute but eccentric, like learning French or collecting scarves. And it's fleeting and incredibly mercurial. And subjective. So fuck it.

So it's all fodder?
As my mom was dying in the family room, I would periodically go into the living room, which, oddly enough, got most all the light the house received, and, sitting on the white couch there, amid all of her dolls, I would write what I would say at her service. I had the piece of paper hidden under the couch, a scrap of folded notebook paper. I would go there, fish it out from under the couch, and consider what I would write.

And your mother was in the family room?
Yes. She was there, at this point half-gone with the morphine. My sister and I expected her to go at any point, really, and so every morning—or anytime we had left her alone for more than half an hour—would race into the room wondering if she'd already be gone. Actually, we wouldn't race into the room, not wanting to

alarm her, annoy her, because she would immediately know what
we were doing, so we would race to the family room and then we
would stand, peeking into the room, watching her chest, fixating
on her sternum, until it moved and we knew she was breathing.
Sometimes it was an excruciatingly long wait, and other times,
if she had a blanket over her or something, we would have to go
further, would have to lean close and search her face for movement—that went on for weeks. But after a while, particularly
when she had lost all consciousness, it was just her breathing, and
we started wondering about timing.

How do you mean?
Well, you can't help start wondering about timing things as well
as possible. Like, everyone was home from college for Christmas
break, and we really wanted it all to end before everyone went
back. I wanted everyone there, had pictured it a hundred times, all
my friends, in their suits and dresses, filing in, heads down, sitting
as a massive group, in the middle. And as matter of fact, that
winter break they were thinking the same way. They were hoping
she'd go while they were home.

But...
But she just kept going and going. Beth started calling her the
Terminator, which I thought was kind of tacky, but—

     You know, as we're talking, I can see my reflection in the
camera's glass. And I can tell I don't look right. I am sneering
involuntarily. My lips curl, my forehead furrows. Jesus, I am not
telegenic. That's going to be a problem, isn't it?

So about the speech...
Yeah, so I'd be there, writing the speech, on the couch, while my
mother was in the other room. Because the couch was white, and I
was always dropping my pens, I was writing in pencil, putting it

in my mouth, revising, starting again. I wasn't sure what angle to take. I didn't know where to start. At her childhood? Should it be a biography of her? A few telling anecdotes? I began again and again. But what I settled on was more about what *I* felt about her death, and where it left *me*.

Interesting.

Yeah, at the time I figured it would be best that way. I let Bill talk a little about her life, about what a good mother she was, some specifics of her personality. He went off on one of his tangents, about how she always supported our collecting habits, how he had collected trains, I had collected bears, Beth dolls— Of course it seemed radically insufficient—I mean, how can that work, a life summed up in—so I was sitting there, and as Bill was talking, I was staring at Father Mike, our priest, to whom I was supposed to give a sign, a sign to indicate that I actually wanted to get up and speak, because in the days before the service I could not decide. But I had prepared a speech, had finished my bit the night before, late, in the dark, in the living room. And so as Bill was talking, I looked at Father Mike, and caught his eye, and even as I was giving him the nod to indicate that I did have something to say, and wanted to share it with the assembled, I immediately wanted to back out again and simply let the whole thing be over, so we could jump into the car, my father's Nissan, it being packed and in the parking lot, and just drive to Florida, be at least halfway by midnight. But then Father Mike was introducing me and I got up and...

What? You just jumped.

Nothing. Something just occurred to me. Anyway, when I spoke I filled everyone in on exactly how cheated we felt, *I* felt. But I was merciful. I said something to the effect that, you know, I *could* stand here and grouse about how she'll never see my children, about how unfair it all was, her being taken a month after my father, about how hard it all was for us. But then I said, my voice getting shakier, that we shouldn't think such sad thoughts, that we should just pick a bright star in the black sky and think of her, and then, to find another, close by, and think of my dad.

Umm...
Yeah, I know, I know. It's horrible, it's cheap and small. And worse, I drew a picture of her on her deathbed.

But what does that—
She was at that point long gone, in terms of consciousness. She mumbled every so often, sometimes sat up with a start, saying something, but otherwise it was just breathing, gurgling, the candles, her hot skin. And waiting, really. We sat there, day and night, trading places, Beth and I, with Toph downstairs usually, Beth and I sitting, watching, holding her hot hand, sleeping there, sometimes draped over her, waiting for the near-end, so we could gather and then wait for the end-end. And during it all, in the dark one night, sitting on a chair to her left, I felt compelled to draw a picture of her, with a red grease pencil on large drawing paper. I sketched it out first, lightly relating the rough shapes, making sure it all would fit on the page, making adjustments. It seemed like I would run out of room on the left. I moved her head farther to the right, so I could fit the whole pillow in the frame. I roughed out the loose shape of the bed, the metal frame. And then I started with her face, actually—I usually don't start with the face, because if you can't find a likeness it corrupts the rest of the drawing, I find—but her face this time was easy, it having a kind of simple geometry in profile, sunken as it was, just barely rising from her pillows, flat from whatever process it was that was making her face sink and flatten, shiny from the jaundice and the excretions coming through her skin, the excretions that would

have been exiting her body elsewhere had the necessary systems been working. Then I drew the tubes, the IV, the bed's aluminum railing, the blankets. When it was done, it was fairly accurate, a nice picture, with a good deal of detail in the middle, less as it reached the paper's edges. I still have it, though it's frayed on its sides... I've never been good about preserving drawings; I keep them, but abuse them. This drawing, for example, of maybe ten thousand I've done in classes or otherwise, could easily be the most important one I've ever done or will ever do, but I just looked for it and found it sticking halfway out of an old portfolio, torn at its corner. How can I be so careless with this memory of my mother? And why did I even draw it in the first place? I mean, what does that mean?

It could be a purely sentimental...
I wonder. But I also remember thinking of taking pictures. At the time, I was painting a lot from photographs, and thought that they'd come in handy later, photographs, that I would take a bunch, from different angles, and use them as source material later.

But you didn't.
No. To be honest, I didn't really even strongly consider doing so, but the point is that I thought of it.

And then you went to Florida.
After the service, we spent twenty minutes or so at a tea and cookies sort of thing in the rectory, and then said goodbye. My then-girlfriend Kirsten was there, and Bill, and my uncle Dan, and after a while we sort of said, See you all later, love you, and then took off, completely wired with adrenaline, driving until midnight, stopping in Atlanta. The next day we drove until there was sand along the highway, and we were in Florida, and we bought new bathing suits, and got sand in the car—the car that our dad would

under no circumstances ever let us drive or allow food into—and
watched HBO at night in the hotel room, and Toph and I played
frisbee during the day, on a white, white beach, and the wind was
warm and wet, and we called Bill at night, and thought about visiting a few relatives we had down there—Tom and Dot, I mentioned them before—but then didn't, because they were old, and
for the time being we were done with such people.

And then you—
I never gave them a proper burial.

Excuse me? What does that—
I don't know where they are.

What do you mean?
They were cremated. They decided, I guess together, God knows
why, and from where the idea came, that they would donate their
bodies to science. We had no idea why—it didn't really gel with
any long-held beliefs that we knew them to have; we had never
heard them talk about it. My dad was an atheist, we knew that—
my mother claimed he worshiped "The Great Tree"—so in his case
it makes some sense, the body donation plan, but my mother was
very Catholic, far more romantic, emotional, superstitious even
maybe, when it came to such things. But all of a sudden the orders
were there—I can't remember if we knew before or after; it must
have been after his death and before hers, come to think of it—and
that's what happened. After they were taken to the coroner's or
wherever, at some point they were picked up by a donor service,
and brought to this or that medical school, where they were used
for God knows what.

This disturbs you?
Well, of course. At the time, we thought it was kind of noble. It

surprised us, the donating, so with everything sort of spinning out of control, we just rolled with it, I suppose in part because it made arrangements easier.

What do you mean?
Well, the casket and all. Or lack thereof.

You didn't have a casket?
No. Nothing. We had services for each, of course, but we didn't bother with the casket, considering it would be empty and all.

So there was no standard funeral ceremony, like at a cemetery...
No.

They have no gravestones.
They have no gravestones. We have no idea where they are, as a matter of fact. I mean, the people from the body donation company promised that after they were done, they would cremate the bodies and then send them to us, but they haven't. At least not yet. It was supposed to be within about three months. But now it's going on about two years.

So you don't have the remains?
Right. Actually, it's kind of funny—they don't call them *remains*; they call them "cremains." But we still think the ashes might be coming. Beth thinks they haven't been returned because we've moved a few times. She thinks they probably tried to contact us and couldn't find us because we moved to the Berkeley sublet and then again, and so threw them out, or whatever. I kind of think they might still be there, somewhere.

Have you tried to contact the donation service?
No. I think Beth has. It's something that we talk about every

couple of months, actually, but less and less frequently. It's hard, because the later it gets, the farther from that time we find ourselves, the more impossible it becomes to even broach the subject. It's kind of embarrassing, really. For me at least. That and the lack of the gravestones, the lack of funerals, the selling or disposing of most of the contents of the house. It was all such a blur, and we were moving so far, and there was so much to be done. I was trying to finish college, commuting back and forth, three days in Chicago and four in Champaign, all spring, and Beth had to do everything else—trying to sell the house, get the estate sale figured out, finding a school in Berkeley for Toph, paying all the bills, selling Mom's car...We were convinced that we would be forgiven anything, really, any lapses in judgment, any mistakes, all the horrible mistakes. Some of the stuff we sold...

You regret all that.
Sometimes. Sometimes Beth and I agree that it's best, the way we cleared out, the clean break we made from home, from most elements of the...you know, it was weird, but a few people frowned upon our taking Toph away and moving to California, thinking that the best support network would be there, in Lake Forest, blah blah. But good lord we could not get far enough away, were sure that we'd all end up this sad local legend, these sorry celebrities, and Toph this ward of the town...no way. And so we didn't do a cemetery funeral or anything, didn't bother with coffins. Beth always says how our parents did not want a funeral, that the whole funeral and gravestone thing was just a racket, was this ridiculous tradition, rooted in commerce, a Hallmark holiday sort of thing, and besides, it was much too expensive. So we can ease our conscience with that, and by assuming that we carried out their wishes.

Do you think they really wanted it that way?
No, not for a second. Beth does. Beth is sure, Beth was there. But

I...I honestly think they can't believe we haven't buried them yet, that we don't even know where they are. It's appalling, really.

Maybe.
But I really think that embalming dead people, dressing them up, putting makeup on them...it's brutal, medieval. There is a large part of me that really likes the idea of them having sort of disappeared, just gone—with us never really seeing them once they passed on, that they just floated away or something, that because they were not buried, that might be—

Do you dream of them?
My sister dreams of them constantly. All the time, and in her dreams our parents are often cheerful, talking and walking and saying interesting things. I have not seen my parents talking and walking and saying interesting things since they died. When we talk about it, when we are not fighting about responsibility and all, my sister and I sit on the couch and she tilts her head and twirls her hair around her finger and pieces together her most vivid dreams. In most of them, our mother is doing something simple like driving or cooking, and when she dreams of my father, my father is skulking around or has just killed someone or is chasing her. But every so often a dream with him in it is a nice dream. And thus I'm jealous, because I'd love to see them walking and talking again, even if it was fabricated in a dream. But I don't dream of them. I have no idea why not, and how to remedy that problem.

Why not just think about your parents just before bed? That would seem to be at least one way of doing it.
I've tried that. I mean, I have tried to try. For instance, right now, I'm thinking Yeah, yeah, I'll do that tonight, thanks for reminding me. But somewhere along the line I will forget. It's happened a hundred times. Why can't I remember to think of my parents

before I sleep? Why can't I simply leave a note on the pillow—
THINK OF PARENTS? Why can I not do this? I mean, the
rewards would be so great—for instance, if I were to think of my
mother just before I fell asleep, there is a fairly good chance that
my dream would bring her to life—the making of dreams as we all
know is often that crudely predictable—and yet I can't bring
myself to do it, to remember, to do the basic work necessary. It's
flabbergasting. Actually, I have dreamed of my father once, sort of.
In the dream, I am driving on Old Elm, a street near our house,
and it's winter, no snow, just gray. I'm driving down the hill, from
7-Eleven to home, and I suddenly see, maybe two hundred yards
away, along a parallel road, through a million bare twiggy trees,
a car, exactly like my dad's. It's a gray Nissan something something, and in it is a gray-haired man wearing an old brown suede
coat, looking almost exactly like my father, except that even in the
dream I'm sort of doubtful that it's him—in the dream, I know
he's gone, and that what I'm seeing must be a coincidence or
mirage, but then suddenly it occurs to me—this is where, in the
dream even, it both conforms to logic and departs wildly from it—
it occurs to me that he could very well be alive still, that his death
made so little sense in the first place, was so sudden and illogically
timed, that...and then the other factors conspire together—that
none of us were there when he finally died, that we have not
received his remains—cremains, sorry—and in the dream it occurs
to me that it could simply be another deception, that maybe he's
alive after all...

What do you mean, another deception?
Well, like all people who drink, and do so while successfully keeping a family and a job, he was an extraordinary magician. The
tricks, once found out, of course, were kind of flimsy, but at the
time, for so long, they fooled a houseful of naturally sneaky and suspicious people. The most famous trick was the AA trick, which

involved attending AA meetings, in our house even, while a few fingers under. It was great. He had gone for about a month to a treatment center somewhere, while we were out East visiting relatives, and when we got home, he was there, sober, dry, triumphant. We were all elated. We felt like we were finally done with all that, our family was suddenly this clean and new thing, and naturally, because he was sober and strong and everything, he'd conquer the world and bring us with him. We sat on his lap, we worshiped him. Maybe that's a bit strong. I guess in a lot of ways we still hated and feared him, after all the years of yelling and chasing and everything, but still, we were resilient, and wanted things to be normal—we were not really sure what normal was, or if we had ever been a part of it, come to think of it—but we were hopeful nonetheless. And then the meetings, including the one held in our living room. We were supposed to stay in bed, but one time I snuck down and peeked through the stairway's railing and saw all these adults, foggy through all the smoke, and our dad there, in the spot on the couch where he sat on Christmas. It was weird seeing all those adults in the house—our parents did not entertain—but the point is that he was drinking even then, probably even that night—we never knew, they didn't know—which is a neat trick, if you think about it. It's a trick I have to respect, being diabolical myself and all.

How could he be drinking undetected if he was home all the time?
Aha. Yes. There wasn't a bottle in the house. We searched the place. My mom was vigilant, we were too. But you know where it was? It'll make you choke, it's so simple. Every so often, early in the mornings—it was the only time he was really alone, and would not rouse suspicion—he would go out, get a bottle of vodka and four or five liters of quinine, and would bring them home.

Then he'd...
Yeah, he'd empty out half the quinine containers, fill them with

vodka, and then toss all evidence of the vodka. So at night, when we all gathered in the family room, watching *Three's Company* or whatnot, he'd go into the kitchen and—oh, this was a great detail—he'd pour the quinine (vodka) into, instead of the short glasses he used to use, a short glass that would indicate, to the casual observer, *alcohol*, he used a *tall glass*. A tall glass and we were fooled! To recap: What goes in the short glass? *Alcohol*. What goes in the tall glass? *A soft drink, of course!* Yes, the tall glass is the container of choice for a nice, cool, nonalcoholic beverage. Can you imagine? He must have felt like the cleverest guy in the world, or at least more clever than his dim-witted brood. This went on for about a year—all while we were flush with pride and hope, believing that he had quit and that there would be no more moving, for days and weeks at a time, to friends' and relatives' houses, no more talk of leaving him, all that, and as we were all rebuilding, all the while—it was incredible. Of course, what's more, with the tall glass (remember: tall glass = soft drink), he was drinking even more, and we became increasingly confused, because while he was ostensibly sober, he was still talking funny after ten, still raging suddenly and implacably, and still falling asleep sitting upright on the couch, at eleven every night.

So after he was discovered, he quit?
Oh God, no. My mother went out on the patio, closed the sliding door and screamed and cried, her arms wrapped around her shoulders, and there were probably a few threats of leaving, all that. But then we kind of gave in. My mother was exhausted, by him and us, the three of us had recently become four, and I suppose she conceded that he was going to drink, that he was born to drink—and was quite good at it, by the way, a pretty functional drinker, not a gone-on-a-bender sort, harmless if not provoked. So with a new baby, moving or leaving suddenly became far more difficult to do (or even to threaten to do) and I imagine at some point our

exhausted mother just came to terms with him—this many drinks a night and no more, blah blah. And when you think about the lengths he went to deceive us, in the interest, of course, of keeping us from leaving—he would arrange his schedule in really any way at all, would do the flimsy, sad little lies, with the quinine and tall glasses, for instance—all so we wouldn't leave—when you think about that, well, he was not perfect, but he was a decent man. And so he reduced his nightly intake after that, readily accepted the truce, drank only beer or wine at home, and as Toph started crawling and then walking, he plateaued. And to tell you the truth, we almost preferred it that way. The whole AA vibe was unsettling, and all those adults in the house, the murmuring and the smoke, it didn't seem appropriate for him, he just wasn't a group sort of guy, buying into all that. In a way, we just didn't want our father to be in AA. He wanted to control or kick it on his own, and that's really the way we preferred it, too. And AA was probably murder for him, with all the references to higher powers and whatnot, the whole gist of which held no water for him. Anyway, after the whole treatment ghost was given up, it was better then because it was all out in the open, we knew the exact parameters of him and he of us, and we could then prepare for eventualities. Which I had been horrible at doing, never knowing what to expect. See, from when I was very small, I had this wild, horror-infested imagination—it was, for example, my firm belief for a few years that when we went to bed the downstairs turned into a laboratory for human experimentation, a cross between snippets I'd seen of *Coma* and *Willy Wonka,* filled with Oompa-Loompa men and bodies in stasis—and that, with even a little of his unevenness, could combine and make chaos and terror where it wasn't necessarily there— I mean, for me, it ended, that thin brittle rope of trust between a parent and child snapped, probably when I was about eight, with the door thing.

Which was...

This was when things were a little messy, when he was a little less in control. And I don't remember what the issue was, but I had apparently done something wrong, and so was supposed to stand for punishment—you know what was funny? We were, when due punishment, in each instance told to "assume the position," meaning to come over and lean over his knees—so quaint, can you believe it?—and of course I wasn't going to have any part of that garbage. Not that he ever really hit us all that hard—our mom was the one who really put her weight into it—but there was something terrifying about his fumbling, his clumsy grabbing...it was just so unpredictable, because we knew enough to know when he was already blurry, so we just didn't want to be anywhere near his area of—you know that game, octopus? Where you run around, trying to get from one side to the other, past all your classmates and then the red line, where they can't touch you, but you can't get near any of the limbs, with their little perfect arms suddenly so perilous, so horrifying?—it was like that in a way, a heightened sense of terror born of doubt, a lack of predictability in his behavior—we just did not want to get close enough to him at night for something weird to happen. So with the verdict handed down and the spanking imminent, we ran. Every time we ran, and tried to get far enough away and for long enough that—and this was usually more wishful thinking than practical—that his anger would subside, or our mother would intervene, or both: a reprieve granted. If the episode took place during the day we'd just run down the street, to the park or the creek or a friend's, and wait it out. But at night—which is when these things usually happened, given we only saw our father, an avid golfer, a few daylight hours each week—of course we (or at least I) couldn't go outside, being sure that it was much worse out there, the neighborhood being populated with the vampires from *Salem's Lot* and the William Shatner mask man from *Halloween*. At night, options were limited to those

within the house, which were many, actually, though each with its
particular merits and drawbacks. Down in the basement you could
hide in the furnace area or the crawl space, but for the area to be
effective one had to keep the lights off, and one never knew when
there would be actual murderers there, in the furnace area or crawl
space, or corpses—highly possible, of course. Then there were the
closets, which were often effective, but in a closet, though one felt
warm and safe, one was found so suddenly—the sliding door
would woosh open and the hands abruptly *there*, grabbing—and so
the best places were either the upstairs bathroom or one's own
bedroom, both of which had simple locks and often held for long
enough for things to settle down on the other side. So on this
particular night, I ran to my room, closed and locked the door and,
while listening to his bellowing from the bottom of the stairs—
this is, by the way, what he did first, inexplicably demanding that
we come down, come down the stairs to allow him to take us with
his hands and drag us back to the couch where he would shake us
around, get us into position, and then do the whacking…
ludicrous. We did not owe him that, I did not owe him that, of
course not, we never deserved spanking because we were perfect,
perfect, perfect, unassailable, or if not perfect at least provoked
into whatever it was we did, and so, while in my room, while staring at the door, hyperventilating, I looked around for ideas. I
looked to the wallpaper—it was the kind that's actually a huge
photograph, mine being an orangey fall forest scene; my mom and
I had picked it out, thought it was so beautiful, had sat on the floor
staring at it after we put it up—and in my room that night I wanted to run through it, through the orange forest, because it looked
like it went deep, the forest, and it was daylight there besides. But
of course I didn't think of really doing that, I wasn't stupid or
delusional but then looked to another wall, to the unpapered wall
over my bed on which I had drawn, with markers, twenty or so little monsters and happy but still presumably fierce Viking men, all

created to protect me as I slept, and to come to life in such situations as this—but they were not coming to life, and why were they not coming to life? The yelling continued and, sure that he was still downstairs, I snuck out of my room and into the hall, grabbed the phone, and jumped back into my room, sliding the cord underneath and again locking the door. I brought the phone to my bed and called the operator and asked for the area code for Boston. Then I remembered it wasn't Boston, it was Milton, outside Boston. I called for information in Milton, looking for my aunt Ruth. Or Uncle Ron. She had done AA, he had been with her, they knew what was what—what should I do? I would ask, they would know, they would intervene...Then the footsteps started coming up the stairs, which they only did some of the time, the times when he was extraordinarily angry and our mother could not calm him down, and as they thumped up the stairs—why did he go so slow, so maddeningly slow?—I hung up the phone—I didn't have time now—and devised a plan. I opened the window over my pillow, then tore the sheet off my bed. The footsteps stopped thumping, meaning he was on the second floor, was just six or seven steps from my door... I twisted the sheet so it looked like a rope or however I had seen it look on TV and as I began to tie it around the bed frame there was the trying of the door, then suddenly my name so loud I jumped, then pounding and demands yelled, and if I could just get this thing tied in time... the thumping got louder and louder and then the sheet was tied, twice-over, I yanked it to test its strength and it seemed okay—it only had to hold for a few seconds, just until I was far down enough to jump—and so I turned my body on my bed and started to scoot back, reaching a leg out the window, feeling my bare foot against the coarse wood of the side of the house...and then the pounding stopped. I was still lowering myself, almost half out the window now, the night was humid, I was able to see the ground, the neighbor's yard, holding the sheet in two hands...I paused, breathing quickly, like an animal, thinking, wondering if he had been called off...so quiet. And then the door came in, an explosion of wood, and he was upon me.

He kicked the door down.
Well, he broke it in, broke off the lock and doorknob, half a hinge and everything.

Wow.
Dramatic, right?

Well, yes. And did he then punish you more severely?
Not really. When my mom heard the sound of the door breaking, she came running and so he only had me for a few seconds before she was in the room and he was in trouble. Ultimately it was kind of vindicating, because this time, like any time we could prove his instability—the extremes of his volatility, I should say, because while sober he was a pretty normal guy, funny even—we felt like we had scored, notched the permanent sort of scorecard that we all kept against him. I used to want to show up to school with bruises, cuts—I knew from after-school specials that that was how it worked, the teacher would see, and then it would finally be out, made semi-public, he'd be given some kind of warning, whatever, and then things would be reined in.

So this was a child abuse situation?
Oh God no. He didn't spank us very hard, once he got hold of us. I don't remember it even hurting.

Oh.
It was my mom who really hit hard. She hit us way more often than he did, but with her you always sort of knew she had it some-what under control, though she did say "I'm gonna kill you!" a bit

too often for comfort. We'd say something smart-alecky at the dinner table, and she'd stomp over and whack us on the head for a
minute, a kind of karate chop maneuver, her muscular brown arm
swinging—we'd cover our heads, just flailing to deflect the blows,
her long fingers knotted with these huge rings, her mother's. After
a while it was mostly funny. At first, it wasn't funny at all, we'd
just lose our shit and run upstairs or run away for a few hours,
yelling "I hate you I hate you," wanting her dead, wanting a new
family, wanting to move in with whatever friend's family we felt
was more together, normal. Of course in an hour we'd be sitting in
her lap again, happy as clams. And as we got older, it just got kind
of funny. Bill started it, I think, by kind of rolling his eyes and
laughing when she'd be karate-chopping his head, yelling "You
damn kids!" or whatever. He'd just sit there and take it, let her get
tired. Then we kind of followed his lead. We were teenagers at that
point, and didn't take it all that seriously, kind of let her get her
rocks off. And after a while even she started to forget what she was
so pissed about in the first place, would be kind of laughing while
she hit us. That's a weird sight, I can tell you, watching her, laughing, hitting Beth or Bill on the head, saying she was going to kill
them, while laughing, too.

But it does give you a certain flinch mentality—a readiness.
You'd see the hand rise, the stiffness of the wrist, the fingers all
together, kung fu–style, and—

Of course, we hit each other a lot, too, we kids spent a lot of
time devising plans to actually kill each other—throwing each
other through windows, down stairs—and so we honestly never
knew what to expect, because the various thresholds of violence, as
you know, can be and were bridged so suddenly, and once crossed,
one seldom goes back. The ante being upped, the terra becoming
ever less firma. So we became jittery, overly defensive, at least Beth
and I, Bill being older, to the point where if our dad came near us
with any corporal intentions, we literally went into a sort of epilep-

tic fit, with arms windmilling and legs kicking. We had florid and dark imaginations, I guess, and coupled with enough public service announcement information, some health class statistics and such…in my case, I guess, it was my imagination more than anything, my morphing him into the murderers and monsters I nightmared about every night, to a degree that I became convinced that there was a better than average chance that, given the wrong set of circumstances, that someday, it would be an accident, but that someday he'd kill one of us. That door, for instance, was never fixed, was left with this jagged bite in it for something like twelve more years. We never got around to fixing stuff like that.

What did he do for a living again?
He was a lawyer, in futures trading.

And your mother?
A teacher. Reward me for my suffering.

Excuse me?
Have I given you enough? Reward me. Put me on television. Let me share this with millions. I will do it slowly, subtly, tastefully. Everyone must know. I deserve this. I have this coming. Am I on? Have I broken your heart? Was my story sad enough?

It was sad.
I know how this works. I give you these things, and you give me a platform. So give me my platform. I am owed.

Listen, I—
I can tell you more. I have so many stories. I can tell you about the wigs they wore, the time, in the family room, that fall, when they both took off their wigs at the same time, that time in the family room, knowing it would terrify me, their heads spotted, hair like

torn cotton, they laughed, laughed, their eyes bright— and the times he fell. I can do last breaths, last words. I have so many things. There is so much symbolism. You should hear the conversations Toph and I have, the things he says. It's wonderful, it's unbelievable, you couldn't script it any better. We talk about death and God, and I have no answers for him, nothing to help him sleep, no fairy tales. Let me share this. I can do it any way you want, too—I can do it funny, or maudlin, or just straight, uninflected—anything. You tell me. I can do it sad, or inspirational, or angry. It's all there, all these things at once, so it's up to you—you choose, you pick. Give me something. Quid pro quo. I promise I will be good. I will be sad and hopeful. I will be the conduit. I will be the beating heart. Please see this! I am the common multiplier for 47 million! I am the perfect amalgam! I was born of both stability and chaos. I have seen nothing and everything. I am twenty-four but feel ten thousand years old. I am emboldened by youth, unfettered and hopeful, though inextricably tied to the past and future by my beautiful brother, who is part of both. Can you not see that we're extraordinary? That we were meant for something else, something more? All this did not happen to us for naught, I can assure you—there is no logic to that, there is logic only in assuming that we suffered for a reason. Just give us our due. I am bursting with the hopes of a generation, their hopes surge through me, threaten to burst my hardened heart! Can you not see this? I am at once pitiful and monstrous, I know, and this is all my own making, I know—not the fault of my parents but all my own creation, yes, but I am the product of my environment, and thus representative, must be exhibited, as inspiration and cautionary tale. Can you not see what I represent? I am both a) martyred moralizer and b) amoral omnivore born of the suburban vacuum + idleness + television + Catholicism + alcoholism + violence; I am a freak in secondhand velour, a leper who uses L'Oréal Anti-sticky Mega Gel. I am rootless, ripped from all foundations, an orphan raising an orphan and wanting to take away everything there is and replace it with stuff I've made. I have nothing but my friends and what's left of my little family. I need community, I need feedback, I need love, connection, give-and-take—I will bleed if they will love. Let me try. Let me prove. I will pluck my hair, will remove my skin, I will stand before you feeble and shivering. I will open a vein, an artery. Pass over me at your peril! I could die soon. I probably already have AIDS. Or cancer. Something bad will happen to me, I know, I know this because I have seen it so many times. I will be shot in an elevator, I will be swallowed in a sinkhole, will drown, so I need to bring this message now; I only have so much time, I know that sounds ridiculous, I seem young, healthy, strong, but things happen, I know you may not think so, but things happen to me, to those around me, they truly do, you'll see, so I need to grab this while I can, because I could go at any minute, Laura, Mother, Father, God— Oh please let me show this to millions. Let me be the lattice, the center of the lattice. Let me be the conduit. There are all these hearts, and mine is strong, and if there are— there are!—capillaries that bring blood to millions, that we are all of one body and that I am— Oh, I want to be the heart pumping blood to everyone, blood is what I know, I feel so warm in blood, can swim in blood, oh let me be the strong-beating heart that brings blood to everyone! I want—

And that will heal you?
Yes! Yes! Yes! Yes!

VII.

Fuck it. Stupid show.

I get the news over the phone, from Laura Folger. I have not been chosen. She tells me how close I was, how much they liked me, how sad my story was (and it was, *it was*), but that mine was one of hundreds, that I was only one of so many, most of them younger than me, carrying around this sort of cross and that kind of baggage, people with the sorriest backgrounds, but that, in the end, they couldn't use more than one suburban white male, that they had to settle on one, and he was not to be me. My spot, my catapult, has been taken by someone named Judd.

"Judd?" I say.

"Yes," she says.

"Judd?"

"Yeah, he's a cartoonist."

Fuck it. It's just as well. It's a relief. It would have been wrong. It would have been wrong, right? It would have been wrong. It's a stupid show, a show that's almost unbearable to watch, everyone on it made hideous, silly and simple, two-dimensional. Fuck it. Let the cartoonist be made into a cartoon. I don't need it, we don't need it. We don't need *The Real World*, we don't need any crutches, we don't need an ongoing role on a television show with a massive worldwide audience and an unquantifiable kind of influence over the hearts and minds of the young and impressionable. No. We will continue, against the odds, with only these simple tools, these small hands. We'll make this thing run on nothing. On fumes, if need be. On our own fumes. Whatever.

In a few weeks, we get a thick envelope in the mail from this Judd, Judd Winick. His stationery has drawings on it, dozens of little characters with funny expressions, in various funny poses. He is for some reason looking for work from us, and so has sent easily five hundred comic strips, what seems to be each and every install-ment from a daily strip he did throughout college.

The cartoons—about a bunch of young people (the protagonist is a lesbian—a fact of life in the '90s, see) living in a brownstone somewhere—are decent, very traditional, crafted well. But not for us. In the month or so since that first issue, *Might* has become something different. We are much less inspired than we were then, and going through with another one seems, on a certain level, more dutiful than impassioned. After all, the last thing we want from this, or at least the last thing I want from all this, is some kind of *job*. We have to avoid that kind of cruelly ironic fate—that we, the loudmouths who so cloyingly espouse the unshackling of one's ideas about work and life themselves become slaves to some-thing, to a schedule, obligated to advertisers, investors, keeping regular hours— Yes, we still care about changing the lives of our peers, and of course the world, and still expect at some point to be sent into space, but on the other hand...we have narrowed our scope and sharpened our knives. We have targets now, we have decided upon good guys and bad guys, friends, enemies (obstacles).

We begin a pattern of almost immediate opinion-reversal and self-devouring. Whatever the prevailing thinking, especially our own, we contradict it, reflexively. We change our minds about

Wendy Kopp, the young go-getter we heralded in the first issue, and her much-celebrated Teach for America. Where we originally praised her gumption and her organization's goals—to bring young, enthusiastic, well-educated teachers into underprivileged schools for two years—now, in a 6,000-word piece that dominates the second issue, we fault the nonprofit for attempting to solve inner-city problems, largely black problems, with white upper-middle-class college-educated solutions. "Paternalistic condescension," we say. "Enlightened self-interest," we sigh. "*Noblesse oblige*," we sneer. We quote a professor summing up: "A study of Teach for America tells us more about the ideological, even psychological needs of today's middle-class white and minority youth than it does about the underclass to whom the project is targeted."

Kaboom!

And because the general public will not believe that we have been chosen to articulate the hopes and fears of a people, to speak for them and everyone and make history, we set out to see what they *will* believe. The cover of the second issue celebrates the magazine's "First Fifty Years," with a grid of twenty or so past covers—October 1964: "The Beatles Are Reds!"; November 1948: "Death: The Hidden Killer"—to prove it. The opening essay, written a month or so after Kurt Cobain's death, touches on a death that touched us all:

> It's so hard to believe you're gone. Even now, I wake with a sense of disbelief. You're gone. Each morning, I rise reluctantly, wondering whether to live the day or just let it wash over me. I walk numbly, listlessly, drifting like a phantom. I feel apart from my body. I am half a person. You're gone.
>
> From the start, everyone knew you were different. There was something more there. A mysterious glow, a strange, unfamiliar beauty. But, somehow, I felt like I'd known you all my life. Maybe I did. Could it be?
>
> I always believed in you. And I believe you always believed in me. You spoke to me, about me, for me. During some of my

most trying times, you shone like a beacon of guidance and strength. A rock. Someone real! I idolized you. I wanted to be you.

Some said you were messed up, disturbed—a bad role model. Some said power changed you, that you couldn't handle it. They said your style was scandalous, your conduct immoral. And that's true. You were abrasive, gritty, and tough. You were reckless. A loner. And sometimes you just made me mad. But that's because I loved you and because, despite everything, I always trusted you. And then it happened. But it wasn't your fault. It was our fault. My fault.

For everything we put you through, that life put you through, that you put yourself through, I'm sorry. Your struggles with fame, with success, with the press—I know you really never meant to hurt anyone. How can a butterfly cause harm? It is with high hopes and a full heart that I say: Richard Milhous Nixon, beautiful butterfly, fly free, fly strong, live forever. I love you.

We seek out those who, like us, had ideas but have run aground. We publish an interview with Philip Paley, a former child actor who played Chakka the Pakuni on *Land of the Lost*, in which he excoriates his parents, blaming their divorce for his semi-indigent state, living in a humble apartment in Hollywood.

Trouble in paradise?

Yeah…My parents divorced when I was sixteen and subsequently all my money got tied up in that divorce. I lost it all. To this day I'm STILL FUCKING PISSED OFF ABOUT IT. Put that in your magazine. My father is a Beverly Hills surgeon with MONEY. And my mother got a really large divorce settlement. I don't talk to them.

And what are you doing now?

I have done every fucking job you can imagine. My first job was at Swenson's scooping ice cream. I was a baker, a gas station attendant, a pastry chef; I worked at EF Hutton as an assistant broker, I worked at a stationary [sic] store, I was a painter. I tore down buildings with my BARE HANDS. A lot of unemployment time.

So there goes the myth that child stars are set for life.
Yeah, it broke the myth for me.

The last page of the issue is a fake ad, featuring five of our friends, for something called Street Harmony Jeans. The five friends-as-models are posed in a corner of South Park, one sitting on a Dumpster, two others draped against warehouse walls, and, at the center, is Meredith pouting at the camera while dropping a quarter into a cup held by a hairy panhandler. The homeless man, played by our motorcycle-repairman friend Jamie, is grinning, giving a thumbs up, and holding a cardboard sign that says:

WILL WORK FOR FASHION

And somehow we think this sort of thing will endear us to advertisers. Not that we need clothing ads. Or tobacco ads. Or ads from big companies. Or anyone, forget it.

But as shortsighted and pessimistic as we've become, we still cling to the idea that the right moves might quickly reverse our fortunes. Thus, Moodie and I sit around, looking at Judd's cartoons, wondering if we should have him come on down, show us more work, talk about contributing. We agree that he is not at all a good fit for *Might*, thematically or aesthetically. He has nothing at all to do with what we're about, really, except that he—

We clamber for the phone. I make the call.

"Yeah, why don't you come down and bring the cameras—er, your portfolio."

Two days later he does come by. He walks in, a regular-looking person with thick black hair, and we get up to greet him, and are then confronted, close at his heels, by a scampering eight-legged insect of black video equipment, lights, microphones, clipboards. Shalini, an MTV devotee, at her Mac across the room, is awe-struck—we had forgotten to tell her they were coming. It's chaos. People walking by on the sidewalk outside stop and press their faces against the window. We bring Judd to our conference table, under the punching bag, and begin the show.

Judd, with his portfolio, pretends that he really cares about having his work published in our tiny magazine, with its ten thousand readers, even though in two months millions will be watching his every quiver. Moodie and I sit with him, pretending that we are editors of a real magazine, one where people sit down to talk about things like this, and that we care about his work, and believe that it belongs in our (real) magazine. We are wearing what we always wear, shorts and T-shirts, having decided, after thinking about what to wear and then remembering not to think about what to wear, to wear what we would have worn had we not been thinking about what to wear. We are happy with our shorts and T-shirts, one side tucked in, just an inch of it on the right side, showing some belt, the rest hanging out—this is our look—it having been arrived at in high school through careful consideration, through the eschewing of so many possible mistakes. We wear no tattoos, because we feel tattoos indicate too much attention paid to one's look and anyway, though the trend is still on the upswing in 1994, we are sure that inside a year, maybe just only a few months, that whole boom will go bust. (How long, after all, could something like that last?) Same with dyed hair, piercings, brandings, creative headwear, neckwear, T-shirtwear, all other indications and accoutrements. We have opted out, taken the ultimate apathetic approach to looks and attire, have moved past the check-me-out look, past the look of rejecting-the-check-me-out-look-in-favor-of-darkly-rebellious-look—have rejected both and have chosen a kind of elegance through refusal—the check-me-out-if-you-must look-but-you'll-get-no-encouragement-from-me look—the look of *absolutely no look at all*. Which is not to say we wouldn't mind looking *good*, Moodie and I, because it would be nice, since we're bothering to slum on MTV and all, to at least be looking appealing, thus increasing our chances of sleeping with Charles Bronson's daughter, or at least the girl from Caffe Centro, the one with the hair down to here, the legs up to there.

We talk to Judd, with both grave seriousness and measured nonchalance, about how and how often we will be working together, all the while choosing our words carefully, needing to sound both articulate and casual, of our demographic, loose but smart, energetic but not eager, because, of course, we are also young people pretending to be young people, putting across an image of ourselves as representatives, for now and posterity, of how youth were at this juncture, how we acted, and in particular, how we acted when we were pretending not to act while pretending to be ourselves. At the same time, it would also be nice to make clear the mistake Laura in casting has made, to have our cameo make clear who the real stars are, stars who far outshine this dowdy Judd person—we the brilliant ringed planets, he just a tiny, cold moon.

And while we must relate to Judd, mano a mano, Judd being on first impression and thereafter a very very nice person, Moodie and I must also try to act cooler than Judd, because we have to make clear that we are not the sorts of people who would be on *The Real World*—or even try out for it!—in the first place. We need to make clear to a casual viewer that, while we are willing to let ourselves be thrust into rec rooms and basements around the world, gazed at by surely adoring teenage girls and their less believing older brothers, by college students eating falafel between classes on couches that came with their apartment, we must make clear to these people that we are on this show only for the purposes of our own perverse amusement—that if you look closely, we are winking, smirking ever so slightly, that all this, our meeting with him, the cameras and everything, will probably be used in *Might* as fodder for some kind of wry and trenchant article or ha-ha chart soon enough. We can play it both ways, all ways. We can look into the eyes of this Judd person, whose eyes look like ours, and we can pour forth to him kindness and understanding, and crack jokes with him and make plans with him, all the while calculating what we might be able to get out of this association, how much of his

sort of access we can get without having to too seriously compromise the purity of our own endeavor by fouling it with his
presence, he who, for his part, is probably only talking to us
because Casting Laura felt bad about cutting me from the team
and so sent him our way, as consolation.

And even while we think we're pulling it off, that we are
acting nonchalantly like ourselves, are looking good, are dis-
cussing matters vital to Judd's career, the importance of these cartoons to us and him, something weird is happening: the camera
guy and the sound guy, slightly older, backward-hat-wearers, are
clearly unimpressed, are almost rolling their eyes at us, because
they clearly see through the whole thing, that we are using this to
get exposure, to prove to all and ourselves that we are real, that we
like everyone else simply want our lives on tape, proven, feel that
what we are doing only becomes real once it has been entered into
the record.

After the first visit, Judd comes by three or four more times,
and, a few months later, when the San Francisco *Real World*s burst
onto the air, Moodie and I are there, in Episode 2. For about eight
seconds, of course, but with that eight seconds, we expect to raise
the eyebrows of thick-skulled and starstruck advertising-buying
proles, not to mention impress people from college and high
school. We get one wish but not the other. The appearance does
next to nothing in terms of solving our financial woes, but on the
other hand, everyone we know and have ever known calls or writes
to say they saw it. How they're able in the blink that constitutes
our appearance to make out who we are is beyond comprehension.
We hear from grade school friends we haven't heard from in eight
years, we hear from old teachers, all no doubt because the words
spoken to Judd, by me in an appealing sort of drone, were
emblematic, unforgettable. Those words:

"If you, you know, don't draw the way you want to draw it's
gonna suck."

The appearance makes us mini-celebrities in the neighborhood, particularly in the eyes of Shalini, who's busy with *Hum*, the
"new voice of the progressive South Asian American twentysome-
thing community." In it are articles about the persistence of
arranged marriages, gang activity in the South Asian American
community, and a health advice column written by her father, a
doctor. Moodie and I design it in exchange for use of her laser
printer and for her thrillingly frequent, unbelievable, semi-erotic
during-work backrubs. Friends, people from upstairs begin to
avoid our office, because each time they step in, Shalini is knead-
ing our shoulders as we moan, grunt, pant, often while being
entertained by her brutal imitation of Indians she calls F.O.B.s—
fresh off the boat.

"Oooh, I tink dat you are dooo dense! Feel da dension in your
shoulders! You need do get out, relax more, go do da dancing, da
partying with da udder youngsters."

She is constantly bothering us about the hours we keep. Also
about our need to work out more.

"You wood look much bedda eev you worked out some."

We offer to fulfill her obvious wish to see us naked by inviting
her to our next photo shoot.

"I don't have to be nude, do I?"

"Actually, yes."

"No."

"No, you won't do it, or no, you don't believe us?"

"Both. No."

But Judd says yes. It's our second big nude shoot. This time we
are setting out to demonstrate what people's bodies actually look
like, the exercise being a response to a familiar complaint, of
course: the media's and advertising's distortion of our perceptions
of our own bodies, how the average person does not and cannot
meet the unattainable expectations rammed down our blah blah
blah. What we want to do, just to see if it'll work as much as

anything, is to assemble thirty or forty friends and acquaintances, ideally being of thirty or forty different sizes and shapes, and have them pose naked. We will then display the pictures on the page, unadorned, in a simple grid, one God-given body after another, making clear how seldom actual people look like the people seen on TV, how all bodies, while not necessarily all beautiful, are at the very least valid, are real and—

Okay. So. We hire a photographer, a sober, softspoken Dutch fellow named Ron Van Dongen, who will do the shoot, this groundbreaking shoot, almost for free. He asks only for the cost of film and a chance to keep the negatives. Yes. So.

In the interest of demonstrating inclusiveness and diversity, in the interest of making clear that differentiating between this one and that one, discriminating on the basis of size or shape or color, these superficial distinctions, is obscene, barbaric, in the interest of setting all this straight, we make calls looking for volunteers:

Do you have any black friends?

Oh yeah? How light?

Really? I thought he was Indian.

How about large friends?

No, we need guys. We already have enough women.

How big is he?

You think he'd do it?

Also, do you know anyone flat-chested?

Like, flat-flat. Bony.

Where is the scar? Is it noticeable?

She has hair where?

In contrast to the first naked photo shoot, this time it's infinitely easier to find people, because at this point we have an actual magazine to show people, and because this time there will be no running-with-penis-flapping, and early on we make two compromises: a) we promise to grant anonymity by cropping the pictures at the neck, and b) we let everyone wear underwear, if not on top at least on the bottom. We do this for them as much as for practical reasons, realizing with a deep, regret-filled sigh that filling our pages with stark naked people, particularly those whose bodies are clearly imperfect, will not help the magazine's struggling newsstand distribution. Yes, it's another heartbreaking compromise—and do know that each one is a five-lane highway through our souls—but this point must reach America, however tattered it is once it arrives.

Judd says he'll be bringing a friend, another member of the cast. We are thrilled. With two cast members present, this will definitely get on the air, this'll be the thing that pushes us over the edge, and when we see the car coming down the alleyway, an old periwinkle blue Dodge or something, a prototypically San Francisco car, a boxy sunwashed old thing, we can feel the pieces coming together, our doing something sociologically huge, with appropriately sized media coverage, a loud point being properly amplified, disseminated to millio—

There are no cameras. They drive up and—

There is no van following them. I meet them at the car, as they park in the alley behind the studio, and, as casually as I can, I look up and down the alley for the van. But there is no van. There are no cameras. We have expected cameras.

"Hey," I say.

"Hey," Judd says.

"So. No camera crew, huh?"

"Naw, they're with Rachel today."

"Oh. Well, good. We sure didn't want those *cameras* getting in our way today, messing everything up."

"Right."

"Cameras can be so distracting..."

"Yeah."

"...in your face, recording everything, all the things you say and do."

"Right. Oh, this is Puck."

"Hey."

"Hey."

I shake hands with Puck. He is wearing long shorts and a white tank top. He is rangy, pale, his eyes alert in a jarring sort of way. As I have his hand, he starts talking. Quickly, without taking breaths, without blinking. When I hear Puck talk I immediately wonder if Puck is on some kind of speed-oriented drug, some kind of hallucinogen. I have seen TV movies about people on such drugs. There was one with Doug McKeon and Helen Hunt, where she takes PCP and jumps out the school window, falls two stories, gets up, runs around, dies. Maybe Puck is on speed. Is this what speed is like? He will not stop talking.

He is talking about *The Real World,* and how he's going to ride it all the way to the top, that there's no stopping him, that he's also a *bike messenger you know that car road cuts racing motocross fuck yeah shit cool all the way to the top.*

He is easily the most unsettling person I have ever met. He has scratches all over his body, including his face. Maybe he has cats? It's hard to tell. He will not stop talking. *Used to ride motocross and there's some fine women in the cast but they seem frigid and yeah, got an agent and party cool shit yeah dude dude dude all right gotta split soon all right dude. Dude.*

He is fantastic and horrible. He is magnetic and repulsive. His eyes are hungry. *Fucking yeah shoulda seen it dumbshits mamas brews ollie rad bitchin.* He pulls up his shirt to show us his tats.

We all mill in the alley, waiting for our turn with Van Dongen. Kirsten, always the good sport, arrives, and Carla, a smattering of interns and friends, their friends. We have called everyone we know.

One by one, we walk in, close the door behind us, and are alone with Van Dongen in the studio. He motions us to step into a U of white screens, and gestures for us to take off our clothes, whatever it is we're planning to take off. We do, and when we do, fumbling with exactly what to do with our arms, our hands, we wonder what he thinks of our bodies. We do not know what to do with our hands. We have them at our sides, then in front of our privates, then behind our backs. What can one do with one's hands when the camera is interested in other things? When he shoots, the flashes in front of us and behind us all woosh at once, and we are frozen in the white. Then it is dark again. He takes about five pictures of each person, a few of the front, a few of the back—we can't afford the film to do more—and then we are done, opening the studio's heavy door to the overwhelming light, a hundred times that of the flashes—San Francisco at midday.

But we approve of these people, those who agree to be naked. We think less of those who refuse to do this, our many friends who said no; we deem them not only overly chaste but stingy, small, lacking in heart, a basic sort of courage. We favor those who pose, favor further those who, like Moodie, Marny, and me (and Puck), offer to pose nude, even though the shots are unlikely to be used. Naked! Naked means something, we decide. Those who pose are our people, people who are living the sorts of grabbing lives we favor, people who cannot say no—with all this, how could we, how could anyone, possibly say no?

In the alley, Puck becomes impatient. *Party shit move chicks fuck yeah motocross X9-45GV boozin gotta split.* As we are talking (or he is talking), a small dog comes to us, literally sniffing around. We play with the dog, and soon discover that the dog, though looking well cared for, has no tags. Shortly after meeting the dog, Puck decides that he will be keeping the dog. When he is done with his shoot, Puck and Judd leave, and over our protests and Judd's, Puck grabs the dog, who no doubt belongs to a nearby resident, and brings him to *The Real World* compound, where he will join the cast.

Shortly thereafter, when I'm at the house, the one time I visit, playing pool with Judd, I see the dog, and see the other cast members lolling about, with seemingly nothing at all to do—the show having cornered them into a weird problem: because they're discouraged from working (boring), or traveling (unfeasible), they cannot produce and cannot move, are left to wander from couch to kitchen to bed, talking and waiting to offend or be offended.

When we get the pictures back, Moodie and I pore over them for hours on end. We study them, try to identify who is who. But because the subjects' heads are cut off, we cannot immediately discern identities, even our own. We cannot tell the difference between one of our interns and a large, furry man who showed up unannounced. We cannot, much to my embarrassment, tell the difference between Kirsten and Carla, who are both thin and unblemished. Most unsettlingly, it takes a second to tell me from Puck—we have the same shorts, the same build, the same stance. The only difference lies in the tattoos—I have none, while he has a bunny, a bumblebee, a bird. Otherwise, we are shocked by the variance of people, the oddness of our peers, how high that large-breasted woman wears her bra, how furry that guy's back is, how unusually shaped that one's shoulders, how flat this one's butt—it's all so much weirder than we imagined. The variety of malformities, the unexpected flaws, the premature sagging, all the tattoos, flowers and snakes, how hairy all the crotches are, bursting from panties and briefs, that one woman who, even with her breasts obvious, convincing, somehow seems too like a man—

These people.

These people are *freaks*.

Worse, Toph thinks he is one of us. Though he had always spent time with my friends—since he was tiny he had known Flagg, Moodie, Marny, et al., had considered them his own friends—lately the confusion had reached a new, distressing level. Though he was doing fine socially, at school, he had been lethargic about pursuing friendships with kids his own age. He couldn't believe the stupid things they said. The girls were hopeless, the boys just a little better. And so he was never hesitant to attend any social gathering of my own demographic, shied away from no one, especially if the atttendees, mostly strangers, were up for a rousing sort of parlor game. It was not uncommon to find Toph, at one of Marny's barbecues, in the middle of fifteen, twenty people sitting on two couches arranged in a V, briefing the assembled on the rules and subtleties of charades, a game I did not teach him but which he knew well and could readily organize. His presence was so expected socially, and at the office—

Paul: "Hey, Toph."

Moodie: "Hey little man."

—that when someone noticed him for being him, we would all have to stand back a second and see him for what he actually was, at least superficially: a seventh-grade boy. Of course, he had a difficult time discerning, himself. He had recently made this clear, when he and Marny and I were driving back from the beach. She and I were talking about one of the new interns, who, at twenty-two, was much younger than we had assumed—

"Really?" said Toph. "I thought he was our age."

He was in the backseat, leaning forward, head peeking between us.

"Oh. My. God," said Marny, and burst out cackling.

It took Toph another few beats to realize what he had said.

I turned to him.

"You're eleven, Toph."

He blushed and sat back down. Marny kept roaring.

But as much as I want to encourage his mingling with his own age group, I fear that if he becomes too involved elsewhere, he won't be ever-available for my own needs. What would one do if one did not have a Toph, sitting in his room, ready at a moment's notice, always willing to run one's errands, to be pushed against a

wall and have his kidney punched, to be brought, as he is at the
moment, to the Berkeley Marina, for the throwing back and forth
of things? To not have Toph would be to not have a life. We go to
the Marina when we want to throw by the water and can't make
the long drive to the ocean. The marina is some kind of landfill jutting, fingerlike, straight into the Bay from University Avenue.
Past the docked boats and the restaurant and club, there is a park,
running parallel, a huge rolling park, mostly treeless and green.
It's a kite-flyers' haven, especially at its farthermost point, the
point farthest into the Bay. It's always crowded with people flying
kites, a few kids, their parents, but the kite-flyers are primarily the
semi-professional sort, with their box kites and dual-handled
remote-controlled F-16 Tomcat kites, kites with the detailing and
windows and cockpits, trick kites with elaborate cantilevers and
thirty-foot tails, swooping up and back, quick diagonals down to
touch the grass, then shooting back up again, their masters looking stern, purposeful, captains at the helm.

They park their campers and vans right there, on the cul-de-sac
that almost meets the Bay, and sit, on folding chairs, chatting about
better brands of string, or conventions for all the kite people, or
how they can better get in our way, *completely get in our way driving
us fucking crazy,* while we're trying to throw. When we go to the
marina, we pray that they will not be there, but this time, like most
times, they are there. We park and leave our shoes in the car, get the
stuff out, Toph with his—

"Hey, you can't wear that hat."

"What do you mean?" he says.

"We're wearing the same hat. You have to take yours off."

"No, you."

"No, you. My hair will look weirder."

"No it won't."

"Yes it will. Your hair's still straight. You know what I look
like with hat-head."

"Too bad."

"What?"

"*No.*"

"C'mon. Please?"

"No."

"*Toph.*"

"Fine."

"Thanks."

"Freak."

We come prepared, with a variety of things we can throw back and forth. First the football, the enjoyment of which never lasts long because Toph's hand is still too small to get around it. Then baseball, which we really need to practice, because the team he's on now is better than the last one, he's with older kids, tall and strong, and he's starting to get spanked, abused, suddenly left behind—stuck in the outfield, sometimes in right field—a humiliation for both of us, after all these years of work. So we do fly balls, trying hard, but not too hard, to avoid hitting the kites, knocking them out of the sky as they bob and weave above us, their strings slashing between us.

He is missing the ball. He is missing the ball because he is experimenting, doing tricks.

"Hey, skip the basket catches, fancyman."

"*Skip the basket catches, fancyman.*"

"Bite me."

"*Bite me.*"

Today we are imitating me.

We drop the mitts and play frisbee, and wait for the awed crowds to form. There is not quite the room here that there is on the beach, or at the park in the hills, and the shorter playing field necessitates a certain delicacy, obviates the need for the brutal force we usually put into the throwing, makes impossible the long, high, epic sorts of throws for which we are known and acclaimed. But we make do, slicing the frisbee through the diagonal kite strings, curving it around passersby, catching it of course in any number of wildly impressive ways—through our legs (but not like some frisbee weenie), behind the back (while jumping, half-twisting, left to right), and after tipping it, two, three, four times, taming it, slowing it to a weak spin, retiring it for the one-fingered catch. We are so good. Everyone thinks so.

In front of us a couple, the man black and the woman white, are walking with their girl, about four, whose skin is the color of a walnut. The girl's skin is a hue much more beautiful than either of her parents', and remarkable in how rudimentarily she is the product of her parents' mixed pigments. Brown and white make light brown—the color of skin mixing like paint.

"Throw it, loser."

"Here."

Toph's throw bends toward the family and almost beheads the tiny girl. The frisbee is picked up by the father, who tries to throw it to me, tossing it like a horseshoe. Poor guy.

The park is a haven for innovative people-combinations. Even more than Berkeley in general, it's a sort of laboratory, the grass perhaps the grounds of a laboratory for experimental people-making—the mixed-race/ethnicity couple capital of the world. Easily half of all couples therein, whether married or dating or on first dates or just jogging together, are somehow mixed—mostly black and white, but often Asian and white (even the somehow less common Asian man/white woman pairing), Latino and white duos, Asian/Latino, black/Asian, a smattering of lesbians. It's been cast by the directors of commercials for banks.

Incidentally, Toph and I, routine-and-inside-joke-wise, are in the middle of a jokes-about-the-dubious-importance-of-race period. We are not sure how it started—surely not by the older and more responsible of us—but it goes something like this:

I say: *Your hat smells like urine.*

He says: *You're only saying that because I'm black.*

Laughs ensue.

The construction works for any situation, really; for example, with sexuality—"Are you hassling me again because I'm gay?"—and religion—"Is this because I'm Jewish? Is that it?" Oh we have fun, or at least I have fun, because he barely knows what he's saying. And of course I'm careful to note that such comedy should stay between us, enjoyed only at home, considering that much or most of the appeal might be lost on his fellow fifth-graders, their parents, or, say, Ms. Richardson.

After half an hour or so of superior frisbee-playing, we rest in the middle of the kite zone, in the grass, watching the tails jump and ripple around us. The Golden Gate is straight ahead, looking small, light, made of plastic and piano wire. The city, The City, that is, San Francisco, is cluttered and white and gray to the left, the Bay flat, blue, rippling noncommittally, dotted with sailboat feathers and motorboats with comet trails.

And then a notion occurs to me: swim to Alcatraz. That would be something, swimming not from but *to* Alcatraz. It doesn't look all that far. Maybe a half-mile? It's always so hard to tell with water. But I could do it, if the water was calm. Breaststroke. What would be so hard about it? Every time I see an island in a lake or bay I think I need to swim there. *I am an excellent swimmer!* I tell myself. As long as I don't panic, or wear myself out too soon, it would just a matter of pacing—

And Toph would do it, too. That would be something, us doing the *to* Alcatraz swim, together. That would be a first, two guys kind of leisurely swimming to Alcatraz together. We'd just plan it between us, a secret, would bring bathing suits one day and just jump off the rocks and go. It's probably illegal. We would be followed by the Coast Guard. Still, that would be amazing, this kind of thing always more impressive with Toph involved—

"Ow. Jesus."

Toph, bored with the rest period, has started picking up the conical pieces of dry dirt produced by the turf aerator, and from about three feet away, he is throwing them at me. He is tossing them carefully at my stomach, watching them bounce off, and chuckling to himself with each hit.

Because, after maybe twenty tosses of the conical dirt fragments, I have still not paid any attention to him, he starts throwing little pinecones. He only has five pinecones, though, so every time he's done throwing all five, he has to walk, on his knees, around me, sneaky-like, chuckling still, to retrieve them. Then he kneel-walks back to his original spot, and starts over.

I tolerate it for three more rounds, then decide to give him the punishment he wants. The fourth time he walks by, I trip him. Then I sit on him. Then he cries. When I let him up, he laughs— "Sucka!"—because he was pretending to cry, which I should have known, since he does not cry, has never cried—but because I have let him up, I have given him room and opportunity for— Jesus. The maneuvers. I dread the maneuvers. He backs up, gets a running start (though still on his knees), and comes at me, doing the maneuver where he slaps his elbow and charges at me. It is one of his three maneuvers. These are the three maneuvers:

a) THE FLYING-OBJECT MANEUVER: For this maneuver, his most commonly employed, he takes an object, like a ball, or a towel, or a pillow, and throws it at me, in kind of an elaborate, arcing motion. Then, while I'm supposed to be distracted by the object arcing toward me, he comes in after me, right behind the object, shoulder first. The objective, one assumes, is to first cause confusion, then strike a critical blow.

b) THE SLAPPING-THE-ELBOW MANEUVER: This one, the one he is doing at the moment, is newer than the flying-object maneuver, and makes a little less sense than the flying-object maneuver. What he does with the slapping-the-elbow maneuver is charge at me, right elbow first, sticking it out toward me, in the sort of position one would have if charging with a knife, or running to show someone a boo-boo. Then, while he is coming at me, right elbow first, he is also slapping the right elbow with his left hand. It's unclear why he slaps his elbow, unless it's for the sake of distraction, like the flying-object trick. Of course, where the flying-object maneuver succeeds to some extent, the slapping-elbow maneuver fails each time, because it is only *bringing attention* to his chosen weapon, i.e., *his elbow*.

c) THE SLAPPING-THE-ANKLE MANEUVER: This is very similar to the slapping-the-elbow maneuver, I guess obviously, except with this maneuver, instead of slapping his elbow, he charges at me while hopping on one foot, holding the other foot, the ankle of which he is slapping. This maneuver requires no further comment.

So at present he is coming at me, on his knees, elbow first, slapping it with his left palm, looking like an angry, masochistic double-amputee. I don't have the energy to move clear in time, so I let him land on my back. Soon we are rolling around on the grass, with me in a few seconds pinning him on his stomach, crossing his legs perpendicularly, his ankle in the back of his knee, then pushing his calf, nutcrackerlike, onto his ankle, inducing pain, tremendous pain.

"Now," he ekes out, his lungs probably collapsed under my weight. "Have you...had...enough...punishme—"

"Have I had enough what?" I'm kind of bouncing on him now.

"Puni—"

"What? You're not making sense. You have to enunciate."

"Pundim—"

"E-*nun*-ci-ate."

People are watching.

I jump off, as I usually do when people notice us wrestling in public, because now, as he's getting older and bigger, and because I have creative facial hair, we do not want people to think what I might be thinking if I were watching a grown sort of man sitting on top of a young sort of boy, in the middle of a park, making grunting sounds.

When it starts getting dark, when the kite people are gone and the joggers arrive, we leave.

When we get home there is a message from Meredith.

"Call me as soon as you get this," she says.

I call.

"It's John," she says. She's just gotten off the phone with John, who she says sounds blurry, and has been talking to her about ingesting the pills he has next to him, on the table next to his couch, in his apartment in Oakland.

"Jesus," I say, closing the bedroom door.

"Yeah."

"Why'd he call you?"

"He said you weren't home."

"You think he's serious?"

"Yeah. Maybe. You should get over there."

"Should I call him?"

"No, just go."

I tell Toph to stay.

"Lock the door."

I'm in the car.

I'm a hero.

John would never do it for real.

He's just looking for attention.

Oh but he might. He might fuck it up.

The traffic will be murder. It's five. Fuck, the traffic's going to suck, fuck fuck. Take the highway? No, no, worse. I get down to

San Pablo, drive south, straight shot, but—why does it have to be five? There is the radio, it needs to be turned up, because the radio gets turned up when there is fast driving and weaving. The radio is up. This is purpose, something is happening. The window needs to be opened. The radio needs to be turned up more now that the window is open. Something is happening.

He'd never do it. Why would he have told Meredith about the pills if he really meant to do it? *Aha!*

John has been seeing a new therapist, is on Zoloft, and has been acting more and more erratic. Meredith and I have been taking turns dealing—

"I've been throwing up all morning," he'll say.

He's always throwing up, dry-heaving, spitting up bile, blood, pieces of his liver. No one knows why. He calls, sounds different, his speech slow, labored.

"Where are you?"

"At home."

"Who's there?"

"No one."

"Then why do you sound drunk?"

"It's the medication."

Down San Pablo. It's almost nice here and there, just past University, all the boutiques—

Move your car, dickfuck! Yes, you, move!

San Pablo into Oakland, where the buildings are crooked and closed and vacant, look like prop buildings, two-dimensional— radio's all the way up, Pat Benatar, oh Pat Benatar—

Drive your truck, dumbassdickfuck, drive! Go, go! Go, Beetle-driving cockfuck! You mother*fuck*er!

This is taking way too long, way too long. He could be dead by now, could be dead. He's not dead. He's acting. He wants my attention, he wants sympathy. The spineless—

Maybe he will do it. Maybe this is it. Cannot be*lieve* this is me

again. I'll have a dead friend. Do I want a dead friend? Maybe I want
a dead friend. There could be so many uses... No, I don't want a dead
friend. Maybe I want a dead friend *without having a friend who dies.*

At his building I worry about getting in— Can I buzz? I can't
buzz. He won't buzz me in, there's no way— I didn't think of how
I'd get in— Fuck, I'll have to climb the fire escape, maybe break
a window, maybe— Shit, I can just buzz someone *else*, any apartment, duh— But they're going to ask who it is and what will I
say? I'm not going to tell them what's happening— Why wouldn't
I tell them what's happening? *Tell* them about dickhead with the
pills! It's not up to me to keep his secrets— Fuck, fuck, but then
ah! here! a woman walking out! timely! perfect!— I'll just go
through, catch that second door in time, not a bad-looking
woman, kind of elfin though, smelling like—what is that smell?
Oh! Jessica Strachan, sixth grade! oh Jessica, I owe you a call, I
have to remember— The elf-woman is kind of cute, actually,
maybe a little old, but—

Fuck. I run up the four flights, three steps at a time, I am so
quick like an Indian and goddamn it even his door is open and
when I burst through and bang the door against the wall for effect
I expect drama or blood or his mouth foaming or his dead cold
blue-green body, maybe naked even, why naked? not naked—but
he's just there, on his futon-couch apparatus, drinking wine.

This fucking guy.

"What the fuck are you doing?"

He just smiles. *What am I doing here?* I hate this guy.

Or else he's already done it.

"Did you already do it?" I'm wired from the drive, the run up the
stairs. "Did you already do it? Fuck you if you did, you fucking
cocksucker."

There are pills on the table, loose, scattered on top of a batik
tablecloth. I point to the pile, the pile just there like a little pill
display, all spread out, like hard candy in a bowl.

"What are these?" I ask, pointing. "What the fuck are these?"
He shrugs.

I scan the apartment. I'm like a cop. A police dog. A robot. I'm scanning for bad things—clues! I'll save his life. I am his only chance.

I go to the bathroom, open the medicine cabinet, dumping everything, more recklessly than I need to, throwing things. I knock over stuff in the shower even. It's kind of fun. I come up with two prescription-looking bottles. Evidence! I stomp out and hover over him.

"What are these?"

He grins. That fucking smile.

"What the fuck are these? Are these those?" I point to the table and back to the bottles. I read the labels. Zoloft. Ativan. Some other stuff. I know what Zoloft is, but have no idea what the Ativan is; it could be hemorrhoidal stuff—

"All right, all right. Listen. You tell me right now what the fuck you took, dickwad, or I'm calling the cops."

Dickwad? Where did I get *dick*wad? I haven't said dickwad for years. Need something more forceful—

"I didn't take anything," he says, chuckling, amused by me. "Don't sweat it. Don't worry," he says, with what seems to be exaggerated drunkenness. Asshole. "It's cool. It's mellow." He's really talking like this. I want to kick him in the head.

"Then where are the rest of these?" I point to the pile of pills.

He does a cute little shrug, his palms up and everything.

"Fuck you, I'm calling the cops. They'll figure it out." I look for the phone. "Where's your phone?"

The phone's on the wall. He's always been neat. Even the empty wine bottles in his pantry are lined up in rows. I start dialing.

"Don't, *don't*," he says, excited suddenly, drawing out the second don't. "I didn't take anything. Ree-lax."

"Ree-lax?"

"Yes, ree-laacks."

"Why are you talking like an asshole?"

He does a gesture indicating drinking, the throwing back of a shot, the kind of gesture you make when you don't have a drink in your hand. But because he does have a drink in his hand, he spills the wine, the whole glass, down his shirt.

"Dumbshit."

I look at the bottle, almost empty. He's alone and drinking Merlot in the afternoon. I have no idea who this person is. His shins are bruised, his hair bed-headed. What kind of person drinks wine by himself in the afternoon? And that swimsuit calendar! I'm calling anyway.

"Aw, fuck you, I'm calling anyway. I'm not having your blood on my hands." (Too.) I dial 911 and feel a little thrill—it's my first time. A few rings and boom! an operator. I'm in charge! I have news! I have a situation! I tell the operator about this asshole—I give John the finger while telling her—who may or may not have taken pills. He probably took something, I add, to make sure she sends someone. I hang up and throw the phone at him.

"They're coming, stupid."

I pace around, looking for more clues. The kitchen. I bang open the cabinets, spill a clump of silverware into the sink. It crashes, a hundred cymbals.

"Hey! What the fuck?" he says.

"What the fuck?" I yell from the kitchen. "What the fuck? Fuck you, what the fuck."

I go back to the bathroom, look under the sink. Nothing. I throw the cabinet door closed. I am making as much noise as I can. I have the right. I'll tear the place apart. I half expect to find anything now—guns, drugs, gold bullion. This is fiction now, it's fucking fiction.

I sit down on the floor in front of him, on the other side of his glass and chrome coffee table. A picture of his parents, a bad snapshot blown up too big.

"They're going to pump your stomach, dummy."

He does the cute shrug again, the little grin. I want to pop his skull like a grape.

"What's the problem? You broke up with someone?" I say, purposely not using Georgia's name, driving the point home. "This is because you broke up with somebody? Don't tell me this is because you stopped dating someone."

"Whatever."

"Jesus."

"Fuck you, you don't know what it's like."

"What what's like?" Suddenly it occurs to me that maybe this is our last conversation. He could be dying, the pills already drowning him, pulling him away. I should be nice. We should be talking about nice things. The drives in central Illinois, those miles, so straight, where you could drive eighty, ninety, the windows down, corn gone, just raw gray fields, where you felt like you were plowing through time itself, like you were a huge loud missile tearing the earth in half, leaving grateful ruin in your wake—but also knowing, we knew, we always knew, that really, at least seen from anyone else's perspective, it was not that way. To cars going the other way we were a quick loud noise, a flash; seen from above—even a crop duster would have given you the perspective—we were nothing like that—not loud, not powerful, not affecting much at all, not leaving any ruin, not making any noise—we were just some little black thing puttering straight on the straight road, producing only the smallest buzzing sound, crawling through this flat, terrible grid.

"So, what's it like? I've had, you know, relationship problems," I offer.

"It's not that. It's this." He points to his head.

"What?"

He lolls his head forward like it weighs a thousand pounds. He's getting drunker every second.

There is a dog barking outside. The dog is going nuts.

"They're dead," John says.

"Who?"

He runs his hands through his hair. Oh the drama.

"This is just stupid."

"So I'm not allowed—"

"Right. You're not."

"You could be getting raped on a Guatemalan hillside, you could—"

"I could be getting what?"

"Listen, all this—I mean, the drinking alone? The wine and pills and everything? You're such a fucking cliché!"

There's a knock on the open door.

"In here."

The cops are huge. They make the room tiny, filling it with black. There are two; they want to know what the problem is. *But don't they know? Didn't the dispatcher—*

When I come to the part about how we don't know what he took or when, I point to John with my thumb and then:

Asshole does the cute shrug for the cops!

But his eyes are starting to look nervous. Maybe he did take something. I almost feel for him now. Then I see him dead. In the emergency room, the doctors doing the thing with the electric things, the Clear! (thump) thing, his body thick and fishlike. Then I look at him. His hair looks best like this, long. The crew cut didn't work. He's almost pretty now, with his tan—

Then dead again. It's like one of those holographic cards, you turn and see one picture, turn back and see the other—

He is telling them that there's nothing to worry about, that he was just having some wine.

"Don't you two fellas have anything better to do?" John asks.

But now I want something to happen. I want release. There has been this buildup, and now something has to happen.

John reaches for the wine bottle, like he's going to pour another glass, right here and now, have another nice glass of wine. One of the cops stops to watch, his pen in his mouth, looking so perplexed his eyes are almost crossed. John stops, puts the wine bottle back, and puts his hands in his lap.

The other cop is writing things down in his pad. The pad is so small. His pen is really small, too. They seem too small, the pen and pad. Personally, I would want a bigger pad. Then again, with a bigger pad, where would I put it? You'd need a pad-holster, which might look cool but would make it even harder to run, especially if you have the flashlight attachment... I guess you need a small pad so it'll fit on your utility belt— Oh, it would be so great if they called it a utility belt. Maybe I could ask. Not now, of course, but later.

John is just sitting there, his hands clasped together, between his bony knees, as if waiting for a valentine. The cops' walkie-talkies start fuzzing, talking, word comes that the paramedics are already on the way. We're told John'll be taken in either way, to be safe, and with that, it all becomes pretty mundane. The cops are casual. They have seen this kind of thing. I too am casual. I almost want to offer them food. I glance into John's kitchen. There's a plate of grapes. *Could I offer you fellas some grapes?*

There's a lunge and John grabs the pills on the table and swallows all of them.

"What just happened?" one cop asks.

There were about twenty-five. Incredible.

"He just took the pills."

"What pills?"

"The ones on the table." *What, are you people blind?*

"What the fuck is that?" I ask John. I want to open his mouth and pry the pills out, like with a cat who's got a chipmunk—

"That was the stupidest thing I've ever seen. Now they'll definitely pump your stomach!"

He's got his eyes closed now.

"You dumbshit! Dumbshit!"

The ambulance comes, another squad car. When we leave the apartment, John's on a stretcher, it's dark and the neighborhood is exploding with red and white, the lights, skipping along the surrounding buildings—flashlight tag.

I follow in my car. I wonder which hospital they'll go to. How do they decide? We are not headed toward the closest hospital. I have never been where this ambulance is going. The ambulance is going slower than an ambulance should be going. It means either that they are not too concerned about his situation, or that he's already dead.

I pull up to a light, next to a bunch of young black kids. Maybe they'll shoot me. I'm in the zone of all probability. I cannot be surprised. Earthquakes, locusts, poison rain would not impress me. Visits from God, unicorns, bat-people with torches and scepters— it's all plausible. If these kids happen to be bad kids, and have guns, and want to shoot someone for an initiation or whatever reason bad kids shoot people like me, it will be me, the glass will break and the bullet will come through and I will not be surprised. With the bullet in my head, I will drive my car into a tree, and as I am waiting to be pulled from the wreck, nearly dead, I will not panic or yell. I will think only: *Weird, this is exactly what I expected.*

As we approach Ashby, I'm trying to remember that riddle, the one about the kid who's sick, and the doctor can't operate on him because the kid's related to the doctor or it's the doctor's son and how can that be?— I can't remember the fucking thing.

I lose the ambulance at a light.

When I get to the hospital, the doctor, a tired, ponytailed woman in her mid-thirties, comes to brief me, but is not sympathetic. "So you're friends with the big actor?"

.   .   .

I call Beth from the waiting room. She goes over to watch Toph. I have to stay until John's stomach is empty.

"How long will it take?" she asks.

"I don't know. An hour? Two?"

I sit in the waiting room.

And oh that Conan. That Conan is killing me. I'm watching the TV from across the waiting room, full of cheap chairs and loud with two children and their mother, a stout woman. They're making so much noise I can't hear Conan. Conan's doing this Live Aid kind of thing, where he's putting together a sort of benefit song, and he and Andy are arguing, because Conan's being this huge prima donna, even though he can't sing to save his life. I can barely hear over the shrieking of the kids. I move chairs so I'm closer. There. Now Sting gets into it—oh, that's a nice touch, getting Sting in there—and he's recording with Andy and Conan. Also that Springsteen drummer, the mailman-looking one with the frozen smile. I am chortling. It's the funniest fucking thing—

I start wishing I had a pen, some paper. Details of all this will be good. This will make some kind of short story or something. Or no. People have done stuff about suicides before. But I could twist it somehow, include random things, what I was thinking on the way to the hospital, about Indian summer, the doctor riddle, about watching Conan. That's a good detail, the laughing while your friend is having his stomach pumped. People have done that, too. Probably on TV even, *Picket Fences* maybe. But I could take it further. I should take it further. I could be aware, for instance, in the text, of it having been done before, but that I have no choice but to do it again, it having *actually happened that way*. But then it will sound like one of those things where the narrator, having grown up media-saturated, can't live through anything without it having echoes of similar experiences in television, movies, books, blah blah. Goddamn kids! The shrieking is the problem. It's fine except for the *fucking shrieking*. So I'll have to take it past that. I'll convey that while I'm living things very similar to things I've seen happen before, I will be simultaneously recognizing the value in living through these things, as horrible as they are, because they will make great material later, especially if I take notes, either now, on my hand, with a pen borrowed from the ER receptionist, or when I get home.

Maybe there's one in my car.

But getting it would be crass.

So instead of lamenting the end of unmediated experience, I will *celebrate* it, revel in the simultaneous living of an experience and its dozen or so echoes in art and media, the echoes making the experience not cheaper but *richer*, aha! being that much more layered, the depth luxurious, not soul-sucking or numbing but edifying, ramifying. So there is first the experience, the friend and the threatened suicide, then there are the echoes from these things having been done before, then the awareness of echoes, the anger at the presence of echoes, then the acceptance, embracing of presence of echoes—as enrichment—and above all the recognition of the value of the friend threatening suicide and having stomach pumped, as both life experience and also as fodder for experimental short story or passage in novel, not to mention more reason to feel experientially superior to others one's age, especially those who have not seen what I have seen, all the things I have seen. Another experience that can be checked off, like skydiving, backpacking through Europe, a ménage à trois.

Oh these fat kids. Look at these kids, these little porkers. Is that a genetic thing? Disgusting, the existence of fat kids.

So I could be aware of the dangers of the self-consciousness, but at the same time, I'll be plowing through the fog of all these echoes, plowing through mixed metaphors, noise, and will try to show the core, which is still there, as a core, and is valid, despite the fog. The core is the core is the core. There is always the core, that can't be articulated.

Only caricatured.

I go in to see him.

He has a tube sticking out of his mouth, one out of his nose. The one in his mouth seems too thick, the setup almost lewd. His face is milky, drawn, as if the tube has drained more than his stomach, has taken everything, a sort of punishment. He's asleep, sedated, morphine maybe, his head pointing up and to his left, in the direction of the respirator. It looks like his hands are tied to the bed.

His hands are tied to the bed. The bindings are thick, black, Velcro. He must have resisted, or swung at someone.

His legs are spread, his arms out, his left hand still looking tense, gripping something not there. Those little chicken legs of his, bruised up and down from bumping into furniture, drunk. And he's barefoot—

It's too cold to be barefoot—

And the floor isn't as clean as one would expect—

Shouldn't it be cleaner? They should clean—

I could clean—

I have seen this before, somehow, this room, I have been here, this room is the room my mom was brought to for the nosebleed, they brought her first to the emergency room, connected her, tranfusions, pouring blood into her—

But this room is much too big, too big and white. This huge room, separate from the rest of the ward, must have been built for more than one bed. As is, it is too dramatic, his bed centered in the floor, all this space.

I am standing across the room, unsure whether I want to touch him, to get any closer. It won't make a difference. He'll never know. He's asleep.

You could put pictures up in a room like this. It would be nice to have some pictures up, like they have in a dentist's office, something to look at while you're being worked on.

But then you'd be dying, and the last thing you would see would be some LeRoy Neiman print from the 1983 Masters and that would be just too terrible, not that there could ever be any appropriate thing to see before you died—

But if you really liked golf...

They should leave the walls blank.

I lean my shoulder against the wall then rest my head against it and watch for a while, palm on the white cinder block. He was such a skinny kid when he was little, always looked smaller, a few years younger because of it—but he was an amazing swimmer, just amazing, in the pool, in the ocean, a beautiful stroke. I try for a second, something to do, to time my breaths to his, watching his chest rise and fall, the rest of his body immobile, the hands in fists, the hands tied down, as the color continues to drain I watch the stupid fucking dickhead asshole sleep.

Then he gets up. He is awake and he is standing, and pulling the tubes from his mouth, from his arms, the nodes and electrodes, barefoot. I jump.

"Jesus fucking Christ. What are you doing?"

"Fuck it."

"What do you mean, fuck it?"

"I mean, fuck it, asshole. I'm leaving."

"*What?*"

"Screw it, I'm not going to be a fucking anecdote in your stupid book."

He is looking through the drawers.

"What are you looking for?"

"Clothes, fuckface. I'm getting out of here."

"You can't just leave. You're drugged and everything."

"Oh please. I can do what I want. I'm going home."

"I'm telling the nurse. You're— You're supposed to stay overnight. And then I stay here until three A.M. or so, when they say that you're safe and sleeping fine, and then with heavy heart I finally go home, to Toph, to more obligation. Then I come in tomorrow and visit you in the psychiatric ward, and then—"

"Listen, dipshit, screw it. This is such fucking garbage. I'm just supposed to lie there with my bruised shins and everything, while you get to play the dutiful friend, always there for me, ooh, ooh, all responsible, while I'm lost and worthless... Listen, fuck it. I want no part of that. Find someone else to be symbolic of, you know, youth wasted or whatever."

"Listen, John—"

"Who's John?"

"You're John."

"I'm John?"

"Yeah. I changed your name."

"Oh. Right. Now, why John again?"

"That was my dad's name."

"Jesus! So I'm your dad, too. Fuck, man, this is just too much. You are such a freak!"

"I'm a freak? *I'm a freak?* Fuck you I'm a freak."

"Okay, *I'm* the freak, *I'm* the freak. Whatever. But I didn't ask you to broadcast all this—"

"What the fuck are you talking about? You're the one who put yourself in here in the first place! You're telling me you took a handful of pills in front of me and two cops and you didn't want attention? Fuck you."

"But that doesn't mean—"

"Yeah it does."

"It does not."

"Listen, I give you the attention you want, and have been giving it to you for years, listening to you ramble about every fucking up and down you have, about how they wouldn't let you join that one gym, and about this breakup and that, fights with Meredith

and whoever else… I mean, it's not really interesting stuff, I have
to tell you, but I've been listening, all along. I mean, I know you
have your therapist convinced that you've had the worst life of all
time—and I can't believe you really told her you had been abused
as a child, you fucking liar!—but you know, your current crop of
problems, and this new drinking thing—it's all just boredom.
Emphasis on the *bore* part. It's *bor*-ing. You're bored. You're lazy.
I mean, every single thing is so boring—alcohol, pills, suicide.
I mean, no one will even believe this shit, it's so fucking boring."

"So leave it out then."

"It's not that boring."

"You're sick."

"Whatever. This is mine. You've given it to me. We're trading.
I gave you the attention you wanted, I bail you out, when you
spend three days in the psych ward, and say how you're still thinking of doing it, I'm the one who comes in and sits on your bed and
gives you the big pep talk—anyway, the point is that because of all
that, all the shit I put in for you—now I get this, this is mine
also, and you, because you've done it yourself, made yourself the
thespian, you have to fulfill that contract, play the dates, go on the
road. Now you're the metaphor."

He's quiet. He has a pair of scrubs in his hand that he found in
a cabinet. He tosses them onto the counter.

"Fine. Put me in the fucking book."

"Really?"

"Yeah."

"You're not just doing this for me?"

"Does it matter?"

"Not really."

"Whatever. I'll get back onto the bed, lie down and everything. You'll have to tie me down again."

"I will."

"And give me more of that morphine, if you don't mind."

"Sure. Sure. Listen, I really appreciate this."

"I know. Get me that tube."

"Here."

"Thanks. Now fix the blanket."

"Here."

"Okay."

"This is going to be great. You'll see."

John has to spend three days in a psychiatric ward. He calls me, and I call back. The phone rings twelve or thirteen times. An older man answers.

"Hello?"

He whispers it.

"Hi. Is John there?"

"Who?"

"A guy named John. Tallish guy, blondish hair."

"Oh, no, no. No one's available at the moment."

"Why not?"

"Well, everyone's in group. They'll be in group for an hour at least. I had to leave group to answer the phone. They asked me to leave and answer the phone."

It dawns on me that I'm talking to a patient.

"Well, can you take a message?"

Long pause. "I'm not sure if I'm allowed to. Wait."

The phone is dropped loudly; I can hear it swinging from its cord. After a full minute or so, he picks it up, breathing heavily.

"Okay, I think I can risk it."

I ask him to tell John I called.

"Okay, John called."

"No, *I'm* calling *John*."

"Oh. Oh." He is fretting. "You're calling John. Does he know you? Are you a relative?"

"No."

"Are you his father?"

"No."

"Well you can't call if—"

"Okay, I'm his dad."

"No you're not. You just said—"

"Listen. I'll call back. Don't worry about it."

"Oh, thank you!"

I come by later in the afternoon.

I am led to the door, and sign the registry. Down the hall is a common room, with blue carpet, a few couches, and a butcher-block table. It looks a little like a seventh-grade classroom. John is through the first door on the left, lying on his side, hands between his legs, on a bed in a dark room. A blanket covers his feet.

I sit on the bed opposite.

"So?"

"Do you smell it?" he asks.

"Smell what?"

"Can't you smell it?"

"No. What is it?"

"The other guy couldn't find the toilet last night."

"What other guy?"

"My roommate, the old black guy out there."

"Oh."

"All last night, on and on. He was moaning, tapping on the window, crying. He was saying, 'I'm dying, somebody please help me, I'm dying.' It was unbelievable."

"Was he dying?"

"No, he wasn't *dying*. He was taking a dump!"

"I thought you said he was by the window."

"He was. He couldn't find the bathroom, so he let 'er go out right there, standing by the window."

"Oh."

"Then he got all quiet, and in the morning, there was shit everywhere. It had gone down his leg, and onto his shoe, and during the night he had walked around—"

"Okay, fine."

"There were shit footprints in the room, in the hallway."

"Okay. So…"

"They moved me to another room for a while. Then they cleaned the floor and moved me back."

"I can't smell anything."

"Yeah, they sprayed or something."

"It actually smells nice."

"They tied me to the bed."

"When?"

"For most of the next day, after I came in."

"Huh." He wants me to be outraged, or impressed. I am not sure which. "Is that standard?"

"It drove me fucking *crazy*. Look at my arms."

He shows me his wrists, rubbed raw, bluish.

"And look."

He shows me his ankles, red and splotchy.

"I mean, have you ever been tied up?"

"Let me think." I think of a few trenchant things I could say. "No, I've never been tied up." Then:

"But I've also never pretended to commit suicide."

"What did you say?"

"Nothing."

"Fuck you."

"No, fuck you."

"You think that was an act? You and that fucking nurse. She was such a fucking bitch. She called me 'Martin Sheen.'"

"You don't look like Martin Sheen."

"She meant it like acting. Like I was acting. *Apocalypse Now*."

"Oh. I've never seen that."

"You haven't?"

"Not all the way through. Not the part she's talking about."

I look at him for a second.

"You look more like Emilio."

He gets up on his elbows to look at me.

"This isn't funny."

"I know."

"They tied me up because they thought I might do it again."

"Why would they think that?"

"Because I said I would."

"But you won't."

"Why not?"

The feces man walks in. His skin is purple and gray. He waves. He sits for a minute on his bed, smoothing the sheet with his palm. Then he gets up and shuffles out.

John leans toward me, whispers.

"See how he walks? They all do that. The Thorazine shuffle."

"Yeah."

"You know I'm locked in."

"I figured."

"As in, I can't leave, even if I want to."

"Yeah, well…"

"I mean, that's weird, right, that these people, who I don't even know, can prevent me from leaving? It's weird, just on a philosophical level, right?"

I agree that it is weird.

"I'm so tired," he says.

"Me too," I say, perhaps too quickly. "We're all tired."

He brings his knees to his chest.

"No, I'm really tired," he says.

He rolls onto his side, his back to me.

He wants to be encouraged.

I put my hand on his shoulder. I can't believe he's going to make me give him the speech. I am livid that he's going to make me give him the speech. I do it, piecing it together from times I've seen it done on TV and in movies. I tell him that there are many people who love him and would be crushed if he were to kill himself, while wondering, distantly, if that is the truth. I tell him that he has so much potential, that he has so many things to do, while most of me believes that he will never put his body and brain to much use at all. I tell him that we all have dark periods, while becoming ever more angry at him, the theatrics, the self-pity, all this, when he has everything. He has a complete sort of freedom, with no parents and no dependents, with money and no immediate threats of pain or calamity. He is the 99.9th percentile, as I am. He has no real obligations, can go anywhere at any moment, sleep anywhere, move at will, and still he is wasting everyone's time with this. But I hold that back—I will save that for later—and instead say nothing but the most rapturous and positive things. And though I do not believe much of it, he does. I make myself sick saying it all, everything so obvious, the reasons to live not at all explainable in a few minutes on the edge of a psychiatric ward bed, but still he is roused, making me wonder even more about him, why a fudge-laden pep talk can convince him to live, why he insists on bringing us both down here, to this pedestrian level, how he cannot see how silly we both look, and when, exactly, it was that his head got so soft, when I lost track of him, how it is that I know and care about such a soft and pliant person, where was it again that I parked my car.

VIII.

We can't do anything about the excrement on the floor. At the *Might* office, we are having a problem with the excrement on the floor. The fecal matter has been coming over the toilet's porcelain lip and onto the tile, then under the door, and there is now a peninsula of brownish sewage in our main work area, which we would complain about, and have something done about, if we were still paying rent. But we can't call anyone to fix anything because the landlord condemned the building four months ago, when it was deemed needy of seismic retrofitting, and no one, especially him or her, knows we're still here. All the other tenants have moved out, but because no one ever formally *told us* the plan, or issued any sort of *official letter,* and because Randy Stickrod is out of town—we have not seen Randy Stickrod for a while—we are squatting.

 We're still not paying contributors, or part-time staffers, much less ourselves. And even though we are able to use the magazine as a vehicle to answer some long-held questions—*Can you drink your own urine? Which butterflies can be safely eaten?*—the perks are not justifying the work, and it's all kind of depressing. We are beat.

We are weak. Marny's nose has been running for two years now. Moodie, who seems to have a perpetual case of mono, keeps a disconcertingly large jug of vitamin C on his desk. We are kept alive only by a constant influx of volunteers and interns, a half dozen at a time. We meet and recruit someone named Lance Crapo (long *a*), apparently an heir to one of the biggest potato-farming families in Idaho. Because he tucks in his shirts and is willing to handle the magazine's business aspects, from advertising to the ever-wondered-about business plan, within a month he's our vice president and acting publisher. And soon we get something named Zev Borow, just out of Syracuse University, who has moved from New York to San Francisco to work, for free, for us.

Like most of the new young help, Zev has more energy than we know what to do with. We send him on errands, we have him file things. We run out of things for him to file, until Paul bets us that he can get Zev to file a gigantic box of record company publicity photos—hundreds of them, none of which we'll ever need, much less in alphabetical order.

It takes him almost a week, but he does it, entertaining us all and for a time distracting us from the fact that in many ways we're starting to hate each other—our frustrations about our stagnancy spilling over into the way we talk to each other—"No, I bet that'll get done real soon, sport"—our self-loathing turned against each other.

Appropriately enough, Zev, largely oblivious and still optimistic, comes up with the next cover story: The Future.

The opening essay:

THE FUTURE: IS IT COMING?

It's fun to wonder about the kinds of things that will happen in the future. Who will do what? What will happen? Those are big questions that are really hard to think about. But try something smaller, like food in The Future: What will we be eating? Will food taste the same, or will it taste different? Will it still be chewy? What about clothes? Will they be tighter, or looser?

We ask a variety of experts what they foresee happening in 1995, and beyond:

THE FUTURE OF WINDOW CLEANING
by Richard Fabry, publisher, American Window Cleaner:
"More and more people will notice professional window cleaning tools...after all, they are pretty. Many are made out of brass and have a nice 3-D sculptured look to them—almost as if they deserve to be shown off in a museum."

THE FUTURE OF BEVERAGES
Susan Sherwood, editor, Arizona Beverage Analyst:
"Overall, people will be drinking less, but drinking better in '95."

Zev writes to William T. Vollmann, soliciting his predictions for the year. Vollmann writes back, in crayon, on the other side of the letter, indicating that he'd like to contribute, but would like to be compensated. Because we have never paid anyone for anything, and have less money now than ever before, we ask if there's anything nonmonetary we can do. He says okay, this is what he wants: a) One box of .45-caliber Gold Saber bullets; b) Two hours, in a warm, well-lit room, with two naked women, to paint them, in watercolor.

Zev runs to the gun shop on Second Street, and one of our part-time assistants, a bartender named Michelle, says she'll model and will bring along a friend. Vollmann drives down from Sacramento with a friend, who sits with Moodie in his kitchen as Vollmann paints Michelle and friend in the living room.

We wait until after the session to hand over the bullets.

The issue's gravamen is "Twenty in their 20s," a ha-ha both on ourselves and on a recent *New York Times Magazine* spread heralding "Thirty Under Thirty," a list that included no one we had heard of, or imagined we would ever hear from again. Most important, it did not include us, and that was perturbing. Our intro:

Slack this: Might presents twenty young movers, shakers and money-makers who can't even spell "slack." Twenty of the hottest, hippest, hard-rockin'est twentysomethings ever to throw on a pair of used jeans and Doc Martens. Twenty who earned their inheritances. Twenty who know that being young, having fun and drinking Pepsi is more than just a slogan. Twenty who'd like to buy the world a Coke, and are already lining up at the counter. Your twenty, my twenty, our twenty…Might's twenty.

In our spread, all of those to watch are famous, rich, attractive, well dressed, and more often than not, the progeny of the already famous, rich, attractive, and well dressed. Brent, Moodie's roommate, dresses as Lt. Sanders, jet-set son of the Colonel. Our newest intern, Nancy, poses as Juliette Tork, rock-star-hopeful daughter of the Monkees' Peter. There is of course a Kennedy (we call him Tad; he has had run-ins), a surname-less model, a black filmmaker ("I want to make fairy tales for black folk"), a Hasidic rave organizer (Schlomo "Cinnamon" Meyer), and a rapper from the Upper East Side (hit single: "Double-Parking Bitch"). For no good reason at all, we send another Scud in the direction of poor Wendy Kopp:

CINDY KAHN, 25, FOUNDER, STREETS FOR AMERICA
Streets for America, an idea born from Kahn's senior thesis at Harvard, is now a multibillion dollar nonprofit corporation. Placing recent college grads on the streets of America's most dangerous cities, the program's purpose is to reinvigorate the country's police force with fresh faces, open minds and good breeding. "All the regular cops seemed to be so stupid and ugly," says Kahn. "It was time to bring some class to law enforcement. You can bet hardened criminals will sit up and take notice if the person who's cuffing them is well-dressed and, say, has a master's from Yale."

And of course we take a swipe at Lead or Leave:

FRANK MORRIS, 29, AND FRANK SMOLINOV, 29
FOUNDERS, ORGANIZE OR EMIGRATE!
These two comprise the brains behind the politically neutral but politically influential Organize or Emigrate! Claiming "somewhere around 130 million members," the organization, in just two years, has managed to produce three pamphlets and a button. But they're

not resting on their laurels. "We won't sit down to an hour-and-half-long meal, or even read our fraternity newsletter, until every man and woman in Generation X has seen our picture in a major magazine," says Smolinov. So what's next? "What we're looking for is a Cabinet appointment," Morris says. "But it looks like Perot isn't going to run in '96."

Zev, with a gesture that says "Who, me?" poses as Kevin Hillman, whose entry strikes eerily close to home:

KEVIN HILLMAN, 26, AUTHOR
"Slacker? Not me," laughs Hillman. He can afford to laugh, too. His book, Slacker? Not Me! has been perched atop the *Times* bestseller list since early January and shows no signs of slipping. The book is simply the transcribed recordings of a week's worth of conversations between Hillman and his friends, captured by accident on a tape recorder. "I just forgot the thing was recording, and when I listened to it, it was just so, so; so damned real!" Next month Hillman guest VJ's with Kennedy on MTV's Alternative Alternative Nation Weekend Rock and Jock Tribute Water Polo Weekend.

Shalini poses serenely, in Indian garb, as electric lutist Nadia Sadique—"equally adept at classical lute, country lute, and bottle-neck-slide lute." Two weeks later we get a call from a producer of *Where in the World Is Carmen Sandiego?* an educational show on PBS.

They absolutely must have Nadia on the show.

We promise to forward the message to Nadia's manager. After a brief discussion, we decide that Nadia's manager will be Paul. We hook up the phone to a tape recorder, and Paul returns the call of the producer.

PAUL: Hello, Mr. Meath, this is Nadia Sadique's agent, Paul Wood-Prince.

[It is my understanding that Paul came up with that, Wood-Prince, on the spot.

PRODUCER: Hello! Yes, I was just given your number. How did we find you?

PAUL: *Might* magazine.

PRODUCER: Yeah, we saw the thing in *Might* magazine. Are you familiar with our show?

PAUL: Yes.

PRODUCER: Oh good. Nadia seems to be exactly the kind of person that we might use for a walk-on on the show, or to illustrate some musical clue. And of course the other thing we love about it is that she plays the lute.

PAUL: [Silence]

PRODUCER: That's sort of an inside joke on our show. Every day we steal something that's called "The Loot."

PAUL: Uh-huh. Right. "The Loot."

PRODUCER: And so if we could have her playing the lute, it would be great. It's just our kind of joke.

PAUL: She's also from Bangladesh.

PRODUCER: Oh yeah, we love that multicultural stuff.

Paul hardballs Meath over dates and fees, and finally books the fictional Nadia on the show for the following month. (We beg her, but Shalini will not go. Nadia is a no-show.)

The cover of the issue features five of the twentysomethings to watch, all looking off the page to some brighter tomorrow, over which are the words:

THE FUTURE: HERE TO STAY!

Just before the issue goes to press, the owner of our building finally catches on that we're still there. We're given a week to get out.

We move our offices from the condemned warehouse to the fifth floor of a glassy office box in the middle of the city. The *Chronicle* promotions department, wanting us closer so Moodie and I can provide lightning-quick service, have let us move in with them—along with Shalini and *Hum*, Carla and *bOING bOING*—giving us about 800 square feet, with floor-to-ceiling windows, for $1,000 a month—which Moodie and I easily pay by overcharging them for our design work.

But the grind has begun. The windows don't open, and even the availability of near-constant jokes about Jews and Mormons fails to stem the tide of frustration, decay. We've reached the end of pure inspiration, and are now somewhere else, something implying routine, or doing something because people expect us to do it, going somewhere each day because we went there the day before, saying things because we have said them before, and this seems like the work of a different sort of animal, contrary to our plan, and this is very very bad.

At home it's returning library books late, and getting posterboard for Toph's map of Africa, and grocery shopping at the place where they know us and know that we don't need a cart to carry the bags to the car, not us, because two men can carry six bags four for me and two for Toph, we love carrying the stuff, side by side, and thus insist upon it. And one night after the grocery store and immediately after a bookstore visit, from the north of Shattuck Avenue, right in the left-middle of Berkeley's downtown there comes a moving, gurgling volcano of lights. White lights popping from motorcycles, police cars yelling in red and blue, and then a slow river of shiny black. A procession. Too late for a funeral—it's already dark—but then, what—

They drive past, and about when we think they'll be out of sight, they stop.

A man walks toward us, from the direction of the caravan.

"It's Clinton," he says. "He's eating at Chez Panisse."

We run.

Toph and I are among the first there. I am wild with excitement. (This was, remember, around '93-'94.) I explain to Toph how thrilling this is, that inside this building is the president, and not just any president—though admittedly that probably would not have mattered—but this is a president that, fuck, we have some

sort of crush on this man. He speaks like a president, not always
authoritative or anything but he can form sentences, complex sentences with beginnings and ends, subordinate clauses—you can
hear his semicolons! He knows the answers to questions. He knows
acronyms and the names of foreign leaders, their deputies. It is
heartening, it makes our country look smart, and this is an important thing, something we have too long been without. Oh many
were the times when Toph and I lay on my bed, my legs on his
back, watching Clinton talk, points a and b and c, *Jesus, how does he
do it?* Toph, I would say, Toph, this man is actually bright, could
be brilliant. This man still reads books; encyclopedic and charming and so seemingly real—he is real, yes, certainly more real than
the last few, who were too old to know—never did we know people that old so they were something else, unintelligible—and
though we hope that he is real even if he is not entirely real he is
more real, and smart enough to seem real, and wins both ways—
And now he is here, mere feet away, eating the fresh and adven-
turous food stylings of California Cuisine!

We decide that we're staying until he comes out. I run to a
phone to call Kirsten. She's in bed but says she'll be there. Toph
runs to the convenience store to get provisions—Fig Newtons and
root beer and caramel.

"No comic books," I say.

"Okay," he says.

"Really. I'm timing you. This is the president, little man."

"Okay, okay," he says.

While he's gone more people arrive. There is a commotion, a
civic bustle just as Frank Capra would have imagined it:

"Charlie, what's all the hullabaloo about?"

"Word is the president's inside!"

"The president? Well, I'll be..."

When Toph gets back there are about twenty people, gathered
on either side of the restaurant's door. Across the street the cars and

vans of the slow caravan stand still, doors open. Agents walk and squint and whisper, doing their agent things, wishing their friends could see them now.

Kirsten arrives, in her pajamas. It's been about twenty minutes, and there are now about fifty people around the door, some across the street, camped near the limos.

We are standing at the very front, to the right side of the door, no more than twenty feet away. We eat the snacks and Toph drinks his root beer, which he's set on the ground, holding it steady with his feet. He is careful about the things he loves.

Another half hour passes and a hundred more gather. There are people ten deep behind us, a throng across Shattuck Avenue. We cannot fathom why people would stand across the street, easily a hundred feet away, when they could be so close, near us.

"Suckers." I tell Toph, thumbing toward those watching from so far away. It is important, I feel, that the boy knows what suckers look like.

To pass the time, we bounce on our toes. We trip each other. We play the game where you're not supposed to look at the circle made with thumb and forefinger and when you do, you are punched on the arm. We stop when given a sidelong look from one of the Secret Service people. *Do we look menacing, or just pathetic?*

Any minute now.

Something occurs to me, though. How much time will Clinton have to mingle? Surely not much at all. So then, how will he decide where in the crowd to plunge? No way will he have time to shake the hands of us all, or even a portion of us, however doting. He will have to choose an area, a slice of us most deserving and representative.

I try to get Toph to take his hat off. He's always wearing the goddamn Cal hat with the smell of urine. He wears it to school, between classes, every moment until bedtime. He is trying to resist the onset of the curly hair—already his hair is thickening—

and the hat straightens it out but now the hat is ruining our chances. The hat makes us look disrespectful. We're a young hoodlum and his ... drug dealer.

"Off with the hat."

"No."

"Off with the hat."

"No."

Good God, the door opens. A few randoms pour out and then this huge grey-haired man. Jesus Christ, he's a big man. His face is so pink. What happened to his face that it's so pink? I ask Toph why his face is so pink. Toph thinks for a second but does not know.

Flashbulbs of course, and the screaming of things, mostly things like We Love You Bill, because everyone does love him now, because he is in the Bay Area, and he is our man, he says things we believe and is so thrillingly articulate, and he knows we love him and has come here to bask, in Berkeley even, at Chez Panisse, our town, our restuarant, and here he is, to be adored and received and thanked and urged on. Because we are in Berkeley and the president is here we are, Toph and Kirsten and I—at the white-hot center of the entire world and history to date.

But Toph can't see, because suddenly some ugly rat bastard has shoved himself in front of us. It's unbelievable. I want to push this guy over, want to throw him to one side. How could we wait for so long and be so devoted and ready, only to have this round-backed asshole devour our chance for an audience with Bill?

This will not stand. I will toss him aside if need be. *But will the president come our way? Will he know that we have been chosen?* Surely he will know. If anyone will know, he will.

After waving to the throng for a minute, Bill heads.... toward us. Of course! Of course! Here he comes! Here he comes! Good lord his face is huge! Why so pink? Why so weirdly pink? Toph is being crushed, his face pressed against the back of this round-backed bastard-man, and so I grab Toph and lift him, and his hat falls off, and Clinton is making his way from our left, where our side began, to us, in the middle. Hands reach toward him, grasping for his flesh, and he reaches into the anemone of fingers and as he reaches toward us I lunge and take Toph's hand and thrust it toward the president's, because close will not do here, chance is not good enough, and just as I throw Toph's little soft hand forward, Bill's fat pink hand is there—perfect timing—and the president grabs and squeezes the little hand of my brother, and I feel the jolt through me because we have completed the moment, have destroyed and begun a new world at this moment when we did all that was necessary.

Toph touched his hand! Oh if only there were a picture. Then, decades from now, when Toph was running for president himself, there would be the shot of he and Clinton touching, like God's finger lazily extended toward Adam's, like the photograph of Clinton shaking the hand of Kennedy.

And who will Toph thank, during his own inauguration? Oh yes, we know who he will thank. He will thank me. He will be there, in his blue suit, so tall and filled out and finally not wearing his urine-smelling hat, and he will say:

"I'll never forget when my brother, who tried so hard and suffered so long, lifted me over the heads of the throng to meet my destiny." Destiny spoken in a whisper, as Vader would, accent on first syllable: *Des*tiny.

Toph is better at it than I am. Half the time, mine go behind me, which is funny on its own, but is not the effect we've been going for. We are doing the thing where we pretend to throw the baseball as hard as possible, with a huge windup, leg-kick and everything and then, at the last minute, instead of actually gunning it, we let it slip off our fingers, suddenly in slow motion, the ball let go with a high, looping arc, the trajectory slow and sorry, a one-winged pelican. Then we catch it and send it back the same way. We've been doing this for half an hour.

Passersby, in their cars, are hating it. They are slowing down, almost to a stop, exasperated that we are playing catch in the street. In a way that indicates that they have never before seen people throwing a baseball in the street, have perhaps *heard* of such a thing, but never thought that, in this day and age, a parent would not only condone but sponsor, would *participate in*, such a practice.

These people, these precious Berkeley people. The man in his Volvo gaping at us like we're skinning babies.

We're actually only stalling. We have an appointment.

We go inside.

"You have the listings?"

"Yeah."

"You have the paper?"

"Yeah."

"Okay, let's go."

We get in the car and go.

After a year and a half of on-again, off-again, Kirsten and I have finally broken up for good, which was mutually agreed-upon, acceptable to all concerned, but which quickly set off a chain reaction too horrible to even menti—

So first we broke up, then Kirsten decided she'd move into San Francisco, which was wonderful with me, we needing distance, and so I would be less tempted to spy on her when curdled with sudden jealousy at one in the morning on a Saturday, convinced that she was at home, on her couch, with someone much more masculine than myself. And all was perfect until Beth, who has just finished her second year in law school, decided that, see, what she'd like to do is, well, she'd like to move, from Berkeley, from a few blocks from us, where she is always handy, within reach, able to provide whatever help we might need when we needed it, to the city, over the Bay, all that water, the bridge, all those miles away, to San Francisco, where she will live with...Kirsten!

Kirsten even called.

"Isn't this great?" she asked.

Then Beth called.

"Isn't this great?" she asked.

It was not great. Toph and I were alone. All was lost. Left to do everything by myself, I would lose whatever grip I still had on anything, and then would take it out on Toph, who would silently absorb my stress, then my rage and the resulting unhappiness of our household, then would insist on going to military school, where he would excel, and would grow up to collect animal skulls and write letters to prisoners. In the end, it wasn't so bad—Beth drove back to Berkeley just about every day—but still to ease the tension, with a few months left on our lease, and middle school over and junior high coming up, we had little choice but to follow. We looked for a place in San Francisco. We are still looking.

We had no idea where to start. Again, I entertained the notion of a loft, a huge loft South of Market, with roof access, endless storage space, a skylight, and walls we can paint on, grace with elaborate murals that will eventually be worth millions, will be preserved and carefully removed and trucked to the MOMA for permanent display. But when we look at the neighborhood, from the Bay Bridge to the Mission, it's all wrong. No trees, too much cement, leather. And once we rule out South of Market, no one seems to be able to agree on an appropriate neighborhood for us.

The Haight? No, no, says Marny. Drugs, homeless people, all those terrible hippie teenagers from Marin begging for change.

The Mission? No, I wouldn't, not with Toph, says Moodie. Drugs, prostitutes, gangs.

And almost everything else is too far from his new school. We answer an ad for a two-bedroom just off Dolores Park, even though Paul says a good percentage of the city's drug traffickers call its rolling green home, and where, only weeks before, a young couple was shot, both killed without motive, in the middle of the day, while lying in the sun.

The rental is owned by an older gay couple who live in the other half of the building. It's big, high-ceilinged, affordable, painted mauve and periwinkle but otherwise perfect. I fill out a form, give them all my information, lie about our income—I have learned that much—and later that night, I write a long letter to them, begging them to grant us the place, reiterating that we were first, that we are quiet and nice, tragic and desperate, chosen to live and suffer and educate. I want to and almost tell them about the dream I had the night before, a semi-conscious dream where I entered Toph's bloodstream—I was some kind of microscopic particle, like in *Fantastic Voyage* maybe, and I entered his bloodstream, and saw the layers of flesh, and the reds and mauves and violets, the muds and blacks, and I was blowing around at thrilling speeds, things shooting to and fro, in the capillaries and out, but then suddenly I was going through the sky—I am not sure at this point if I was still inside Toph or not; could Toph's frame also encompass a sky—and there were the usual stages of blue then atmosphere-white and then soundlessly into ebony space, seeing the world, with roundness, below. I somehow think this story, this kind of thing, will endear us to them, but then worry if it'll be a case of, you know, too much information.

I drive to the twenty-four-hour Kinko's to fax it so they'll have it in the morning, will read it when the sun arrives and will love us and cease to entertain other offers. In the morning he calls.

"David?"

To gay men I am David.

"Yes," I say.

"That was a nice note you faxed."

"Thanks." Relief. It's done. The eagle has—

"But we're really looking for a gay couple."

It's unbelievable. With the San Francisco rental market tightening to an all-time high—driven, in large part, by the endless flow of *Real World*–worshiping postcollegiates—we are treated like vermin. We are below gay couples. We are below married couples, unmarried couples, female roommates, male roommates. Landlords do not answer our calls. We see one place, a light-filled two-bedroom in just the right neighborhood, which we know we are the first to see—we are always the first—and though the pudgy landlord is himself a single parent, and though we hand him all our bank documents proving our net worth and ability to pay this rent, he gives the apartment to—

"Who?"

"A doctor."

We are appalled. We are shocked, *shocked* that in this day and age two such as we would be discriminated against, solely because one of us is twenty-five, dubiously self-employed, makes only $22,000 a year, and lives with his twelve-year-old brother, who, it says on paper, pays almost half the rent—

Oh, rental stories are not interesting.

But suffice it to say we had to debase ourselves thoroughly to get this place, in a quiet neighborhood, close to his new school, close to a movie theater, close to a grocery store from whence we can walk the whole way home, carrying our bags without car or cart. Like men. In the apartment is a huge west-facing window for Toph and a retirement-community-facing window for me, which is depressing but fitting if you really think about it, and I relish the sacrifice I have have made, giving him the bigger room, the light-filled room with the bay window. And we gorge ourselves on San Francisco. We're suddenly a five-minute bike ride from the beach, Baker Beach, rolling with dunes, the Pacific on the left and the Golden Gate on the right, and we're a few blocks from the Presidio, choked with pine and eucalyptus, recently decommissioned and all but abandoned. We bike through it, a ghost town of white stucco and wood set against lawns of parrot green, everything sprawled loosely, casually, on some of the most ridiculously valuable property in the world. There is no sense to the Presidio, its areas of raw forest, unkempt baseball diamonds near million-dollar homes, but of course there is no logic to San Francisco generally, a city built with putty and pipe cleaners, rubber cement and colored construction paper. It's the work of fairies, elves, happy children with new crayons. Why not pink, purple, rainbow, gold? What color for a biker bar on 16th, near the highway? Plum. Plum. The light that is so strong and right that corners are clear, crisp, all glass is blinding—stilts and buttresses and turrets—the remains of various highways—rainbow windsocks— a sexual sort of lushness to the foliage. Only intermittently does it seem like an actual place of residence and commerce, with functional roads and sensible buildings. All other times it's just whimsy and faith. Just driving to and from Marny's, in the Castro, is epic, this hill and that hill—oh, the sorrow of flat, straight Illinois!—this vista and that, always the hills, the curves, the maybe our brakes will fail, the maybe someone else's brakes will fail—it's always a kind of adventure in faded Technicolor, starring a vast cast of brightly dressed losers. Always there is something San Franciscan reinforcing all everyone has come to think about the city, The City, they say—the homeless people wear bathing suits and do handstands on the sidewalk, and shamelessly defecate, unmolested, on busy street corners. Activists throw bagels at police in riot gear, bicyclists are allowed to choke Market Street traffic but are arrested for trying to ride over the Bay Bridge. The first time we visit Haight Street a man staggers past us, bleeding profusely from the head, followed ten seconds later by another man, also bleeding from the head, yelling, apparently at the first bleeding man. He is holding a tennis racket. There are the endless signs of the concerns of its residents, the different things considered objectionable, grapes and granulated sugar among them, to cars in the city, skateboards downtown, tunnels through Marin. Street signs are amended:

STOP
DRIVING

STOP
MUMIA'S EXECUTION

The buses are attached to strings or wires or something, and driving behind them requires often waiting, having reading material on hand, for these buses do not for long stay attached to the strings or wires—suddenly there will be a spark, and the bus will stop and the driver will get out, walk to the back of the bus, and yank on the string or wire, smiling cheerfully, oh ha ha, because here there really isn't all that much of a hurry, for anyone, anywhere, least of all for those who take buses. There are eighty-year-old twins who haunt Union Square, and the alleys breathe urine, and teenagers slum in the Mission, the Haight—"Brotherman! How 'bout a slice of that pizza?"—and the wind tunnels off the Pacific, speeding down Geary, through the Richmond, attacking Toph's west-facing bedroom window.

And at the new apartment, the sliding is good. The layout is long and narrow, and there is a hallway connecting all the rooms, and because the hallway is wood-floored, and about thirty-five feet long, we can, with the door to the building's stairway open, pick up three or four feet in momentum, so, with those three feet and another sixteen or seventeen needed to build sufficient speed, it still allows for a good twenty feet or so of superior sliding, even more if Toph's door is kept open and the chair at his desk moved.

But Toph is the only one in his new school who lives in an apartment. Many classmates live nearby, but all own their homes, huge perfect houses in Presidio Heights, with maid's quarters, driveways, garages. When I see the school roster, and see that "#4" after our address, I hate it. I want to call the school and have them remove it. He's started seventh grade and, outside of the one teacher, a kind man who feels it necessary to ask him once a day how he feels, all is well and normal and he has immediately become unbearably popular. Within a month there were three bar and bat mitzvahs, two birthday parties, various other social events, and I am relieved, enormously relieved despite the endless driving involved, for this activity, the popularity, buffering the shock of the move.

I drive him to a get-together at the house of a girl in his class. When, three hours later, I pick him up from the party, he is shaken, bewildered.

There has been Spin the Bottle.

"Really?" I say. "Spin the Bottle? I had no idea that still existed. I mean, I don't think *I* even played that, ever..."

He had been surrounded. It had been only him, one other boy, and six girls. He had been trapped, set up. He was the new boy and they were fighting for dibs.

"So did you kiss anyone?"

"No."

"No? Why not?"

"Because I hardly knew them."

"Well, sure, but..."

"I didn't feel like it."

I don't know what to say. Most of me, the vast majority of my being, wants to spend the next few weeks talking only about this, not only siphoning every possible detail out of him, drunk as I am with vicarious curiosity, but also overwhelmed with the need to rattle him for being such a *pussy*. I weigh my options carefully and, because I am a master of strategy, decide that the only way to get any information at all is to add as little as possible in the way of, say, ridicule to the conversation. I am careful also not to project my own regrets on him, the opportunities missed, the girls never kissed, the junior high dances I missed—the fact that I do not want him to have these regrets, any regrets. We discuss the subtleties of the evening all the way home, and at home on the couch, long past his bedtime, while watching *Saturday Night Live*, and after that.

"Were they cute?"

"I guess. A few. I don't know. A couple weren't from my school."

I am enthralled, hoping not to jinx it, his openness with regard to the girls, because it's one of the first times he's talked to me about it, given that I usually giggle and snicker, and so, accordingly, he usually chooses to share these matters with Beth.

But Beth, as a first-year associate, has lately been too busy. We are seeing her less and less, which is a problem, but not as much of a problem as it would have been even a year ago. Toph is at the age where I feel like I can leave him for a few hours, and because we are only twelve blocks from his new school, he can walk. I do drive him the first few times, and when he's too late to get there himself, but otherwise, because I have been up until three at the computer, changing the very face of the world, I sleep through his morning. He wakes up and makes his lunch, his breakfast, ingests it with the cartoons and then, when he's leaving, I often, easily once a week, raise my head from the pillow long enough for:

"Hey."

"Hey."

"How's it going?"

"Good."

"You better get going, you're almost late."

"I know."

"What'd you eat?"

"Waffles."

"You eat any fruit?"

"An apple."

"You did?"

"Yeah."

"How you getting there?"

"Bike."

"Your chain still broken?"

"Yeah."

"Wear the helmet."

"Bye."

"Wear it!"

Because his chain has been stuck, or broken, for weeks—we've gotten it fixed twice but it quickly reverts to its useless, congealed form—he has been doing what amounts to a coasting sort of thing to school, where, without sitting on the seat, he has one foot on one pedal, and pushes off with the other, using the bike like a skateboard, or scooter. He had described it to me, but I had not seen the routine until one day, when, after he left, I was walking to the bathroom to pee before going back to bed, when I noticed his lunch was still on the kitchen table. I ran out after him, and he was gone so I drove to the school, not expecting to see him en route but there he was, heading toward the first traffic light, at California and Masonic. It was unbelievable. He was doing the thing with the pedals and the pushing off, like riding the bike sidesaddle—it looked like he was joking. No normal child would ride a bike like that. And of course he wasn't wearing his helmet. I honked and stopped him at the corner.

"Your lunch."

"Oh."

I was too tired to say anything about the helmet.

I feel wretched with guilt much of the time, know in my heart that because I do not make him breakfast and drive him to school, he will grow up to skin rabbits and recreate with crossbows and paint guns— But then again, in comparison to some of the other parents, I'm Dr. Spock. There is, for example, the case of the one divorced mother of a kid in Toph's class. About fifteen of us, parents, are out in the Marin Headlands one afternoon, standing by our cars in the parking lot, waiting to pick up the kids, all of whom have been on a two-day camping trip. The mother, tanned and leathery, with long blond hair and pink lipstick, wearing a long rugby jersey over white stretch pants, is talking, blithely and while gesturing extensively, about how she deals with pot in her home, vis-à-vis her other son, a sophomore in high school:

"I figure if he's gonna smoke, he's gonna smoke." She shrugs elaborately. "So I let him fire up at home. At least I know where he is, what he's doing, that he's not driving around or something."

Though she is talking to another parent, she is glancing my way. I have the feeling she expects me, because I am closer to her high schooler's age than she is, and, because I have creative facial hair, to be sympathetic to her point of view.

But I'm too stunned to speak. She should be jailed. And I should raise her children. Maybe I'm the only one qualified to raise all these kids—so many of these parents are too old, dusty. Worse are those like her, who dress like their children and use their expressions. But "fire up"? Who says "fire up"?

I tell Beth the story, and she is entertained, as always, by the inadequacies of our fellow parents. She and I are collaborating peacefully, tag-teaming, doing the parent-teacher conferences together. We are a circus family, a trapeze family, with perfect timing, great showmanship, tight green outfits.

We decide holidays on a case-by-case basis. Church is out completely, as are most of the related holidays. Thanksgiving is observed halfheartedly, since neither Toph nor I care much for turkey, and don't eat stuffing and that cranberry-Jell-O-in-a-can job. But Christmas we do. Bill, Beth, and I get copies of Toph's list and split it up. Beth handles the stocking and the clothes. Bill handles a few things from the list, but otherwise takes the opportunity to buy for Toph books he finds vital to the development of any budding libertarian—one year bringing both William Bennett's *Book of Virtues* and the *Dictionary of Cultural Literacy.*

A few days before, Bill comes up from L.A., and we try as best as we can to set up the presents in the way our mother did. At Christmas, as with all holidays we still bother with, we celebrate it in a way that's at once an homage to our parents and their way of going about things, but more often a vicious sort of parody.

Our mother was a Christmas extremist. Weeks of eight-hour shopping days, lists tendered and revised and revised again, presents pushing outward from the tree, almost to the foyer—a relentless effort to top previous years, to make it look not just joyous or extravagant, but obscene. My father, a fan but a less out-wardly enthusiastic one, had a ritual, wherein he, because he was the father goddammit, and had been up half the night putting the goddamn presents together, would rise late, and would come down, at oh maybe ten or so, not to watch us open our presents, but to make for himself and eat a full breakfast. Coffee, danish, bacon, orange juice, grapefruit, newspaper, everything—and at the most leisurely of paces. As we waited, cross-eyed with anticipation, kids from the neighborhood, most of whom had been up since four or five, would frolic outside our windows with new sleds, taunting us, riding by on their Green Machines, pushing the pedals with new moon boots, shining in the winter sun, utterly fabulous.

This Christmas we're dying because Beth and I have been doing the routine. Bill has been sitting, disapproving but still laughing, arms crossed, shaking silently. The routine, which begins after we've woken up and before Toph has started unwrap-ping, goes like this:

BETH: Okay, you can open them now.

ME: No, actually, wait. (*Picking lint from shirt, then slowly, slowly untying and then tying shoes*) Okay...now.

BETH: Actually, hold on. I have to use the bathroom. (*Sounds of water from the faucet. Then silence. Then flushing. More water. Then tooth-brushing)*

BETH: (*Reappearing from the bathroom, refreshed, straightening sweater*) Okay, I'm ready. Go ahead.

ME: Wait a sec, wait a sec. You know what would be delicious about now? Grapefruit.

BETH: Mmm. Grapefruit.

ME: Let's have some grapefruit, then you know what? We could all take a nice walk.

BETH: That would be so nice.

ME: Fresh air, some exercise...

BETH: And closer to God...

ME: And closer to God.

BETH: We can have Christmas tomorrow!

BETH: (*Thinking, clicking tongue*) Oooh. Tomorrow's no good. Thursday?

ME: Thursday's bad. And the weekend's tight. Monday?

At this point Beth and I are choking, crying, contorted, looking to furniture for support. We knock ourselves out.

Toph is waiting, unimpressed. He's seen the routine before.

Addressing Toph's presents is up to me, and the night before, I do everything I can to spruce up the task, to forge new ground. Some I address to fictitious recipients, or to other kids in the neighborhood. Many of Toph's presents I address to myself. Those that actually bear his name are misspelled. Or else I do what I do when filling out school forms: I get his name wrong, writing "Terry" or "Penelope," then cross it out and write his real name, smallish, below. I sign a few from "Us," a few from "Santa," but prefer this:

FROM: God.

He doesn't know who to thank. He does not want to seem overly cavalier when reaping the booty, and we exploit his eagerness to please. A package of colored clay is opened.

"Thank you," he says.

"Thank who?"

"I don't know. You?"

"No, not me. *Jesus*."

"Thank you, Jesus?"

"Yes, Toph, Jesus died for your Christmas fun."

"He did?"

I turn to Bill. Bill is staying out of it.

"He did," I say. "Beth, did he not?"

"Indeed he did. Indeed he did."

Work becomes ever more depressing, routine, improved only by the occasional near-death experience. To wit: It is any day at all when I am at my desk, working on a spread debunking raves, one in a long line of contrarian articles pointing out the falsity of most things the world believes in, holds dear. We have debunked a version of the Bible written for black kids. We have debunked the student loan program. We debunk the idea of college in general, and work in general, and marriage, and makeup, and the Grateful Dead—it is our job to point out all this artifice, everywhere, and the work is rewarding, bringing truth to an unsuspecting—

I am kicked from inside. A kick with metal-tipped shoes. I am at my desk. It's like a cramp, but more like a spoon poking from my insides out, jammed from inside, a spoon trying to get out of me, fuck. I am used to odd pains, usually caused by too much caffeine with too little sustenance, but usually not during the day— they come in the morning, or late, late, when I stare at the screen and think of that winter—

I continue to work. But when the pain should be subsiding as pain always subsides it does not; it grows, the pain, and thinking it might have something to do with my bowel movements or lack recently thereof, I stand to walk to the bathroom and just as my eyes see the hall to the bathroom the picture is jarred and then the landscape is tilted, and then I see the office from a Batman camera angle—*that's* new!—and then everything is blue— The carpet. I'm on the floor. Now there are five spoons, smaller spoons in the same place, kind of twisting and digging, clumsy people in there, dancing with pointy shoes, stomping even, my right side the dance floor. I come to the realization that I am...I am writhing on the carpet. I look up at the couch, maybe three feet away, and must make it to the couch. The couch is my home, the couch is the answer. If only I can...reach...the...couch...

No one is noticing. Have I been shot? I have not been shot. There was no shot. But what if it was one of those silencers? It could have been a silen— I have not been shot. But I am dying. Surely, surely. I am dying. Finally.

I can't talk. I try to eke out words—Help. Me.—but all I produce are little pants, dog breaths, my words taken by some ghost as they leave my—

I am dying, finally. Fuck I knew it. I deserve it. You know this, everyone knows this. It's AIDS and I had it coming, what with that One Time When the Condom Broke with the Woman Who Had *Been Around*. I get a vivid picture of the where—a crooked-walled little third-floor apartment overlooking south San Francisco, the dawn coming while I stood by the bed, her on her hands and knees—and the who, yes of course, I know, it all comes to me in flashes, God*damn* I should have been checking that rubber as we were going along but oh we were plastered, we barely knew what we were doing, had gotten a ride from a mutual friend, who dropped us off, he knowing what was about to happen—we had run, *run* down the block to her place—

Fuck, Toph, I am so sorry. Will I even have time to call you? Who will take you? Beth? Alone? No— Fuck, Bill'll have to move up—fuck, where will he work? There's that one think tank, where Flagg works, but— What if he wants to move Toph to

L.A.? Oh I'll have to make sure that doesn't— But Toph likes
L.A., actually, so— Oh look at how those clouds are moving,
through the window, up there, all white, with a little gray, as if
lightly bruised and—

Fuck! The pain! I'm giving birth!

Why are these people not noticing? Why is it not considered
unusual that I'm writhing on the floor? Have I writhed on this carpet before? I try to think of when that might have happened—

Someone from next door, the *Chronicle*, notices first, through
the glass, and comes over; then it's people everywhere. I am helped
to the couch to rest there, then the asking of questions about where
and how bad and why. Maybe I am kidding.

"Are you kidding?" asks Paul.

"Fuck you."

I refrain from saying I'm dying. I'm only about 95 percent sure
that I'm dying, and don't want to alarm anyone. But soon I will
know. I say *hospital, hospital*.

"I'll take you," says Shalini.

"Thank you yes," I say.

I stumble to the elevator, scraping along the wall, leaning on
Shalini. Shalini smells so nice, oh you smell nice Shalini. I'm
dying, Shal, dying. Jesus I'm hunched over, I can't even walk. I
need someone to carry me. Shal can't carry me. God*damn* it! *I have
to tell— He should know—* At the elevator I almost want to turn
around and tell someone to call Toph's school, to have him meet
me at the hospital but I can't walk all the way back maybe I can
tell the guard in the lobby, and he'll call up to the office, and then
someone can call Toph's school— Oh but the fucking message'll
get butchered fuck fuck— No, Toph shouldn't know, I don't want
him to see me die— I'll slip away like Dad, during the day, sly-
like, that'll be the way, we've had our time, we don't need a goodbye fuck this elevator is fucking slow Shalini you smell so good.

In the car I am almost crying, because the pain is ten times what it was when it knocked me to the floor. But I am tough, I am army tough. But this is fucking breaking me in half, this is acid all over me, acid being kicked into my side with steel-tipped shoes by a hundred little Nazi fuckers, all inside me—fuck! Can AIDS kill like this? Yes, yes. No, no, no. Maybe. Oh I knew it when that happened, that condom broke, I knew it was wrong from the beginning, that sex and with her and my life and guilty guilty. And Toph! All squandered!

Oh this is worse than the time when we went rafting, when the American River was way too high, when we went, all of us, and then we hit those rapids, plunged down, all fell from the raft, and I was in the froth, quickly swallowed a gallon, couldn't get straight, couldn't stay above water, trying to look, to see where Toph was, if he had fallen, but couldn't see, was mostly underwater, and thought about how ridiculous this would be, how stupid to be drowning on some little rafting trip, what a pathetic way to go, and helpless to save Toph, wherever he was. But when the river turned and slowed, I found my balance, scanned the river, now flat, and there he was, Toph, alone on that huge raft, the only one who had not fallen out. He was grinning like crazy.

It's too sudden for AIDS. Something has burst. It's my appendix. Is that fatal? Of course! Always! No, no. Then what? What is it? I must be dying. Internal bleeding. A tumor! A bleeding tumor!

"I'm dying, Shal."

"You're not dying, hon."

"Then what the hell is this? What if I'm dying?"

"You're not dying."

Shalini is driving too bumpily. She is driving on all the bumpy streets. Carelessly. She is stopping too often, and braking too suddenly, because she's so careless. Goddammit, Shal.

"Shal, can you drive…more mellowly?"

"I'm trying, hon."

"Hold my hand," I beg. I want to rest my head on her right

thigh. I want to sleep. Then I'm struck, for a second, by a kind of exhilaration. I don't have to be at work. Moodie'll have to finish the stuff that's due tomorrow. I'm doing something important, something that is more crucial than anything else I could possibly be doing—oh what relief, not having to choose, not having to feel guilt about wasting time, idling, doing this when I should be doing that—no decisions here, only survival—

So easy, so simple!

How can the pain be getting worse? It's shooting now—planets explode inside me. *I've been hit, I've been hit!* The sky is blue like always, this perfect San Francisco sky maybe I will die before I even get there— Oh Shal, why are you wearing that tight ribbed shirt today, the day that I'm dying? Why didn't we ever date, Shal? Before seat belts—not before seat belts but before everyone wore seat belts—my mother used to whip her arm hard against our chests when she stopped short, as if her arm could do anything, would do anything when we hit, her arm so flimsy and I am so flimsy, there for a few years, protection for a few years, sorry Toph, sorry, sorry, I am weak and am being taken, as I expected to be taken— I will not be buried: I want my ashes, or my whole body, dropped from a cliff; a helicopter, a volcano, into the ocean…Oh but which ocean?

Which ocean?

Which ocean?

In the waiting room they first ask me about insurance, which I do not have. I had had insurance for a few months a few years ago, but then they stopped sending bills, I think— But I can pay, I will pay, I swear I can pay, here are credit cards, please take this thing out of me. Please I cannot stand up I will sit here, just over here and answer the questions no actually maybe I will lie here, across these chairs, my head on Shalini's thigh, actually maybe I will go into that next room where I can lie down on the floor and

MOTHERFUCKER! MOTHERFUCKER! I can yell. MOTHER-
FUCKERMOTHERFUCK!

It's a kidney stone. I wake up and am drugged. Kirsten is there. I
haven't seen Kirsten in weeks. Beth couldn't get out of work, so
called her. Kirsten takes me home.

"I thought I was dying," I say.

"Of course you did," she says.

I lie down on the couch. Kirsten leaves.

Toph stands above me.

"Hey," I say.

"Hey," he says.

"Hey."

"Hey."

"Okay, enough."

"You okay?"

"Yeah."

"So. What about dinner?"

"What do you want?"

"Tacos."

"Can you deal? I don't think I can move."

"Do we have stuff?"

"I don't think so."

"Do we have cash?"

"No. Take the ATM card."

He walks to the ATM and gets money and then to the grocery
store and gets beef, spaghetti sauce, tortillas and milk. While he's
gone I doze for a minute, dreaming of persecution. I wake up suddenly, knowing this is not good, this lying on the couch, incapac-
itated. I will sit up straight, nonchalant. No one's dying. Does he
think I'm dying? Maybe he think's I'm dying. He thinks I may be

dying but am not telling him. No, no. He does not think this. He
is not me.

He comes in with the groceries, walks past me, into the
kitchen. "You want me to cook?"

"Yeah, can you?"

"You want fruit, too?"

"What do we have?"

"Oranges, half a cantaloupe."

"Yeah, yeah. Thanks."

I doze off to the sound of the beef crackling in the pan, and
when I wake up he is clearing off the coffee table, putting the piles
of papers and magazines and his math homework underneath, in
stacks corresponding to their former places on top of the table.
Then he goes back to the kitchen. He comes out with two plates,
fully arranged, with the piles of just-burnt-enough beef, the
tortillas folded on the sides of each plate, a bowl with the fruit
cut into manageable portions, oranges and cantaloupe, all wet
and orange. He goes back to the kitchen and comes back with
the milk.

"Napkins."

He goes back and gets the roll of paper towels.

We eat. I doze again. I wake up at one point to the tapping of
fingers on the Playstation. The next time I open my eyes it's dark;
he's gone.

I walk to his room. He's asleep, in a sort of crash position, arms
splayed out, mouth wide open. His forehead is hot, like things
inside are burning.

IX.

Robert Urich says no. We were so close. It would have been so perfect. His publicist seemed to like the idea, she was going along with us and it, laughed a little at the idea—at the very least she found it diverting. Urich was just the kind of person we needed: a star (or, at the time, near-former star), a household name who for whatever reason had fallen off the national radar, someone whom everyone knew and maybe even cared about at one time or another, but who hadn't been seen for some time. We needed a celebrity who the public, the press, not to mention the hard-to-fool Internet community, would believe had indeed died, but whose passing did not make national news. The celebrity, therefore, couldn't be so big that it would be implausible that his death was first reported by a small, mediocre San Francisco bimonthly.

But who? Urich was our first choice, because a) we, like everyone, had been huge fans of *Vega$*; b) we knew he had some sort of sense of humor, at least as evidenced by a few self-deprecating comments made on this or that talk show with regard to his role in the seminal *Turk 182!*, also starring Timothy Hutton; and c) he was slated to star in an upcoming series called *Lazarus Man*.

Lazarus Man. Too perfect.

"It's just not right for us," his agent said.

Then Belinda Carlisle. We decide that Belinda Carlisle, too, would be perfect.

"She lives in France," says her publicist.

We run through other possibilities—Judge Reinhold, Juliana Hatfield, Bob Geldof, Laura Branigan, Lori Singer, C. Thomas Howell, Ed Begley, Jr. We consider Franklin Cover, the actor who played Tom Willis in "The Jeffersons," but then don't bother calling him, remembering that we cast him in what could have been considered a negative, or at least kind of pathetic, light, in an interview a year earlier. An exchange:

Is there anything else you'd like to say to our readers?

Well, no, I have nothing to say, except help me get a job teaching somewhere! If anybody knows of any position at a college that needs an acting teacher, let me know.

Then genius strikes. There is one man from the world of entertainment who might have thought of this himself, one man with a brand-new middle name, Hellion, one man who tours with a multimedia show featuring slides of dwarfs and retarded people.

Crispin Glover.

He's perfect. So perfect.

Marty McFly.

We call the agent. The agent has no idea what we're talking about. We fax the letter, altered to include flattering comments about all of Glover's work, including his invented nickname. Then we wait.

A day later the phone rings.

I pick up the receiver and put it to my ear, in the way customary to those answering phones.

"Hello," I say.

"This is Crispin Glover."

He is calling from Tennessee, where he's filming a movie with Milos Forman. *Crispin Glover's on the phone!*

He has read the proposal and he loves the idea. He has, as a matter of fact, been wanting to do something like this. He wants to do it, and he wants to do it whole hog—wants to really fake it, wants pictures, proof, and wants then to go underground, to set up a system where no one close to him will give it away, wants to leave it be for months, have the funeral, the eulogies, the comments from other actors, all that, the whole nine yards, and to then come back alive, triumphant! It'll be great. This will be the thing that'll put us over the top. I am on the phone looking over the center of San Francisco, the park and the giant SFMOMA humidifier and a sliver of the bridge and hills, and I am weak from the excitement.

"This'll be great!" I say.

"Yeah, yeah," he agrees. "So what kind of timeline are you on?"

He can't do it. He can't see why we can't just push the thing back a little bit, or do it next issue... but he doesn't see, he doesn't see that all six of our advertisers cannot be kept waiting, and our hundreds of subscribers cannot be kept waiting. We'll call back if either of our schedules changes.

"You know who," I say.

"No," says Moodie.

"He's our only hope."

"No way."

"We have no choice."

"Oh man."

"He'll be fine."

"Fuck. Okay."

Adam Rich.

Nicholas from *Eight Is Enough*.

We already sort of know him. One of our contributors, Tanya Pampalone, had gone to grade school with him, and they had kept in touch. With her entree, we had worked with him twice previously. First, we had run a short interview with him, in which he talked to Tanya about his shoes and an umbrella he planned on buying. An excerpt:

TANYA: *How many pairs of shoes do you have?*

ADAM RICH: Ten, I'd say ten. I have one umbrella. I just bought this umbrella. When I bought this umbrella, it had stopped raining and I thought that I had better buy an umbrella and it won't rain anymore and I'll have it for the next time. But it has continued to rain and it has rained continuously since I bought this umbrella.

TANYA: *Do you think it's because you can predict the future?*

ADAM RICH: No, it's probably because I bought the umbrella.

We call Adam at his L.A. condo and explain the concept to him. He listens. We explain that it'll be this elaborate hoax, that it'll be serving a higher purpose, that of satirizing the media's interest in celebrity death, parodying their eulogies, that this will make national news, and that outside of the feeling good he'll be able to do as a result of his role in providing this educational service to a needy America, everyone will think he's bleeding edge for even associating with us.

You'll be in on every step, we say. You'll have full approval on everything. "It'll be great," I say, believing it will be great. I have in my heart the firm belief that if he plays this right, it will mean not only the final breakthrough for us, but, perhaps more important, the certain revival of the career of Adam Rich.

I picture him sitting in a small and dingy Hollywood condominium, surrounded by junior Emmys or whatever, his hands on a Nintendo, a fridge full of yogurt and ice cream sandwiches, his days spent gardening, watching satellite TV.

He agrees.

"This is going to be great," I tell Toph. We're in the bathroom. He's sitting on the toilet; I'm cutting his hair.

"He agreed to this?"

"Yeah, yeah, totally. Put your chin up."

"And what's the point of this again?"

"You have to get your chin up."

"Okay, so…"

"The point is, we're making fun of these celebrity eulogies you see in magazines, where—"

"What's a eulogy?"

"Like a tribute. These eulogies where, when celebrities die, suddenly everyone cares, they're given these massive funerals, people cry, people weep even though they've only known the guy on TV, some character he's played, lines he's read…"

"Huh. And people will believe this?'

"Yeah. People are dumb."

I turn his head toward the mirror, comb his hair straight down, comparing the left side and right. I have again done a masterful job. He still looks like a prepubescent heartthrob—the nose upturned, the hair long in the front—even though it's starting to thicken, darken, curl and kink like mine. I do not like seeing myself next to him. Next to him I am a monster. The facial hair I am cultivating is ridiculous, grotesque. My sideburns do not meet my hair, and are so sparse that they look less like facial hair, and more like leg hair. Worst of all, the goatee I'm working on is failing miserably, because I can't even grow hair on the sides of my mouth, giving me a perpetually in-progress, fourteen-year-old's look. I am wrinkled, bloated, with deeply carved laugh lines, and my eyes are too close together, and too small, squinty, mean. And my nose is shapeless, too big. Next to his face, his twelve-year-old face, smooth, proportionate, soft, harmonious, I look distorted, as if digitally manipulated, my skin pulled the wrong ways, everything stretched or compressed, grotesque.

"People are going to be pissed when they find out," he says.

"Well, we hope so. These are the people we want to upset. Anyone who cares about him in the first place, who would at all be moved by the death of someone they saw on TV, deserves to be duped. I mean, why should anyone pay attention? Why should some dramedy star moron loser be mourned by millions, when other people are not? When the average person, who lives a happy and maybe even in some ways heroic life, can only attract twenty or thirty people to a funeral, when— I mean, it's unfair, it's abominable, right?"

"Huh. Well, to tell you the truth, I think it's kind of sick."

"That's what we think."

"No, I mean, I think what you guys are doing is sick. You're using Adam Rich to make a point—"

"Of course."

"That point being that you people are just as good as celebrities like him. You think he's vapid, dim-witted, with his stupidity arising, first and foremost, from the fact that he is famous and you guys are not. The fact that at nine he was hanging with Brooke Shields, that a hundred million people know his name, a hundred million more his face. And no one knows yours."

"You're breaking out of character again."

"I mean, you people cannot stand the fact that this silly person, this Adam Rich person, who you feel is nowhere near as smart as you people, who did not go to college and did not write captions in the yearbook or run the school's art gallery or whatever, who has not read the books you have, has the *gall* to be a household name (or was at one time) around the world—for something, like acting in a dramedy, that you find unimpressive. So you make fun of him, first with the umbrella interview, and now with this so-called well-meaning hoax—I mean, can it be any more gruesome and transparently symbolic, you people killing this contemporary of yours, a kid on TV when you were kids watching TV, this victim of your predatory mentality, who you claim is in on it all but who really has no idea of the scale of, the potential consequences of this thing—and certainly not your motivations, the bitterness simmering just below the surface, the desire to dirty him, humiliate him, reduce him to you, to below you—I mean, does he have any idea about the jokes made at his expense at the office? Could he ever imagine the malice involved? It's disgusting. I mean, what *is* this? What does this mean? Where does anger like that come from?"

"It's not anger."

"Of course it is. These people have already attained, at whatever age, a degree of celebrity that you assholes will never reach, and you feel, deep down, that because there is no life before or after this, that fame is, essentially, God—all you people know that, believe it, even if you don't admit it. As children you watched him, in the basement, cross-legged in front of the TV, and you thought you should be him, that his lines were yours, that his spot on *Battle of the Network Stars* was yours, that you'd be so good on that obstacle course—you'd win for sure! So doing all this, when he's no longer such the world-conquering celebrity, gives you power over him, the ability to embarrass him, to equalize the terrible imbalance you feel about your relationship to those who project their charisma directly, not sublimated through snarky little magazines. You and everyone like you, with your Q & As or columns or Web sites—you all want to be famous, you want to be rock stars, but you're stuck in this terrible bind, where you also want to be thought of as smart, legitimate, permanent. So you do your little thing, are read by your little coterie, while secretly seething about the Winona Ryders and Ethan Hawkes, or even the Sari Lockers—

"Remember the Sellout Issue? When everyone went to L.A. and New York to interview all these budding celebrities so you could make fun of them? There was that girl from *Father of the Bride*, and the guy from "Baywatch," the Australian guy, and of course the Doublemint Twins. You had to make them all look like imbeciles, even while in person you were smiling with them, joking, being kind, accepting theirs. Same with Elle Macpherson.

And Natalie from "Facts of Life." And then poor Sari Locker, the sexologist."

"That was different."

"Right. You get a call from her publicist, a cold call because you people are on some general Gen X magazine list, and even though you would never have any real interest in the twenty-four-year-old author of *Mindblowing Sex in the '90s*—"

"*Mindblowing Sex in the Real World*."

"Fine. So you say, sure sure, let's do an interview, chuckling to yourself—you can't wait to hang up the phone and tell everyone, wanting only to tear her apart. Then while you're in New York, you have dinner with her. Dinner goes well and you have drinks. During dinner and drinks—like, three or four hours of talking—she's a little pushy and self-promoting, but also extremely generous—you had not bargained for that—and wants to hear all about me—that part shocked you—and about our parents, and says so many nice things, and during all this, while she's being kind and listening and everything, all the while you're balancing your two prevailing interests: recording her words to later use against her—because, she, too, had the temerity to be relatively famous and attractive (with a master's from Penn)—while also, more pressingly, trying to get invited back to her apartment."

"I almost did."

"Yeah, you took a cab with her, watched her get out, didn't know if you should make a move or whatever, and let her go, thinking, there goes my big chance to score with the sexologist."

"I almost did."

"And then you still went back and wrote a bitchy little thing about her."

"She wasn't offended."

"Maybe she's got thick skin. Maybe she didn't read it. But don't you see this is a kind of cannibalism? That you're just grabbing at people, toys from a box, dressing them up, taking them apart, ripping their heads off, discarding them when—"

"Weird that you mention Sari. She's actually coming to town."

"Oh Jesus. You're not going to see her?"

"Yes I am, young Toph. Yes I am."

"I don't get it."

"Nor should you. Much too complex for your tender mind. Put your head down. I have to wipe off your neck."

I brush the hair from his neck with a towel.

"Toph, there are so many things you have yet to learn."

"Right, right."

"Just stay close to me, and you will glean."

"Right."

"Fear not."

"I fear."

He looks perfect.

"You look perfect."

He's grimacing.

"It's too short. It's brutal."

"No, no. It's perfect."

When Toph is gone, servicing his new, to-be-truthful-kind-of-annoying social life, things are sort of weird at home. At the moment he's at Gabe's house and there's nothing to do. It's not that I'm bored. Am I bored? I go into the hallway and lean my back against the wall. I look at my shoes. I should not wear white socks with these shoes, because the hole at the left pinkie toe becomes so much more pronounced with this bright white fuzz protruding. When was he supposed to get home again? He hadn't said. I should call Gabe's house. But would that look anxious? I don't want to look anxious, do not want to be a parent who is jealous of his child's time with friends, much like Mrs. H—, whose son we liked but who only let him out occasionally, because, we all felt, even at twelve we felt that she was afraid that he would come to like us, his peers, more than her, his mother. I straighten the rug in the hall. I find the broom and sweep. I open the refrigerator and throw away a heavy bag of blue oranges. And baby carrots, now brown and soft. I go to my room, open the blinds. Across the street, at the retirement home, an elderly woman is out on the porch, moving slowly, watering her plants. I go back to the kitchen and pick up the phone. Who to call? I put it down. I turn on the computer. Get up, turn on the oven. What to cook? We have no food. I sit down, look at the computer and turn it off and stand up, staring toward the door. I lean my head against the molding near the window. What if my head became attached to the wall? I could be half of a pair of Siamese twins, attached at the head, the other half was actually this wall. I could be half man, *half wall*. Would I die if not separated? No, I could survive. I would stay attached to the wall. Toph would feed me, and I would have a specially pre-pared chair, tall enough, so I could sit— But how would I change my shirt with my head attached to the wall? I think about this for a few minutes. Then it comes to me: Button-down shirts! Oh, but the bathroom problem... I'll need a bedpan. Or a catheter. I could do this. I could.

But my head is not, in fact, attached to the wall. I remove my head from the wall.

If he got home by four there'd still be time to play. Is it too windy? Will he be too tired?

The bell rings.

I look out the window and down. It's him. A surge runs through me.

"Where's your key?"

"I forgot it."

I make the obligatory scoff. *You flake ha ha!* I throw him my keys. They clink on the sidewalk.

I watch him put the key in, turn, push, disappear into the wall.

Should I scare him when he walks in? No, no, he knows I'm here. Punch him? Pour something on him? *Shit, no time!*

"Hey."

"Hey."

"So? Was it fun?"

"Yeah."

"What'd you do?"

"Nothing. We got pictures today."

"What pictures?"

"School pictures."

"You got them when?"

"Today."

"No. I mean, when did you take them?"

"I don't know. A month ago I guess."

"You didn't tell me. What did you wear?"

"A yellow shirt."

"Which one?"

"The dark yellow one."

"Was it clean?"

"Yeah."

"Let me see the picture."

"You're not going to like it."

"Why?"

"You'll see."

"Are your eyes closed?"

"No."

"Are you giving the finger?"

"No."

"Then why?"

"You'll see."

He digs the pictures, letter-sized, carboard backing, in a plastic sleeve, from his backpack and hands them to me and Good fucking God no. No. No. No. No. This is bad. This is so bad. This is unbelievably bad. This is so unbelievably bad. They'll take him away now. They'll take him away for sure. If ever they needed a reason now they have one good God. It's proof of everyhing. The proof they want.

"Toph, this is bad."

"It's not that bad."

"It's so bad."

"It's not."

"It's horrible."

"Whatever."

"No, you whatever yourself whatever whatever. God. Damn. You look like you're about to cry. Jesus. You like you're pleading for help."

And he does. Yes he is tan and blond and cute—he does look very cute, his eyes exceptionally blue here—but he's looking out so forlornly, so helpless, soft, neck extended, eyes almost watery... Fuck. This is so bad. This is worse than the Phone Voice Problem. The Phone Voice Problem we have addressed over and over, and it's improved but still hasn't been resolved, fixed.

For years he's been answering the phone like this: *he/ lo?*

And of course people wonder. What's wrong with Toph? they ask me when he hands me the phone. And always I have to be cavalier. *That's just Toph! ha ha*. But he does sound like he's been bawling, like he's locked himself in the bathroom and I'm banging on it, yelling over his sniffling, and he's just starting to control his breathing when someone calls and that's when he says Hello?... And worse, he achieves this same tone every time, day or night, always this crinkly slow *he/ lo?*, at the edge of 12-year-old sanity and suffering. So I've been imploring him to sound normal. Please sound normal, Toph, you are normal, we are normal so just sound normal please can't you? Don't sound like I've been beating you, like you're in the bathroom hiding from me, because I have been there, have hidden from parents before, have been on the other side of a door being struck with all conceivable parental force, have searched the bathroom for places to hide, have found a place in the closet where the bath toys are kept, under the lowest shelf, and I have hidden there, and have seen, darkening the white slit of light under the door to this closet, his shoes, and then the white light everywhere as the door is opened, and have had my shoulder grabbed and...and he's been working on it, especially when I make him do it in front of me, my arms crossed in front of me, watching, coaching, making a chipper smiley face for him, eyebrows shooting skyward... *happy!*

And now here we are again. This picture thing goddamn. I should start packing his stuff up. Will the foster family be nice? Will he take good pictures for them? Foster families. Foster families.

"Toph, this is so bad. You know what people will think. You just know. I won't be able to go to the school now."

He's making a milkshake.

"Can you turn that thing off?"

"It's almost done."

"Jesus, Toph. I can't do the next open house, I can't see them now because now they've got the proof they want. Your teachers! They must think I'm beating you. Do they talk to you like I'm beating you?"

"What are you talking about?"

"This is so bad."

"Why?"

"You're not unhappy."

"Yeah, so."

"So you're not allowed to look or sound unhappy."

"Fine."

"Because that's what people expect."

"Sorry."

"And you didn't tell me the pictures were even happening."

"They sent a notice."

"They did not."

"Fine."

This could be the time to escape. We should pack and go. They might be on their way already, the child welfare people. What kind of car would they drive? A big truck or something. *Or undercover!* We're surrounded already. We could go out the other door, by the laundry room. We go out the door, wearing disguises—what disguises? Capes! We *do* have capes!—we go out and get to the car and then get provisions, some fruit, salted meats, yes, then we head for where? Mexico? Central America? No, no—Canada. Then we do home-schooling. We farm and do home schooling. Oh, but Canada. Will he start saying *aboot*? We both will. And *sorry* like *sore-y*. Can't have that. We'll have to be vigilant...

"I just don't get why you didn't smile."

"I thought I did. I did for some of them."

"And they picked this one?"

"I guess."

Maybe this was part of their plan. They pick the sad picture so they can take him away. Or else the photographer is some kind of child slave trader. He's hooked in with the child welfare agency and he gets them to give him the kids and then sells them to white slavery operations in...where are the white slavery operations, anyway? And what kind of cars do *they* drive?

"I just wish you'd help me out here, Toph."

"I said sorry."

"I mean, you know how bad this makes me look, makes us look? They're going to be bringing over more fruit baskets now. They're going to be baking us bundt cakes."

"What's a bundt cake?"

"It's like a big donut."

"Huh." He's halfway through his milkshake. Trying to put on some weight.

I look at the picture again. So pretty, in a way. The yellow shirt matches his hair, so blond after that sunny September and all the time at the beach.. And the background, light blue, just right, matches his eyes. The eyes that say *Help Me!* And there's not one but six of these pictures, a grid of them, then four bigger ones below, and then this huge one Jesus christ! All these pleading Tophs, Eleven Tophs saying *Look at my sad life, you people, you viewers of junior-high pictures! Class, teachers, see my eyes, which have seen too much! Erase my past, start me over, let me be like you and everyone, normal and happy happy. Watch me smile for my school picture! Save me from him, because every night before dinner he's asleep on the couch and so dead to the world, and when he can't get up he tugs on my shirt and begs, he makes me cook for us and then later, once awake, he's so tense, staring at the screen, writing something he won't let me see, and he falls asleep in my bed and I have to push him out and then he's up half the night and—*

"So what do you want for dinner?"

"Taco."

"We had taco Sunday."

"So?"

"If you cook it you can have taco."

"Do we have meat?"

"No. You have to get it."

"Can I get something else?"

"Like what?"

"Root beer."

"Fine. Wake me up when it's ready."

Will I ever get this picture out of my head? Will we ever live it down? Is it as sad as it looks? I know it means nothing but how can it look so transparent? Do any of the other kids look so sad? The girl whose mom and dad are getting divorced—is she crying? God no. These kids, they know the score. They know to protect their parents. But not Toph. All I do—I changed his sheets last week!—all that, and he gives me this.

My mom used to kill us when we took school pictures without

her knowledge, before she would approve of our outfits. Of course, there's a reason we didn't tell her about Picture Day, and that reason is spelled P-L-A-I-D. Did everyone wear that much plaid in the early 70s? It's uncanny, but it seems like every picture we took before fifth grade featured plaid in some way, mostly in the pants category. And we matched, all three of us.

"You know, we can't send this out to anyone. I can't even show it to Bill or Beth."

"Then don't."

"I won't."

"Then don't."

It might be right then that Marny calls. It might be the day before, or the day after, or the next week. I am at home, and Toph is on the couch, sighing through his math homework. The stereo's on, and I have one speaker against the wall fighting the neighbors' must-see Thursday night lineup. The phone rings.

"Shalini's been in an accident."

"What? A car?"

"No, no. You know that deck that collapsed in Pacific Heights?"

"Oh. No."

"She's in a coma. She fell four stories and landed on her head. They don't know if she's going to make it."

We go. I think we go right then. Maybe we wait until the morning. No, it must have been then, it must be right then that we go. Maybe it is not night that Marny calls. Maybe it is day, and I leave Toph alone. Or maybe I lock—

This is it:

It is midnight. Toph is in bed. Carla calls me from L.A.—she and Mark have moved to L.A. Shalini's mother has called her, and Carla has called me. I leave. Shalini could be gone.

As I walk down the stairs, I know that someone will take this opportunity to do something to Toph. I know it every time I leave Toph home alone, which I do often now, no more baby-sitters because he is thirteen and can be left, as long as the door to the apartment is locked, and the door to the building is locked, and the back door, that which leads down to the laundry room, is locked, then he's fine, although that lock is weak and worthless, and so of course that's the way through which the bad man will come. He will come through the back, because he has been watching, has been waiting for me to leave, knows I will be gone for a while because he has been listening to my phone conversation, and watching me through binoculars or a telescope. And when I leave he will come in, with his rope and wax—he is friends with Stephen, the Scot, *of course!*—and will take Toph and do things to him, because he knows I am out to look at Shalini, who is in a coma, who fell from a building.

I pick up Marny. Moodie meets us at the hospital.

Shalini's family is there, the parents, her sister, a dozen cousins, uncles, aunts, some in saris, some not, other friends. The halls, shabbily shiny, are filled with people in small clumps, sitting on the floor, walking in and out of the waiting room, which has been entirely commandeered. One of the girls there had been at the party. We learn more details. It had been in Pacific Heights. Shalini had gone with a friend. They had walked around, ended up on the back deck, outside. There were maybe twenty people on it when it went, the supports giving way, and all the young people floating down. The friend Shalini had come with was dead. A dozen others were hospitalized, or had been and were released. Shal the worst among them. By all accounts she was lucky to be alive. Her head had broken her fall.

We wait in the hall, sitting on the floor. Then standing, walking, whispering. They are operating. Or maybe they have already operated. They have done many operations maybe—twenty, thirty, a hundred. At some point—maybe it is the next day—we are told we can go inside the closed ward where Shalini is being kept. At the entrance to the ward we pick up a receiver, and a nurse answers and another comes to open the door. We walk past other rooms and then there she is—

Her face is broken, her eyes closed, inflamed, huge, red and purple, blue and red and purple and yellow and green and brown, her eye sockets black. She's on a ventilator. They had told us about the knit cap, and there it is, covering her head because they shaved her head and removed part of her skull to alleviate the brain's swelling. Her legs stick straight out, as if in splints, and are wrapped with fluid-filled leggings, blue and soft, like the masks worn during sleep—

Christ, they haven't even cleaned the blood off her, at least not all that shit over her eye, I mean that's—

But her arms are perfect. Her arms are smooth and brown, without a mark or bruise or blemish.

There is no one else in the room. Marny and Moodie and I don't know what to do—if we are allowed to touch her, whether to touch her or whether to talk or just stand nearby, or just say hello, or pray, or walk by and leave— Don't you talk to the comatose? They hear, correct? Like an unborn child they hear.

We stand on the other side of the room with our hands over our mouths, whispering sideways, unblinking, until an Indian woman, a cousin or friend, comes in and, without acknowledging us, walks straight to the sink, washes her hands, dries them, walks straight to Shalini and picks up her hand, holds it in both of hers and talks to her.

"Hello, Shalini. Hello, darling…"

There are already flowers.

Shal's mother comes in. She tells us that we have to wash our hands. We do, and then walk to the bed and touch Shalini's perfect arms. They are warm.

After a few minutes we are ushered out. Zev is in the hallway.

We tell him what we know. He's bouncing from one foot to the other, bug-eyed, nodding a lot.

We wait.

Days pass. Her chances are bad, then good, then iffy, then better, and soon the doctors become confident that she will at least be stable, though still comatose. No one is sure if she will pull out. The fall was so bad. She was standing on the platform and she— We did not know the girl who died, but we all seem to have a feeling that we've been at that house, have been on that deck— More people fly in. Carla and Mark come up from L.A. Shalini's relatives, dozens of them, appear. The waiting room overflows at all hours. We meet Shalini's friends, her aunts, uncles, men in suits and gray-haired women in saris. We eat the food in the cafeteria. We leave the hospital and it is bright outside, it's always sea blue and sunny, and we go back to work, and then come back, and then eat and sleep and Shalini sleeps. We bring bagels sometimes, and sometimes we feel welcome among the relatives, and other times we do not feel as welcome. Usually Shalini's mother's eyes are watery; other times she is pacing, arms crossed, stiff-backed, demanding things of the doctors. She is a doctor herself, and has assembled an elite team to care for Shalini. We meet Shalini's college friends, high school friends, cousins. *We're going to the store, do you want anything?* You can't go in today. The doctors are in there. Come back tomorrow. *No, we'll stay.* Why will you stay? We must stay. I have done the waiting and the vigils, and have negotiated with doctors, and have held hands and known visiting hours. I know the rules: We are to stay. And we are not to ask questions of the parents. If we want to know something, we are to ask a cousin or a friend. We are not to smile, not to laugh, at anything, unless the family smiles or laughs first. We are to dress neatly. We are to be punctual if we are expected. We are not to miss visiting hours, and not take up too much time once inside, keeping waiting the college roommate or uncle from India. Most important, we too must suffer. Everyone around the ill must do what they can, in terms of sacrifice and struggle, or malnourishment or sleep deprivation, to suffer too, and to stay close while suffering; to leave the bedside, to leave the hospital, is to weaken the curing forces, to enfeeble the efforts toward recovery. While the ill are ill, if you can be there you should be there. I know these things. Bizarre, self-sacrificing gestures are important. On days that you cannot possibly come visit, you must visit. When you get home one night, and Toph says, "So, are you going to pretend to be a parent tonight, or what?"—which he means as a kind of joke, because you two have been eating fast food for weeks, and you've been napping on the couch every night after dinner—you should take a breath and know that this is okay, that this sort of thing, this struggle and sacrifice, is essential, that he does not understand but someday will. And even after you have gone in to see Shalini, and have seen her cuts healing and have held her perfect small hot hand, you must stay in the hallway, talking to anyone who might want to talk—it is unclear whether Shalini's mother wants to talk to us, or feels obligated to talk to us, but we assume that it's the former and so we stay for hours. One day I bring a teddy bear for Shalini. I bring the tiny mohair bear that I have kept in the door compartment of my car for years, since my mother passed, because I think that there is something of her in this bear— I look into the two black pinhead eyes of this tiny, ancient orange bear, with tiny jointed legs and arms, his fur worn and scratchy, and there is something of my mother there, it being the only object that evokes her so, in an inexplicably strong way that makes me unable to look into the tiny black pinhead eyes of this bear, because when I do I think of that funny little voice my mother used when she would make this little bear talk, when I was four, five, six, when we would be playing with the bears in the little house she had built and decorated with tiny furniture for them, when she would get one of these little bears out, put him in front of her mouth, and, in a high gravelly voice, say "Hello," and then "Let me tell you a secret," she would say, bringing the bear close to my ear, allowing me to imagine what secrets he was uttering—I would feel the tickle of the coarse fur on my ear and would giggle crazily—it would drive me mad with astonishment, rapture. I would absolutely lose my mind. And so one day I take this bear from the car, move him for the first time in maybe three years, and I bring him into the hospital, his prickly fur like a burr in my hand, and I will go in to see Shalini, who is sleeping, with the wool cap on, on the walls pictures of her standing and happy with her mother, her sister, her eyes now less swollen, bandages off, skin collapsing around the wounds, regenerating, and I will be in there alone and I will nestle the bear in between her arm and torso, and I will back up and see the bear sitting there, no more than four inches tall, its tiny black pinhead eyes staring back at me, and will feel pious and proud and will let myself believe that it means something that I have done that. That the bear will be magic and I will save the day and bring Shalini back.

Another day John, who does not know Shalini, calls to offer his condolences.

"I read about it in the paper," he says.

"Yeah."

"They're going to nail that landlord. He's got about a hundred other violations on his record."

"Yeah."

"Is there anything I can do?" he asks.

"No, I don't think so."

Pause.

"So I was spitting up blood again today..."

Adam Rich doesn't want his death to be a suicide. Doesn't jibe with his persona. He wants to be murdered.

We settle on his being killed by an unemployed dinner theater stagehand in the parking lot of the Asp Club, a fabulous Los Angeles nightspot. He likes that, a violent death, and better yet, at a location that makes clear that even hours before a sudden and bloody death, the guy knew how to party. We will, in recounting his life, get around his long-ago substance abuse problems, while nodding vaguely to them. Instead of drugs, we decide he'll be addicted to vitamin C, because, while starring on "Code Red" with Lorne Greene, he become hyperaware of the importance of fire safety, and believed the supplements would make his skin flame-retardant. We will talk about his interest in motocross and painting, and reveal to the world that Nicholas from "Eight Is Enough" was more than an actor, that he was indeed one of the burgeoning auteurs of Hollywood—that at the time of his death, he was working on "a genre-bending blockbuster, incorporating multimedia and interactive elements"—a mysterious, much-anticipated project known around Hollywood as "The Squatter Project." He is liking all of this, this idea of the untimely death of a genius.

The story begins:

> It is said that to fly too close to the sun will cause you to fall. Adam Rich—actor, idol, iconoclast—flew too fast and flew far, but on March 22 he flew too close to the sun. His peers, his loved ones, and a nation mourn....

Toph is on the couch, hunched over his history book. I am walking up and down the hall, snapping my fingers.

"Please stop," he says.

"No."

I am wired. Big night. Sari in town. Toph going to bar mitzvah thing, then Sari. Okay. Okay. Okayokay.

We cook dinner quickly and then he has to change—

"Why do I have to change?"

"Because it's a religious event, right. Where is it again?"

"I don't know."

"Well, did you get an invitation or anything?"

"Yeah but—"

"Well where is it?"

"Don't you have it?"

"Me? Why would I have the thing?"

"I never saw it."

"C'mon. Jesus Christ."

He calls a classmate and gets the details and of course we are late and he comes out of his room wearing the pants I was afraid he was going to be wearing, the ones with the ink stains on the pocket.

"Don't you have clean pants?"

"I would if someone did laundry every once in a while."

"What? What? These were never in the wash, smart-ass. You have to put the clothes in the wash first, you little..."

"Why would I put them in the wash if I never wear them?"

"Goddamn it, for occasions like these, duh!"

I drive him to Union Square, to that hotel where Fatty Arbuckle did whatever he did, and when he gets out of the car I am happy to see him get out of the car, the little dickhead. I go back to the office, where Moodie and Paul and Zev are working on Adam Rich's final interview, which we are purporting to have obtained, exclusively:

Q: *Who do you admire most?*

ADAM RICH: Spencer Tracy, James Cagney, Babe Ruth—especially the Babe. Here's this guy who everyone—players, women, alcohol—tried to keep down, but he just kept pointing to the fence. That's kind of what I try to live up to. Every morning I get up and I point to that fence.

Q: *So every morning you play baseball?*

A: No.

Q: *Huh. Well, that's a pretty good attitude to take. You seem to be very accepting of the peaks and valleys of the typical Hollywood career.*

A: It's about having a vision. It's been frustrating for me lately as an actor. The most important thing I've learned is that the past can be a block to the future.

Q: *Surely opportunities exist?*

A: Yes, but I'm not gonna throw emphasis on my past to make a buck.

We have only a week left to finish the issue, not to mention the *Chronicle* work, a whole campaign for the paper's columnists, due the next day:

HERB'S BLURBS: READ HERB CAEN
JON CARROLL: LET'S GO CARROLLING

As usual, we make it look easy. I drive back to the hotel, so I can get Toph, then bring Toph home, then go back to Union Square, to Sari's hotel. I slow down in front of the Fatty Arbuckle hotel, hoping to catch Toph on the steps, waiting for me outside. He's not there.

I drive around the block and when I come down Polk again and pause in front of the hotel he's again not there, and there's a motherfucking cable car behind me, full of idiot people hanging off—*whee!*—so I drive around again, and when I come to Union Square, tourist clusterfuck, I—

Fuck it, I'll just park underground and so I do, and then run to the hotel, into the lobby, in my shorts. I am already almost late for Sari. She will be waiting. She has to fly out tonight, she had a convention today and is flying out tonight, but by the time I get Toph and drop him off, she'll be gone—

Fuck. There are some kids walking out with their parents, but he is nowhere. He is not in the lobby, as other kids awaiting their parents are, and he is not on the steps, as a normal child might be, and not in the doorway, and not by the elevators or front desk. When I ask, a willowy girl in his class says that no, she hasn't seen him for a while, but that some kids are still upstairs, maybe he's up—

I ride the chrome and mirrored elevator up, assaulted by the garish red carpeting, then the view, it's an outdoor elevator, view of the whole city how nice, and upstairs the room is all glass, there are balloons sadly resting on the floor, a DJ packing up his equipment. Two kids are left, dressed up, one in suspenders. Toph is not among them. I ride the elevator down with one of them, ask him but he doesn't know where Toph is.

Out the front door, the steps, into Union Square, another ridiculous cable car, tourists everywhere, no Toph.

Sari will be gone. My one chance with the sexologist, squandered by this inconsiderate little—

I go to a phone and see if he's called. He has not called. Back to the hotel, scan the lobby, back up the elevator, look at the view so nice, inspect the party room again, which is almost empty now, only a few parents, who look at me quizzically while I look at them desperately—but cannot talk to them because I am not them and do not know what to say—if I explain it will only confirm their low expectations of me, strengthen their fear and pity for little Toph. I ride down again, and in the mirrored elevator I look like a madman and maybe he's dead. He was taken, of course, he was taken like Polly Klaas was taken, and is right now being molested and dismembered. Or first driven to another state. Not possible. Of course possible. It's probable, *all probable!*

Sari will not wait. Oh to be able to just fucking once do something, be able to do something simple and normal like shacking with the author of sex manuals, just that one little thing—goddamn can I just have this *one thing*—

Oh wait. That's it. He's gotten a ride from a friend, yes, a ride—the little dickweed, without telling me, he got a ride from someone else. If I find him at home—

No, no, he's still here. I'm sure of it. I look in the hotel's phone room, the restaurant, the bar— Why the bar? Why the bar, dumbass? Think, think! Then up the elevator again, oh ha ha what a nice view, and such a leisurely pace, this elevator, then off and in the party room, no one left. Then down, then outside. Then into the park across the street. Then around the block, and he's definitely gone now, he's as good as dead, been taken, of course, the same age as Polly Klaas, right? Oh God. I will become Marc Klaas. I'll initiate legislation—Toph's Law—I'll start a foundation—

Then back into the lobby, where he is standing by the door, his shirt untucked, his hair matted, looking outside, through the hotel's thick gold glass doors, on his tiptoes.

I grab him and say nothing until we get to the car, and inside the car with the windows rolled up—after he gives me his excuse, involving his thinking that I would be picking him up at the *other* door, a door *other than the door at which I dropped him off*, after I patiently listen, interesting…interesting…without swearing, trying not to yell— I do not want to do these things, these things are not what we're about, no yelling, no swearing, that's verboten, no anger, no outbursts, no threats of doing this or that, hitting him here or there—instead I calmly, slowly, softly, as if reading Chaucer to senior citizens, avail him of my way of seeing things—

"Goddamn it, Toph! That makes no goddamn sense! The *other door*? Why the other door? Are you *kid*ding me? God*damn* it! God*damn* it! God*damn* it! This shit can*not* happen. Sorry pal. This can*not* happen. I mean, please, Toph, please, this kind of thing is just ridiculous [raising voice, to his and my surprise] *fucking ridiculous*! I mean, this shit just can*not* happen, there is no room for this kind of shit. [Pounding steering wheel] God*damn* it! God*damn* it! God*damn* it! I can*not* be driving endlessly around the city looking for you, wondering when I'll have to call the police, wondering what Dumpster they'll find you in, molested and torn apart and— God*damn* it! Jesus fucking Christ, Toph, I had just about written

you off, I went through that hotel ten fucking times, I was picturing you in a million pieces, that Polly Klaas killer guy giving me
the finger at the trial, everything. Fuck this, man! There simply is
[pounding steering wheel] no margin for error, here, my man.
There is no margin for error! [Pounding steering wheel with each
syllable] No! Mar-gin! For! Err-or! Listen, you know this, we know
this, we've always known this, that the only way we can do this is
with a certain amount of efficiency. We have to be thinking, we
have to be on our toes! We have to be on the same page, have to be
anticipating, thinking, we have to have presence of mind! Things
are pulled taut, Toph, pulled taut! There is no give! No give!
Everything is too tight, brother, everything is just right there, like
that [clenching fists], see that? Tight, taut [jerking fists apart,
miming the testing of a knot in a short piece of rope]! Everything
is pulled taut!"

"You just passed our street."

I drop him off at Beth's, watch him step into her red foyer, wave to
Beth as she waves to me, watch the door close, see them start up
the stairs, knowing he'll tell her everything.

I cannot worry now.

Not when there is Sari.

I do not know what, exactly, Sari wants. Maybe she's getting
revenge. This could be her getting back at me for having fun with
her book, making me come up to the hotel room, which will be
empty. Or when I walk in, someone will douse me with something. Whipped cream. Tar. This whole thing is a big setup. It's a
trap. I would deserve it, certainly. I deserve anything, everything—no attack would surprise me. But it's worth the risk. To be
with a sexologist! She will know everything, full of tricks, tips,
explosive things, will pull things out of me that I didn't know
were there—

I call from the lobby.

"I was about to leave. I have to catch a plane in two hours."

"I'm here."

"I'll come down."

I am waiting to see the sexologist. Sari. Sexologist. Sari. Sexologist. But how bad is this? Friend in a coma, Toph at Beth's, maybe crying, shaken up at least—it's the first time I really exploded—*did I explode?* I exploded, I sounded like them—

And I'm waiting for this woman who I have known all of three hours— The elevator splits and she is there, with the suitcase, striding toward me and, when close, smelling so good—

We decide to skip dinner, to go straight to my house. We'll have an hour before her flight leaves. We get in my car and there is rain, and the Tenderloin is gauzy and bright, and on the way home all the green lights are timed, and then we are alone in my room—

I am with the sexologist! All is lush. We are progressing, still clothed but progressing—on a bed with the sexologist, on a bed with the sexologist, on a bed with the sexologist—what does that mean, to be here with the sexologist? There is nothing better, yes? This is it, right? I am not married, and I will die soon, three years, maybe five, and Shalini would be wanting us all to be enjoying ourselves, even with—*especially with* a sexologist in from New York, a one-in-a-million chance here, I know, Shal knows—and thus I'll be adding joy to the world, not depriving. Deprivation does no one any good. I will be adding something to the world, this experience to the world and more so, Sari and I will be further weaving ourselves into its fabric, by doing things, anything, anything at all, one is weaving oneself into the fabric—

It is okay for me to have sex with the sexologist while Shalini is in a coma. *How could we say no?* Our being together means that something is happening, and the happening of things equals a moral good, which equals an irreducible good, which = existing = defiance = pulling = pushing = proof = faith = connection + hand-holding = affirmation = swimming to the rock and back + holding breath under water all the way from one side to the other = the fighting of fights, tiny fights, big fights, any fights = the proving of points, all the time = denial of the tide = flouting of decay = force − restraint − moderation − nail-biting − no-saying + wall-punching + volume-turning-upping + quick-lane-changing + car passing + light-making + yelling + demanding, insisting, staying, getting = defiance = handprints, footprints, proof = tree-shaking, fence-cutting + taking + grabbing + stealing + running = engorging = no regretting = insomnia = blood = soaking in blood and what Shalini needs is the connection, the pumping of blood, the use of the lattice! She needs her friends not only there by her side, but she needs us being as close as possible, not only to her but to each other, creating friction, noise, and if possible, she needs us having sex, having sex with each other and projecting that energy to her, the bursting and love—it all connects, aha! *Shalini would want us having sex!* And then, with Sari, just mild groping at this point, with our eyes closed, then the thumping of empty shoes on the wooden floor, the thinking of all the things you think about with your eyes closed while feeling and positioning and rubbing like, for example, space travel. Walking on Mars, in a *2001: A Space Odyssey*–style spacesuit, everything dusty, red. Then images from a lavishly illustrated book owned throughout adolescence positing what space travel might look like, three thousand years hence, the moon-sized spacecrafts, the towers miles high on planets heretofore uncharted; then Shalini's eyes, closed and purple; then your lack of a condom, and then your giving AIDS to Sari, and your having to tell Sari, a year hence, when you are diagnosed, and having to wait— No, you'll do it through the mail, being unable to face her, you will have moved to Greenland or Franz Josef Land by then, or else you will still be here, and will tell her in person, and will ask her to marry you, and together you will fight through AIDS, because—no, she won't want anything to do with you, asshole—

The door to the building opens and closes. Then the door to the apartment opens and closes. Then the door to the bedroom opens. Toph.

"Oop," he says.

I walk out. It's the first time he's caught me. Not that we were all that engagé. But still.

He's looking in his closet. Just standing, looking.

"What are you doing here?" I ask.

"What do you mean?"

"You're supposed to be at Beth's."

"She didn't have any food. She sent me home."

"Listen, head back there and eat. Tell her she has to. Tell her to order something. I'll come get you in an hour."

He leaves.

I return to Sari. She's standing, to go.

Then to the airport.

Silence. Idle talk.

Outside the car we hug.

She passes through the airport's glass and I watch, blinking stupidly.

It's unclear what we've done, whether something happened, whether we broke through, whether proof was provided.

Accompanying Adam Rich's final interview is a full-page photo of Adam, mid-laugh. The caption reads: "Didn't Fear the Reaper." The spread is great. It looks perfect, everything down to the last detail—photos of him growing up, the one with Brooke Shields towering above him, even a bizarre shot of him, at age nine or so, with Moodie's new girlfriend Michelle (she and Adam went to the same school for the arts). It's all pitch-perfect, everything dead-on, believable. This will be big, we think.

"This will be big," we say.

"Yes, this will be big," we say.

Things finally seem aligned for us, with our rental situation seemingly stable, advertising somewhat better, the staff at a maximum, with six or ten or twenty interns, and now our new East Coast helper person, a twenty-two-year-old actress/waitress named Skye Bassett whom Lance has somehow roped into running around New York for us, doing meetings, planning an upcoming party, running errands.

"An actress?" we say.

"Yeah, did you see *Dangerous Minds?* She was one of the kids in the class. It was a big role. She's on the box and everything."

"So... what does she want with us?"

It is a standard response. We are suspicious of anyone who offers to help us, worried about anyone who actually does. Those, like Zev, who move across the country to do so, for free, well...

I rent the movie soon after and sure enough, amid the black and Latino kids—at-risk youth, see—there is a pretty white girl with dirty-blond hair. She is tough and wears too much makeup. She has speaking lines and everything, and now she's running around New York for us. She waitresses thirty hours a week at the Fashion Cafe, acts or auditions twenty hours more, squeezes our garbage in somewhere between. When she phones she is manic and funny, with a husky voice. She is one of us, and with her, and with this Adam Rich thing, it really seems like we might be turning a corner here, maybe we should really make some kind of push, actually put together a kind of business plan and get a bunch of millions of dollars and finally dominate and have bridges and grade schools named after us, arrange for the trip in the space shuttle, and maybe Shalini will get some money, too, maybe she'll get back in there and do her thing because Shalini has been in the coma for about two weeks when Marny and I go one day, a bright weekday at about noon, and are led inside, where Shalini is there with her eyes open.

Jesus fucking Christ.

We freeze. We had not been told that her eyes were open. We want to run and tell her family.

Her eyes are open, but not open in a vacant sort of way, but open-open, absolutely. She's looking at us! I move a little to the side to see if her eyes will follow me, and they do, slowly, slowly, but...she must be...

"Hey Shal!" Marny says.

Awake!

We wash our hands and come over to one side of her bed—maybe we forget to wash our hands—and lean over in the usual way, holding her arm, all the while her eyes are following us, at least one eye is following us. The other eye is not moving, but she's really watching us, with those huge eyes or eye, looking completely amazed by our presence—the stunned, mute look of a newborn. God her eyes are huge, the whites of her eyes so gigantic, bigger than before it really seems, maybe twice as big as before.

The world is in bloom. She is back, we have not lost her, she's obviously back, and hearing us, and will soon talk, and then, maybe in a few days, be up and about and then back to work, chatting, creating, assembling, and finally resuming the backrubs.

One of her friends comes in. We give him an urgent sort of look, casual but urgent, not to alarm anyone, but *Jesus Christ*!

We tell her to wiggle her toes and she waves her foot back and forth.

It's spectacular.

It's Jesus and Lazarus and Christmas.

Afterward, though, in the waiting room, we are told by one of the doctors that even with her eyes open and her seeming to be cognizant, she is still, technically, comatose. That it is not unusual, for someone still comatose to open one's eyes, to respond to basic commands. We can't for the life of us figure out what that means.

To us it's obvious that she is awake, is back, and that it might have been us, Marny and I, that made it happen.

We leave, dizzy, catapulting. The cars in the parking lot shimmer, the sky is full of doves and big dancing puppies, all singing early Beach Boys songs. I put my arm around Marny as we walk to the car, and by the time we get to the car I have a fantastic idea. My idea is this: Marny and I should have sex. In the car.

My head is on some new planet, a just-found planet that's full of flora and fauna and winged deer and snakes that harmonize and I am so giddy that when we get in the car I just sit there and grin. At Marny. We both are alive, and have known each other for all these years, and have made it this long, so long, we are so old and tired and have not been killed and have not fallen from a bridge or balcony or rickety deck. I am really thinking that the very best way to commemorate it all is for Marny and I to be naked with each other, and sweating—at her apartment, mine, in the car, it doesn't matter. The beach, the park.

I need to take my clothes off. I can't drive. We sit in the car, in the hospital parking lot. I can't do anything else. I can't go back to work. Sex is the right thing.

"She was staring at us," I say, thinking of sex.

"It's incredible," Marny says, not thinking of sex.

"She looked amazing, exactly like her—I mean, her eyes were following us!" I say, thinking of Shalini's eyes, then of sex, and about whose apartment, mine or Marny's, is closer.

"Yeah, it was definitely her, so alert," Marny says.

I pause and look at Marny and hope that my thoughts, those relating to sex, seep into her brain, or are already there. She looks ahead, through the windshield, hoping that any moment I will start the car. When she turns back to me I am still looking at her, with the grin—I don't know how to broach the topic—now a shy grin. Maybe a shy grin will work.

"I know this sounds really strange," I blurt, "but I'm really horny right now."

There is a short pause as she diagnoses the depth of my confusion. That I am not kidding. I am thrown, because for a minute there I thought she might be on my planet, which also has waterslides, but as it turns out she is not, after all, on my planet.

"I think we should get back to the office," she says. She is right. She is good. She never gets upset when I do this. It was a dumb idea, a revolting idea. All wrong. Bad!

I ask her for a hug. She complies. While hugging, I get another very, very good idea: that Marny and I should have sex. I drag the hug out for a minute, across the bucket seats, thinking again that maybe she's warming to the idea, that maybe she'll change her mind and we'll complete this circle...

She pulls away, pats me on the shoulder with three mini-pats, like those used to pet reptiles. Okay. I turn the car on and back up and drive out of the parking lot, and we head back to the office, the city looming up ahead, all jagged and white, all the buildings standing there, smiling, chuckling, a bunch of huge happy people. They understand.

Adam Rich insists on being picked up at the airport. I have paid for him to fly up, so he can come to a party for the release of the issue and do a few radio interviews. I had gently suggested that the shuttles to and from SFO were just great, and cheap, too, I take them all the time—but there had been a long pause, and he had then, as he had before, let me know that I was not dealing with just some high school friend coming into town. I was dealing with a major Hollywood presence, someone whose stamp had long ago been put on that *zip* code—*a made man*. He was Adam Rich! No airport shuttles for Adam Rich! No half-assed motel rooms for Adam Rich! Get serious!

Perchance was Adam starting to believe the auteur bit, the genius-working-on-"Squatter Project" deal?

I pick him up in my Civic. I am late. I am running through the carpeted hallways. I run up the escalator, to the gate, then down, to the baggage claim. I will have to page Adam Rich. He will not like this.

"Is that you?"

I turn around.

"Adam."

"You're late."

And there he is. Adam Rich.

I guess I knew he was kind of short. I knew this. I will not act surprised. He is impeccably tanned, buff almost, with gelled hair, a goatee. He is wearing precisely the outfit he wore in the photo shoot—tanktop, surfer shorts, sunglasses. He looks pretty great.

We walk to the car.

When we hit San Francisco, the first thing he wants is a cigar. He must have some good cigars. He has been enjoying cigars, he insists, long before their enjoyment became so faddish, and wants me to stop at a place he knows of on Market Street so he can pick up some of this brand and that, the kind you can't just get at the 7-Eleven.

I have made a reservation at a hotel near Van Ness. I have never seen the hotel before, had found it in the phone book.

"You'll like it," I say. "It's close to...stuff."

It's not close to anything. But it was cheaper than any other place I called, and their ad was clear, and had by far the nicest illustration.

We pull into the parking lot. It's a sort of Red Roof Inn, just off busy Van Ness, close to a car dealership, about three blocks from the Tenderloin. There is no air-conditioning, no pool.

He is not happy. He is exasperated. He wants to be near the water, as he clearly indicated when we spoke on the phone. We

drive to the Wharf. Once there I stop at a pay phone and look
through the yellow pages. He is waiting in the car, sunglasses on.
Ten minutes later I have a place, a Best Western, with A/C, a pool,
five blocks from the sea lions. I drop him off and pay for the room.
Over the next two days, I will do anything he wants, for we feel we
owe him, because the issue, the cover of which reads:

> Fare Thee Well, Gentle Friend
> Adam Rich, 1968–1996
> His Last Days
> The Final Interview
> The Legacy He Leaves

has hit and hit big—relatively speaking, of course. When the issue
was making its way to newsstands we sent out, from our Brother
600 fax machine, a press release to exactly one media outlet, the
National Enquirer, fully intending to lie to them about the article's
veracity. In the interest of diverting questions from us, thus keeping the hoax alive for as long as possible, we planned to pin the
story, and its fact-gathering, on its elusive British author,
Christopher Pelham-Fence. All inquiries would be directed to
him, though, oddly enough, he would be unavailable for a week,
as he was on assignment in, we think, Romania.

Eight minutes later there was a breathless call from a producer
from *Hard Copy*. We had not faxed *Hard Copy*.

"Why haven't we heard about this?" he wanted to know.

"Man, that's a good question," we said.

"Have you talked to any other TV outlets?"

"No, you're the first."

"Good, good. Can you get us his family? Friends?"

"Um, sure. Yes. Maybe. Yes."

The logistics were getting complicated too fast. Who will play
his mom? His dad? The neighborhood grocer?

"Well, first," we said, "we'll have to track down, you know, Mr. Pelham-Fence. He's got all the details."

We were caught unprepared. We assumed that they would take our word for it. (*Well, if an obscure, error-filled magazine in San Francisco says so, then it must be true...*) We didn't think the makers of *Hard Copy* were sticklers for things like facts. A few minutes later, the producer called again.

"The LAPD has no record of the murder."

"Oh. Well—"

"Not that they would have to, but—"

They wanted to believe it as much as we wanted them to.

"Well," we say. "Um..."

Twenty minutes later, he called again:

"There's no record of it anywhere in Southern California. Is that where it happened?"

"Well. Um. Yeah. We think."

"Do you have any more information? What day was it again?"

"Um... [Flipping wildly through the magazine for the article]. If I...remember correctly...it was...you know, you really should talk to Mr. Pelham-Fence. Of course, he's in Bucharest at the moment...and it's what, three A.M. over there by now, and—"

We hung up and strategized. We tried to get Paul or Zev to be Pelham-Fence. They both refused.

"No way."

"I can't do a British accent."

The producer called again.

"No one's heard anything about this. We called his manager, and he says it's news to him."

Within an hour of the fax, the jig was up.

"Listen, guys, what's going on here?" the producer wanted to know.

We told him. A hoax. Funny.

He was unamused. He was angry. He hung up.

It was over.

Or not. Not for Adam, for the machinery had been set in motion, and it would be a few weeks before it would slow. An AP reporter, apparently slow on the uptake, tracked down *Eight Is Enough* dad Dick Van Patten, in rural Missouri, wanting a comment on the untimely death of his TV son. He was beside himself. He reportedly sobbed. It was all over the Internet. People debated it in chatrooms; most of those who knew it was fake were furious. Most people weren't sure. Adam's friends and ex-girlfriends spent days in shock, believing he was gone. One girlfriend, assuming he was dead, called his home number, just to hear his voice on the answering machine one last time. Adam picked up. She swooned. He called us, in a panic.

"Listen you guys. This is way out of control. My relatives are fucking freaking out."

We sent out another press release, this one explaining our big ha ha, asserting that its phoniness should have been obvious to all (knowing that it was not), that the humor was self-evident (but of course). The notice is complete with a short note from Adam, telling everyone, at our urging, to "lighten the fuck up."

But then came the backlash. They tore Adam to pieces. There was a piece in the *Enquirer*, segments on *American Journal*, E!, mentions in dozens of AP papers, a spread in the *New York Post*. Most of the stories, given an excuse and a motive, dredged up his past, a semi-sordid melange of drug abuse and petty larceny, with very unflattering results. And almost to the last, they accused him of using this stunt, this fake death—*this egregious manipulation of public sentiment*—as a cheap way of getting his name in the papers.

The next morning, I pick him up at the Best Western, for the first of two radio interviews.

"So what are you working on these days?" asks Peter Finch, the compassionate disc jockey at KFOG.

"Well, I'm putting together a period piece. A costume drama."

"Great. Wow. And you'll be..."

"Producing and directing."

Adam is amazing. I expected disaster, expected that callers would tear into him, that the DJs would make fun, but everything stays above-board, and Adam is composed, assured, well-spoken— still a performer, still in control.

Afterward, he comes back to the office, signs copies of the issue, his signature confident, full of strong lines, grand loops, one of which, a short while later, Zev and I bring to Shalini.

She has been moved to a new hospital, down the street from Toph and me, in a bright room with a view of Nob Hill. She is cognizant, has had ten or twelve or thirty operations on her head so far, will have a hundred and fifty thousand more. We entertain her and her mom, reading her letters aloud, and filling her in on office goings-on. Her short-term memory is shot, so she doesn't really remember Zev too well, and has to be reminded of many of the people we're talking about.

"Oh, you know who's in town?" we say. "You'll love this."

"Who?"

"Adam Rich!"

"Oh. My. God! Why?"

"Well, we did this issue, we did this story where we pretended that he was dead and—"

I am thinking this is a great story, but in the middle of the story I glance at her mom, and her mom is not liking the story. This story is perhaps not appropriate. Of course it's not appropriate. Her mom, so small, has been by Shalini's side for months, through countless edge-of-oblivion situations, the all-nights wondering and listening to breaths, everything I know, and still I come in and say these things—

I'm an idiot. I look to Zev for help, but he hasn't seen the look from Shal's mom. I change the subject.

We stay for a while. They've moved most of the stuff from the old room to this one. The pictures of her family, friends, the big black and white ones of her, the stuffed animals, flowers, her portable CD player, books. I didn't plan to look for it, but then it occurs to me and I can't help but look around. It is no longer wedged between her arm and torso. It is not on the sidetable, or on the windowsill. I casually step around the room, eyes scanning, thinking that maybe it's here, but in a place of honor. It could be in a glass case somewhere.

But there is no glass case.

The bear is gone.

I don't know what it means that the bear is gone. The bear's eyes were my mother's eyes and I put the bear on Shal's bed so that she would be healed and now the bear is gone and everything is still uncertain.

The only sure thing is that I can't be trusted with anything.

The party for Adam is awkward. We have spread magazines all over the club, and all the attendees are walking around with them, leafing through, Adam's face staring out, glassy-eyed, already a phantom. And so when I walk around with Adam, introducing him to people, everyone is confused. They look from their magazines to Adam and back. They do not know what to make of him. He is both a '70s icon, a fragment of their childhoods, and a purportedly dead person. Both facts preclude him from walking among them, trying to get a few of the more diminutive women at the party to come back to the Best Western to swim in the pool. "I think Adam Rich just hit on me," one friend says. "Is that really him?" they ask. "What's he doing here?" Even when he gets up on the small stage to speak, people still do not understand. *But it says, right here, in this satirical magazine, that he's dead. How could—* Those who catch on are still unimpressed. The fact that he is at this party, thrown by an obscure magazine at a mediocre club, means that he, by being here, by association, is himself unimpressive. To have him walking around, in this small nightclub, all crushed velvet and rounded bars, would mean that he would be desperate enough to fly up from L.A., to work this crowd, to slum in San Francisco, reminding everyone of what he once was, what he might be again— It was freakish. Or sad. Could he really be doing all this for attention? Could he really be milking his own past to solicit sympathy from a too-long indifferent public?

No, no. He is not calculating enough, cynical enough. It would take some kind of monster, malformed and needy. Really, what sort of person would do that kind of thing?

X.

Of course it's cold. I knew it would be cold. I would have to have known it would be cold—why wouldn't it be cold, in late December, good god of course it's cold in Chicago in late December. I had lived here for a hundred years, knew the cold. I had loved the cold, embraced and mastered the cold, had raced with Pete to the lake when it was frozen, had studied the massive icicles, ice walls, waves frozen in mid-curl. I had objected when clumsy or cruel kids would break the formations, to hear the sound, to see them fall. I had brought my Walkman down, headphones under hat, piously learning the lessons of Echo and the Bunnymen while throwing rocks across the lake's ice, watching, listening to the beedlebeddlebeedlebeddle of the rocks hopping across the dull smoked glass, extending, the ice but not the rocks, endlessly, indistinguishable from the sky, the horizon vague, like a line erased or smudged. I knew the snow, the difference between pack and powder, how if you added some water to powder you could pack it, that if you packed a snowball and ran the hose over it and let it sit for a minute you'd have not a snowball but an ice-ball that if thrown accurately—all too accurately—would create a massive gash in the cheek of your brother Bill. I knew about the walls of my nose feeling like the hard frozen walls of a cave in a mountain in the arctic, toes frozen into pebbles, only dimly related to me, in my shoes, the sting of the wind against my legs, through my papery jeans. I knew all this.

So why why why didn't I bring a fucking coat? Sadder still, I didn't even think about bringing a coat. I did not forget, no, no. I never thought about it, not once.

I feel the cold when walking off the plane, and worse while thumping through that little hallway between airplane and terminal. Nothing can keep the cold away. I am cold already. I no longer have much use for the cold, will not be sledding this trip, and it hasn't even snowed. Its only use is as a forced and obvious metaphor, as foreshadowing. But I half-wish it were just raining. It is freezing and gray and night in Chicago, and I am wearing a pullover made of cellophane.

Toph is in L.A. with Bill and I am in Chicago. I will rent a car at the airport and will go back to my hometown, and will look up Sarah Mulhern, whose bed I ended up in one night a few weeks after I heard my mother would die, and will visit my father's friends, and the bar where my father (on the sly) used to go, and will maybe go to his office, and will go to the funeral home, and will go to my old house, ghosts in pocket, and will see my parents' oncologist, and will see worried friends, and go to the beach to remember what winter looks like there, and I will look and see if I can find their bodies.

No, no, I know I won't find their bodies—they were cremated, of course, eventually—but I have long dreamed, because I am misshapen and think it might be an interesting story to tell, of coming closer to finding them, at least seeing the building where they were brought, the medical school—you know what I really want to see? I want to see the face of the doctor or doctoral student or nurse or whoever it was who used my parents as cadavers. I have pictures of them, not real pictures but images in my mind of them, in a great, armory-sized room, its floors shiny, dotted with stainless steel tables, all with tools, small machines for picking and drilling and extracting, with long thin cords, and there are medical students, five to a table, the tables spread out in a way that is perhaps too spread out, not cozy but overly spacious, gridlike, eerie by way of rigidity. God knows what they do with two cancer-ridden bodies like that—if they're used as tumor case studies or examined for their parts, like rusted cars on blocks, stripped, their colonized areas ignored in favor of their comparatively benign legs, arms, hands—oh God, my dad used to do a trick at Halloween, with a hand. We had a realistic-looking rubber hand, had had it for ten years, it was always around, and at Halloween he would scrinch his own arm into his sleeve, then put the rubber hand where his own hand should be. When a trick-or-treater would come to the door, he would open the child's sack and drop first candy, and then the hand, into the bag. It was great.

Oh my gosh! he would bellow, waving around his handless arm. *Oh my gosh!* The child would be terrified, speechless. Then my dad would compose himself, and calmly reach into the bag. *Let me get that...*

So I plan to find out which medical school received them, and then I will go to the medical school, and will find the teacher who at the time was in charge of the use of cadavers, and I will knock on his door. I will. I have no courage for such things but in this case I will, I will surmount my— This is what I will say, brightly, when he opens the door, the doctor, when he cracks his door to see who has knocked:

I don't know what I'll say. Something scary. But I won't be angry about it. I want only to take a look at the man. Offer greetings. I want him to be shorter than me, in his late thirties, forties, fifties, frail, bald, with glasses. He will be dumbstruck by my introduction, afraid for his life, my shadow darkening him, and then I will close in on him, all casual confidence, and will ask something, something like:

"So tell me. What did it look like?"

"Excuse me?" he'll say.

"Was it like caviar? Was it like a little city, with one big gleaming eye? A thousand little eyes? Or was it empty, like a dried gourd? See, I have a feeling it might have been like a dried gourd, empty and light, because when I carried her, she was so light, much lighter than I expected. When you're carrying a person, I just thought of this, when you're carrying a person, why is it easier to carry them when they hold tight around your neck? Like, you're supporting their full weight no matter what, correct? But then they grab you around the neck and suddenly it's easier, like they're pulling up on you, but either way you're still carrying them, right? Why should it make a difference that they're holding you, too— The point is that at the time, before when I was carrying her, when she was reclining on the couch and watching TV, in general I was kind of thinking that the thing in her stomach might be terribly heavy. And then I lifted her, and the weird thing was that she was so light! Which would mean that it was something hollow maybe, not the writhing nest of worms, the churning caviar, but just something dry, empty. So which was it? Was it the dried gourd, or the festering cabal of tiny gleaming pods?"

"Well—"

"I have been wondering for many years."

He will tell me. And I will know.

And then I will be at peace.

Oh I'm kidding. I kid you. About being at peace. This trip is about the fact that things have been much too calm in San Francisco— I am making enough money, Toph is doing well at school—and thus completely intolerable. I will return home and look for ugly things and chaos. I want to be shot at, want to fall into a hole, want to be dragged from my car and beaten.

Also, I have a wedding to go to.

I stay in Lincoln Park with two grade-school friends, Eric and Grant. The night I get in we go to the place on the corner.

Grant is still working at his father's halogen light factory, in the shipping department. We talk about when his dad, who we think is perhaps unnecessarily holding him down, will promote him. He is not sure. Eric, our high school valedictorian, is a management consultant. His last assignment involved a month at a pig farm in Kentucky.

"What do you know about pig farming?" I ask.

"Nothing," he says.

He makes gobs of money. He owns the condominium they live in; Grant pays rent for a room in the hideous red brick thing, imposing and square, three stories.

I note how ugly their building is.

"Yeah," Eric says, "but look at it this way: If you've got the ugliest house on the street, you never have to look at it."

Eric is good at these sayings. It's unclear where he gets them, but he and Grant now talk like this, full of salty wisdom, the lessons of the Plains. Grant, for a long time our only friend whose parents were divorced, has long been sage-like, the old soul among us. His walk was slow; he sighed before he spoke. He grew up in the apartment complex near the high school, and when we'd drop him off he'd say, "Roll up the windows, lock the doors—we're entering the ghetto." And this made us laugh.

We play pool. After updates on Moodie, et al., the usual subjects are touched upon:

1) Vince Vaughn, who we've all known since fifth grade, who everyone from home now watches closely, vicariously, fingers crossed, second-guessing his career choices from afar.

"You see him in *The Lost World?*"

"Yeah, he was okay."

"They didn't give him much to do."

"No."

"He needs another *Swingers*."

"Right. Something ha-ha."

2) Their hair: They both have interesting hair news. Grant continues to lose his, unabated, and Eric has finally abandoned the hairspray he'd been using since high school that made him, though fully coiffed, look like he was wearing a hairpiece.

"It's nice," I say, looking at it.

"Thanks," he says.

"No, really, the way it's kind of feathered like that, all natural, kind of floaty. It's nice."

"Yes. Thank you."

They are also going to the wedding, the next day, the wedding of Marny's sister Polly, who is marrying someone we do not know. We have all been invited, about fifteen of us, the friends of Polly's sister, and so we're using the wedding as a sort of reunion. Everyone will be there; most are coming tomorrow, the day after. Grant and Eric are curious why I am here for five days, and I tell them enough so that they understand but not so much that they will worry.

We leave the lights off when we get home. They have moved the weight bench to make room for a futon for me.

"Thanks," I say, getting under the comforter.

I am afraid Grant will tuck me in.

"Good to have you," he says, and pats my head.

In the dark I hear Grant in the next room, his dresser drawer squeaking, and Eric upstairs, in the bathroom, water running.

I sleep like I have not slept in years.

• • •

In the morning I begin. I have borrowed a coat from Grant, and have brought along a tape recorder, a notebook, and a list of things I want to do while here. The list consists of about fifty items, was typed out and laser printed and then added to on the plane. The list starts with the things mentioned above:

Wenban [the funeral home]

924 [the street address of my old house]

Stuart [my father's friend]

Haid [Dr. Haid, their oncologist]

Sarah [in whose bed I woke up all those years ago]

Bar [the bar, in the next town, I know where it is but not its name, which my dad frequented]

Beach [a sandy area abutting Lake Michigan, where people gather to meet, sunbathe, play in the water]

The list goes on. The idea, I suppose, is the emotional equivalent of a drug binge, the tossing together of as much disparate and presumably incompatible stimuli as possible, in a short span, five days, together constituting a sort of socio-familial archaeological bender, to see what comes of it, how much can be dredged up, brought back, remembered, exploited, excused, pitied, made known, made permanent. In the interest of overload, I've continued, on the plane, in bed, to add to the list, tangential or random things—phone calls and unexpected visits to people I haven't seen in five, ten years, people I never talk to—wanting to throw anything potentially provocative or brutal into the mess. For instance, handwritten in the margin there is:

Wooden [a grade school friend who was sent to military school for reasons unexplained to me, but who wrote a very nice condolence note that winter of ours, though we hadn't spoken in easily seven years; I'm thinking I'll maybe pop by his house, because I never wrote back to him, and would like to see what he

looks like, how he talks, maybe say hello to his mother, who, one
night when I slept over and could not sleep because we had
watched *Grizzly*—sort of like *Jaws* with fur—had heated milk in
a pan for me, had whispered kindnesses in the kitchen]; Aunt Jane
[who lives in Cape Cod; a phone call?]; Fox [Jim Fox, of
Abramson & Fox, my dad's old pinstriped boss, a bent-over and
sour man, who, as Beth and I were cleaning out our father's desk
a few weeks after, came into the office and said this, in an unkind
way, the way one would talk about a child who was found masturbating too often: "Well, we all *knew* he was dying"]; Donation
place [organization that picks up and then distributes cadavers to
medical schools]; Medical school [the one most likely to have used
the cadavers]

The list continues. Other friends, friends of my parents, the
few college friends who made it to either funeral; grade school and
high school teachers; the park at the end of our street, with the tiny
frozen lake; Mrs. Iwert, whose lawn I used to cut and whose gardening I used to do (to see if she's still alive); my mother's friends,
coworkers, on and on.

And: On the side of the page, the page with the list, is this
word, written in large letters, crooked though, scrawled left-handed.
It stands large, in all caps, next to the computer printout portion
and all the handwritten additions. I added it at a pay phone at
O'Hare, while talking to Toph in L.A. right after my flight landed.
The word is:

DRUNK?

Which is my question to myself regarding just what state I would
best be in while doing this business in and around Chicago. As I
was talking to Toph about what he and Bill were doing in L.A.—
that day they had gone to a batting cage and seen a movie (Bill gets
to be the fun one)—it occurred to me, with great clarity, that I
should be drunk the entire time. The drunkenness, I guessed,
would add to the whole endeavor a haze of mystery, not to mention

a romantic fluidity that I could not otherwise count on. I should be desperate, raggedy, semi-coherent, stumbling from place to place. It seemed much more fitting than being calculating and sober, would strip things to their core, would eliminate a layer or two of self-conscious white noise, would allow me to do more asinine things.

On the other hand, though, it would be hell on the documentation. Could I really take appropriate notes and make comprehensible recordings...while tanked?

I get my rental car and while driving to Lake Forest I have not yet ruled out the drunk-all-the-time notion. Though I've never been intoxicated more than three hours in a row without falling asleep, and have rarely been drunk more than once a week, I leave the option open, resolving to decide at the wedding, where I will surely be soused—at that point, I can choose, if the mood seems right, to continue the binge, stock up, have some with me at all times, in a thermos maybe—

The driving though. The driving would be hard.

I head north to Lake Forest. The highway, 41, in late December, and the entire Chicago area, looks as mothy and sad as it's supposed to. No snow, just silvery cold and exhaust, black slush.

In twenty minutes I'm outside my old house and I feel nothing. I'm in Lake Forest, on my block, across the street from my house. I'm in the car, listening to a college rock station, and the thing that's occupying me most of all is the state of the neighbors' yard. Something is different. Have they cut down trees? It seems as if they have cut down trees.

The car is getting foggy inside, and I am not crying. As I wound up my street, I was sure that I would do something emotional when I saw the house—a part of me hoped briefly that it would not be there, that it had been removed, carried off by a tornado. Or that the new owners had razed it, built from scratch. But then, at the bend of the road, it was clear that it was still there, is still here. They have painted blue the wood that we had left gray, but otherwise it looks the same. The shrubs I planted in front, to discourage the toddler-Toph from running into the street, are still there, have not grown.

I rip a piece of paper from my notebook and write a note—

Dear resident of 924 Waveland,

I used to live here, most of my life. I would love to come inside and look around, but didn't want to arrive announced. If you're amenable to the idea, please call me at 312-------. I'll be here until Saturday.

—and put it in the mailbox. I do not expect much from it, because in their position I am not sure I would invite me in. Maybe I would pretend to be on vacation, would lose the letter.

I go to the train station in town to use the pay phone. It's freezing. I am looking for Sarah, whose number I don't have. I don't know where she lives—last I saw her she lived at home, with her parents—or if she still lives in the area, or in the state. I try a Sarah Mulhern in Chicago.

"Is this Sarah?"

"Yes?"

"Sarah Mulhern?"

"Yes."

"Sarah Mulhern from Lake Forest?"

"Uh, no."

"Sorry."

I hang up, blow hot air into my hands. I'm a moron. Someone will see me here, back in town for the first time since I left, using the phone outside the train station. No one uses this phone. Then again, no one will be surprised. They will have expected something like this, from me—they know what happened, will assume that I've finally hit bottom, that I'm homeless and on crack. Did I ever belong in this town? Another wrong number and then:

"Sarah?"

"Yes?"

"Sarah Mulhern?"

"Yes?"

"Sarah Mulhern from Lake Forest?"

A pause and then, slowly, "Yeah..."

It has been four years. But she's warm, right away she's warm. We talk about the last time we saw each other, when we had to sneak out of her house in the morning so she could drive me home, how her dad would have killed me.

"He died last year, you know."

"No, I didn't, actually. I'm so sorry."

Jesus. I'm not sure what I say at that point, but soon enough I ask if she's going to Polly's wedding; they were in the same class. She is not. I ask her if she has time for lunch, coffee in the next couple days.

She says any night is fine.

The wedding is wonderfully normal. I had wanted desperately to be at an unsurprising wedding, as rigid and traditional as possible. The idea of them frightened me enough to begin with, but deviation from rote made weddings somehow more absurd. I could not shake the memory of Beth's ceremony, six months earlier. The groom was a nice young man named James, baby-faced and blond, and the whole affair took place on a deck in a cluster of cottages near Santa Cruz, high above the Pacific.

Beth had long dreamed of having the wedding on the beach, to be barefoot, to be in white, on the sand, windblown, all of us in front of the shushing waves, at sunset. But the permit was impossible to get, so she settled for this group of little houses, beach or no a wonderful setting, all buttery green and white-white—though Toph and I barely made it.

We were already late, had gone to get Toph some pants, and were driving through San Francisco in our little red car, up Franklin's rolling thoroughfare, toward home to get changed.

We stopped at a light at the top of the hill. Then a thump, a jump forward, a crash of glass. We had been hit from behind by some kind of truck, something huge.

It was a woman, mid-forties, in a Jeep Grand something. A huge car. In the woman's car was a family, two teenaged daughters, the husband, all tall, well dressed, normal. They looked down from their truck with mild concern. The sun was right overhead, and I stood under it for a minute, in the road, the shattered glass flickering on the road. Toph and I walked to the sidewalk and I sat down, dazed. He stood over me.

"You okay?" he asked.

"Move over. I can't see you in the sun.

"That's better. No, I'm fine."

"What are we going to do?"

"We have to go. We're already late."

We had an hour. Our car had been halved. There was no back bumper, no back window, the hatchback's door was twisted, shattered, unhatchable. We exchanged names and information, and the woman offered to call a tow truck, but there was no time, and when I tried it, the car started, so we left. Back home, changed and then back in the car, back down the hill, onto the highway, the wind screaming through the car's naked frame, south to San Jose, where we picked up Bill at the airport—who thought the car situation very funny, sitting in back, the wind pouring in—even while I feared with all my soul that the gas tank had been damaged, that we were leaking fuel, that the fumes would spark and we would all explode en route, that it was all too fitting—

We rolled in, rumbling and pathetic. The grounds were white with fog, the green was gray, the ocean invisible. Toph and I had nothing approximating formal clothing, were wearing wrinkled white shirts and my father's frayed ties. Everyone knew who we were, that we were *them*.

We met the minister, a lesbian agnostic named Reverend Jennifer Lovejoy, with the flowing robe and wild, steely hair. We said hello to our family's representatives. First, our cousin Susie, out from rural Massachusetts, who had been shopping in the small beach town earlier, and was wearing a thrift-store hat she bought, straw, eight inches tall, with four woven birds perched on it. And then Aunt Connie, my father's sister, a synthesizer composer (her music is called Sacred Space Music), who had come down from Marin, at the last moment, a surprise, though without the talking parrot or cockatoo usually perched on her shoulder. Before long she had cornered me and John—who showed up just beforehand, had been drinking tall boys on the way—and had for fifteen minutes debated with us the likelihood that the government was hiding knowledge of alien visits from the public. She of course knew first-hand of the coverup, having been receiving, for some time, messages from outer space through her computer. I asked how she knew the messages were from outer space and not from, say, AOL. She looked at me with pity, in a way that said, "If you have to ask..."

Bill and I were supposed to walk down the aisle with Beth, to give her away. She had asked, and we had said yes, of course, that it would be nice, an honor—but then, as Bill and I waited outside in the clearing fog, she decided that, come to think of it, she did not want to be "given away," did not like the patriarchal implications of the custom, that she would walk down the aisle alone, under her own power. And so Bill and I sat in the front row and waited, as Connie complained about the quality of the pre-wedding music (Mark Isham, she guessed, with a sniff).

But the music would change soon enough. When Beth and

James came walking down the aisle, under a sky that had cleared and was now immaculate, the first notes wafted toward us, piped through two speakers on the deck—it was not the wedding march. Or Pachelbel. It was—I was panicked, scanning the crowd for a reaction because I was almost sure that this song was—oh, now it was unmistakable, this song—

This song was "Beth," by KISS.

Not an instrumental version. The original recording.

And she was barefoot.

Did she think this was funny? Surely she couldn't—

There was a cliff only thirty yards away, and I wondered if I would be noticed, if I could just slip away quietly, as they were all watching the entrance, and fling myself over.

For Polly's wedding, my first since Beth's, I am clinging to the hope for simple, tradition-bound Protestant solidity. It is at a church, First Presbyterian in Lake Forest, which is a good start, and they've asked us to wear tuxes, which is just fine. The reception is at Shore Acres, the country club in the next town where Bill spent a summer waiting tables. A nice place. Completely respectable.

At the reception, what everyone wants to talk about is the English teacher's sex change operation. One of the high school's teachers, and my former (intrepid, spirited) J.V. soccer coach, has announced that after a spring regimen of hormones, and a surgical procedure over the summer, he will be returning, in the fall, as a woman. We cannot believe it's happening. It's the best thing we've had since Mr. T.

When the subject is exhausted, there is the inevitable:

"How's Toph?" from Megann.

"Still limping."

"How old is he now?" from Kathy.

"I forget."

"Where is he?" from Amy.

"Funny you should ask. He's been hitchhiking…"

Conversation dissolves and we stare at each other. They know I am not them. I am something else. I am deformed, am a hundred years old. I will spend the next day looking for the remains of my parents.

"How's that magazine going?" Barb asks.

"Probably not for long."

"Why?"

I explain. We're all exhausted, tired of having other jobs, that we'll either get some funding soon and move it to New York, or fold. It's the last thing I want to talk about, think about. I don't want to talk about my failures, or theirs. Maybe we're all stunted. Is anything happening for any of us? The celebrity of the night is the date of a girl Marny went to college with. He's the host of a children's television show in Chicago, and has just starred, with one line, in *Space Jam*, not to mention an even larger role in a recent Jack in the Box commercial. He performs for us—jokes, does imitations of other guests. We adore him.

Half of us are talking about moving. Flagg has already left for New York, for grad school, and I'm vaguely thinking about moving, too. But what I really want is to just swim around in a warm baby pool of these friends, jump in their dry leaf pile—to rub them all over myself, without words and clothes.

But we are all sitting, needing to talk, to catch up. There is a band. They are playing '50s hits. There are three female singers with bouffants. They are going all out, these people. Older couples start dancing. I do not like the older couples, who dominate this wedding of two young people, these older couples everywhere, dancing in a jittery way, each either too slow or much much too fast, like that one woman, in gold lamé, doing some kind of Latin maneuver, as the band plays the Beach Boys, like she's trying to crush ants with her high heels. She wears, as they all wear, an expression that says *Oh yeah!* or *All right!* or—

I want to jump through the plate-glass window and into the

club's backyard, and then run to the cliff and jump down, into
Lake Michigan. Or at least go outside and walk around. But it's too
cold. And I don't have the shoes. I can go upstairs. I can grab
everyone and we can leave. I want us all to be in one big bed,
naked. Maybe not naked—

The bride and groom leave, and the old people leave, and the
guy who shook my hand in the bathroom, insisted on it as we stood
at neighboring urinals, is thrown out for getting into a kind of
physical sort of fight with his girlfriend, and then everyone is gone
and we are the last ones, all of us sitting around, the sweat dried on
us, debating where to go, someone's house, a bar, it's only midnight, and we end up at Megann's, eating cookies in her kitchen,
looking at the pictures on her refrigerator, as we had a hundred
times before, keeping quiet because her parents were asleep upstairs.

We had all taken spots in the various empty beds, so I wake up in
Megann's brother's room. He's at college, and the room is dark,
thickly carpeted, full of mahogany furniture and hockey trophies,
team pictures. A stick signed by Denis Savard.

I drive Marny home.

Then back to work.

An hour or so later I'm walking across the yard of my old
house. There's a new mailbox. They've fixed that broken post,
repainted the front door.

Already I feel bad for these people. These poor people.
They've made a mistake letting me in. What will happen when
this happens? They should not have invited me. I would have
understood if they had not invited me. But the father called and
said I could come and here I am. This will be bad. Things will happen. I will slip and tell them things they don't want to hear.

No, no. I will be good. This will be fine.

The door opens and they are all there. *Do they always answer the door together?* There are three young children, all under seven, two boys and a girl, the father with a sweater and a mustache, the mother with a bobbed haircut, the children hiding behind them, peeking behind their legs. I shake the man's hand. They let me in their house.

It makes no sense for them to let me into their house. The only thing they know about me is that I once lived here. I wonder if they know what happened there. I assume they do. The parents at least. Not these perfect little children. I will not tell.

We walk straight into the kitchen and the light! The place is filled with light. I look around quickly, trying to find the source of all this light. The walls have been repainted. The wood paneling is gone. Other walls are missing. They've knocked down walls! Cabinets are gone or moved and replaced. There's a new window, or the window is bigger. I can't tell. I can't tell what's different. It all looks different. And small. It looks like a house for small people. But these people are regular height.

We tour. They have renamed the living room the family room, and vice versa. They've removed the wall-to-wall white carpeting, revealing perfect wood floors, and there's new paint everywhere, the ceilings are fixed, and skylights! We talk, and I ask questions about how they did this and did that. I ask technical questions.

"Is this new molding?

"Is this drywall?"

And I quickly become not the former inhabitant of this place, not some masochistic oddity, but a friendly neighbor with an interest in decorating.

Upstairs, the bedrooms are cheerful, pinks, light blues for kids' rooms. My room is unrecognizable. The orange forest wallpaper is gone, my drawings are gone. The carpet is gone, the mirrors on the closet gone. The broken door has been replaced.

Everything is so neat, so tidy, the toys bright, rounded. The children's bathroom has special children's fixtures, little blue and red and yellow toothbrushes. The master bedroom—that's where the skylight is. We had never thought of a skylight. Good god, a skylight. It is so bright, this room, and where there was a walk-in closet full of my father's suits, where it smelled so much of him, the leather belts and smoke-drenched suits and shoe polish there is now—there is now a Jacuzzi.

I ask them how, how all this—

"We put a lot of time into this house," the father says. He makes a soft whistling sound, underlining just how much work it had needed.

"Yeah," I say. "We kind of let things slide there for a while."

We go back downstairs, the kids following us around. The laundry room has been repainted, the carpet replaced. The bathroom by the garage no longer has the wallpaper with the groovy expressions. Through the small tall bathroom window, the backyard looks much the same, white with snow, the hill dotted with plastic toys and red sleds.

The sky is white. I am at the beach. I'm at the beach because I need a phone, and refuse to conduct this business at the train station, in the middle of town. I call Eric and Grant's machine to see if the oncologist has called back. He has not. The beach is empty. The cold is savage. It couldn't be above ten degrees.

I walk from the parking lot along the brick-sidewalked promenade, inspecting the benches, each paid for and dedicated. I decide that I will buy one of these benches, that I will dedicate a bench to my mother, maybe one for him, maybe one for both—it would depend how much they cost. Most of the benches' inscriptions simply list a name, but on one, near the phone, it reads:

> Roses are red
> Violets are blue
> We like the beach
> And hope you do, too.

Good lord. I can do better than that.

I'll get a bench. I'll get Beth and Bill to chip in. Finally we will do something. We can afford this. We owe this—

Which reminds me—I gasp, audibly, alone on the beach— that Toph's high school financial aid forms are due the next day. We have applied to five or six private high schools, and now must submit an application for aid to a national processing center. I did not do it before I left, had left it for the plane, and now here I am, at the lake, with three hours to make it to the FedEx box.

I go to the car and get my backpack, return and lay the application's pages out on one of the picnic tables near the guardhouse. As always, I am immediately stumped by the questions. I don't know or quickly forget everything in this arena—Social Security numbers, bank account numbers, the amount we have in savings. Beth will know.

I use the pay phone under the awning of the snack bar, soaked from the icicles melting above it. I wipe away the puddles, the water warmer than expected, and call Beth in San Francisco. Beth knows why I am in Chicago, but does not understand why I am at the lake in December.

"I don't know. I am. There's a phone here. It's cold."

"I have to call you back."

"Beth. It's freezing."

"I'm on the phone. Give me the number there."

"It's like zero degrees here."

"It's what?"

"There are no degrees here, Beth."

"I'll call you back in ten minutes."

I give her the number, and lie down on a picnic table. I experiment with staying warm. Is it warmer when sitting still, or when moving? I guess I know that it's warmer when moving, but for a minute I entertain the notion that I can lie still, and can *will* my blood to circulate. With my eyes closed, my breath loud, I direct my blood to speed up, imagine that I am watching it, picturing conveyors and Habitrails... I doze for five, ten minutes, thinking of life on other planets.

The phone rings. Beth is annoyed.

"Listen, do we have to do this now?"

"Yes."

"Why?"

"Because I have to FedEx it today."

"Why?"

"Because they're due tomorrow."

"Why didn't you do it before now?"

"That doesn't matter now."

"——"

"Listen, I'm still at a pay phone. At the beach. By the lake. It's winter. Winter is cold. Can we just do this?"

"Fine."

We go over the numbers.

"Thanks. That's it. Bye."

Out of habit—I tend to call Bill shortly after Beth—I call Bill and Toph in L.A. and get his machine. They are no doubt at the beach, a real beach, warm, watching women play volleyball. I ramble into his tape recorder for a while and hang up. Two men jog by, wearing Chicago Bears sweat suits. As they putter by, they watch me, because I am sitting on a picnic table, with a pen in my mouth, surrounded by papers. I finish filling out the forms and stuff them into my backpack.

On the way to the parking lot, past the snackbar, I put my face against the guardhouse window. Inside, just behind the desk of whoever sits behind a desk at a beach, is a picture of maybe fifteen lifeguards, posed in bathing suits. All in orange, all grinning, all with extremely white teeth, blond hair, silver-white hair. There are a few I recognize. The picture must be five, six years old. And there, in the back row, is Sarah Mulhern. She looks much as I remember her—tan, blue-eyed, sad-eyed, blond, curvy. I knew she was a lifeguard, but had never seen her guarding here, had been at the beach hundreds of times but had never seen her or this picture. And now—

It's too weird. I make a note to write that one down.

At the car, I drop my backpack inside and walk back and call Beth again.

"Listen. I have a question for you."

"Yes."

"You know about those ashes?"

"What?"

"You heard me."

"Oh no. Whose?"

"Both, either."

"What about them?"

"Well, you never got them back, right?"

"Right."

"And they never called you about them or anything?"

"Yeah they did."

"What do you mean?"

"About a year ago they called."

"They did? Who did?"

"I told you this."

"You did not tell me this."

"I did. They called, and they had the ashes. Mom's at least. They'd been trying to track us down."

"Where?"

"Chicago, Berkeley, San Francisco, everywhere."

"What did you say? Did they send them?"

"No."

"No? Then where are they?"

"I said we didn't want them."

"You didn't."

"I did. What do we want with some stupid ashes?"

"But without consulting me or Bill? You just—"

I have to stop asking questions. Every time I ask a question, of Beth, of anyone, expecting something benign, or even mildly upsetting, the answer is much weirder and more terrible than I could have imagined—

"I just what?"

She's angry now.

I'm too weak to do this.

"Nothing."

She hangs up.

This is just too— I had loved how vague it was before. *Where are they?* Well, that's a good question. *Where were they buried?* Another interesting question. That was the beauty of my father's way. We knew that he had been diagnosed, but not how sick he was. We knew that he was in the hospital, but then not how close he was. It had always felt strangely appropriate, and his departure was made complete, as was hers, by the fact that the ashes never found us in California, that we had moved, and moved again, and again, dodging, weaving. I assumed the remains had been bungled, that the medical school, or whoever, had neglected their obligation, that someone had erred, forgotten. But now, knowing that Beth knew, and that they're really gone, discarded, that we had a chance—

I had actually entertained, however vaguely, the idea that I might actually find them, that at the medical school they might have them stored somewhere, in an…ash storage area, in some vast warehouse of unclaimed remains—

But now to know—

Oh we are monsters.

I stop at a pay phone at the 7-Eleven, on the border of our town and the next, now closed. I call Stuart. His wife answers.

"Oh hi!"

"Hi."

"Where are you? In San Francisco?"

"No, actually, I'm in Chicago. Highwood, actually."

"Oh my gosh. Well then, you're right near him. He's actually in the hospital."

"Oh God."

"No, no, it's just an infection. He's fine. His leg. It's a freak thing. It's all swollen. He's just in for a few days."

"Well, I was actually hoping to talk to him, or both of you for a few minutes, but I'll call again when—"

"No, go visit him. He's at Highland Park Hospital. He'd love it."

I tell her no, I couldn't, it'd be weird—

"Don't be silly. Go."

Ten minutes later I'm there, in the parking lot, in the car. From here I can see my mom's old room, the New Year's birthday room. I get out and walk around the building, to the emergency room. The doors woosh open. I want to be in the emergency room and have something happen. I want to be back the night of the nosebleed. They took her here first, boosted her white count, stopped the flow.

The waiting room looks tiny, all peach and pink and mauve, like a Florida condo. I sit on one of the soft, loungy chairs.

Nothing happens. Nothing returns.

On the TV, the 49ers are playing.

The receptionist is watching me.

Fuck it.

I leave, walk around the building. In the lobby I get Stuart's room number and call him.

He asks me if I am in town and I say that yes, I am. He says that I should come over sometime, that he's just in the hospital for a few days but after he gets out, should be out tomorrow—

I tell him that I'm already here.

"In Highland Park?"

"Actually, I'm in the building. In the lobby."

"Oh. Why?"

I lie. "Well, I'm supposed to see this doctor here at five-thirty, the oncologist, and I..."

"Well, it's almost five-thirty now."

"Oh, well, that's not totally firm. I can see him afterward."

"So you want to come up?"

"Yes."

"It's D-34."

"I know."

He is on the fourth floor. This is the same building that played host to my mother's various stints, the same building where my father died. The same floor. Probably the same floor.

The last time I saw my dad I was with my mom, Beth, Toph. We walked down this hall, pushed open his door and were assaulted with the smell. Smoke. They were letting him smoke in the hospital. The room was gray, hazy, and he was sitting there, on the bed, his legs crossed at the ankles, his hands clasped behind his head. Big smile. He was having the greatest time.

I push open the silent, heavy door and there is Stuart, the only friend I knew my father had.

The moment I step in I want to leave. The room is dark, and his torso is bare. The only light is above his head, a fuzzy round halo of amber light above his head.

Oh this is weird. He seems much more sick than he was purported to be. Why is his torso bare? Oh this is weird. Maybe he's dying too. Gray hair, all over his body.

We shake hands. He has grown a beard, gray and neat.

I sit down, in the dark, at the end of the bed, by his feet.

I mumble for a while.

I ask him about his infection. His leg is discolored, inflamed.

It's gargantuan.

I no longer feel like asking Stuart the questions I planned to ask him, the ones I was writing down half an hour ago, in the car, in the parking lot, while listening to '80s rock on the radio. I force myself to start, stuttering about why I wanted to look Stuart up, ask a few things...

The first words Stuart says are:

"Well, I'm not sure how much I can enlighten you about your dad's soul."

His voice is measured, even. His arms rest on his torso, bathed in the room's ocher light, the room otherwise brown.

This would be the way to die. This is drama, this is appropriate, at night, with the lighting just so. My father's way was all wrong, alone, the middle of the day.

He had fallen again, this time in the shower.

He called out, to Beth. Beth ran to him, dragged him to the bed. Then the ambulance. He was supposed to be in for a week or so, getting his strength up, not unusual. He had been diagnosed only a few months before. A week after he was admitted, the doctor had called, said things were not looking good, that it could be any time.

My mother scoffed. She and Beth went in.

They sat for a time in the room, in the smoke.

"Come back later," he said. "I'm taking a nap."

They drove home.

"He's not going to go today," said my mother, amused by the worrying. "He's not going to go today, or tomorrow, or next week. He just went in."

In an hour he was gone.

"He was the best driver I've ever seen," Stuart is saying. "The way he would insinuate himself—that was his word, *insinuate*— 'Watch me insinuate myself into this lane...' he would say. It was incredible. He'd change lanes, drive on the shoulder..."

I tell Stuart the story about how, when he got that car, the Nissan 280, the only new car he ever owned, the first thing he did was customize it. He put an ashtray on the side door, and cut the shoulder straps on the seat belts. We all knew he was not a fan of the seat belt law, thought it was a violation of civil rights, patently unconstitutional. But the odd thing was that, in addition to cutting off the shoulder strap on the driver's side, he cut the one on the passenger side...

The door opens. It's Mrs. Stuart.

"Oh, you did come."

I look up and shrug.

"I'll leave you alone for a few minutes."

She leaves.

The phone rings. Stuart picks it up.

"Oh hi. Can I call you back?"

His meal comes. He offers me his cheesecake.

"No thanks."

"Soup?"

"No thanks."

I ask Stuart if he thinks my father felt alone when he died.

The phone rings. He stays on longer this time. When he gets off, he does not come back to my question, and I don't ask again.

Mrs. Stuart returns and we all talk for a few minutes. Then I leave. In the parking lot I talk to the tape recorder for a while, already having forgotten most of what Stuart said.

In the morning, Grant and Eric and I eat breakfast at a diner, watching people pass, the jeans and leather jackets of Chicago winters.

"So what did you do yesterday?" Grant asks.

"Not much," I say. "Went back home, drove around."

I remember that I saw his mom. Grant's mom walks miles every day, on Western Avenue. I had driven past her.

"Did you say hi?" he asks.

"No, I didn't realize it was her until too late."

"Oh, that's too bad."

"Yeah."

"So what are you doing today?"

"Probably going back up."

"What for?"

"I don't know. Not much. Maybe I'll go to the high school."

Grant looks at me for a second. Maybe he knows.

"Well, say hi to L.F.H.S."

Mr. Iacabino, the owner of the funeral home, is not in. The man who is in is younger than me, and wears glasses behind bright, startled eyes. Chad. I step in, stamping the snow from my feet. I tell him that I'm hoping to get some papers, that I'm collecting things, that my parents had come through this way, that I was looking for any paperwork they might have.

"Let me make a call," he says.

He disappears to call Mr. Iacabino at home, leaving me in the coffin display area. There are eleven coffins in the room, each named according to its style and purported quality. The town being what it sometimes is, the coffins are extravagant, each shinier and more elaborate than the other. One is called The Ambassador. Another seems to be made of steel. I write some of the names down in a notebook I will later lose. I will not be buried, I assure myself. I will disappear. Or maybe by the time I die, there will be machines, utilizing advanced laser technology and fiber optics, that will evaporate people shortly after they pass away, without actually burning them. Experts in the operation of the machine will enter shortly after a death, assemble the machine—it'll be highly portable—and with the pull of a few levers, the person will disappear, instantaneously. There will be none of this interment, no carrying bodies around, inspecting them, embalming them, dressing them up, buying holes in the ground for them, this building elaborate boxes for them, boxes reinforced, double thick—

Or I'll be launched into space. Or by then people, dead people, will be raised atop mile-high white towers. Why not mile-high white towers, as opposed to six-foot holes? There would be obstacles, surely, for engineers and architects, and the problem of space. But space could be set aside. There is Greenland, for instance, vast and white like heaven—

"See anything you like?" Chad asks. He is behind me.

I chuckle. Good one.

He has a file folder. We sit down at a table, black and glassy, used for the planning of services.

"This is what we've got," he says.

In the folder are pages recording that Wenban Funeral Home received both bodies, had held a service for my father, and had overseen the donations.

The forms and records for my father's service are signed by my mother; those for my mother are signed by my sister. I like these papers. They are proof, the only proof we have.

"So this is everything?" I ask.

"That's it," Chad says.

I ask if he can make copies of the papers. He says he doesn't see why not. He'll go downstairs; it'll just take a sec.

The stairs are cut out of the middle of the foyer. I watch him walk down.

On the wall behind me is a display of headstone offerings. Sizes, materials, choices in style of type and order of information. The options are many—you can have the name first, the dates first, no dates at all. Or, before the name, a slogan—"Beloved," "Eternal." I should probably get a stone. A stone would be good. A stone would save me, would salvage all the damage we had already done, all the things we had given up or lost.

Chad walks up the stairs. He has a small brown box. He puts the small brown box on the table in front of me.

"This is weird," he says. "But I was just down there, by the copier. Just for the heck of it I looked on the shelves, and saw this."

The label on the cardboard box, handwritten:

Heidi Eggers

"You mean this is..."

"Yeah, this must be the cremains. They must have been sent to us at some point. I'm not sure why they hadn't been sent to you..."

I touch the box.

Good God.

Chad stands. "I'll go back down and make those copies."

He leaves again.

Fuck. God. Fuck.

The box is about a foot long in each direction, and is closed with clear packing tape. It's simple, brown, square—as it must have looked when it was mailed. The label indicates it was sent from the Anatomical Gift Association in Chicago. *How long has it been here?* I can't make out the postmark.

I have to call Beth. I will not call Bill. Bill won't want to hear this. But Beth—

I won't call Beth, either. Beth will be upset.

Chad returns with the copies.

I thank him and collect the papers, put them into a folder in my backpack, and stand up. I pick up the box and—

I have no idea what I thought it would weigh, but it's heavy. Ten pounds or more.

I wander outside.

The cold is startling. I turn my back to the wind, protecting the box. I walk to the car sideways, open the passenger door and put the box on the seat. I walk around the car, tiptoeing on the ice, open the door and get in.

I turn to the box.

The box is my mother, only smaller.

The box is not my mother.

Is the box my mother?

No.

But then I see her face on the box. My sick head makes me see the face on the box. My sick head wants to make this worse. My head wants this to be scary and unbearable. I try to fight back, to know that this is normal, all this is normal, but I know that I am a monster, that I should not have come here, that because I am looking for bad things they are being given to me and I should not have asked for this in the first place, that because I have been asking for this and more it will get worse and more brutal. My eyes blur. I shake. I want to put the box somewhere else—in the trunk maybe—but know that I can't put the box in the trunk. The box which is not my mother cannot go in the trunk because she would be livid if I put her in the trunk. She would fucking kill me.

Late that night, I get back to Grant and Eric's, and they are watching a movie where Al Pacino is blind. Al Pacino is angry and talks with an unplaceable accent. He is maybe Canadian. We are all sitting in different parts of the room—Eric in a comfortable chair, Grant in a comfortable chair, me on the couch between.

We are watching TV, drinking beer from bottles. We are completely normal. With Grant and Eric, in their condo in Lincoln Park, in Chicago, we are regular, I am regular. We are kicking back. I can kick back. I am *kicking back*.

I am trying not to think about the box. About how, forty feet away, in my rental car, on the floor of the passenger side, is the box. I could not bring the box inside, and I have not and will not tell

Eric and Grant about the box, and, fearing that someone, perhaps one of them, might pass by the car and see the box and know what it is and be horrified and think me a monster, I have covered it with a towel.

Al Pacino is wearing an elaborate military uniform, and is yelling at a high school–aged guy in a school uniform. I have come to the movie late, so it's unclear why he is yelling at the guy in the uniform. They are in some kind of swank hotel room.

"Why is he yelling?" I ask.

"Shh!" says Grant.

"Is he blind?"

"Shut up. It's almost over."

The phone rings. Eric answers, tosses it in my lap.

"You."

"Who?"

"Meredith."

It's Meredith, panicky.

"Is it John?"

"Yeah," she says.

"Is he—"

"No, no. He's okay, but he's threatening again. He sounds drunk."

I take the phone upstairs and into the bathroom.

"Does he have pills? What?"

"I don't know. I didn't ask. Maybe he'll do his wrists."

"Did he say anything like that?"

"No. Maybe. I don't know. I can't remember. But you have to call him. I've been on the phone with him for an hour and I'm losing my fucking mind. He says he tried to call you but you weren't home."

"I'm in Chicago."

"I know that. I called you, stupid."

I call John.

"What's the problem?"

"Nothing."

"What do you mean, nothing? Why am I calling you?"

"I don't know. Why are you calling me?"

"Meredith said you wanted me to call."

"I tried to call you."

"I know. I'm in Chicago."

"What for?"

"A wedding."

"Get off!"

"What?"

"Nothing. I was talking to the cat."

"You're talking to the fucking cat? Listen, I don't have time for—"

"Fine. Sorry I'm such a bother."

"Okay. So. What's the problem? What is it? Are you threatening?"

"I've just had a rough couple of days."

"Now you sound drunk. At first you didn't sound drunk. Are you drunk or not? Give me some parameters."

"No, it's just this medicine."

"Wait. What medicine? What does that mean? Did you already take something? What is this? Is this it?"

"Is what what?"

"Did you already—"

"No. Jesus. I'm just sleepy. I had a beer."

"You're supposed to be sober. You can't drink on the antidepressants, stupid. You were sober the last time we talked, right? You're supposed to be sober. How long did that last?"

"It's one beer. Don't sweat it, my man."

I hear Eric and Grant walking up the stairs, going to bed. Under the door I can see the lights in the apartment go out.

Part of me is bracing for the gunshot. John has been planning it all along, is lulling me into thinking things are fine, and any second he'll do it, to make sure I hear it, to make sure I know it was my fault. I will have a dead friend.

Then again, this is kind of lucky. The timing, that John would be threatening suicide the same day I have been given the box, during the week when I have been looking for gruesome things— What are the odds? Fantastic.

There's a knock on the bathroom door.

"Yeah?"

"You okay?" It's Grant.

"Yeah. On the phone."

"All right, son. We'll see you tomorrow."

"Night."

"Who was that?"

"Grant. Now..."

"I ran through the crackhouse again," he says.

"What crackhouse?"

"The one off San Pablo, near Emeryville. I ran through barefoot this time."

He has done this before, has told me about the running through the crackhouse. He wants me to be impressed. If it is true, which I doubt, I am impressed. I can't let him know this.

"And why?" I ask. I know why.

"I was feeling weird. I wanted to see what would happen."

"And?"

"Nothing. People just looked at me. Someone said 'Fuck, dude.' That was it."

"Huh. So what's the issue this time?" I want to know why we have to do this again. I want to know if he's going to make me give him the talk again. I will refuse.

"I don't know. I went out, and I—I don't know, when I got home, I just felt all black, tarry. I don't know. That makes no sense, I guess, I just felt like I was under this net or something, I mean, sometimes I get into these holes—shit, I don't know, I'm just so tired of it, it's so—fuck, you wouldn't understand—"

"I wouldn't what?"

"I just don't—"

"I can't believe you'd say that. You know me. I wouldn't understand? Do you know what I've been doing today? Where I've been tonight? Do you know what's on the floor of my car?"

I tell him about the funeral home, the box.

"Jesus," he says.

He likes that. He is suddenly sober-sounding, animated.

This is what he wants, I can tell. Already he is sounding more animated, sober. He wants to share stories, wants to be reassured that however sick he feels, and scared, and ashamed of the contents of his head he is, that I am far worse off. As always, I oblige. I tell him about how, after the funeral home, I spent the night driving around the frozen, broken South Side of Chicago, looking for something to happen. I was talking into my tape recorder, staring at groups of kids in their huge jackets, wanting again and again to get out, throw myself at them—"Hey guys! What's up?"—to maybe get punched or hit over the head with something, or chased—that's what I really wanted, maybe, to be chased—but it was so cold. I tell him that whenever I stopped at a light I expected a car to pull up in the next lane and that, without turning around, I would know. There would be a crash of glass and a pounding deep into my grassy childhood, and I would see my own blood all over the window. Or I would be at the light and someone would slimjim the side door—no, not someone—a black man in an army jacket, the man I always picture when imagining being killed in such a way, always an army jacket—and he would jump in next to me—I'd have to move the box—where would I put the box? Backseat. And then he'd make me drive to the lake, out by the aquarium. He'd have me get out, and would walk me over to the edge of the parking lot, facing the water. He'd tell me to kneel, and I would, and then without a word, he would shoot me twice in the back of the head—

"That's weird," he says. "I always see it in my own house. I'm tied to a chair, and my mouth is taped, and when I see his gun raised toward me, I can't move, scream, all I can do is try to stop the bullet, with my eyes. I always have some weird sense that I can maybe stop the bullet with my eyes."

"You know what's funny," I say, "the thing I was most worried about when I was down there, in the South Side, driving around and talking into the tape recorder? I was worried that after I was shot near the lake, that the murderer, who really only wanted the car, would for some reason find and play the tape, the one where I'm describing my imagining someone like him killing me, and all this stuff about finding the box, and that this murderer would think I'm this racist weirdo—"

"Jesus."

"That's what I was worried about! I was worried about what the guy who killed me would think of me. Then I worried that the cops, who would eventually find the car in Gary or Muncie or wherever, would find my tape recorder and the tape inside, and would play the tape, looking for clues or whatever, and they'd be horrified too, would be horrified and would also laugh, would make copies and give them to friends—"

"No." At this point I'm no longer worried about John's vague threats. I no longer expect the gunshot. It has worked before, always works—by now he's more worried about me than himself.

"So what happens tomorrow?"

"Tomorrow I see Sarah."

"Oh man. You have to tell me how it goes."

"I will."

I expected her to meet me on her building's doorstep, in her coat, maybe pulling on her coat, saying Hi how are you, warily. But she has come to the door, without a coat, and has let me in.

Sarah Mulhern. I have come to pick her up. We are going to dinner. I am inside her home and she is glowing.

We sit on her couch. I move a pillow.

"You want a drink?" she asks, getting up.

"Sure."

"A beer?"

"Yes, thanks."

She goes to the kitchen. Her apartment is immaculate. She has the lights turned down.

She comes back, puts on an album by a guy we went to high school with. The guy, my older brother's age, plays piano at the Deerpath Inn, the one hotel in town, and has named the album Deerpath. We talk about how the guy should maybe get out of the town for a little while, get some perspective. We talk about her teaching (seventh grade, in a western suburb of Chicago), the career of Vince Vaughn.

We go to dinner, drink during dinner, run through my eating habits, ha ha, and stay late. We talk about the swim team we were both on, how lame I was and how incredible she was, how her name, when it was spoken over the scratchy loudspeaker, to the rest of us meant grace and power, how she never lost a race, how that fueled my long-standing crush, and about the time her little brother caught me in the club's locker room just after I had stepped in someone's feces.

"I never heard about that."

"He thought it was mine, though."

"The feces."

"Yeah, from then on, to him I was the guy who shat himself at the club. And there was no way to explain it. Telling him that I had walked into the stall and hadn't noticed the excrement all over the floor..."

"That would have been harder, probably."

"Right."

I briefly consider telling her about the picture of her I ran into at the beach. I decide against it. It's weird enough as it is.

We go to a bar and run into people we know, all of whom are clearly confused by seeing us together. We have never been seen together, are two years apart, and I haven't been back to Chicago for years and years. I see Steve Fox, who I've known since kindergarten, this grown person whose eight-year-old smiling face I have in albums, pictures from Cub Scout birthday parties. We talk for a minute—where to start? Should we have hugged? Has he gained weight?—but Sarah is uncomfortable. In Lincoln Park, there are too many people we know; it's overload. We leave, find a small ugly bar, drink until we both feel like we can do what we are both expecting to do, and walk back to her apartment.

As we are on her couch, she suddenly pushes me up and back, her hands on my chest, arms extended and she looks at me in a wild-eyed sort of way—eyes so round-seeming in the dark here, those whites so white!—that at first I interpret it as a sign that my superior kissing technique has her overwhelmed. She looks at me for a second.

"You look older," she says.

Right away, I think: symbolism. *I look older.* It's also symbolic that, as we sit on the couch, in the dark, the light through her large windows, the weak yellow light from the streetlamp, brings her father into her face. I had only met him a few times, and never saw that strong a resemblance but now— Now her eyes are darker. It occurs to me that her smoking, as she did when we were at the last bar, is also symbolic. That must mean something, that she says I look older, that she looks like her dead father, that she is smoking like my dead father, that we are opening our mouths on each other even though, outside of having lived similar lives, walked the same path from the parking lot to the pool at the Lake Forest Club, swum the same laps at dawn, we barely know each other. All this means something. What does this mean?—

After a few seconds we are again fiddling our tongues around in each other's mouths, turning our faces left and right. But why that weird look she was giving me? Every time I open my eyes, her eyes are open. It's unsettling. Maybe *she's* unsettled. She is. I know why.

She knows I have my mother's box in the rental car.

That's it. She can tell. She can tell that I've been driving around with it, right there on the passenger seat, sometimes on the floor, next to Burger King bags, apple juice bottles, like we were on some kind of road trip together— And she can tell that last night I was talking to my maybe-suicidal friend, and that I wondered if I wanted him to do it, and she knows that yesterday, I paused when driving by Ricky's family's house, and she knows that not an hour later, while I was at the library in town I actually ran into Ricky's mom, who I had forgotten worked there, and Ricky's mom had given me a hug, and we talked about Rick, whom he was dating, all that, and I said nothing about anything much, because if I talked too long she would know too, and would know that I wanted to tell the world about her husband, and she would know as Sarah no doubt knows that as I was driving through the cemetery in Lake Forest, the one by the beach, all the gravestones with puddles around them, thin puddles frozen, that I was listening to the Danny Bonaduce radio show, the *Partridge Family* guy, which was bad enough while driving through a cemetery, but then on the show was a familiar voice, someone talking about sex, who was that?— And it was Sari Locker, Sari Locker was on the *Danny Bonaduce Show*, on the radio, in the cemetery, talking about how you can put condoms on with your mouth. I was so shocked that I stopped the car to indicate my shock, to punctuate it to myself, to anyone who might be watching, even though I wasn't actually so shocked that I needed to stop the car. And Sari said something mean to him, something about his recently canceled TV show, and after she was off the air, he ripped into her, calling her names, and by that time I was on my way to that bar in Highwood, the one my father stopped at on his way home every night—that's why he always came home at seven-twenty, on the dot, no matter the traffic, Sarah knows that when I was at the bar, in the afternoon, freezing out, mothy gray, I sat at the bar and ordered a Sprite, and then sat, having no idea what I was doing there, what I was looking for at the bar that my father went to. Maybe I expected pictures of him somewhere, his name still on the chalkboard by the pool table. I didn't know. Such great handwriting he had— I looked at the pictures of the bowling teams, somehow expecting him to be among the— I mean, of course, he never bowled much—

We are still moving our mouths over each other's mouths, and her eyes are probably still open—

and when I was sitting there, I wished for a minute that I had a picture of my dad, so I could hand it, like a detective, to the bartender woman, so she could say, "Yep, sure I know him. Came in every night..." But instead I just sat there. There were novelty mugs everywhere. A bumper pool table. "What a Feeling!" was playing on the jukebox. It really was "What a Feeling!"—

I open my eyes and Sarah's are open again. It's like she's holding her breath. But who can blame her? She knows, she can tell. She knows that after the bar I went to a pay phone and called the Anatomical Gift Association, and found out where most of the bodies go, to the University of Illinois at Chicago Medical School, and then I drove there, to the West Side of Chicago, drove around, lost for an hour amid the blight, the blocks crumbling, the acres and acres crushed, as if walked on by giants. She knows that I finally found the school, and the building where the head of the anatomy department was, and how I parked down the street, and had to jump the fence of a construction site to get into the build-

ing, and how, once in the building, I was afraid that I would be
found out, that they would see my eyes and would call security, so
I skipped the elevator and went to the stairs, opened the heavy
metal door and—

We move to her bed and we fumble, undress.

—the stairwell was about eighty degrees. Ninety. It was
withering, and I had to walk to the seventh floor, where the doctor
was, the man I was going to confront about taking my parents and
doing things with them. Why was the stairwell so hot? I was
drenched by the fourth floor. Doctors walked by me, going down
as I was going up, and I had to act casual, normal; I was a student,
I had to look like a student. It was like being inside a heating duct,
the heat like wind, coming from below, and by the time I got to
the seventh floor I felt faint, and burst open the door, and felt the
cool air sing into my lungs—

Sarah is saying no to something I am trying to do. I am
fumbling with something, trying halfheartedly to do something,
but feeling so tired, too, my head so heavy—

And when I found the doctor's name on the listing, spelled
with those white movable letters on the grooved black board, I
walked to the corresponding door, and was going to confront this
man, at least look into his face, have it do something, tell me
something—

I am falling asleep, so exhausted, so I pull Sarah's back to my
front and fall asleep—

and then opened the doctor's door. There was someone right
there, a middle-aged man, right there, a man at a desk—only
inches from my face, and it was the moment that I could finally—
"Oop, sorry!" I said, and closed the door. Then I took the elevator
down, tapping the walls on the way down, leaning toward the
doors, vibrating, jumped out and then down the steps from the
building, back through the construction site, walking quickly,
jogging a little, then back to the car, in the car, with the radio

turned up, back onto the highway, then back to Grant and Eric's, where they were watching cable and I told them nothing.

In the morning I sleep to nine, ten, ten-thirty... and don't wake up until Sarah begins to pointedly make noise around the apartment. The room is all white light, the bed so warm still. I have nowhere to be. I want to never leave. I have no plans. I want to chat. I look at her yearbook from her school. I look at pictures of her and her students. They seem to really love her, and this is so good, that we're back here, in a different place, but together these years later, and it is perfect because now we are connected again, and this is some sort of bridge that was in disarray but is now rebuilt, redesigned, and new, pristine, wonderful— This is great, we'll keep in touch, and when I'm in town we'll get together, and when she's in San Francisco—

Maybe we should go get some breakfas—

Then I'm at the door and I'm leaving. I do not know why I am leaving. Something happened. She tells me that she has to go to the school to do some things, or she's meeting a friend for lunch, or her sister, her mother. It's all hazy. I'm putting on my shoes at her door, feeling the winter air coming through the gap, looking up at her as she says something else, "Happy New Year" maybe, and then she has the door open, and we hug quickly and then I'm on the sidewalk, walking back to Grant and Eric's.

I make the trip stiff-legged, cold, trying to remember the words she said. I run the last exchange through my head over and over. Was it: "Well, now that you've gotten what you wanted..." or was it: "Was that what you wanted?" It was something like that. What did it mean? I try to make the words work, to make them sound familiar, have them make sense. Gotten what I wanted? Was that what she said? Sure, I had, I thought I had, that we had been reconnected, all this time collapsed— Fuck, I don't even know what I wanted.

Everything was tied together again and now this. I do not

understand this. Are we bound or unbound? I have closed the loop, only to have it come undone again.

By the time I get to the beach, in Lake Forest, the next night, it's dark, about nine or ten o'clock. I have to leave Chicago the next day. Last night, New Year's Eve, was uneventful, quiet. We had all walked a few blocks to a party thrown by someone from Eric's office, stood and talked to each other, ate their carrots and celery. We left before midnight and a few minutes later were back home, eating chocolate chip mini-cookies and watching *The Nutty Professor*— I park facing the water. I get out of the car and put on Grant's coat, put the tape recorder in the jacket pocket. In the other pocket, I have a notebook and pen. I lean through the car's door and get the box from the floor. Then close the door and put the box on the hood of the car.

I will do it now. This makes sense. This is the right thing.

I don't want to see what's inside. I check to make sure no cars are coming down the beach driveway. Of course I want to see what's inside. I use my car key to cut through the clear packing tape on the top of the box. I am careful not to cut too deeply, for fear of puncturing the bag I expect the ashes are within; even so, I half expect the ash to billow out, it being light, like dust, and so I squint and turn my head so as not to inhale it. I open the box, spreading the flaps like skin. No ash breathes from inside.

Inside there is gold. A golden canister, the size and shape of a container one would keep on the kitchen counter, for cookies or sugar. I am overcome with relief. This is better than the cardboard box, more fitting, even if it's only tin. Then again, there's something about the gold canister, something sinister, evocative of the Ark of the Covenant, in the movie, with the ash within it—all the bad things that happened to the men who tinkered with the Ark, who disturbed its contents...what if—

Jesus, I'm no fucking Nazi!

But look what I'm doing, with my tape recorder and note-book, and here at the beach, with this box—calculating, manipulative, cold, exploitive.

Fuck it.

I open the canister. It comes slowly; there is some kind of suction from within. I remove the top. Inside is a bag of kitty litter, tied at the top.

Fuck. Someone switched the ashes with this fucking kitty litter. This is not it. Where is the ash, the ash like dust? This is not ash. I move the box to the hood of the car, to see it better. These are little rocks, pebbles, Grape-Nuts, in white and black and gray. I open the bag. Dust rises, a small amount, just for a second, the bag exhaling, its breath smelling—I am terrified of smelling its breath, fearing death? some faint trace of her smell?—but it smells just like dust, a simple dusty smell.

And then I sense her watching. I do not do this often, do not often have (submit to?) visions of her sitting atop some cloud, looking down, Family Circus–like, robed and beatific and drawn with a dotted line, but at this moment I see her suddenly, watching me, not from a cloud, but instead just there, or half there, superimposed on the blue-black sky just over me, and she is just shaking her head, disappointed, disgusted.

But isn't it her fault? Surely it's her fault. Did her eyes make me this way? The way she watched, stared, approved and disapproved? Oh, those eyes. Slits, lasers, needles of shame, guilt, judgment— Was it a Catholic thing or just a her thing? At the very least, it had something to do with me not masturbating until college. I figured that part out a while ago.

With the bag open the colors and shapes of the pebbles become clearer. They are six or seven different colors—black, white, light gray, dark gray, gray-yellow, yellow-gray, creme—different shapes, smaller, bigger, mostly roundish but some oblong, some longer even, like fangs—nothing like the light gray fine ash uniformity I expected and wanted. Oh this is infinitely more gruesome. You can almost differentiate between the pebbles—what is the white? Bone? Are the black pebbles the cancer, or are they the parts that were burned more thoroughly? What do they use, anyway? An oven? An oven, right? So would it follow that parts of the oven were hotter than others? The white must be bone, clearly. Wouldn't this all be bone? What else would survive the heat? Nothing, nothing, unless some parts, this or that organ, were simply burned to a crisp, like coal—coal is organic matter. The black must be the cancer.

 Then what is gray?

 I walk to the water, and across the sand, which, on this beach, largely man-made, is not really sand at all, but is—I see the correlation now—also like kitty litter, that being, come to think of it, what we called it as teenagers, when our decrepit and eroding natural beach was replaced with a many-million-dollar beachfront, with a promenade and jetties and protective barriers. Kitty litter is what we called the sand; we hated it because after a day of walking on it, or playing volleyball, your feet would be wrecked, sanded raw. I walk across the kitty litter, in my shoes, it crunching like gravel, loudly, and then to the jetty, a foot-wide girder of rusted steel, extending out into the lake, forty feet long maybe, until it is met by a low makeshift wall of huge white granite rocks, a pile of giant rocks in a half-circle, forming a wall protecting the beach from waves. I am holding the gold canister in front of me, like an offering. I do not know why I am holding it in this way.

 I jump a few rocks, until I am on the outer part of the rock wall, facing out toward the water. It is a wet sort of gray and blue—foggy almost, the sky and the water smudged together no more than thirty feet out, the water murmuring quietly, its depth, even only fifty or so feet out as I am, seeming—

I will slip and fall, hit my head, pass out, fall into the quiet lake and drown. This is the kind of thing that happens. There is no one here, I will not be saved, I will be gone. Then they will find the rental car, and my—

At least the tapes will be destroyed, soaked in my jacket, with my notebook.

This is stupid, this throwing the cremains into Lake Michigan. Lake Michigan? Ridiculous, small, tacky. Why just a lake? A Great Lake, sure, but— I should be at the Atlantic. I should be on Cape Cod. That would be something. I could drive to Cape Cod. I have a car. I could drive to the last house we rented out there, the one with Aunt Ruth, before she died, when I saw her, Ruth, through a crack in the bathroom door, without her wig on, her fiery red hair gone— I'd have to call the rental company, confirm that I could rent here, drop it off there—I would drive to the Cape and then fly back to San Francisco—how long would that take, the drive? We did it dozens of times, Chicago to Cape Cod, we three kids, Mom driving, eight hours a day— fuck, the drive would take me at least two days, and I have to meet Toph at the airport tomorrow, he'll be coming up from L.A., we timed it so we'd both be at the airport at the same time, fuck, I can't do Cape Cod. Maybe if I called Bill... Fuck it, then I'd have to tell him about this, and he'd be disturbed and— Fuck it. It makes sense here, it makes sense to be doing this here, now, it makes sense. It is good. It is the first of the year, after all—

Jesus.

It's her motherfucking birthday. I cannot believe that this happened again. Why do I not connect these things? Why do I know her birthday is approaching but do not remember on the actual day, do not remember until I am on a jetty in the lake with her— That does it, that's a sign, screw it, that means this is good, no doubt. She loved the beach, her favorite place, loved to come and set up her chair near the water, her feet in the water, eyes closed, absorbing the sun, me behind her, in her shade, cool, with my blanket and bottle—

I put my hand in the bag and grab a handful it's so light! I don't know what I expected but this lightness I did not I cannot believe I am holding I am sick to be holding—

I throw. In the air it spreads out in a wide diagonal, and drops into the groaning lake with a series of pitititits. I throw again. Some spills. I should not spill. It's spilled, right there, by my left foot, about eight particles—I'm stepping on them! Of course I am! Of course I'm stepping on them, how fitting! How expected, asshole! I lean over to pick up the particles but I already have a handful in the other hand and as I crouch down some of the other handful spills on my right side—Jesus! Jesus fucking Christ! *Why can I not do this right?*

I stand up quickly and throw, this time some of the cremains sticking to my palm, which is now sweaty—fuck! I try to kick the spilled cremains into the water, down below the rocks, through the crevices—what I need is a hose or something—

But should I really be kicking my mother's ashes? I try to pick them up again, too many, too many and then I crouch down again— Fuck, maybe this is illegal. I had heard that this was not legal, that these cremains were not sanitary, that one needed permission or could only do it on the open sea— I turn around to see if anyone is here. No, no other cars. But someone's going to come here tomorrow and find them and then report it and connect it to me, because the funeral home guy, Chad, with his ham radio, will be listening to a police frequency—

With the back of my hand I brush the fallen grains into the crevices—and am suddenly reminded of the way my mom cleared a fogged windshield, quickly, violently almost, with the back of her hand, her rings clicking against the glass, as we drove through some or other sudden storm, all of us in the Pinto, on our way somewhere, the mall, the Cape, Florida. And for a second I wonder if her rings will be in the bag. Oh shit. Her rings will be there, half-melted, like a prize in a box of Cracker Jacks. No. Beth has the rings? Beth has the rings. Of course.

How lame this is, how small, terrible. Or maybe it is beautiful. I can't decide if what I am doing is beautiful and noble and right, or small and disgusting. I want to be doing something beautiful, but am afraid that this is too small, too small, that this gesture, this end is too small—   Is this white trash? That's what it is! We were always so oddly white-trashy for our town, with our gruesome problems, and our ugly used cars, our Pintos and Malibus and Camaros, and our '70s wallpaper and plaid couches and acne and state schools—and now this tossing of cremains from a gold tin box into a lake? Oh this is so plain, disgraceful, pathetic—

Or beautiful and loving and glorious! Yes, beautiful and loving and glorious!

But even if so, even if this is right and beautiful, and she is tearing up while watching, so proud—like what she said to me when I carried her, when she had the nosebleed and I carried her and she said that she was proud of me, that she did not think I could do it, that I would be able to lift her, carry her to the car, and from the car into the hospital, those words run through my head every day, have run through every day since, she did not think I could do it but of course I did it. I knew I would do it, and I know this, I know what I am doing now, that I am doing something both beautiful but gruesome because I am destroying its beauty by knowing that it might be beautiful, know that if I know I am doing something beautiful, that it's no longer beautiful. I fear that even if it is beautiful in the abstract, that my doing it knowing that it's beautiful and worse, knowing that I will very soon be documenting it, that in my pocket is a tape recorder brought for just

that purpose—that all this makes this act of potential beauty somehow gruesome. I am a monster. My poor mother. She would do this
without the thinking, without the thinking about thinking—

Oh fuck. I throw more. I do it as fast as possible. I crunch my
hand into the bag and grab a handful of the tiny rocks. I pull it out
and they spill from my grip. I pull my arm back and more tiny
rocks trickle between my fingers, falling down between the huge
white rocks under my feet. I throw. The pebbles spread out and
ditdtdtdtdt into the water. I consider specifics—should I throw
them all in one place, or redirect the throws each time? Should I
hold on to some for later, to deposit elsewhere? Yeah, yeah. This
seems like the best idea—I can hold on to some, half maybe, and
throw the rest elsewhere...in Cape Cod! In Milton! I can spread
parts all over the country, at all of her favorite places! I can spread
them all over the world! The Atlantic, the Pacific! But then the
airport, the plane. I'd have to carry them on the plane, would have
to explain the box to the airport security people. I'd have to put
the box on that conveyer, and then— Do cremains show up in that
radar machine they run your bags through? Maybe they'd ask me
to open the box, demonstrate it like they do with laptops. Does it
look like gunpowder? Maybe it does. I could check the cremains at
the ticket counter. No, that would be bad. That would be worse.

I grab again and throw. This is good. Good enough. No, this
is great, this is best. This is where she spent her last years, by the
water. I start throwing faster and faster, grabbing and throwing,
flailing almost, dust everywhere. My coat is snowed with dust. She
is aghast. I am pathetic. This is what I've done. This is what it's
come to—winging her remains into the lake. No, she's not watching me. She's gone. She has an afterlife but I will not, because I do
not believe. I'll be exhausted by then anyway. I'm exhausted now,
I am so tired. I'll jump in the lake. Not to kill myself but just to
do it— The drama! I won't survive. If I took off my clothes I'd
make it. With the clothes on I'd sink. My heart would seize up and

I'd sink. I could do something else, something dramatic. I'll drive the car into the lake with me in it. Maybe with me not in it.

I throw and throw, into the gray. I know I will slip and fall into the lake and die. Oh the irony! Just like that one woman, who was throwing her mother's or husband's ashes from a cliff and a wave came over the cliff and took her, too. Maybe it was a sister. No waves here. I will simply slip and dribble off, into the lake. I have to shake out of the bag the last bits of the cremains. I should keep some. I could keep just a few bits, as souvenirs. Souvenirs! What kind of asshole— What a fucking sick dickhead, souvenirs, thinking of souvenirs. I shake out the bag. I do not like to have to shake out the bag, like shaking a goldfish out of a baggie. Can the ashes swim? Do they dissolve? I am done and sitting down and my breath, quick and heavy, is visible, because it's fucking cold all of a sudden with me not moving. The water undulates, so slowly, is hundreds of feet deep and there are a million fish right there eating the ashes. There is no difference between the sky and the water, and I can feel the water rising around me, and I am already under the water, and all of the water is inside something larger, and I look at my feet to make sure they are secure because I am inside something living.

I drive to the church. It's only a few minutes from the beach, straight through the heart of town, past the library and the barbershop.

I park and walk toward it, the air damp, cold.

The door is open. It is about eleven. I open it a crack and peek inside, sure that this must be a mistake, that this church cannot be open at this hour.

Inside all the lights are on, though dimly. I walk slowly inside. The church is empty. I stop in the glassed-in back area designed for latecomers, wailing babies.

The church glows red. The nave is tall and white, and in the center is hung an almost-life-sized Jesus, cast in gold, crucified, suspended by wire. So many times I had worried about the Jesus, that the wires would not hold, that it would fall, would land on the priests, the altar boys. I was much more comfortable when the priests were off to one side, during the reading of a psalm or liturgy. When one would stand in the center, right under, doing the consecration, lifting that chalice over his head, oh that's when I was sure it would fall—it was just so precariously hung, just those two thin wires.

This church is so small. I look out over the pews and the church is tiny. The pews are so low, and there are so few rows. It was never so small before. I walk into the church's main chamber. Up the center aisle, on the red carpet.

I walk to the first pew, where I had sat the last time I was here. I had been in the front row and had been turning around beforehand, waving to a few people as they came in. I was sitting with Toph and Kirsten and Bill and Beth. We were huddled together in the pew, on its near end. We had been to the church, but had never sat so close to the stage before. My mother sat us in the middle, or the back, and we were thankful, because then the priest and his coterie could not tell if we knew the words we were supposed to know.

I sat in the pew, holding Kirsten's hand, playing with Toph's, dizzy, wearing my blue blazer, waiting for the service, all the glory. I had known for months what it would be like, had pictured it, the whole thing. There would be light. It would be day. There would be light through the high stained-glass windows, prismatic—no, the light would be direct, direct, clear, wide, golden. The crowd would be endless, the church full like it is at Christmas, at Easter, the side aisles overflowing, the entire town there almost, all of the relatives, her brother and sisters from out East, the cousins, my father's enormous extended family from

California, all her former students, all the other teachers, all my friends, Bill's, Beth's, high school, grade school, college, Toph's, their parents, the grocers, the doctors, nurses, strangers, admirers, everyone in their overcoats, their dark deep colors, silent and reverent, the back entry area crammed, overflowing. Oh but others would be outside the church, a hundred on the steps, in the courtyard, wrapped around the building, down the street, a thousand or so, waiting just to—to know that they were there, to validate, to help prove— In the church the service would start but priest after priest would stand and begin to speak but then would be overcome and would have to give up, would shuffle to their red velvet chairs, yield the podium to the next and then would weep, shaking, their faces resting in their long-fingered hands. We would be there, in the first pew, the beautiful and tragic Eggers children, soaked in blood, stoic, as a hundred or more would stand before us and speak of her, all the gifts she granted them, and her life would be recounted in glorious detail, every moment, all the holding together and sacrificing and—

Then the ceiling would go. The barrel vaulting would rise, and the entire roof would quietly unhinge itself and lift up, would rise straight up, and disappear and the church's huge wooden cross-supports would fly up and away, and would quickly get so small, tiny in the rich blue sky, and would become birds. The church would double in size, would triple, the space expanding, suddenly taking in all those waiting outside, and then become bigger, would take in everyone she had ever known, millions, all with their hearts in their two hands, offering them to her. The angels would come. Thousands, slender, winged and bird-boned, descending and circling, all with sharp, small eyes, and they would be laughing, full of mirth, why not, this was happy, happy. My mother would be there. No coffin, no remains, but her, ephemeral, huge, her head as big as the nave, the angels moving around her, tiny by comparison, her hair, her original hair, feathered up huge the way she liked it, before she lost it, replaced by the darker, tighter curls. And her squinty smile, all the crinkles at the corners of her eyes, smiling to see us all there, knowing all those she had touched were there, that they were giving back, giving at least this much back. Oh such a celebration. And we and she would all be so happy not to see her as some embalmed thing, some rubbery and gruesome thing, but instead as this wonderfully glowing bright visage, above us all, and she would be first smiling the big closed-mouth smile she smiles, then that big small-toothed smile she smiles, then she would be laughing, someone would say something funny and she would laugh that way she laughed, silently, crazily, out of breath, it was so funny whatever someone said, who said that funny thing? Who? Maybe I said it, maybe I said it, maybe I said it and made her laugh like sometimes we could, really bust her up, so that it was just killing her, this laughing, her eyes struggling to stay open, to see, because when she laughed, my mom almost immediately teared up, and had to wipe her tears with the side of her forefinger— Oh that's when you knew you had really said something funny, when she would be crying, wiping her eyes, you had her then, you really wanted that, there was no greater thing, no achievement so great, so stirring, you tried to play it casual, deadpan, but you were so proud and thrilled, watching her, you wanted her first to say Stop! Stop! because you were so funny but you would continue because you wanted her to laugh more, to really laugh until she would have to rest, to half collapse on the kitchen counter while you were sitting at the table after school, Oh you're awful! she would say. Stop! Oh but to see her laugh you would say anything, and she so loved a good laugh at someone's expense—Bill's, Beth's, yours, her own, and at that moment everything would be wiped away, all the times you feared her or wanted to run away, or wondered how she lived with him, protected him, you wanted only her laughing like she did when she was on the phone with her friends—Yes! she would shriek, Yes! Exactly!—

then afterward she would sigh, breathing heavily and say Oh that's funny. God, that's funny. That's what she would say, and she would say something like that as the church walls disappeared and the nave evaporated and the angels flew faster, elliptically around her and we would all be feeling vibrations from it all, or they were all inside us, too, moving elliptically, or through our blood and there would be music, ELO maybe, *Xanadu* maybe, did she really like it or just tolerate it for our sake? She would hum along a little, move her fingers back and forth a bit and Oh we would have such a time! Then she would have to go. She would have to leave but not before saying goodbye, *See yoooo!* she would say, raising the last part, a high note, faux formality, and then turning from us to touch the small golden cheek of that golden, broken, and crucified Jesus, suspended in the air—the nave gone but it still floating, the golden thing, she would touch it gently with the back of her tanned, ringed hand, that lucky bastard, and then she would be gone, and we would all collapse right there, in the opened church, and sleep for weeks and weeks, dreaming of her. Oh it would be something, something fitting, proportionate, appropriate, gorgeous and lasting.

I stand up and walk to the podium—it was a hundred steps that day but now only two. Then I had a piece of paper, I had brought it, the one from under the couch—I had tried to recopy it onto a better sheet of paper then ran out of time—and I put the piece of paper on the podium and looked up and over the—

Where were the people? It was not a crowd. It was a scattered thing, a few here, a few there. Everyone loved her; where were they? Everyone of course knew and loved my mother, everyone, but where were they? This could not be, would not do, a life and then this, this forty people. Where's the woman who cut her hair— Laura? Was she there? Is she here? All the volleyball women? Did they come? There's one, Candy, but— Where is her family? Where are her sisters? There is only Uncle Dan, who has come, he says, "to represent the family." And the cousins? Her friends?

There are some here, but my God there were so many more! This is the crowd that was at my *father's*. It should not be the same crowd, the same number! They were not the same, these two lives. Where are the people from town? Where are the parents of her former students? Where are my friends? Where are the world's people to honor her passing? Was it too gruesome? Are we too vulgar? What is happening? All she put in, all she gave for you people, she gave everything for you people and this is— She fought for so long for all you people, she fought every day, she fought everything, fought for every breath until the last, sucking everything she could out of the air in that brown living room, gasped again and again, it was unbelievable, yes, she grabbed at the air, grabbed for us and for you, and where are you?

Where are you motherfucking assholes?

XI.

BLACK SANDS BEACH IS only ten minutes from San Francisco. It
depends where you leave from, of course, but from anywhere near
the Golden Gate Bridge, it's ten minutes, maybe fifteen, which is
weird, considering how raw and remote-seeming the place is, exotic
even, its sand actually black, about five hundred yards of it, from
one bracketing cliffrock to the other.

On the bridge, Toph is making cow sounds at the people walking, because it brings us both to tears. He is leaning out his window
mooing.

"Mooo."

He has the window all the way down.

"Mooooooo."

The tourists are not hearing, it doesn't seem, because the wind
coming over the bridge from the Pacific is wicked and relentless,
as it always is, and the tourists, couples and families, all under-
dressed in T-shirts and shorts, are being abused by the gusts, are
barely staying upright.

"Moooooooooo."

Toph's not even trying to make it sound cowlike. He's just

saying the word—it's just a person saying Moo. He does a few where he kind of barks it, angry-like, but in monotone.

"Moo! Moo!"

It's hard to convey why this is funny. Maybe this isn't funny, but we're dying. I can barely see; it's killing us. I try to drive straight, wiping my eyes. Wispy clouds hurtle over us, cotton pulled apart by children. For the last group of tourists, he does a little stutter thing with the mooing.

"I say, I say, I say," he says, "I say, I say, I say"—he pauses for a second, then does a quick "Uuuh," then:

"Mooooooooooooooo."

The bridge ends, the torn-cotton clouds breaking up immediately, then it's clear, Easter blue, and we're on 101, but just for a second—two exits and then we get off at Alexander, then come back under 101 and up the Headlands drive. As we climb with the road, right away above the Golden Gate, the clouds are suddenly below us, rolling through the bridge, fleece pulled through a harp.

We did not go to the test. An hour ago we skipped the city's mandatory high school test, the one Toph had to take if he sought admission to Lowell, San Francisco's vaunted public high school. A week ago we had gone to the school administration building, a white colossus on Van Ness, to sign him up.

"I know we're late but we're hoping to sign up for the test."

"Who are you?" said the woman behind the counter.

"I'm his brother. His guardian."

"You have guardianship papers?"

"Guardianship papers?"

"Yes, something proving you're his guardian."

"No. I never got any papers."

They needed something.

"Like what?"

"Like guardianship papers."

"There's no such thing as guardianship papers."

I was guessing.

The woman sighed.

"Well, how do we know you're his guardian?"

I tried to explain, but had nowhere to start.

"I just am. How can I prove this?"

"Do you have a will?"

"What?"

"A will."

"A will?"

"Yes, a will."

"Oh Jesus. This is incredible."

I thought of the will. Beth had the will.

"The will doesn't stipulate anything." I lied again. The problem with the will was that in the will, I wasn't even listed as the guardian; Beth was. It was a technicality, something we had all decided on that winter; Beth and Bill would be the executors, be listed officially, and I wouldn't have to be involved in the money, the paperwork. This had come up before, the guardianship thing, the proof—*where is the proof?*—and always I had been afraid of being found out. All this time, *a fraud!*

"Well, without guardianship papers, or a will, we can't do anything."

I had brought all his school records, school notices to parents, letters proving our residency, both of our names above the address. *We are a team. We have been a couple for years—* The woman was unimpressed.

"Why would I lie about this?"

"Listen, a lot of people from out of town want their kids to go to Lowell."

"Are you kidding me? I'd come down here and pretend my parents were dead to get him signed up for a goddamn test?"

Another sigh.

"Listen," she said, "how do we know they're even dead?"

"Oh God. Because I'm standing here saying so."

"Do you have death certificates?"

"This is disgusting," I said. "No," I said, another lie.

"Any notices, obituaries?"

"You want me to bring you an obituary?"

"Yeah, that would work. I think. Wait a second." She turned and conferred with a man behind a desk. She turned back to us.

"Yeah, that would work. Bring an obituary."

"But I won't have time..."

"For both of them."

Always proving this! Always reminded, never more than a few words into conversations, arguments, this fucking story— that's why I lie, make things up, why at this point, when making appointments with the dentist, whoever, I just call him "my son," as cruel as it feels coming out—

I called Beth from a pay phone. We only had twenty minutes until the office closed. Beth drove down with both the obituaries, little paragraphs about each of our parents in the *Lake Forester*, and the will, with two minutes to spare. And we placed them on the counter, on top of Toph's birth certificate.

And now, a week later, on the day of the test, as hundreds of kids are scribbling graphite into meaningless ovals, we're driving through the Headlands, on the way to the beach. It was only a few seconds ago that we actually realized that we were missing it—

"Oh Jesus," I said.

"What?" he said.

"The test!"

He put his hand over his mouth, expecting me to turn the car around, scramble like we always scramble, think of excuses; he was so used to it by now, the rushing, me banging the steering wheel in traffic, swearing at the windshield, the knocking on windows when doors were locked, the exceptions begged—

"Forget it," I said. "Doesn't matter now."

It doesn't.

We're leaving.

Two days ago we decided that we're not staying in San Francisco, and so we won't be applying to Lowell, won't be needing that school, anything here, because we're leaving the city, leaving the state, in August will get up and fly out of California and will go back—actually, farther, over Chicago and to New York. We're leaving again, amid all the tongue-clicking and head-shaking, we have to leave even though we'll see a little less of Bill and Beth, we'll move again—

"I think it's good to move around, see stuff, not get stuck," Toph says, and I love him for saying that. He knew I needed him to say something like that, and there isn't a chance in the world I'll ask him if he means it.

San Francisco was getting small, and everyone is dying. The summers are getting colder, and the falls aren't what they used to be. The kids in the Haight are younger all the time, more of them than before, sitting all day, all night at Haight and Masonic, with the sticks, the hacky sacks, nowhere to go in those stupid floppy reggae hats. And the drive to work was getting unbearable, the repetition too sad, especially at night, when after putting Toph to bed, locking the door, I would go back to the office—the drive just harrowing, the routine—I had even changed routes, had started driving down Geary, all the way down, past the prostitutes, a change of pace, and it was diverting for a week or so, all the cars slowing down, stopping, the cops hunting, laughing—but then even that was a routine, and so we have to leave, because the people are pissing on the streets, during the day now, anyplace, all the time people are pissing on the streets, defecating on Market Street at noon, and I'm getting sick of the hills, always the hills, the turning of wheels to park, and the street cleaning, and those fucking buses attached to the ropes or wires or whatever, always breaking down, those motherfucking drivers getting out and yanking on

that rope, the stupid buses just sitting there, in the way, everything
just sitting there, stuck, in the way—

Everything weirder, the extremes more pronounced, the con-
trasts too strong.

Toph and I keep going up the hill because you have to go up to get
to Black Sands, first straight up the hill, the road winding in and
out, past all the tourists stopped for the view, looking down on the
Golden Gate, and every time we double back toward the bridge,
the view, biblical, presents itself, the view where one sees Treasure
Island, and Alcatraz, then (l–r) all of Richmond, El Cerrito,
Berkeley, and Oakland and then the Bay Bridge, then the white
jagged seashells of downtown, the Golden Gate, blood red, then
the rest of the city, the Presidio, the avenues—

But we keep going, and as the road continues, winding up,
the cars thin out, and at the very top of the hill/mountain, there
are only a few sightseers left, and they are turning around to go
back down, three-point turning right at that WWII–era tunnel at
the top, because it certainly seems like the road ends, right there,
at the top of that hill—

But then the road continues, and there is a gate, a flimsy
metal gate, right there, and it is open, it's probably always open.
We keep going, not slowing, and as Toph and I continue through
the parking area and descend through the gate, two young tourists,
Dutch fellows with the customary dark socks and shorts, are
gawking, not knowing what we're doing—we are some kind of
fantastic superhero team in a space-age vehicle, not bound by laws
of country or physics.

The road, now a one-way, heads straight for the water, and it
looks for about twenty yards like we're going to go straight over,
it really does for a few seconds there—and if we did we would be
ready, of course, would do the thing where we get out of the car at

the same time, one door each, then the timed perfect dives—so we go slow, then the road starts bending right, and then down, and in a second we're driving parallel to the water, a few hundred feet up of course, for a while without even a visible cliffside to the left, just a sheer drop—and then suddenly we see the Headlands whole, green and mohair hills, ocher velour, the sleeping lions, the lighthouse far to the left, unbelievable given we're ten minutes from the city, this vast bumpy land, could be Ireland or Scotland or the Falklands or wherever, and we snake down, with the road bending back and forth along the cliffside, and Toph, as always, keeping his eyes away from the edge, understandable, not appreciating when I drive no-handed, using only my knees, for a little while, lookee here, ha ha, look at this!

"Don't, asshole."

"What?"

"Use your hands."

"You can't call me that."

"Fine. *A*-hole."

And as distressing as this, his first curse, is—the first I've heard, at least—it's also kind of thrilling. Wonderfully so. To hear anger from him is a great relief. I had worried about his lack of anger, had worried that he and I had been too harmonious, that I hadn't given him enough friction. He needed friction, I had begun insisting to myself. After all the years of normalcy and coddling, it was time to give the boy something to be pissed about. How else would he succeed? Where would he find his motivation, if not from the desire to tread over me? Always there had been just mutual devotion, and compliance, and his kind eyes and young pure wisdom— But now this! I'm an *asshole*. Such a relief. A breakthrough, the truth finally clear and unavoidable! I should have noticed the signs earlier. While wrestling lately, on the floor, and that one time on the tennis court, when I gave him the wedgie, did he not fight back with more conviction than ever

before? Did he not achieve a nice, effective sort of headlock and
hold it, with startling tenacity, for much longer than comfortable?
Did his body not tense up, his grip tighten, his eyes have in them
a certain abandon, betray some rage from some distant place? Yes,
yes! Now we are omnipotent.

Finally!

"You can't say A-hole, either."

"Okay."

"A-hole's even worse."

"Fine. Dickhead."

"Dickhead's fine."

At *Might* there had been an endless succession of fruitless lunches
with various people who Lance had found, people with money who
expressed some interest in helping us. It was always someone in
their early thirties who for whatever reason had come into enough
wealth to spread it around. "All right," Lance would say, his hands
as parentheses, "this girl is heir to the double-stick masking tape
fortune, and she..." or "Okay, this guy cashed out of Microsoft and
has about three hundred mil he's putting into progressive
media..." We would meet them for drinks or lunch, in the back of
Infusion 555, or at a picnic table in South Park, and we would talk,
explaining our plans, vaguely conveying our hopes, doing the best
we could to articulate the fact that we wanted to be successful
without being seen as successful-successful, wanted to keep doing
what we were doing, with the option of opting out if we ever got
bored, wanted to conquer the world in a way that no one would be
able to tell that that's what we wanted, trying not to let on how
tired we all were, how unsure we were that we really wanted to do
any of this anymore, actually—

And midway through the meetings the prospective benefac-
tor would, as she or he pushed the ice around with their straw,

explain how they'd have to talk anything over with their parents, or their lawyers and advisors and—

It was just as well. We hated the meetings, hated each other half the time, hated coming in every day, wondered why we were still doing this stuff—

We had been given a month's notice on our lease. We had already been extending our stay, every month begging for one more, asserting that we were so close to getting some kind of funding, that we needed some money so we could arrange for a place to move to, first, or maybe we'd move in with whatever company agreed to help us out— So Lance went to New York as a last-ditch thing, meeting with people much too small and much too big to help. He called back every day, with news of no news. He was staying with Skye, just as we all did when we were all in New York. We had had a big party out there, and Skye organized the whole thing, free drinks, a DJ, and had slept at her boyfriend's so we could all stay on her floor, four of us in her bedroom, sleeping bags and throw pillows, and at the party, when the police had come to shut it down, it was Skye, and her mom of all people, in town from Nebraska, who had begged the police to let us go on, because, her mom said, "These are just good kids, and they've worked so hard for this," something to that effect, Skye sad-eyed, batting her lashes, and the police let us go on.

Lance called from Skye's the day he was supposed to come back because he was staying an extra day. Skye was sick, was in the hospital with a fever, food poisoning maybe.

"A viral thing," he said.

Moodie and I met with the founders of *Wired*, went in to pitch the notion of their taking us under their wing, the perfectness of us with them despite how many times we had made fun of their magazine, we expected the meeting to be casual, easy, short on details and long on broad strokes. And of course we were wrong. We were woefully unprepared. What we wanted was just enough money to

get this next one out, and some kind of office arrangement, a
corner of their floor maybe, we had a few weeks to get out of our
place, anywhere would do, really—

They wanted numbers and plans. Sitting around their gleaming black table, we fumbled and joked and did our best to sound
confident, ambitious still, disguising our exhaustion, gesturing to
each other—

No you go ahead, finish—

No you were saying—

and we said that yes, of course there will be a new design team
and better proofreading, and yes, we would stop making fun of
advertisers and that yes, we are in it for the duration, that our
projections this and our plans that and TV shows and a Web site
of course, of course, and some concessions on the covers, some
familiar faces maybe, celebrities even, if they're the right kind,
done the right way, sure, some profiles, we'll tinker to make the
thing available to a broader audience, operate with a small staff,
same as always, we'll stay here, move in with you guys, or move to
New York, whichever, it'll be so great—

After handshakes we walked out, past all the workstations,
the rows and rows, the heat of all the computers operating at once,
the tangles of wires, past the kitchenette and the reception area
painted neon orange, the girl at the desk dressed just so, and in the
elevator down to Third Street we recapped—

You think it went well?

Yeah, yeah, they love us—

but we both knew it was over, and the great, oddly wonderful thing was that neither of us really cared anymore—oh we cared,
yes, but we were ready. I wanted it to be over and Moodie did even
more so, and Marny was more than tired of it all, Paul, too. Zev
and Lance were still pushing to continue, still felt there was
reason, but they also knew—we had long prepared them—that the
floor could give out any day, that the floor had been built to give

way. And so there we were, knowing that three, four years, all these hundreds of thousands of hours, were going to end without our having saved anyone—

What was conquered?

Who was changed?

—with no spot on the Space Shuttle, that all this—what had it all been? It had been something to do, some small, small point to make, and the point was made, in a small way, and so fine— Moodie and I walked through South Park on a flawless July day, the park full of new people, all of them beautiful and brilliant and young, and we were tired and walked through them and back to the office. It was fine. Finally, the strange comfort of knowing the end, its parameters and terms. We had two weeks to finish the now-final issue before we had to be out of the office, so we took the stuff we had already planned—cover story: "Are Black People Cooler Than White People?"—and added, throughout, countless references to the end of the magazine, to death, to defeat.

The first-page essay:

Death, like so many great movies, is sad.

The young fancy themselves immune to death. And why shouldn't they? At times life can seem endless, filled with belly laughs and butterflies, passion and joy, and good, cold beer.

Of course, with age comes the solemn understanding that forever is but a word. Seasons change, love withers, the good die young. These are hard truths, painful truths—inescapable but, we are told, necessary. Winter begets spring, night ushers in the dawn, and loss sows the seeds of renewal. It is, of course, easy to say these things, just as it is easy to, say, watch a lot of television.

But, easy or not, we rely on such sentiment. To do otherwise would be to jump without hope into a black and endless abyss, falling through an all-enveloping void for all eternity. Really, what's to gain from saying that the night only grows darker and that hope lies crushed under the jackboots of the wicked? What answers do we have when we arrive at the irreducible realization that there is no salvation in life, that sooner or later, despite our best hopes and most ardent dreams, no matter how good our deeds and truest virtues, no matter how much we work toward our varied ideals of immortality, inevitably the seas will boil, evil will run roughshod over the earth, and the planet will be left a playground in ruins, fit only for cockroaches and vermin.

There is a saying favored by clergymen and aging ballplayers: Pray for rain. But why pray for rain when it's raining hot, poisoned blood?

And then, a few days later, we looked again at it, hoped it didn't sound glib, callous—Zev wrote it and he was still so young—because Lance had just came back from New York, from all the running around, he and Skye, looking for money, any sign at all. We wanted to know how everything went—it was all academic by now but we were curious anyway, morbidly maybe— wanted to hear funny rejection stories, tales of indifference—and I don't remember why we were all there in the office, all at once in the middle of the day, but Lance came in and dropped his backpack on his chair, and sat down, slumped in his chair. Then he stood up. He paced for a minute. He stood by the filing cabinet, next to Marny's desk. He had a look on his face, an almost-smiling look, his mouth sort of smiling but also kind of quivering, his eyes focusing on something small on the floor between us. He had his hand in front of his mouth, to hide whatever his mouth was doing. *Was he smiling?* He was smiling. His head was tilted. Something was funny. This was going to be good.

"Skye died."

"What?" someone said.

"She *died*," he said.

"What do you mean? Who?" We were all talking at him.

"She *died*."

"Who?"

"Skye."

"No."

"Fuck you, dickhead. Why is that funny?"

"He's serious. Are you serious?"

"That's not funny."

"No, listen, she *died*. She *died*."

"No."

"What does that mean?"

"How?"

"It was a virus and it attacked her heart. She was there just for a few days. They couldn't—"

"No."

"Holy shit."

"Jesus."

"No."

Marny and I drove out, just over the Golden Gate, not far from where you have to turn up to get to Black Sands, to get a picture for the last issue's last page. We wanted something that would articulate everything, one image, and had chosen the tunnel on Route 1 that leads to Sausalito, carved through the mohair Headlands. It was a simple tunnel, a half-circle, dark, its end not visible, with the entrance framed by a thin rainbow painted on long ago. We had parked and then walked along the highway, and Marny had watched for cars while I stood in the highway's middle lane and took the picture, which in the end didn't really come out all that great, the rainbow faded and unclear, the tunnel not dark enough.

But that was it, the final image. It was either that or the letter Paul had opened a few days before, as we were already packing up, from Ed McMahon. In large bold black type:

MIGHT MAGAZINE

HAS DEFINITELY WON

FROM $1,000,000.00 TO

$11,000,000.00 CASH!

. . .

We dedicated the issue to her, to Skye, of course. Our sad little gesture. Man, we said, you should have seen Skye. Actually, you still
can. Go rent that movie, *Dangerous Minds*. She's there, walking
around, talking. She didn't write the lines she said, and was probably only nineteen or twenty at the time, but there she is, forever,
walking and talking, snapping gum. Oh she was something.

. . .

The walk down to Black Sands is long, steep, but the view, all
wildflowers and ocean, is astounding. As Toph and I stomp down,
men are walking up, in pairs, sweating, stopping to rest—the
walk up is a thousand times what it is going down. As we walk
down together I become conscious of our proximity, mine and
Toph's, and am preoccupied with making sure no one gets the
wrong idea. He's almost as tall as me now, and has that boy-toy
look that with us together, at this beach in particular, could easily
be taken as a NAMBLA kind of thing, and if the wrong person
saw us, surely they would report us, and then the child welfare
people would come, and then he'd be in a foster home, and I'd
have to bust him out—we'd be fugitives, underground, and the
food would be terrible—

   It feels like some place very far away, this beach. The patrons of
Black Sands are primarily naked gay men, some straight naked
men, some straight naked women, with the rest a mixture of
clothed people like us, and the occasional Chinese fisherman. We
drop our stuff in the middle, where the families, when they dare
come down, set up and sit. We take off our shoes and shirts, scan
the beach, left and right. Toph has an idea.

   "You know what I think?"

   "Yes. No."

"I think everyone should be able, just once, to make an inan-
imate object come to life and be his pal."

I have to pause. Should he be encouraged?

"Like what?" I ask, nervously.

"Like an orange."

He scratches his chin, something he actually does when
thinking these kinds of thoughts.

"Or a hammer."

John was slithering, crawling, breaking up. He was in rehab, then
left and for a while was living in Santa Cruz with a woman, forty-
five at least, who he met in NA. I had stopped keeping track, did
not ask why he was in NA in the first place, was not aware that he
had a problem that would necessitate NA—it was accelerating
with him, he was trying to do all the problems he could do in the
shortest possible amount of time. I wondered if that was the plan,
some sort of experiment or performance art—if it was I would have
respected that, that would have been cool but it was not, actually,
that way, that calculated. We went to see a counselor, I brought
him in after a while, talking to us, she called me an "enabler," and
so we left that counselor and he slept on the couch and then he was
better— He would disappear for weeks, then resurface, calling
from a library, from Oregon, had run through everything he had
inherited, now needed two hundred dollars for the room he'd been
living in, *the Red Roof people were losing their fucking shit*—and then,
finally, after getting punched in the head one night at the Covered
Wagon by a guy he knew, he wanted to go back into rehab.

Meredith and I split the cost of a private place, three weeks'
worth, because he had no insurance, and would not go into the
county one, if he had to go into the county one he might do something—he would not be able to handle that kind of shit, man—
and so a few days before the private place I picked him up, from

some place in the Oakland hills, the house of another woman he was seeing, two kids in the window—

"Dude, thank you so much for putting up the money. I really want to tell you how much I appreciate that. It makes all the difference in the world. The county place was full of druggies and hookers. I could not handle that, I swear, would not have made it."

I open the window.

I have nothing to say to him.

"There's a part of me," I say, "that wants to let you out of the car right now, on the fucking bridge."

A minute or so of silence.

I turn up the radio.

"Then let me out."

"I want to let you out, asshole."

"Then let me out."

"I mean, are you trying to break some record? Like, right now, you're sitting here, seemingly normal, with your hands in your lap and everything—but then, when do you put on the freak suit? When does that happen? I mean—"

He is rhythmically clicking and unclicking the knob to the glove compartment.

"Don't."

He stops.

"I mean, why can't you just fucking…" I want to say *chill*. But that would sound wrong.

"…chill? Why can't you just fucking chill?"

He's with the glove compartment again.

"Stop it."

He stops.

"I mean, all this is getting so fucking boring."

"—"

"It's really fucking boring. For a little while it was kind of fun, having you do all this made-for-TV shit, but not anymore. It's been boring for a while now."

"Sorry dude. Sorry I bore you."

"You do. All this unbelievable whining, uncertainty, the wallowing—"

"Please. Look who's talking. You're one to talk about dwelling on this shit, your family shit. You're the one who—"

"We're not talking about me."

"Yes we are, of course we are. We always are. In one way or another, we always are. Isn't that obvious?"

"Listen, fuck you. I didn't need to come out here."

"Then you shouldn't have."

"I'm going to toss you out that fucking window."

"Then do it. Do it."

"I should."

"I mean, how much do you really care about me, outside of my usefulness as some kind of cautionary tale, a stand-in for someone else, for your dad, for these people who disappoint you—"

"You are so like him."

"Fuck you. I am not him."

"But you are."

"Let me out."

"No."

"I'm not this. I can't be reduced to this."

"You did it yourself."

"I am more than this."

"Are you?"

"I cannot be used to get back at your dad. Your dad is not a lesson. I am not a lesson. You are not a teacher."

"You wanted this. You wanted the attention."

"Whatever. I'm just another one of the people whose tragedies you felt fit into the overall message. You don't really care so much about the people who just get along and do fine, do you? Those people don't make it into the story, do they?"

There's a truck next to us, three kids in the bed. It will roll.

"All to help make some point. I mean, isn't it odd that some-one like Shalini, for example, who really wasn't one of your clos-est friends, is suddenly this major presence? And why? Because your other friends had the misfortune not to be misfortunate. The only people who get speaking parts are those whose lives are grabbed by chaos—"

"I am allowed."

"No."

"I am allowed—"

"No. And poor Toph. I wonder how much say he had in this whole process. You'll claim that he had full approval, thought it was great, hilarious, etc., and maybe he did, but how happy do you think he is about all this? It's disgusting, the whole enterprise."

"It's too big for you to understand. You know nothing about us."

"Oh God."

"It's enlightenment, inspiration. Proof."

"No. You know what it is? It's entertainment. If you back up far enough, it all becomes a sort of show. You grew up with comforts, without danger, and now you have to seek it out, manufacture it, or, worse, use the misfortunes of friends and acquaintances to add drama to your own life. But see, you cannot move real people around like this, twist their arms and legs, position them, dress them, make them talk—"

"I am allowed."

"You're not."

"I am owed."

"You're not. See— You're just not. You're like a...a cannibal or something. Don't you see how this is just flesh-eating? You're...making lampshades from human sk—"

"Oh Jesus."

"Let me out."

"I can't let you out here."

"Let me out. I'll walk. And I don't want to be your fuel, your food."

"I would do it for you."

"Right."

"I would feed myself to you."

"I don't want you to feed yourself to me. And I don't want to devour you. I don't want to use you as fuel. I don't want anything from you. You think that because you had things taken from you, that you can just take and take—everything. But you know, not everyone wants to eat each other all the time, not everyone wants to—"

"We are all feeding from each other, all the time, every day."

"No."

"Yes. That's what we do, as people."

"For you it's all blood and revenge, but you know, there is more, or rather less, to all this than that. Not everyone is so angry, and so desperate, and hungry—"

"You can have me."

"Ick. No."

"I'll make you stronger."

"I'm done with you."

"You are not. You will be back. You will always need. You'll always need someone to bleed on. You're incomplete, John—"

"You just missed the exit."

Shalini's party was huge. It had been a year since her fall, and she was out of the hospital, had gone home to L.A., to live with her mom and sister. She was improving daily, could do just about everything again, though her short-term memory was still jumbled, unreliable. Everything from a year ago forward was gone. She could often not remember what had happened the day before, the hour before. She had to be told about the accident almost daily, and each and every time the story was told she was floored. "Wow," she would say, as if the story were not about her at all. But her memory, she was working on it, had flashcards, had a tutor, a diary where she kept notes, the events of the day, a paper memory of things that had happened. She had come so far, and the prognosis was good, so for her twenty-sixth birthday, her family had planned a huge party at their house, all kinds of food, a DJ, dancing, torches around the pool, a hundred people, more.

Toph and I drove down. I didn't know what to bring as a present, so did what I had been doing regularly at that point: I asked Toph to make her something. He had been making a series of Jesus figurines from colored bakeable clay—Jesus in a tuxedo and cane, mouth open ("Showtunes Jesus"), Jesus with a blond wig and pink woman's suit ("Hillary Jesus"), and Jesus in a white sleeping bag with a red cross atop it ("Sleepover Jesus") complete with a tiny can of itching powder. They were dead-on renderings, and were always appreciated by their recipients, but he claimed he didn't have time anymore to make things for *my* friends. And my second idea was shot when he refused to give up the Book of Mormon he had ordered though a 1-800 number. Well.

When we got to L.A., I dropped him off with Bill in Manhattan Beach and drove on to Shalini's, stopping at the mall on the way, where I bought a cat calendar, a book about Menudo, some paperweights—$54 for a few seconds of laughs. I found her house, high on a hill, on a wide dark street. There were cars everywhere, both sides of the road; I had to park blocks away. You could hear the music from five hundred yards, could see the lights in the backyard. I was terrified. I hadn't seen Shal in months, did not know what to expect.

I knocked on the huge door and when I was let in there were

people everywhere, presents stacked on the table, on the floor, huge beautiful presents, there were people in the living room, and the family room, and back there in the dining room a whole crowd doing something, and then maybe fifty more in the back, on the patio, around the pool, surrounded by torches, the backyard bathed in fiery light. Her mother said Shalini was upstairs, resting. I walked up the carpeted stairs and followed the voices down the hallway. In a bedroom overlooking the pool there she was, sitting on her bed, looking bright and sparkly, completely the same.

"Hello dahling!" she said.

We hugged. She was dressed up, a silk blouse, a miniskirt.

I told her about how my car broke down on the way to L.A.—it had—how I borrowed and drove Bill's to her house, how great the party seemed to be going, all the torches in the backyard, all the people, the pool—

She looked out her window, down at the pool, glowing like a sky, the people silhouetted against it.

"Yeah, but what's it all for?" she asked.

She didn't know why everyone was here. You could see her searching her memory for a reason, finding nothing.

"It's your birthday," I said.

Her sister, Anuja, and I explained the birthday party.

"But why the big deal? I mean, I know I'm pretty popular and everything, but really!" She laughed a little laugh.

Anuja and I sketched it out as vaguely as possible, mentioned a fall and a coma, an incredible recovery. And as always, when we were done with the story, Shalini was utterly amazed.

"That is in*cred*ible," she said.

"Yeah," we said. "You were lucky." No one mentions her friend who died, the one she came with.

"I mean, thank you, *God*," she said, in her Valley way, rolling her eyes. God sounded like *Gawd*.

Eventually she came downstairs, and she danced for a while,

on the parquet floor they'd assembled by the pool. They did the
presents, and there was a dinner, and Carla and Mark were there,
and everyone else from all those hospital days. The view, and the
warm winds coming up from the ocean, made it as euphoric as it
was meant to be. People walked around with tears in their eyes,
especially Shalini's mother, who I had seen no other way, for as
long as I had known her. As things wound down, and Shalini was
upstairs resting, I walked with her mother to the door.

"You know, I went looking for the landlord," I said.

"What do you mean?"

"The landlord, the one who owned the building." I tell her
how I followed the trial in the papers, the trial of the landlord
responsible for the faulty deck, how I went to the courthouse half
a dozen times, looking for him, wanting to sit in on the hearings,
wanting to see the man. I planned what I would do to him if given
a moment alone—that, if I found myself in a dark vacant place
with him, I would shove my fist through his head.

"Did you see the trial?" she asked.

"No, I kept going to the wrong room, or they would have
rescheduled it. They were always rescheduling it. I kept sitting in
empty courtrooms, waiting—

"Tell Shal I had to take off."

I left knowing that I might not be back. I said I would be
back—maybe next Thanksgiving—but I knew that we were leaving California, Toph and I, we were exhausted and felt hunted—

Everyone else was leaving or was gone. Flagg had moved to New
York for grad school, then Moodie moved there for a job, and then
Zev, and Kirsten went to Harvard with her new boyfriend—he was
in law school, she was after an MBA, a nice couple, an untroubled
couple, and I surprised myself by being endlessly happy for her—
and we're going, too, because going to work every day is starting

to tear me into little pieces, that stupid drive every day, the same roads, hills, and because I still don't have health insurance, and we're sick of that tiny, loud apartment, and living next to all those horrible people who don't understand, who should be like us and understand but they don't yet understand anything at all, and I'm tired of living across from that senior citizens' home, having to wake up and see them, puttering on their porches, getting dressed up to walk down to the community center, to put on their rubber caps and swim so slowly in that pool—

There are too many stupid echoes here, everywhere. Even a beach like Black Sands brings her back, how in her last half-year, she would watch from the car. At Toph's flag football games, Beth and I would sit on the sidelines, cheering, making unkind remarks about the coach, while she stayed in the car, parked in the lot high above the field. We could see her, leaning over the steering wheel, squinting to see the action.

We would wave. *Hi Mom!*

She would wave back.

She couldn't make the walk down to the field, couldn't make the trip down to the beach the last time we were out here, when Beth graduated and I flew out, when after the ceremony she, Beth and Toph and I drove down the coast, through Monterey, and when we got to the beach in Carmel we told her we'd be back and ran down the high dune, ran down to the water, Toph only seven then, his first time in California. Beth and I pretended that we were throwing him in the ocean. We hit each other with long stretches of brown, rubbery seaweed. We looked up at the car and we waved.

She waved back, high above the beach, overlooking. And after we rolled around more, and poured sand on Toph's hair and made Beth kiss a dead jellyfish, we walked back up, knowing our mother had seen everything, was so proud of us all, watching from above.

But when we climbed the dune and were closer to the car it almost looked like she was asleep.

She was asleep. Her hands in her lap.

She had not waved.

So today the wind is perfect. There's hardly any at all. This beach, Black Sands, usually has some kind of wind coming from the water, which fucks things up, sending the frisbee deep into that frigid water, forcing me to wade in in my shorts stiff-legged to retrieve it. But today there is no wind, and there is almost no one else here, which means we have most of the beach, or at least our part of it, to ourselves, which is really something, even if for an hour.

We've gotten so much better. I mean, we started out really good, when he was smaller, when we first came out here—he was years ahead of anyone his age, would dominate games of Ultimate at his summer camp, they worshiped him, the other kids—you should have seen the younger kids crowd around him, oh and when he would take off his baseball hat and let his long blond hair fall forward—this one time a boy was awestruck: "You shouldn't wear a hat," he said, "your hair is amazing." This little boy, I was right there, it was Parents' Day. But so throwing-wise Toph didn't used to have the range he does now, and the tricks, he can do tricks— and I've always had the tricks I can do, like the one where I run up to the frisbee as it's coming at about chest level, and when I'm almost there I jump at it, do kind of a 180 in the air—it's probably a 360, actually, when you think of it, because I— Yeah, so I spin around in midair, coming at the frisbee as it's coming toward me and when I'm perfectly— When I have my back to the frisbee in midspin, that's when I catch it, so it's like a behind-the-back catch, in midair, but ideally, with the spinning and all, I land— get this—facing Toph. A 360. That's a pretty cool trick when you can get it to work, which is only so often, for me, even though I'm really fucking good— So the point is that Toph does that one now, and he's way more consistently good at it than I am. He still fucks it up a lot of the time, bats the frisbee away, which makes me cringe because we break our frisbees every couple months, and it's always something like that, a batting of the frisbee that cracks the thing right in half, always happens right when we get to the beach, or wherever. It's thick plastic, too, of course—we use only the really heavy frisbees—

But so he does that trick, which is a cool one to watch, but he also does, almost prefers, all these stupid tricks, really stupid fucking tricks, tricks that aren't really tricks at all, they're just stupid things, because he's always been more interested in doing goofy stupid shit than doing things normally, keeping score, that sort of thing— So he's got one trick where, when the frisbee's coming, he'll just lay down on his stomach for as long as he can, and then, at the last possible moment, he'll stand up and then...take a few steps and go catch the frisbee. That's it. It's a pretty stupid fucking trick, right? I mean, it makes no sense at all, when you think about it, it's the most unspectacular thing in the world. But he cracks himself up with that one, truly. Laughing like an idiot—

The morphine was taking her under, but her breathing was still strong. It was erratic, but you should have heard the breathing—when it came, it was strong, forceful, it was a yanking of air. Her limbs weren't moving anymore, now she was still, her head back, and just the breathing, like a sort of uneven snoring. More and more like snoring, the grinding, the gasping. We stayed up all day and night because you did not know. We moved chairs close, curled in them and slept, held her hand, and soon the tide came in. It started with a different sound in the snoring. Something rounder, more liquid. Then almost a gurgling. Her breaths became more strained, pulling both air and also these bubbles—what *was* that sound?—and Beth and I were there, on either side, and the breaths were pulling, yanking at something like a boat still tied to a dock, the motor revving but something holding, holding. The breaths were pulling more and more. And the gurgling, the bubbles became more prominent in the breathing, she was pulling at a tub of water, or fluid, then a lake, a sea, an ocean, pulling at it— The fluid kept coming, the tide inside her rising, rising, her breaths shorter, like someone being filled as the water climbs and there is no longer anywhere to— But there was intelligence in that breathing, and passion in that breathing, everything there, we could take that breathing and hold its hand, sit on its lap while watching TV, the breaths were quicker and shorter and quicker and shorter and then shallow, shallow and that's when I loved her as much as any other time, when I knew her as I thought I knew her—oh she was out, she was gone, a week into the morphine maybe, and she could go any minute, her systems were falling apart or gone, no one had any idea what was keeping her going but she was sucking in that air, she was breathing so erratically, weakly, but she was doing it so desperately, each breath taking all that she had, her small person, with her beautiful tanned skin shiny, Beth and I draped over her, not knowing when— But she would just breathe, and breathe, suddenly, anxiously, unyielding— And I only hope it wasn't regret, that there wasn't regret there, in those breaths, though I know there was, I dream there was, when I hear the breaths, I can hear the anger— She could *not fucking believe* this was actually happening. Even while sleeping under the morphine and when we were only waiting, expecting, she would snap back, would rise suddenly and say something, cry out, a nightmare— furious about this bullshit, that something like this was actually happening, that she was leaving all of us, Toph— She was not ready, not even close, was not resolved, resigned, was not ready—

And while we're throwing there's a naked man walking, I first see him as he walks right past me, between me and the water. He's about my height, skinny, pale, bony butt, and he walks past me, down the shore toward Toph. At first I'm worried about Toph having to see this man, not just his butt but his whole frontal action happening, this man, walking toward Toph, unabashed, proud even, and for a while, for fifty yards at least, as he approaches, I watch Toph, watch him to see if he looks, or laughs, or is disgusted at this human nakedness, all pale and unadorned, pathetic and silly and maybe desperate, maybe needing something, needing to be looked at by strangers—and God knows what kind of freaky looks the naked guy'll be giving him, the kinds of freaky looks naked guys are always giving— But then I'm watching Toph's face, and he doesn't even look at the man. He does his best to avoid him, overconcentrating on his throws, looking serious, like this throw is so insurmountably important that he could never be bothered by this naked man—it's funny, actually, impressive, really—and then the man is past him, is gone, walking on toward the end of the shore, toward that spooky cliff jutting into the breaking waves, and Toph will never have to see the naked man again—

And we will be ready, at the end of every day will be ready, will not say no to anything, will try to stay awake while everyone is sleeping, will not sleep, will make the shoes with the elves, will breathe deeply all the time, breathe in all the air full of glass and nails and blood, will breathe it and drink it, so rich, so when it comes we will not be angry, will be content, tired enough to go, gratefully, will shake hands with everyone, bye, bye, and then pack a bag, some snacks, and go to the volcano—

Toph does another trick where, okay: First, I throw the frisbee to him, and he catches it normally. And then, while he's standing there, he just, he just slowly and methodically puts the frisbee in his mouth, like a dog. And then once he's got it in his mouth, he does a little jump, like that's how he caught it. Catch, put in mouth, then little hop. It's hardly even funny, that one, it's just sorry, it's so dumb. And he does it in front of other people, which is the tragic thing, he thinks people'll laugh, which is just so— He laughs, of course, loves it. But he still can't do—I'm not even sure he's tried it—my big trick, the one where I cartwheel and catch the frisbee with one hand while I'm upside down. That's a great trick, a crowd-pleaser, but he hasn't tried it and I'm not sure why. But he throws well, and you have to throw well to make the cartwheel trick work, you have to throw it low, two or three feet off the ground, and not too fast, and not too floaty—just a nice even throw. And it has to go to my right, because I can't do the trick going to my left. So even though he can't do the trick, he's essential to my doing it, because he's the only one who can throw it the right way, consistently, which is okay for now, but he'll do it soon enough, he's doing everything earlier than I ever did, beats me in every sport, basketball I cannot get a shot off anymore, they come back in my face and he revels, he yells in triumph, is already almost my height, is six inches taller than I was at his age, will surpass me within the year.

It's never too gusty on this beach, it's just balmy, the air waving around, loopy and soft, which makes you wonder why anyone ever goes to Ocean Beach, which is always insanely windy, pointless for anything, and you can't swim there either, and the wind just destroys any kind of throw you want to do unless you're just standing next to each other and dinking it back and forth like a couple of pussies. To throw and have it be any fun we need some calm, because we need to *wing* that fucker. And of course people stop and watch us, we're so fucking good. People young and old, whole families, gather to ooh and ahh, thousands of people, they've brought picnics, binoculars—

Not like we're frisbee geeks—we don't wear fucking head-bands or anything— We're just good, so good— We throw it high and far. We just get as far apart as we think we can get— And so we sent flowers and Lance, who was always closest to her, wanted to go out for the funeral but just came back from New York— And so we sent a wreath from all of us, and never had to see her embalmed and cold, could just think of— And everything that seemed possible at twenty-four, twenty-five, is now just such a joke, such a ridiculous fiction, every birthday an atrocity— And we now keep the gold tin on the kitchen counter, and inside are my father's business cards, and a tiny sweater my mother knitted for a teddy bear, and some change, and some pens, and a cap to something, maybe a camera lens, that we haven't been able to match with its mother and—

Oh fuck I was going to say: so Toph's got this other trick where he catches it normally— I'll throw it straight to him, a totally regular throw, and after he catches it he'll take a few steps forward and do a little forward roll, a somersault, with the frisbee on his head, like he caught it mid-roll or something— You should see him now, he's so tall all of a sudden, he'll be some kind of giant, seven, eight, nine feet tall—surely the tallest guy in our family, ever, always—

We're best at the long high throws. Like when you take four or five steps and rip it— It's almost like a shotput approach, the steps, four or five quick, one over the other, kind of sideways-like—and then you slash away with that fucker, it's such a violent act, throwing that white thing, you're first cradling it to your breast and then you whip that fucker as hard as you possibly can while keeping it level, keeping it straight, but otherwise with everything you can send with it you whip that fucker like it had blades on it and you wanted it to cut straight through that paperblue sky like a screen, rip through it and have it be blood and black space beyond. Oh I'm not going to fix you, John, or any of you people. I tried about a million times to fix you, but it was so wrong for me to want to save you because I only wanted to eat you to make me stronger, I only wanted to devour all of you, I was a cancer— Oh but I do this for you. Don't you see I do this for you? I have done this all for you. I pretend that I do not but I do. I eat you to save you. I drink you to make you new. I gorge myself on all of you, and I stand, dripping, with fists, with heaving shoulders— I will look stupid, I will crawl, drenched in blood and shit, I will— Oh look at those birds, on their stiff tiny legs and— There is nowhere I stop and you begin. I am exhausted. I stand before you millions, 47 million, 54, 32, whatever, you know what I mean, you people... and where is my lattice? I am not sure you are my lattice. Sometimes I know you are there and other times you are not there and sometimes when I'm in the shower with my hands scratching around in my head I think of you all, all your millions of heads and legs, standing under buildings shuffling them around, carrying them, taking them apart, making new buildings— And I am with you there, when you're under that fucking building all centipedey and everything you motherfuckers— And when Toph catches his, he flexes with a fury, his muscles just these taut strings, his mouth open, teeth straight and pushing so hard against each other. And when I catch I do it, too, I flex and yell and vibrate— Can you see this? Goddamn, look at that fucking throw did you see Toph throw that goddamn thing, the trajectory on that fucking thing? it's going way past me but I can run under it, I am barefoot and run like an Indian and I can look back and it's still coming, I can see Toph in the distance, blond and perfect— It's up there and rising, Jesus fucking Christ it's small but then it stops up there, it slows and stops all the way up there at the very top, for a second blotting out the sun, and then its heart breaks and it falls— And it's coming down and the sky is all white with the sun and the frisbee's white too but I can see the thing, I can see that fucker I can make it out and I can run under it I know where that fucking thing is, I will run under and outrun that fucker and be under it and will be there to watch it float so slowly down, spinning floating down I beat you motherfucker and I am there as it drifts down and into my hands, my hands spread out, thumbs as wings, because I am there, ready to cradle it as it spins just for a second until it stops. I am there. I was there. Don't you know that I am connected to you? Don't you know that I'm trying to pump blood to you, that this is for you, that I hate you people, so many of you motherfuckers— When you sleep I want you never to wake up, so many of you I want you to just fucking sleep it away because I only want you to run under with me on this sand like Indians, if you're going to fucking sleep all day fuck you motherfuckers oh when you're all sleeping so many sleeping I am somewhere on some stupid rickety scaffolding and I'm trying to get your stupid fucking attention I've been trying to show you this, just been trying to show you this— What the fuck does it take to show you motherfuckers, what does it fucking take what do you want how much do you want because I am willing and I'll stand before you and I'll raise my arms and give you my chest and throat and wait, and I've been so old for so long, for you, for you, I want it fast and right through me— Oh do it, do it, you motherfuckers, do it do it you fuckers finally, finally, finally.